Mondo Mandingo

Mondo Mandingo

✦

The "Falconhurst" Books and Films

Paul Talbot

iUniverse, Inc.
New York Bloomington

Mondo Mandingo
The Falconhurst Books and Films

iUniverse books may be ordered through booksellers or by contacting:

iUniverse
1663 Liberty Drive
Bloomington, IN 47403
www.iuniverse.com
1-800-Authors (1-800-288-4677)

ISBN: 978-1-4401-7596-1 (pbk)
ISBN: 978-1-4401-7597-8 (ebk)

Printed in the United States of America

iUniverse rev. date: 10/6/2009

This book is an unofficial companion to the novel *Mandingo*, the novel's sequels, and the play and motion pictures based thereon. It has not been authorized or endorsed by any publisher, author estate, motion picture studio, production company or distributor affiliated with the novels, plays or films discussed herein.

The views and opinions of individuals quoted in this book do not necessarily reflect those of the author.

The illustrations are from the private collection of the author (unless noted otherwise). The film-related promotional photographs and publicity materials reproduced herein date from the original release of the films and were released to media outlets for publicity purposes.

Contents

Acknowledgments

My extreme thanks is extended to Steve Carver, Ji-Tu Cumbuka, the late Richard Fleischer, Tim Kincaid, Kathrine McKee, Laura Misch, Ken Norton, and Sam Sherman for graciously sharing information on the films discussed in this book. I made intense efforts to contact every living actor involved with *Mandingo* and *Drum*, and I am highly grateful to those that did agree to be interviewed. Special thanks to Mr. Carver for loaning me his personal collection of photographs, notes, and other papers relating to *Drum*.

Thanks also to attorney G. Franklin Rothwell, who was involved with the Lance Horner estate from the mid-1970s to the early 1980s, for providing me with information on the publishing history of the Falconhurst books and on the personal lives of Kyle Onstott and Lance Horner.

I am greatly indebted to my friend Chris Poggiali, a brilliant film historian/researcher, for providing me with endless reams of print information on many of the novels and films discussed in this book. Additional information, material, and/or assistance was provided by Dennis Bartok, Chris Bickel, Tommy Faircloth, Glenn Gardner, Stewart Grinton, Tim Mayer, Mike Malloy, Nathaniel Thompson, Michael Weldon, and David L. Wilson.

The photographs from the Broadway production of *Mandingo* are by Fred Fehl and appear here courtesy of Gabriel Pinski.

Thanks also to the helpful and courteous staffs at the Billy Rose Theatre Division at the New York Public Library for the Performing Arts, the Library of Congress Copyright Office, and the Thomas Cooper Library at the University of South Carolina.

Thanks to Charles Brower, Sam Bruce and Leslie Haynsworth for proofreading and editorial advice. Also to Trey Mooneyhan for technical assistance and page layout.

And finally, I thank God and my incredible family.

Introduction

"MANDINGO. Not just a novel—an Electric Shock!" This was the only text on a mysterious postcard that was sent to American booksellers in early 1957. *Mandingo* was the first piece of fiction to come from its publisher and the initial novel by Kyle Onstott, an eccentric, seventy-year-old dog-breeding specialist who had based his heavily researched story—about a family of slave breeders on a pre-Civil War Southern plantation called Falconhurst—on bizarre legends.

The postcard's hyperbole underestimated the response to *Mandingo*. The novel became a literary sensation and a publishing phenomenon that created a whole subgenre of pulp known as "slave fiction"—a category that easily ranks as one of the more lurid to appear in mainstream bookstores. *Mandingo* also birthed thirteen official follow-up novels set at Falconhurst that were published over the next three decades. Throughout the 1960s and 1970s, store racks were stuffed with sensational paperbacks whose covers showed frail Southern belles succumbing to shirtless, muscular male slaves. Onstott's long novel was whittled-down considerably for the paperback edition and shortened further for international printings, but no one who has read *Mandingo* in any form has ever forgotten it.

After three aborted attempts at a film version (as well as a failed stage adaptation on Broadway), a *Mandingo* movie finally arrived in 1975, courtesy of Italian producer Dino De Laurentiis. The permissiveness of the film industry in the 1970s—when new cinematic ground was being broken and previously taboo topics were being explored—enabled a faithful, no-holds-barred *Mandingo*. The result was the best film on slavery ever made. It features a fine screenplay, excellent performances, gorgeous production values and superb, stylish direction by the vastly underrated Richard Fleischer.

Mandingo was one of the most talked-about films of 1975 and a worldwide box office hit. Audiences were drawn to the compelling, uncompromising depiction of slavery. With its unusual story, graphic violence, fisticuffs, and naked male and female bodies (both black and white), the film earned its hard-R rating and provided something for everyone. It also received some of the most vicious reviews to ever come from American critics.

Drum, De Laurentiis' lavish, but troubled, sequel that arrived a year later, was directed by young action specialist Steve Carver. While no masterpiece (or blockbuster hit) like *Mandingo*—few films are—the follow-up was a solid action programmer that proved popular with audiences. *Drum* is less stylish than *Mandingo* but just as sexy and bloody and it has a bawdier sense of humor.

I have always been intrigued by Kyle Onstott's creation. I remember seeing, as a young boy, huge newspaper ads for the *Mandingo* film in 1975 and being haunted by the forbidden artwork of two interracial romantic trysts and the provocative tagline: "Expect all that the motion picture screen has never dared to show before." Also during that decade, I frequently saw "slave fiction"—with cover art of black studs and swooning blondes—displayed in the paperback racks at the local drug stores.

I finally saw the *Mandingo* movie in 1982 when it was shown—uncut—on Home Box Office. The next day, my fellow high school students—both black and white—excitedly discussed the violent and sexual images. A teacher who overheard our conversation and had also watched the film remarked, "We're not here to discuss black pornography."

Over the years, I would frequently revisit *Mandingo* (and *Drum*) via videotape. Decades later, after yet another viewing of *Mandingo*, I began to research extensively the film's production and I finally read Onstott's unabridged novel after locating a yellowed, brittle copy. I had to find out what kind of man would write such a story and why. During my research, I was especially privileged to speak at length with *Mandingo* director Richard Fleischer shortly before his death.

Since its release almost thirty-five years ago, *Mandingo* has been an unfairly maligned film, especially in America, where film buffs have accepted its reputation as a bad movie. For decades, historian/critic Leonard Maltin's influential annual compendium of capsule movie reviews (currently titled *Leonard Maltin's Movie Guide*) has branded *Mandingo* and *Drum* with "BOMB" ratings. The *Mandingo* listing notes, "Trashy potboiler will appeal only to the s & m crowd....Stinko!," and incorrectly claims that Susan George plays James Mason's "oversexed daughter."

In a "Worst Films Compendium" in Harry and Michael Medved's popular

1980 book *The Golden Turkey Awards*, *Mandingo* was called a "celluloid bag of clichés and pat situations about a plantation in the South that bears little resemblance to what Scarlett O'Hara left behind. Prize fighter Ken Norton, as a rebellious stud, punches away at a script that could never last fifteen rounds." (*Drum* was also on the list and was described as a "slimy sequel.")

More recently, *Mandingo* has been reevaluated. Director Tim Hunter (*The River's Edge*, 1986) wrote in a 1996 issue of *Movieline* magazine: "this epic potboiler...probably sheds more light on the roots of racial hatred in this country than any dozen more politically correct films on the subject."

Film critic and professor Robin Wood, in his lengthy 1997 essay "*Mandingo*: The Vindication of an Abused Masterpiece," claimed, "No film is more urgently in need of revaluation than *Mandingo*....In my opinion it is the greatest film about race ever made in Hollywood....I am encouraged by the experience of showing the film to large classes of students, by the generally powerful impression it makes, and, especially, by the enthusiasm of black students, who find at last a pre-[Spike] Lee Hollywood film about race to which they can relate unconditionally....[O]ne of the most audacious films ever to come out of Hollywood...it remains an extraordinary achievement, still unrecognized as such. *Mandingo*'s hour has come: it was vastly ahead of its time."

Robert Keser on the online *Film Journal*, 2006: "*Mandingo* reflects its exact historical moment just as it unflinchingly confronts all three hot wires of American history—race, class and gender—to dramatize a squalid chapter of capitalism without restraints....[A] remarkable and deeply political film." Brian Baxter in a 2006 Fleischer obituary for *The Guardian*: "the single most important film on the subject, a vision so wholehearted in its condemnation of racist barbarity that any so-called excesses can be readily excused." Dennis Cozzalio in his blog *Sergio Leone and the Infield Fly Rule*, 2008: "no corny sex-and-slavery romp...but instead a serious and agonized attempt to grapple with a period in American history that it seemed was still too hot to handle....A movie that gets under the skin of blacks and whites, in 1975 and in 2008, and lives there."

While more elusive today than *Mandingo*, *Drum* has a growing cult following among offbeat movie buffs as well as grindhouse and blaxpoitation scholars, who love it almost as much as its predecessor. *Drum* is unlikely to be reevaluated by mainstream critics, although it was a surprising part of the program at the Harlem Week Black Film Festival in 2002, where a 35mm print was screened with other hard-to-see, but more acclaimed, black-themed films like *Porgy and Bess* (1959), *The Incident* (1967), and *Thomasine & Bushrod* (1974).

The Leonard Maltin guide lists *Drum* as "a new and dreadful low in lurid characters and incidents." In her 2009 biography on Warren Oates (star of

Drum), Susan A. Compo calls it a "tawdry sequel" and adds, "*Drum* is corn on the cob…grim, difficult to watch—even for laughs.…*Drum* was financially successful among the lowest common denominator."

I hope that this book will lead more people to discover or revisit and reevaluate the *Mandingo* novel and film, as well as some of the other books and movies inspired by it.

Book I: The "Falconhurst" Novels

Chapter 1:
Kyle Onstott and *Mandingo*

"Since my childhood in Illinois, I have always been horrified and strangely drawn to slavery," Kyle Onstott told *Newsweek* in 1957. The seventy-year-old writer was granting a rare interview promoting the just-published *Mandingo*, his scandalous, immediately popular novel set in 1820 at Falconhurst, an Alabama slave-breeding plantation.

Kyle Elihu Onstott was born on January 12, 1887, in Perry County, Illinois, in the small town of Duquoin, named after Jean Baptiste DuQuoin, a part-French, part-Native American chief of the Kaskaskia tribe that once dominated the area. Onstott's parents were Donald Morrison Onstott, of Bavarian descent, and his second-cousin Barbara Pyle, originally from Kentucky. (Her previous husband was another of her second-cousins.) Donald Onstott became the successful owner of a general store after moving to the Duquoin area around 1850 to take advantage of the activity from a newly built railroad station. Kyle Onstott got his middle name from his paternal grandfather, Elihu, a Perry County merchant and county commissioner.

During his youth in Illinois, Onstott heard many ominous and sadistic local legends involving slavery. Relatives and acquaintances from his mother's home state would tell him similar, equally bizarre Kentucky-set stories. These sinister tales would be recalled decades later during the writing of *Mandingo.*

Although he was fascinated by antebellum slavery and would go on to write a best-selling epic set throughout the South, Onstott never lived lower than Illinois and had no family background in slavery. His maternal great-great grandfather had been a (hard-drinking) doctor in Kentucky, but that side of the family, despite their affluence and Southern residency, never owned any slaves and were opposed to the institution.

In 1904, at age seventeen, Onstott moved with his parents from Illinois to Pasadena, California. He would spend the rest of his long life in that state. By 1920 the thirty-three-year-old was still living at home with his widowed mother.

All of Onstott's paternal male ancestors were hardworking, and many had gone to college, including his half-brother, maternal grandfather and great-great grandfather, who had all become doctors. But while Onstott was an insatiable reader and history buff, the future author never pursued a formal education or held a steady job. He looked down on those that worked for a living. The money he inherited from his parents was apparently enough to sustain him.

In 1921, the thirty-four-year-old was licensed as an all-breeds judge by the prestigious American Kennel Club. Onstott made his meager living by writing about dog breeding and by judging dog shows, which kept him traveling throughout the United States and Canada. His acquaintances on the dog show circuit included silent screen comedy star and avid breeder Harold Lloyd.

Among his Pasadena neighbors and his dog show colleagues, Onstott was known as a mild-mannered, quiet, well-groomed eccentric, who loosely rolled his own cigarettes with Prince Albert tobacco and often burned holes in his costly suits. His tall, gaunt build, dark wardrobe and skull-shaped face made him look like an undertaker. He began each day with a glass of grape juice mixed with six packets of Knox gelatin. He always skipped lunch and began his dinner with a chemistry beaker full of gin. Onstott was a Democrat, an agnostic, and a heavy reader of world history, classic literature, and the Bible.

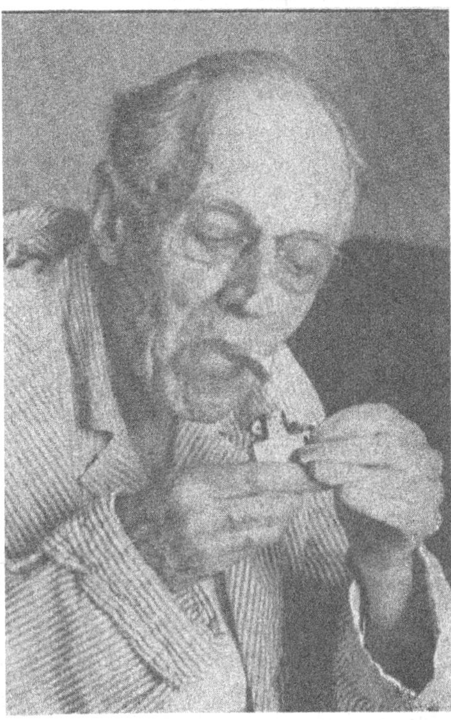

Kyle Onstott in 1957, shortly after Mandingo was published.

He was also a shy, closet homosexual, but when he did converse, he had no fear of expressing his opinions on any subject.

Onstott never married, but in 1927, at the age of forty, he decided to start some sort of family by adopting his neighbor: a twenty-three-year-old orphaned college student named Philip. The young man changed his last name to Onstott, and when he graduated from college and got a well-paid teaching job, he became his adoptive father's provider. Philip Onstott later married a woman named Vicky, who became close to her father-in-law. Many years later, *Mandingo* would be "Dedicated to Vicky and Philip, of course."

Onstott took dogs seriously and slept under the bedcovers with his favorite dog. He was an elected board member of the Grand Canyon German Shepherd Dog Club and was one of only seventy of the 1,078 members of the American Kennel Club who were authorized to judge all of the canine breeds. In July 1934, *Time* published a letter from Onstott that berated the magazine for a dog-related error:

> If one shrugged when other news publications erred, one would soon be musclebound [sic]: but when *TIME* makes a blunder it is as if Emily Post should suck her soup....The locution Boston bull to denote a Boston terrier irritates a dog man like ants in his armor. There is not, was not and has never been a breed of dogs rightly called Boston bull, although an illiterate public persists in applying that name to the Boston terrier, just as the same public for some unaccountable reason calls a cocker spaniel, a cockerel spaniel. Per-haps [sic] it thinks one bovine and the other galline [sic]. My florist has a standing order for orchids to *TIME* every week, but one more error about dogs (Do your worst with whatever else you will!), and I shall cancel it.

Philip Onstott would later tell the *Washington Post*: "My father did what he did best: nothing at all. Basically he was an all-breed judge in American and Canadian dog shows and he wrote books about dogs for about $500 each; what he didn't know, he'd make up." Onstott's first published book, *Your Dog as a Hobby* (co-written with fellow Pacific Coast breeder-judge Irving C. Ackerman), was put out by Harper and Brothers in the fall of 1940. Onstott followed it the next year with *Beekeeping as a Hobby* from the same publisher.

Philip Onstott—a student of clinical psychology, sociology and anthropology—helped his adoptive father write *The Art of Breeding Better Dogs*, which was started in 1938 but not released until 1946 when it was put out by Denlinger's, a tiny, family-owned "pet book" publisher in Virginia. Kyle Onstott was listed as the sole author, but later printings (by another publisher) as *The New Art of Breeding Better Dogs* gave Philip a "revised by" or coauthor credit. The book stayed in print into the 1980s and is still considered a classic in the field.

Around 1947, at age sixty-five, Onstott started researching and writing his first novel. Philip Onstott explained, "When I was a grad student, Kyle said, 'Why in the devil can't we write a book that will make some money?'" The adopted son was then studying Western Africa and the Mandingo (a.k.a. Mandinka) people, many of whom had been captured and shipped to America during the days of slavery. This information was only the beginning of the massive research and numerous notes that Onstott would incorporated into *Mandingo*.

In a 1959 article for *True: The Man's Magazine*, Onstott discussed the shocking true history that he dramatized in *Mandingo*:

> American slavery was the absolute chattel ownership of one human being by another human being. The owner had the legal right to do as he chose with or to the owned; the slave had no right whatsoever....Most slave owners regarded their slaves as we might today regard domesticated animals...They were candidly and openly referred to as "niggers," which appellation they did not resent; it is only since emancipation that the term has come to be one of oppression...
>
> No law concerned itself with the rape of a slave. Her owner could use her as he saw fit....Many plantation owners provided their male guests with a yellow wench for a bedmate as a part of their hospitality....On some plantations the virgin slave girls considered it an honor and a right to be deflowered by their master or by some other white man and looked forward to their visit to the "big house" for that ceremony...
>
> The deliberate breeding of slaves to satisfy the demands of the market is frequently disputed and even denied. But it happened.... Many planters expected and demanded that each of their slave women produce for them one child every year....Some planters hired their overseers partly on the basis of their vigor and good looks, trusting that the overseer would lighten and improve the slave population by blending his blood into it...White college students from the North [would be brought South] during their summer vacations to act as stallions for the slave women, thus providing offspring of a color lighter than the mother's....

Generally, a slave girl took pride in the sexual attention of a white male; if she were made pregnant by a white man, she would boast of that pregnancy and the resultant child....If the mother were a slave, so was the child, irrespective of its paternity. Yellow slaves were more valuable than black or brown ones, and the begetting of slave children with white fathers was profitable...

The [slave] owner's child usually had his own slave—his "play boy," a slave child who had been especially chosen and delegated to serve and amuse him....Play boys were the companions—and often the victims—of their young masters day and night....The white youth was provided with a whip to use on his play boy as he saw fit....Some white fathers provided their sons at or before puberty with "bed wenches,"which was presumed to forestall homosexual play with their play boys...

Any sexual relations between a white woman and a Negro slave were unthinkable. Such as did occur were certain to bring ostracism for the woman and death for the slave...

Some masters were kind to their slaves and considerate of their feelings and welfare....Other masters were brutal and sadistic....On many plantations there were stocks in which slaves were placed and flogged and left for a day or two. Often they were anointed with molasses or treacle which would attract flies, bees and other stinging insects....Ears were cropped, nostrils slit or noses amputated....Pronged iron or brass collars were riveted around the necks of slaves. The prongs, three or four inches or more long, prevented them from lying down; they had to sleep in a sitting position...

Castration of male slaves was not a common practice, but it was done, probably more frequently than has been reported. The father of this writer, returning to his home from a trip through the South in 1896, reported seeing and talking to a hotel servant, a so-called porter, in Corinth, Mississippi, who formerly had been a slave and who bore all the stigma of castration, the long bones, the flabby flesh, the smooth, unbearded [sic] cheeks. He declared himself to be a castrate, although the writer's father did not examine him...

There are so many tales of the burning of slaves at the stake

> and of the tearing of living flesh from a slave with hot pinchers and the owners' flogging of slaves to death that to attempt to deny or to contravert [sic] them would be as fatuous as futile. But, while murders of slaves by owners did occur, I must assume that they were not frequent, for the very good reason that slaves were valuable property…
>
> It seems incredible that one person could have owned another, dealt with him as property is dealt with, bargained about and transferred ownership in him—less than 100 years ago….Slavery was an unjust and brutal institution, one that the white man, although he has repented, cannot live down.

Some of the more-extreme material presented in *Mandingo* came from stories that Onstott remembered hearing more than four decades earlier. While a youth in Illinois, the writer's lifelong curiosity about slavery began when he heard legends about a creepy local mansion called Hickory Hill that was known as "the Old Slave House"—where blacks had been imprisoned, tortured, and forced to breed.

During the antebellum years, slavery was illegal in Illinois, but many of the state's white men were violently racist. In the early 1840s, a gang of white vigilantes regularly stormed the area to brutally assault liberal whites and free blacks, including a young black female who miscarried after she was viciously beaten by a gang member.

Hickory Hill (a.k.a. the Old Slave House), Onstott's partial inspiration for Falconhurst

Operating out of the state at the time was a highly organized underground network of criminals who would profit not only by capturing and reselling runaway slaves from the South, but by kidnapping Illinois's free blacks.

The most infamous, successful, and sadistic of the illegal slave traders in Illinois was John Hart Crenshaw. Born in 1797 in Gallatin County, Crenshaw was illiterate, but clever. He dabbled in several ventures, but was most successful in the salt business—the first major industry in Illinois. Starting in 1828, Crenshaw leased a number of the state-owned salt springs, but because of the brutal nature of the work, he could find few men willing to work them. Throughout history, the unpleasant, strenuous process of salt mining was often done by slaves and prisoners. Although it was illegal to own slaves in Illinois, Crenshaw was allowed to lease male and female slaves from Kentucky to work in his mines, which were located in the ironically named village of Equality. By 1830 Crenshaw was leasing 746 slaves, aged ten to fifty-five. Also working his mines and his home were the many indentured black servants that Crenshaw had under personal contract—with terms lasting twenty to forty years. The mine workers were brutally mistreated by the overseers and Crenshaw, who was known to use a branding iron on insubordinates.

Crenshaw had an intense hatred and fear of blacks, especially those that were free. He supplemented his sizeable salt fortune with his equally lucrative side business: illegal slave trading. Starting in the mid-1820s, Crenshaw (often using an assumed name) and his associates (including his two brothers) kidnapped and sold numerous free blacks, mostly women and preadolescent children. In the early years of this operation, the Crenshaw ring would store their human inventory in a large cave located near one of the salt mines. The victims would be taken later on a long wagon trip down the dusty roads leading to slave territory, or on a one-night ride to the Ohio River, where they would be shipped to Kentucky for sale throughout the South, for a usual fee of $200 to $600 each.

In 1838 Crenshaw chose an isolated location on his 30,000-acre plantation and started building a three-story mansion to serve not only as his family's elegant residence, but also as a haven for his secret activities, with a specially designed interior layout. Four years later Hickory Hill, as the house was called, was finished. On the back wall of the mansion's first floor was an unusually large double door that could be opened for wagons to load or unload stolen black people. A secret underground tunnel led to the river, where the captives could be transported by boat. The wagon entrance was near a hidden, narrow stairway that led to the third floor.

The infamous top floor of Hickory Hill had a twelve-foot-wide, fifty-foot-long hallway with a dozen small, cell-like rooms where the kidnapped free blacks and the rebellious leased slaves would be imprisoned, punished, and tortured. The rooms were windowless and unventilated. Narrow, double-stacked wooden bunks without mattresses took up most of the room space, which was made even more crowded by the slanted roof. The rough wooden floors and walls had iron rings to hold shackles. Often, eight to ten captives, usually young women and children, were held in each room. A few of the cell doors had tiny, barred windows that faced the hall. The smallest cells were not much bigger than a coffin and were reserved for those being punished.

Except for one small window at each end of the hall, there was no light or ventilation on the third floor. In the summertime, the temperature inside would be well over 100 degrees. The hallway had leg irons, neck collars, and two whipping posts where slaves were hung by their thumbs and brutally flogged, sometimes to death. The posts, the walls and the floor were permanently stained with splattered blood.

In a 1997 letter to historian Jon Musgrave, Melissa Galloway-Theiss recalled what she heard from her grandmother (one of Crenshaw's great-grandchildren): "I was told of the whipping post, how Mr. Crenshaw enjoyed beating these dark skinned people. I was told he'd force all to watch, including his own children....Further I was told Crenshaw would use the women to satisfy his own needs."

Located on the Ohio River near the salt mines was a small island that was frequently used as a hideaway for runaway slaves—until Crenshaw had his henchmen stock it with flesh-eating hogs. Whenever kidnappers heard screams coming from the island, they would row there to capture and resell the usually maimed runaways.

The victims of Hickory Hill included Crenshaw's own cook and her seven children, who were taken from their own home by Crenshaw's accomplishes, stored on the notorious third floor of the mansion, sold several nights later to a slave trader for a $2,000 flat fee, then bound and taken by wagon to Texas, where they were separated and auctioned. During another journey, a kidnapped male drowned when the ferry sunk in the Ohio River.

Crenshaw's illegal slave trading, his vicious treatment towards his captives, and his abuse of his salt workers were open secrets of the county. Even in his legitimate business dealings, he was known as a cheat and a scoundrel. But Crenshaw was also a devout Methodist and a prominent, leading citizen with major political influence and wealth. As much as one-seventh of the state taxes collected by Illinois came from Crenshaw. Sunday school classes were taught on the second floor of Hickory Hill, just below the lurid activities. The guests at an 1840 Hickory Hill ball included a young political debater named Abraham Lincoln, who spent the night at the mansion after the party ended. Some overnight guests at Hickory Hill would comment on the violent sounds that came from the third floor.

During his forty-year career as a kidnapper and slave trader, Crenshaw was indicted twice by a Gallatin County grand jury for kidnapping. He was acquitted both times, partly because of his status and partly because the main witnesses were black and it was illegal for blacks to testify against a white man.

In 1847, Crenshaw's left leg was brutally severed. Some folks said he was pushed into a blade at his sawmill by a vengeful slave. Others recalled Crenshaw savagely whipping a black female for over-boiling his laundry, then getting attacked by the girl's enraged, axe-wielding father, who was chopping wood nearby. The slave's fate is unknown. Crenshaw ended up with a wooden limb. (The only existing photograph of Crenshaw shows him holding a crutch.) The same year he lost his leg, the fifty-year-old entrepreneur lost his lease on the salt mines due to his nonpayment of taxes. But his other dealings—both legitimate and illegal—kept him busy and wealthy.

At some point, the reprehensible Crenshaw learned that he could make money not only by selling already-existing blacks, but by breeding his own. From 1856 to 1859, a prized item in the Hickory Hill inventory was Robert "Uncle Bob" Wilson, a six-foot-five, 250-pound descendent of the Mandingo empire. Originally from Virginia (he took his original owner's surname as his own), Wilson was twenty years old when he was purchased by Crenshaw for around $5,000 and brought to Hickory Hill. He was given a private room on the third floor where young female blacks, usually screaming and crying, would be imprisoned with him. Once pregnant, the now-more-valuable females were then shipped south to be sold at a high price. Sometimes Crenshaw would sell only the baby and send the mother back to the third floor to be rebred. Prior to Hickory Hill, Wilson had provided his unique services on six other plantations throughout a half-dozen states. During this era, he fathered around 300 children, mostly male.

In the early 1900s Wilson met and told his odd story to an Illinois teenager named Kyle Onstott. Fifty-five years later, without using Wilson's real name, Onstott would write in an article:

> In my own youth, I knew one old Negro, a former slave named Jim White who had been a stallion slave at the time of the emancipation....By the time he had reached his teens, he had developed such strength that he was a prime candidate for stallion duties and was sold to a Mr. White... It was not until several weeks had gone by at the new plantation that he learned the purpose for which he had been bought. One day his new owner appeared at the barn where Jim was working,

accompanied by an obese woman slave much older than Jim.

While the master commanded Jim to remove his clothes, the woman arranged herself on the splintery floor. She offered no comment or objection as the master explained to Jim what was required of him. After an initial period of reluctance and shame, Jim accomplished his task.

He later learned that his new owner's purpose in breeding him first to a woman so grossly fat and old was merely a test. The owner believed that the woman's breeding days had passed. He was amazed when she became pregnant from this single mating service, but he never brought her again. He brought others, however, to the gin house or the barn or the fields, wherever Jim happened to be. All of the women were generally older than Jim, either pure-bred Negroes or first-cross mulattos. None was so unpleasantly gross as the first one.

Jim was called upon to serve one or two women a week, sometimes three, and on rare occasions four. He was kept at public stud at a fee of $10 and was used twice in the same day if need be....As soon as White determined the boy's fertility and decided not to sell him, he branded him "H. White" across his shoulders. It was done with a red hot awl, with Jim lying prone on a bench. Jim denied that the process had been painful and said that all of White's Negroes had been marked in similar fashion.

Spreading wide his nostrils, Jim showed me a hole in his septum, also made with an awl. He declared he had been forced to wear an iron ring in this hole in his nose, like a bull. His master attached a leather strap with a snaffle to the ring to lead the slave around to show him off to any outsider who considered using him for stud....Jim got religion and became a preacher, alternating his calling of slave stallion with the ministry....Jim White was the only such stallion this writer ever knew personally.

The Civil War ended John Crenshaw's repulsive slave trading and breeding industry. In 1864 he sold and moved from Hickory Hill. Still active in real estate and other businesses and living only two miles away from his notorious former estate, Crenshaw died in 1871 at age seventy-four. His personal fortune had somehow dwindled to a mere $8,000.

After being sold by Crenshaw in 1859 and leaving Hickory Hill, Robert "Uncle Bob" Wilson ended up back in Virginia, where he saw the hanging of abolitionist John Brown. Wilson fought in the Confederate Army during the Civil War, and came back to Illinois as a free man, where he worked as a farmer, a well digger, and a personal servant. The intelligent, charismatic former slave practiced voodoo (he snorted "voodoo powder" throughout his long life) and Christianity and became a mule-riding, traveling preacher. He quoted the Gospels and sang spirituals (learned at his first plantation) throughout Illinois and much of the South, including Kentucky.

Wilson looked back in disdain at his "duties" of the past, but he didn't hide his background and willingly told his "stud slave" history to dozens of male and female strangers as well as to several reporters for Illinois newspapers. In 1941, at the age of 105, the unconscious Wilson was found on a Chicago street and taken to the Elgin State Hospital for Veterans in Illinois, where he spent the rest of his life. He died in 1948 at age 112.

First edition dust jacket

Sometime after the Civil War, the Hickory Hill mansion became known in the area as the Old Slave House. The young Onstott was among the thousands of Illinois residents who heard the brutal true history of the house and the legends of how later guests and trespassers would hear eerie sounds of wailing, crying, and rattling chains inexplicably coming from the empty third floor. In 1930, the then-current owners began charging admission to the house and were soon selling up to 300 tickets per day to curious tourists eager to view the notorious top floor of the allegedly haunted mansion. One of the tiny, dark rooms on the third floor was called "Uncle Bob's Room" or "the Breeding Room." The house was still a popular tourist attraction when it closed to the public in 1996. The Old Slave House was purchased by the state of Illinois in 2000, but attempts to raise money to restore and reopen the controversial historic site have been unsuccessful.

In addition to Crenshaw's Hickory Hill, there was another mansion in Gallatin County whose pre-Civil War owners dabbled in kidnapping and illegal slave trading. This house had a basement with prison cells and big iron rings in the walls to attach to the captives's chains. A brief, obscure 1915 report on this mansion noted: "[M]any tales are told of the prisoners held there and dark doings of long ago." Among African Americans in Illinois's nearby Richland County, there were legends that a local house there had been used for slave breeding. Although these other two sites were nowhere near as famous as the Old Slave House, it is possible that the curious young Onstott had heard about them also during his years in Illinois.

Kentucky—the birthplace of Onstott's mother, who lived with her son for at least the first three-and-a-half decades of his life—also had a long history of lurid slave-related activity that intrigued the author of *Mandingo.* Slave kidnappers and traders operated out of that state's caves from the 1820s through the 1840s. Kentucky also had its share of legends involving antebellum slave studs, including a tale about a farmer that kept a virile, insatiable male slave chained up in a cabin with barred windows. When the prisoner wasn't breeding with females, he was feasting on his steady diet of gunpowder and raw meat.

As Onstott wrote *Mandingo,* he blended his (and his adopted son's) extensive research into a fictional story about a series of bizarre, shocking events that take place in 1832 at and around Falconhurst, a slave-breeding plantation in Alabama, near the Tombigbee River and the town of Benson. Falconhurst is ruled by the wealthy, rheumatic, hot toddy-guzzling Warren Maxwell, and his limping but virile eighteen-year-old son, Hammond. While buying and selling slaves, and frequently "pleasuring" himself with his female possessions, Hammond purchases the physically perfect Mede, a rare descendant of the Mandingo tribe, whom Hammond trains as a bare-fisted fighter. Hoping to create an heir for Falconhurst, Hammond marries his sixteen-year-old blonde cousin, Blanche, only to neglect his wife in favor of Ellen, one of his slave "wenches." Seething with jealousy and lust, Blanche eventually summons Mede to her bedroom, leading to a violent and gruesome conclusion.

Philip Onstott recalled, "My father's method of writing was to put a Ouija board on his lap, and then he'd get a box of big white paper and a box of soft pencils. He didn't bother with things like paragraphs, chapters or page numbers. While he'd write, he'd just drop the pages on the floor. Then I'd come home, gather the pages and put in paragraphs, number the pages, and try to edit. He hated to go back over what he had written. He'd say to me: 'You don't expect me to return to my vomit, do you?'"

Writing entirely in longhand, Onstott worked on *Mandingo* for six years and came up with an enormous, awkwardly structured novel containing dozens of unforgettable and well-defined (if not especially well-developed) characters. In Onstott's depiction of the South, slave breeding, rape, homosexuality, alcoholism, pedophilia and incest are presented as casual, regular occurrences, and the techniques of physical punishment are graphically described. (After a slave is beaten, the wounds are coated with pimentade—a mixture of salt, cayenne pepper and lemon juice.)

Onstott also vividly detailed the era's various diseases, ailments and backwoods remedies. The characters's numerous meals were described with phrases like: "The chicken was indeed stringy muscled, but was cooked so done that it fell apart from the bones." Among the novel's many unforgettable sequences was when the decrepit Warren Maxwell slept with his feet pressed against a slave boy's belly to "dreen off the rheumatiz through the feet jest as good as any nekid dog."

Hammond Maxwell is the novel's main character and the most developed. The young heir is often uncomfortable with the family business and feels intense guilt when he physically punishes a slave. "I reckon I wasn't cut out fer threshin' niggers," he says at one point. Hammond is only attracted to black women, and when he meets his blonde cousin and prospective wife, Blanche, Onstott writes: "He would have to get used to the whiteness of female flesh. Its pallor seemed to him not quite healthy, somehow leprous, cold." (Notably, "Blanche" means "white" in French.) Onstott later notes: "[Hammond] believed it to be the skin color and the odor of white bodies that he did not like, wheras in fact it was a need to possess, to command, to order his sexual object, in a manner he was unable to do with a woman free and white....His choice was not between white and black (or yellow), but between free and chattel." The youth bluntly states, "White ladies make me puke." (Hammond Maxwell would appear in all but one of the many later Falconhurst books.)

The many *Mandingo* characters all add to the book's atmosphere, if not always to the plot. Among the slaves are: the hefty house servant Lucretia Borgia, who is respected by the Maxwell men and runs Falconhurst in their absence; Agamemnon (or Mem), a lazy, whiskey-sneaking, and frequently beaten house boy; the Amazon-like Big Pearl, who mates with Mede, her fellow Mandingo (and brother); Jason, Ellen's effeminate cross-dressing brother; Topaz, a powder-snorting prize fighter whose lack of ears is due to having them chewed off in brawls; and Shote, a morbidly obese boy who constantly begs for food while wandering around naked. Also notable are Lucretia Borgia's identical adolescent twin boys Alpha and Omega, nicknamed Alph and Meg. Alph is used by the elder Maxwell as a rheumatism cure, while Meg has an intense crush on (and begs to be beaten by) Hammond. Both boys blackmail Blanche into having sex with them.

Most of the Falconhurst slave names were borrowed from mythological, historical, or biblical figures—including Brutus, Genghis Khan, Jupiter, Lancelot and Aphrodite. Warren Maxwell explains, "I like names out'n history or names of heathen gods." Ganymede (Mede) was among the names taken from Greek mythology. In several stories (including Homer's *Iliad*), Ganymede was a stunningly handsome, perfectly formed human male who was adored and captured by Zeus. As one *Mandingo* character notes, "The boy served Zeus as a cup bearer, that is he poured his wine, and for other purposes."

Onstott's white characters include: Charles Woodford, Hammond's cross-eyed, devious, and bi-sexual cousin, who is also brother and lover of Blanche; Doc Redfield, the local veterinarian who also treats slaves; Mister Roche, a flaming French homosexual of New Orleans who purchases the twin boys as "bed-bucks;" and assorted white trash like Brownlee, a sleazy slave trader, kerchief-wearing thief, and pedophile; Madison Church, a blubbering, cherubic, gay teen desperate to buy a "pet" from Hammond; and Aristotle, a fat, dim-witted adolescent who defecates on himself during epileptic fits. Each (white and black) character's facial features, skin tones and bone structure are described in vivid detail as are wardrobe, daily schedule, living quarters, personal hygiene, body scents, bodily functions and mating rituals.

The book's dialogue can be hard to decipher, and some readers would be frustrated by the constant use of Old South slang and colloquialisms. Each character is poorly educated and all of the dialogue is presented in a strong Joel Chandler Harris-like dialect. For example:

> "I better look at them young bucks I traded fer yestidy. Do you reckon they's somethin' the matter with 'em

> that I didn't find? That son-of-bitch too gladsome, seem like, about that trade. Wish you fetch 'em shotes up to the gallery, finish your dinner."

Onstott's fascination with breeding and genetics—originally noted in his dog books—is evident in *Mandingo*, which often reads like a well-researched manual on breeding humans. Many of the slave characters in the novel are the result of interracial or incestuous mating.[1] The novel's author didn't understand or approve of a slave owner's physical punishment of his property. According to his first guide book: "The dog whip is happily a thing of the past. It belongs with the rack and the thumbscrew….We no longer seek to break a dog." In *Mandingo*, Onstott wrote: "To the Maxwells [the slaves] were cattle, valuable cattle and irresponsible, cattle reared and conditioned for sale. It was as unprofitable to abuse Negroes as hogs or horses. The owners took pride in the husbandry, care and comfort of their servants." The Falconhurst rulers are presented as decent men. At one point, Warren Maxwell says, "One way our niggers does own us, and we owns them. They feeds us and we feeds them. Nothin' I craves more than good niggers, fat and well and happy—and a-growin.'"

In 1953 Onstott was in Richmond, Virginia, to meet with William (Bill) Denlinger at Denlinger's, the publishing house that had released the author's last, and most successful, dog-breeding book. After his father's recent death, Bill Denlinger had become head of the family-owned firm that had been printing non-fiction pet books since 1926. Onstott and Denlinger were planning another book about dogs, but the publisher wanted to branch into fiction and asked to read the Old South novel that the author had mentioned. When Onstott went back to his then-current home in Sacramento, he packed up the 1,300-page handwritten *Mandingo* manuscript and shipped it to the publisher. "Kyle sent me a cardboard box full of pages and pages of longhand, a legible scrawl," Denlinger recalled in 1975. "After dinner, I laid down to kind of glance at it, and I watched the sun come up the next morning. If the book could do this to me, I felt it would do it to other people. I decided it was something I wanted to take a fling on."

Reading the Denlinger version of *Mandingo* today, it seems unlikely, if not impossible, that the publisher did any editing at all to Onstott's original manuscript. The long-winded, often plodding hardcover edition has fifty chapters, which range in length from two-and-a-half to fifty-two pages. Hammond Maxwell's frequent, endless journeys go on for hundreds of pages that have nothing to do with the narrative. Pointless new (admittedly flavorful) characters are constantly introduced only to disappear immediately.

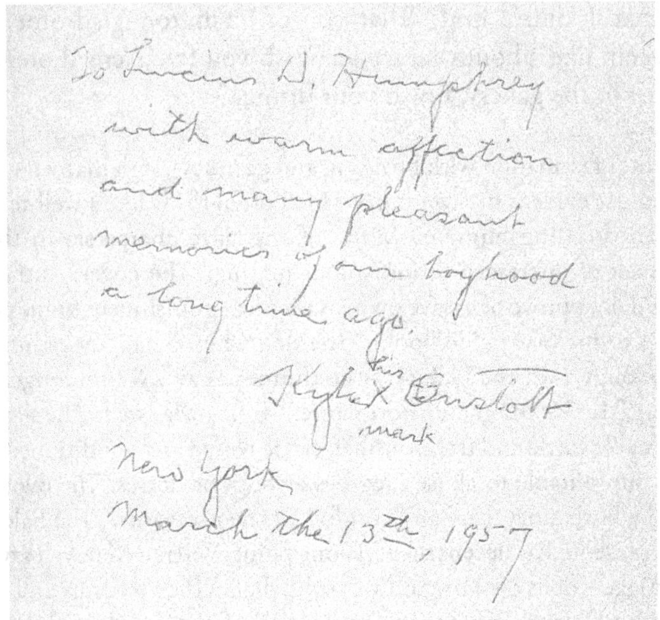
To Lucius D. Humphrey
with warm affection
and many pleasant
memories of our boyhood
a long time ago.
his
Kyle X Onstott
mark
New York
March the 13th, 1957

Inscription by Onstott in a first edition of Mandingo.

Denlinger may not have spent any time editing *Mandingo*'s content, but he spent $25,000 on the book's promotional campaign, which included sending advance review copies to the press and raffling off a free car at a convention for booksellers. Denlinger's financial risk was minimized by his contract with Onstott, which gave the publisher an atypically hefty 25 percent of the *Mandingo* royalties for ten years. The book's copyright was put in Bill Denlinger's own name instead of in Onstott's, which would lead to hefty royalties for the publisher when *Mandingo* went on to spawn a long series of sequels.

In January 1957, Denlinger hired a clever New York public relations firm to create and mail several thousand oversized teaser postcards to American bookstores. The first group of cryptic cards read only: "MANDINGO." This was followed by a second card with a few early reviews ("You've GOT something there") plus the novel's price and Denlinger's address. A final postcard said, "MANDINGO. Not just a novel—an Electric Shock!"

Ten thousand hardcover copies of the 659-page, 375,000-word *Mandingo* were printed just before the official publication date of Monday, March 11. A single salesman was sent to unload the books throughout the country.

The *Mandingo* dust jacket gave a subtle indication of the graphic text with a crude (and ugly) drawing of a white antebellum couple looking suggestively at a shirtless male slave and a cleavage-bearing female slave. In the front matter was a "Publisher's Note" that described the story's (allegedly authentic) social climate and hailed Onstott as "a master story-teller who ranks among the literary great of our time." The $4.95 price, mainly necessitated by the hefty page count, was at least one dollar more than most hardbacks of the era.

Novels dealing semi-explicitly with the slave trade had been around before, but no previous author had ever presented American slavery as bluntly or graphically as Onstott.[2] Many people wanted to read *Mandingo*, but few could find a copy in their local bookstore, and Denlinger was soon printing the 30,000th copy. In early May 1957 the independent novel entered the best-seller lists. Hollywood film director Samuel Fuller (*Pickup on South Street*, 1953) was among those that added it to his personal library. The surprised seventy-year-old Onstott, who wasn't fond of his own novel, explained at the time, "I didn't expect to find a publisher, but when Bill Denlinger wanted to take it, I decided that he'd do a better job of exploiting it than a bigger publisher. He has." Philip Onstott added, "The book doesn't have any significance, but it's like eating peanuts."

The critics were just as shocked and titillated by *Mandingo* as the public. The Reverend Daniel A. Poling, *Christian Herald*: "This over-length novel is a literary Chamber of Horrors. Never has anything in fiction so appalling, so terrible, and alas, so nauseating but at the same time so convincingly authentic come into this reviewer's hands. The book is so revolting that it becomes an emetic. *Mandingo* is the all-out other side of ante-bellum slavery, the side Lincoln glimpsed at the open market in his visit to New Orleans. If ever the hungry motion picture industry films this one *faithfully* and if the now flaccid Motion Picture Association gives it a seal, *Baby Doll* [1956] will look like a children's Christmas card. Also censorship may become a serious threat and this reviewer is against censorship."

Earl Conrad (author of a number of books on black history), *Associated Negro Press*: "*Mandingo* has aroused in me a wild enthusiasm. It is just about the most sensational, yet the truest book I have ever read....If the book abounds in sex in all manner and form, it has to be borne in mind that Kyle Onstott is dealing with a slave-breeding plantation.... Nobody else has done this, or even attempted it...and it is natural that Onstott should tell how the white masters plunged into the thick of that fascinating work with their divine right of seduction, and with the whole orgiastic unchecked nature of the chattel system itself....I think it will be read soberly, solemnly, even if fearfully, as men and women everywhere ask of themselves, Can this be true? Was this our land? Did we do this?

When you are done you will know, in large measure, why there was a Civil War."

Ted Posten (the first African American reporter for a major metropolitan daily paper), *New York Post*: "May well become one of the most discussed works of the year....The shock lies not so much in the cruelty and violence...but in its cold-blooded examination of the system of American slavery."

W. G. Rogers, *San Mateo* (California) *Times*: "For reading this book and reviewing it—with one eye closed and trying to see as little of it as I could—I have to blush, for this is raw stuff. But there's been a buzz-buzz-buzzing about it in book circles: A New York publisher wanted to get it away from this Virginia house, there are 20,000 copies in print already, it out-Peyton Places *Peyton Place* so the rumors go. The worst of them are true. This is about a stock farm, a Negro stock farm in the days before the Civil War and, if this is the truth about the South, let us all stop complaining about moonlight and magnolias....This is a vulgar and vile and unspeakable way of life. The author claims it's authentic. He has been accused of anti-Negro bias, but he is certainly no less anti-white."

Texas-based CBS radio and TV humorist John Henry Faulk: "*Mandingo* is one of the most compellingly powerful novels I have ever read. Mr. Onstott has taken the institution of human slavery as it existed in the South and woven a novel peopled with all those enmeshed in slavery's evils—slave-owner, slave-trader, slave—victims all! It is interesting indeed that it has taken America nearly a century to produce the 'Great Novel' on slavery....I love the Southern people, but I always wondered, 'How can they be such animals?' Like Uncle Lee—how can he make such a sharp distinction between his wife and the white women, and the Negro women sexually? The answer is, they regard them as animals. And this book, *Mandingo*, came near explaining it." (Faulk would later be known for his libel suit against the Joseph McCarthy committee.)

The Lexington, Kentucky *Herald-Leader*: "morbid, revolting, interesting, sadistic....A fascinating story which strikes a conclusion with a sledgehammer blow fit to rock the reader in his tracks."

Dallas News: "Onstott leaves nothing to the imagination...it is like no other book ever written about the South."

Raleigh (North Carolina) *News and Observer*: "Onstott spins the factual details of the slave-bound economy of the South into a historical novel that will establish his position as a master storyteller."

Emerson Price, *Cleveland Press*: "A huge novel compounded of such horror as I have not before encountered in the literature of any people. Indeed, it is a tale of such dark evil as to forbid full description...it carries with it the

Artwork for first paperback edition.

power of absolute conviction, and this quality may demand that we revise our notions of American history, for it confounds us with the evils of our past."

Another Cleveland reviewer wrote that *Mandingo* "might be one of the best books ever written." A critic down South called the book "a slimy mess" while some Southern scholars dismissed the content as "far-fetched." Most disturbed of all was a reviewer for the Ft. Lauderdale *News* who felt that "Each volume should have a little package of bicarb attached to the last chapter."

Amazingly, the novel's most notorious and highly promoted incident—the intercourse between mistress Blanche and slave Mede—takes place completely off-stage, doesn't happen until the huge book has almost ended, and is one of the few actions that isn't described graphically. Yet this forbidden tryst between the blonde Southern belle and the dark, muscular slave is what *Mandingo* is best known for. Similar interracial pairings would occur in each of the official Falconhurst sequels and the many imitators.

In May 1957 *Newsweek* sent a reporter to Sacramento to interview the elderly author, who was then recovering from pneumonia, at his home. Onstott told the magazine, "I've always felt that the human race could be regenerated by selective breeding. But *Mandingo* isn't the sort of thing I mean." The article, which called the book "mammoth, shocking, [and] meandering," was accompanied by a photo of the frail, bespectacled writer with thin white hair and sunken cheeks. He wore a seersucker suit and was lighting one of his hand-rolled cigarettes.

Encouraged by the phenomenal success of the hardback sales, which ultimately totaled 2.7 million copies, Denlinger sought a paperback publisher for *Mandingo* and sent a copy to Fawcett Publications.

Fawcett was a successful family-owned publisher that had been around since 1919 and by the mid-1950s had offices in New York and Greenwich, Connecticut. In September 1955, Fawcett created their Crest imprint to specialize in paperback reprints and genre fiction. Vice president Ralph Daigh described Fawcett's current market as "department stores, drug stores, book stores, gift shops, specialty shops, in many places where you will see softcover books on sale side-by-side with hardcover books." He explained, "From our entrance into the paperback business, we paid authors at a more generous rate than had been the custom....It caused quite a sensation in the trades....Giving the author a bigger share of the pie paid off handsomely."

Crest editor-in-chief William C. Lengel decided to look at *Mandingo* after he heard that one of his readers was enraged by it. Lengel felt that the lurid novel would appeal to the huge market that craved sensational paperbacks and paid Denlinger a then-hefty $25,000 advance for the *Mandingo* American softcover rights. (Onstott and Denlinger retained all subsidiary rights.) Over the next thirty years, Fawcett would publish twenty-six Falconhurst-related paperbacks.

Crest determined that softcovers of the complete *Mandingo* would not only be too costly to print and cumbersome to bind, but would also be too thick to fit into the spinning metal racks that most stores used to display paperbacks. An edited version of the novel, running slightly over 638 pages, was prepared for the paperback market. Most of the deletions included the long, often pointless chapters that detailed Hammond's frequent road trips and stopovers.

While the Denlinger hardcovers for *Mandingo* had subdued dust jacket artwork and a "Publisher's Note" that almost seemed to apologize for the content, the Crest cover (like most paperbacks of the day), went for the hard sell. It featured an enticing painting of a riding crop-clutching white man leering at a submissive young black woman wearing a sheer frock that exposes her protruding nipples. The back cover copy screamed:

> HUMAN BREEDING FARM! Behind the hoop skirts and hospitality, the mint juleps and magnolia blossoms of the Old South was a world few people knew existed—a world of violence, cruelty, greed, and lust.
>
> *Mandingo* brings to vivid reality the smell and hassle of the slave-breeding farms and plantations, where men and women were mated and bred like cattle.
>
> You may rave about *Mandingo* or you may hate it, but you won't be able to lay it down, *because it is a terrible and wonderful novel!*

To assure readers that none of "the good parts" had been removed from the paperback (and to appease the Federal Trade Commission which required abridgments to be labeled as such) the cover boldly announced the Crest version as an "Uncensored Abridgment." The paperback also contained a one-page note called "What Is Mandingo?" that described the tribe and featured a facsimile of Onstott's scrawled signature at the bottom.

Mandingo hit the paperback racks in 1958 and became a pop culture sensation. The Crest release came at a perfect time. By the late 1950s, softcover books were available at 95,000 stores throughout the United States, and over a million paperbacks were being sold daily. At the time, Crest was not a major player among paperback houses, but their status quickly changed when *Mandingo* became their first big seller. By 1959, well over a million paperbacks of Onstott's novel had been sold.

Among the many readers of *Mandingo* was journalist Kathryn Wright, who met Onstott when he came to Billings, Montana, in May 1959 to judge a dog show. She later recalled:

> A tall, old, gaunt man leaning on a cane carved from gnarled wood came into *The Gazette* newsroom...Kyle Onstott. The name rang a bell. I had just finished his novel, *Mandingo*, and

> I stared at the author of this book of shock, horror and sadism. He stared back with dark eyes that looked as if they'd seen everything this side of Hell and beyond. The eyes blazed like coals from a cadaverous face topped by a lank shock of white hair…"I have just read your book, Mr. Onstott," I said. "It's fascinating." His thin wide mouth curled sardonically. "Weren't you shocked?" he asked. "Sure. But it was interesting, especially since it's—." He cut me off. "Since it's true. I research the hell out of an era or event. Then I put these people in to show how it was." He turned his back on me and started talking dog show to the sports editor. 'Mr. Onstott," I said. "Well," he glanced my way, his quavery [sic] voice full of irritation, "what do you want now?" "If I run to the book store and get a copy of *Mandingo*, will you autograph it for me [?] I don't have a copy here." He nodded.

Onstott inscribed Wright's copy: "I'll exchange this autograph for any publicity the Gazette [sic] can give the Billings dog show."

The October 1959 issue of Fawcett's rugged, heavily circulated *True: The Man's Magazine* included Onstott's fine article "Cruel Masters," which was written in the same flavorful, descriptive, and detached style as *Mandingo*. The article began: "My fictional novel *Mandingo*…so impressed the editors of *True* that they asked me to write the factual story of slavery in America. They imposed no editorial restrictions whatsoever, asking only that I authenticate such facts as I put down." Billed on the cover as the "shocking story of the barbaric American slavers by the author of *Mandingo*," the long, compelling piece demonstrated Onstott's extensive knowledge and research. Included were authentic illustrations of slave abuse, excerpts from actual notices that offered rewards for the (alive or dead) capture of runaway slaves, and the vintage advertisement: "my Nigger Dogs…in prime training [are] ready to attend to all calls of Hunting and Catching runaway Niggers….From $15 to $25 will be charged for catching; according to the trouble."

Mandingo was too hot to be printed only in America. In 1959 Denlinger made a deal with the British publisher Longmans, Green and Company. Their hardcover of *Mandingo* was abridged even more than the Crest paperback and ran 423 pages with a dust jacket featuring dull, non-suggestive images (painted by Ronald Glendenning) of a black woman picking cotton, a white man on a horse, and a white woman and a black man standing with an antebellum mansion in the background.

English readers and reviewers were as stunned as the Americans had been. London *Sunday Times*: "*Mandingo* shocks, shakes." London *Evening Standard*: "What remains vivid in the memory is [Onstott's] picture of an extraordinary and almost unbelievable pocket of the not-so-distant past." *Time and Tide*: "All the more horrifying because it is so calmly and quietly written....Not for the squeamish or self-complacent." London *News Chronicle*: "A novel of flaring colour."

At the end of the 1950s, after moving to San Francisco, where he would spend the rest of his life, Onstott began work on a new novel. His story was set in California farming country during the first three decades of the 1900s and dealt with the tensions between white landowners and Mexican laborers. The main character was honey farmer Manuel O'Brien, a sixty-three-year-old offspring of Spanish and Irish immigrants who was struggling to raise his infant son on his own. Onstott had lived in California at the time the story was set and based the novel on his actual observations.

Onstott stopped work on this book in 1960, but his written pages and notes were put together in 1985 by author Harry Whittington to become the (very weak) novel *Strange Harvest*, which was published only in England and promoted as "The final masterpiece from Kyle Onstott, author of *Mandingo*."

In March 1960, Hollywood gossip queen Louella Parsons announced in her syndicated column that Onstott was writing the screenplay for a new film version of *Uncle Tom's Cabin* (Harriet Beecher Stowe's classic 1852 anti-slavery novel) for producer Eugene Frenke (*Heaven Knows, Mr. Allison*, 1957; *The Last Sunset*, 1961) that was to star popular vocalist Johnny Mathis. Parsons wrote, "I question the wisdom of making it now with the civil rights bill and the trouble in the South. The story is being brought up to date, but I would say it will be tricky business trying to satisfy both the rabid southern whites, and the equally determined Negroes." It's unknown how far Onstott got on the script, but this unlikely project was never shot.

Mandingo first appeared on British paperback racks in 1961 via Pan Books, a successful London paperback house known for its exceptional cover art. The publisher (its name and logo derived from the mythical half-man/half-goat creature) stood out in the crowded market by focusing on sensational subject matter. The typically stunning Pan cover for *Mandingo* featured a painting of an alluring young black woman (with erect nipples) leaning against a post while in the background a whip-wielding white man looked down from his horse at a shirtless black man.

First British paperback edition.

During the 1950s, the cost of book production had risen, and even the abridged versions of *Mandingo* proved to be too long for Pan, whose paperback version was released at 377 pages, a full *263 pages less* than the edited American softcover. But this abridgement was a skillful editing job. Instead of merely removing large chunks of text, a meticulous editor went through all of the book's paragraphs to remove varying amounts of extraneous material. Pan turned Onstott's novel into a leaner and more accessible read, and their version is the best edition of *Mandingo.* It was the size of an average paperback and could be easily hidden in the pocket of an embarrassed reader. Regrettably, among the many characters deleted for this edition was Mad Church—the white, plump, effeminate, constantly crying, "play boy"-craving teenager. Like most of the people encountered on Hammond's journeys, Mad Church contributed nothing to the narrative, but he was one of Onstott's more memorable creations.

Mandingo quickly sold over a million British paperbacks, and Onstott was awarded a "Pan," a gold-plated statue of the publisher's logo that was given to the firm's top-selling authors.[3]

African American writer Richard Wright, author of the 1940 novel *Native Son* and other works about race relations, was an early reader of *Mandingo* and was so impressed that he convinced a contact in France to publish a French translation. Throughout the 1960s and 70s, *Mandingo* was a worldwide publishing sensation with editions ultimately printed in Korea, Norway, Denmark, Japan and Italy. The Italian edition contained a glossary that defined such words as "Masta," "Miz" and "Pone."

Back in America, *Mandingo* was a perennial paperback bestseller. It stayed on the racks and in print until the late 1980s. The Fawcett/Crest version went through several cover designs and endless printings. By the mid-1970s, the novel had sold over five million copies and was ranked thirty-third among the bestselling books released in the United States from 1895 through 1975.

But *Mandingo* was far from the final word in the Falconhurst story. The last chapter featuring Kyle Onstott's characters wouldn't be printed until thirty years after they were created.

American paperback, mid-1970s.

Notes:

1 Biracial children of the antebellum era had been featured in earlier fictional literary works, notably in *The Quadroons* (1842) and *Slavery's Pleasant Homes* (1843)—two short stories by abolitionist Lydia Maria Child—which told of the ill-fated, mistreated mulatto female slave who was the offspring of the daughter of a white slave owner and a black slave.

2 Popular earlier novels about American slavery included Frances Gaither's *Follow the Drinking Gord* (Macmillan, 1940) and *Double Muscadine* (Macmillan, 1949), Norman Collins's *Black Ivory* (Duell, Sloan and Pearce, 1948), and biracial author Frank Yerby's *Foxes of Harrow* (Dial Press, 1946).

3 The British hardcover and paperback deleted the "What is Mandingo?" opening page of the American paperback. The "Publisher's Note" in the American editions that featured a facsimile of Onstott's signature was abridged in the British versions as an "Author's Note" with the initials "K.O." at the bottom.

Chapter 2:
The Lance Horner Entries

Among the earliest readers of *Mandingo* was Lance Horner, a middle-aged aspiring novelist who adored Kyle Onstott's novel and wrote letters of praise to its author, urging him to write more books set at the Falconhurst slave breeding plantation. But it would be Horner himself who would end up writing *Mandingo* sequels.

Kenric Lancaster Horner was born in New York on August 4, 1902, to George and Estella (maiden name: Lancaster) Horner. Lance Horner served in the Coast Guard during World War II and became a long-time advertising art director and copywriter in Boston. He was also an antique dealer (with two shops in Massachusetts), a constant traveler, a patron of the arts, an amateur weight lifter, and a bullfighting fan. Like Onstott, Horner never married, was interested in slave history, intrigued by the black race, known as an eccentric, and began writing novels late in life. Unlike Onstott, he was open about his homosexuality.

In 1956, the year before *Mandingo*'s release, Horner had published his own first novel at the age of fifty-four. *The Street of the Sun* revolved around slavery in 18th century Cuba and, while not as explicitly as Onstott's book, dealt frankly with the trade and contained many elements that would appear in later novels set at Falconhurst, such as slave auctions and interracial sex that produces light-skinned blacks who pass for white. Horner referred to Cuba as his "second home" and, like his later books, *The Street of the Sun* was very descriptive of the setting's culture. The painting used for the dust jacket was done by the author. From 1956 until his death in 1973, Horner would write fourteen epic-length novels and all would be published.

Publisher Bill Denlinger had been looking for a lurid, similarly-themed novel to follow *Mandingo* and found it in Horner's *The Tattooed Rood*, which covered the Spanish Inquisition and slave trading in Havana. Denlinger secured the *The Tattooed Rood* copyright in his own name and released the book in hardcover in 1960. To make it stand out in store windows, the book was promoted as "A new novel by the author of *Mandingo*" and credited to "Kyle Onstott with Lance Horner" despite the fact that Horner had written it alone. *Independent Press-Telegram* in Long Beach, California, called it "as lustful a book as you're likely to come across, jam-packed with action and sweeping violence and adventure." *The Tattooed Rood* wasn't a *Mandingo*-like sensation, but when Fawcett/Crest released it to the paperback market in 1961, it became a steady seller and stayed in print for a decade as it went through several cover designs and numerous printings.

Meanwhile, *Mandingo* paperbacks continued to fly off the racks, and it was obvious that readers would gladly buy more grisly novels about Falconhurst and its master and slave residents. But Onstott had not been especially proud or fond of *Mandingo* and wasn't interested in writing a sequel, especially since he was now a wealthy old man and was collecting enough in royalties to last well beyond his limited lifetime. To get a sequel, Denlinger made arrangements with Onstott and with the tireless Horner, who was eager to write about Falconhurst. Under the agreement, Horner would write a follow-up and mail his completed chapters to the *Mandingo* creator for editing and approval. Onstott would be the sequel's sole copyright holder and would be billed as the book's lone author.[1]

Using research from his many trips to Africa and New Orleans, Horner came up with a hefty epic called *Drum*. Structured as three "Books," the novel deals with three generations of male slaves of Royal Hausa descent: Tamboura, a captured African prince taken to Cuba in the late 1700s; Drum, son of Tamboura, who lives with his white mother, Alix, at her New Orleans whorehouse in the 1820s; and Drumson, offspring of Drum and slave girl Calinda, who becomes a slave breeder in Alabama of the 1840s. *Drum* does not become an actual sequel to *Mandingo* until the third "Book," when the now thirty-year-old Hammond Maxwell brings Drumson to Falconhurst, where the reader is reintroduced to Onstott's characters that were still alive at the end of *Mandingo*. (Patriarch Warren Maxwell survived the first book but is dead before *Drum* gets to Falconhurst.) At one point, the drunk, delirious, and remorseful Hammond imagines that Drumson is the resurrection of Mede.

Each "Book" ends tragically with the death of the main character. (Drumson is decapitated while helping to defend Falconhurst from a slave uprising.) While the multi-part *Drum* gives equal pages to all three protagonists, the novel's title comes from the second story's main character, presumably so that this follow-up would have a memorable one-word title like *Mandingo*.

While not quite as flavorful a writer as Onstott, Horner was a good storyteller and provided *Drum* with rich characters, quotable dialogue, and exciting action. It is apparent that he was interested in and had researched the period. *Drum* doesn't skimp on *Mandingo*-like graphic scenes of bodily functions, punishment, humiliation, and fisticuffs or interracial sex—only this time even more homosexuality was added to the mix. The openly gay Horner always added lewd (white and black) homosexual characters to his novels and often included gay sex scenes. Horner would frequently write about "glabrous" male skin and would describe male nipples as "copper pennies."

Among the notable characters in the Falconhurst section of *Drum* is Sophie, Maxwell Hammond's spoiled, cross-eyed, sadistic, twelve-year-old daughter. One slave explains, "Ain' a buck on this plantation but what afeared of that Miz Sophie. She a bad 'un. Likes to play round wid de boys and ain' no one kin stop her. No boy dast to go to Masta Hammond an' tell him. All scairt for fear he kill 'em." Sophie had been introduced in *Mandingo*, where she was born before her mother, Blanche, had the scandalous, fatal tryst with the slave Mede.

Reiterating Onstott's previous depiction of the era's sexual atmosphere, Horner wrote in *Drum*:

> The youths of the period were hot-blooded and impetuous; the maidens, despite their magnolia-petaled [sic] purity, were at least curious. If the slaves enjoyed the sexual acts, why should not they? And they did…many a week-ending young man-cousin carried away the memory of having deflowered the plantation's resident charmer. Just as Hammond had discovered that his bride had already been initiated by her own brother, so had many another Southern bridegroom discovered that the supposed virginal little missy whom he had married was most practiced from having "played house" with her brothers, cousins and friends and, occasionally, from having encouraged the advances of some mulatto house slave.

Although Bill Denlinger had commissioned *Drum* and had the rights to have his own company publish it, he felt that the sequel to a bestseller would be better served by a major publisher and arranged for the New York house The Dial Press to release the novel as a 502-page hardcover in 1962. The Dial dust jacket featured a white couple admiring a proud black man and a submissive black woman as they are displayed at auction.

Drum was promoted as "by the author of *Mandingo*" on the dust jacket, but a page in the front matter read:

This volume is dedicated, with his permission,
to my good friend and valued collaborator
LANCE HORNER
to whom I am profoundly obligated for the
assistance he has given me and without whose
insistence, aid, and persistent encouragement
the book would never have been finished.

The Dial hardcover of *Drum* was well-received by the public and some critics. Edna L. Vercini, *Bridgeport* (Connecticut) *Sunday Post*: "*Drum* is not for the fainthearted or weak-stomached. It is full of violence and cruelty. It is a startling, sensuous, shocking novel—and it is a dramatically written, fascinating story which will hold your interest to the last line on the last page. Onstott pulls no punches in this book....Here is the South without the scent of magnolias or the rustle of hoopskirts and without any attempt to gloss over the brutal acts of an era in which slave trading and slave-breeding were a way of life in part of this country....*Drum* is a compelling and powerful saga of an authentic and shameful slice of American history."

Virginia Kirkus Bulletin: "*Drum* is the story of three generations of Negro slaves...we follow three strong and handsome men through sex-and fight-filled lives to sudden gory deaths...This is an immensely readable novel.... Mr. Onstott writes with a ruthless skill."

Another reviewer wrote: "It is so superlatively filmic as to be a potential companion piece to Hollywood's best adventure films." (An exciting movie version would appear in 1976.)

Fawcett/Crest released a paperback *Drum*, which, unlike the *Mandingo* paperback, was unabridged. The cover art did not focus on the interracial aspects and instead presented a black man in a skimpy shirt standing proudly while a light-skinned black female crouched beneath him, clutching his leg. The British hardcover and paperback were released by W. H. Allen and Pan, respectively. W. H. Allen would also handle the British release of all of the later Falconhurst entries.

The substantial paperback sales of *Drum* encouraged Horner to visit the plantation once again and write *Master of Falconhurst*, again with editorial input from Onstott. The two authors met in person only once or twice during their nine-year acquaintance, but they developed a close relationship through numerous personal letters in which they discussed not only the fictional Falconhurst, but their real-life sexual fetishes.

Lance Horner, 1956.

Horner saved his correspondence from Onstott. One person who read the letters years after both authors had died would describe much of the content as "embarrassing" and one that revealed Onstott and Horner's mutual fondness for brown-skinned young boys.

The third Falconhurst entry, like *Drum*, is broken up into three "Books" and the story is again told mostly through the viewpoint of a male slave. The main character this time is Drummage, the son of the previous novel's Drumson and a favorite of Hammond Maxwell. While Hammond fights in the Civil War, the clever and charismatic Drummage marries the master's daughter, Sophie, and effectively controls the plantation. At the conclusion, Drummage is killed by a band of vicious, hooded white men and Sophie dies while giving birth to a new Drum—the pale-skinned, part-Mandingo, gold-haired son of Drummage.

Master of Falconhurst is a rambling but readable 470-pager with a major subplot about Apollon Beauchair, a vain, light-skinned biracial con man who passes himself off as white and tries to seize Falconhurst by bedding Sophie. (A large birthmark on Apollon's pale buttocks gives him away.) Black characters passing for white was a favorite plot device of Horner's and would be used many more times in the series.

In this entry Hammond Maxwell, the main character of *Mandingo* and part of *Drum*, dies (unceremoniously and off-stage) of dysentery while at war. Also killed off were Sophie (described as having "her mother's vapid good looks and her nymphomania, along with her limited mental capabilities"), Ellen (Hammond's slave mistress), and the now eighty-year-old Lucretia Borgia (all from the first two novels), as well as Augusta (Hammond's second wife, first introduced in *Drum*). Several new characters pop up briefly and pointlessly, including three runaway slaves, whose escape attempt ends almost immediately when the grown male in the group decides to rape and kill both of his conspirators—a woman and her teenage son—in a bizarre vignette that has nothing to do with anything else in the book.

Once again, the fictional Falconhurst drama is blended with actual historical events and organizations including the Civil War and the Ku Klux Klan. (A small illustration appears on one page to depict an ominous note from the Klan.)

Master of Falconhurst contains probably the most effective and concise passage of the series describing life on the notorious plantation:

> The entire plantation at Falconhurst centered around its cash crop— its slaves. The produce of its fields was to feed them, its dairies gave them strength and vigor, its hens laid eggs for them to eat, its spinning and weaving sheds produced clothes for them to wear, and this complete, concentrated endeavor produced the finest specimens of Negro manhood and womanhood that ever stepped up onto an auction block...Nobody at Falconhurst worked very hard or was driven very hard. The Falconhurst slaves were not work horses and one of the greatest difficulties was to keep them all busy... Such was the easygoinglife of the plantation slave at Falconhurst where there was little cotton to be chopped and picked and no white overseer to curse and whip.

In 1964 *Drum* publisher Dial Press handled the hardcover printing of *Master of Falconhurst* and came up with an unattractive dust jacket painting that depicts the plantation and, presumably, Drummage and Sophie. (This would be the last book of the series to be published in hardcover in the

United States.) The sole writing credit again went to editor Onstott, but the true author was mentioned in the front matter: "I wish to acknowledge the collaboration of Lance Horner in the writing of this book and extend to him my gratitude for his valuable assistance."

Like its predecessors, *Master of Falconhurst* received a number of stunned and surprisingly positive critical notices. The Ft. Wayne *News Sentinel*: "Not for the fainthearted or weak-stomached. It is full of violence and cruelty. *Master of Falconhurst* is a startling, sensuous shocking novel, a dramatically written, compelling story which holds the reader's interest to the last page."

The Austin, Texas *American*: "A book of violence—of violent love, of violent suppression and punishment of Negroes, and of violent death....*Master of Falconhurst* is likely to be extremely shocking but hard to put down."

Bridgeport (Connecticut) *Sunday Post*: "There is cruelty, lust and hatred in *Master of Falconhurst*, and the mirror which it holds up to the post-war South, with its carpetbaggers, Ku Klux Klan, and Union League, does not reflect a pretty part of our American heritage...the book is a compelling tale, the work of a master storyteller. It is a worthy successor to Mr. Onstott's other novels—and, we would hope, the predecessor of still further segments of the Falconhurst saga."

Dallas *Times-Herald*: "Onstott writes skillfully, ruthlessly, through sex- and fight-filled lives to terrible and quick gory deaths....*Master of Falconhurst* is fiction, but under the author's masterful skill and knowledge of genetics and anthropology, this novel becomes stark realism."

The Worcester (Massachusetts) *Telegram*: "A powerful, lusty and honest novel....The combination of authentic detail, compelling writing and an outstanding story line make this novel a highlight of the current publishing season."

Lexington (Kentucky) *Herald-Leader*: "fascinating, revolting, morbid, interesting and sadistic...strikes with a sledge-hammer blow fit to rock the reader in his tracks."

George Panton, *The Sunday Gleaner* (Kingston, Jamaica): "Nowadays people tend to know just what is historical writing, and what is a fictional treatment of the facts, with extra details added to titillate the reader....Onstott has come out with another saga of the black man's burden in the United States of America—not at present, but in the times just before and after their Civil War....Both white and colored [characters] in this novel are full-blooded, so it is no wonder that there is much sexual activity....This novel is tongue in cheek....It has the ingredients that please the undemanding reader—the reader that is, that does not want his novels to be literature."

The Fawcett/Crest *Master of Falconhurst* paperback, billed as "the fiery new novel by Kyle Onstott [,] the bestselling author of *Mandingo* and *Drum*," was soon available with a cover blurb from the *Boston Herald* hailing it as "Lusty, Violent, Cruel and Mighty." The attractive, surprisingly non-exploitive cover painting featured three antebellum characters standing in front of a column—a distinguished black house slave, a white man in a long coat, and a beautiful dark-haired white woman in a cleavage-revealing gown. Its probable that the artist of this nicely designed illustration knew nothing about the novel's characters, but these images seem like good representations of Drummage, Hammond and Augusta. (A later Fawcett printing featured alternate, and more typical, artwork of a shirtless, muscular black man standing over a petite white Southern belle with heaving cleavage.)

Horner took a break from Falconhurst—but not from slavery—with his next project. *Rogue Roman* was a long period epic billed as "a savage novel of a slave whose passions fed the fires of Rome and overturned an empire."

Like the Falconhursts, *Rogue Roman* contains slaves with the "odor of musk" and vignettes where well-endowed male slaves have their genitals and foreskins fondled and examined. It is one of the author's weaker books with a tedious, convoluted plot and reams of laughable dialogue. ("You bully, you brute, you stinking gladiator, you hired prick, you paid screwboy!") One scene has the naked, aroused main character standing before a female cast member as they perform a play. Horner writes: "Containing himself no longer and in view of half of Antioch, he exploded in a spasm of drama such as no theatergoer had ever seen."

Rogue Roman was published as a paperback by Pyramid Books in 1965, and Horner received sole author credit for the first time since his first novel in 1956. But Onstott's name was still on *Rogue Roman* as writer of the foreword: "A remarkable book....It is not for the prudish, but for those readers who can endure the truth, it will provide the same thrilling experience it did for me.... It came to me in installments as Lance Horner, with whom I have collaborated on several books, wrote it....I particularly enjoyed it because of its candor and the fact that nothing was being withheld from the reader....[Some] incidents were stimulating as, for instance, the description of the orgies."[2]

While *Rogue Roman* was not originally handled by Horner's regular house, Fawcett re-released it in 1969 with cover art by Frank Frazetta and an "author of" credit that tied Horner to the Falconhurst series.

Horner focused on Roman male slaves again in his next novel, *Child of the Sun*, which dealt with an insatiable gay emperor. This time, editor Onstott was credited as coauthor and was billed above Horner. W. H. Allen published a British hardcover in 1966, but *Child of the Sun* didn't hit American racks until 1972, when Fawcett issued a paperback version with a Frazetta cover.

Fawcett's belated releases of *Rogue Roman* and *Child of the Sun* indicated that the publisher didn't think their readers would be particularly interested in Roman slavery. But while Fawcett definitely wanted another novel about Mandingo slaves, there was a problem with continuing the Falconhurst series. In *Master of Falconhurst* many of the characters that had been around since *Mandingo* (including protagonist Hammond Maxwell) had been killed off, and the plot involved the end of the Civil War and the emancipation of the slaves. Much of the lurid appeal of *Mandingo* and the sequels was due to the books's frank depiction of the slave trade and the resulting interracial mating. Now that Horner's pen (with Onstott's approval) had ended the peculiar institution, further entries could not be set on a slave-breeding farm.

A post-slavery sequel to *Master of Falconhurst* would probably have alienated fans of the series, but Fawcett and Horner solved this problem by bringing back the beloved dead characters and re-shackling the freed slaves in prequels set at and around Falconhurst prior to the Civil War. *Falconhurst Fancy*, the first of the prequels, begins about eighteen years before the events of *Mandingo* and is set primarily at Dove Cote, a plantation "in the next county." The story focuses on Dovie Verder, a gorgeous but neglected and sexually frustrated Southern belle. When she is widowed, Dovie satisfies her "animal craving" by purchasing the magnificent slave Colt and begins a forbidden and, of course, ill-fated affair with this "fancy" (a slave-breeder term for an exceptionally beautiful specimen.)

Warren and Hammond Maxwell pop up briefly, and pointlessly, during the novel's fifteen-year chronology, most prominently when they sell Colt to the heroine, but the plot has nothing to do with earlier Falconhurst books. Much of the "Raising Slaves 101" from *Mandingo* is repeated and there are graphic passages on slave auctions, genital inspection and whippings ("He looked like a hunk o' meat what the buzzards bin a-pickin' at."). Once again, a light-skinned black tries to pass for white.

Dovie Verder is a decent pulp romance heroine with more depth than most females in the Falconhurst books, but *Falconhurst Fancy* is one of the weaker Horner entries and reads like an already-completed Southern Gothic that was tenuously tied into the series for marketing purposes. The novel ends abruptly and appears to be setting up *Dovie of Dove Cote, Book II*, but while she would appear in future entries, none would feature Dovie prominently.

Other new *Falconhurst Fancy* characters that would reappear later were: Ransom Lightfoot, a corn-drinking, ruggedly handsome (but slovenly and unwashed) white trash sadist who finds whipping slaves "pleasantly erotic"; Fronie, the gorgeous octoroon; and the six-fingered rich white man Tommy Verder, who rapes both Dovie and Fronie, resulting in the mute heir Tommy (a.k.a. "The Dummy") and the white-skinned (except for dark spots on his stomach) Calico. The latter character would become one of the major and most popular figures in later books.

Fawcett distributed *Falconhurst Fancy* in the summer of 1966 under their Gold Medal Books imprint, which had recently been created for titles that skipped hardcover release and debuted in paperback. The cover blurb read: "They Sent The Colt Out To Stud—Only This Time, The Colt Was A Man," while publicity noted: "[Onstott and Horner] believe that *Falconhurst Fancy* will trigger the same kind of controversy that greeted the other books." Cover art depicted a shirtless black man standing over a frail blonde. This was the first Falconhurst to use this visual theme, but the image of a powerfully built, shirtless black man being lusted after by a submissive white woman would later become associated with the series and the many, many imitators.

Publishers Weekly: "Long, lurid, with its sexual variations fully rung, this is just what Mr. Onstott's fans want."

Falconhurst Fancy was the first "paperback original" of the series and the first to give a writing credit to Horner, even listing his name before Onstott's. Horner had once again sent the manuscript to Onstott for editing, and also shipped the old man some costly paintings of male nudes. (The *Falconhurst Fancy* copyright would be co-owned by Onstott and Horner.)

The next year, Horner's name was before Onstott's on the cover of another slavery novel without the Falconhurst slaves. Horner frequently traveled to Haiti and would have lived there if the country had not been ruled by a totalitarian government. His research led to *The Black Sun*, a typically long epic set in the Caribbean during the 18th century. The premise dealt with a white plantation owner who was (surprise!) attracted to black women. In addition to interracial sex between master and slave, the story included homosexuality, voodoo, and a slave revolution. With artwork depicting a white gentleman holding the hand of an elegant black lady with a parasol, Fawcett released the paperback in early 1967 as "the towering new novel by Lance Horner and Kyle Onstott [,] author of *Mandingo*." This would be the last time that Fawcett would put Kyle Onstott's name on the cover of a new book.

In June of 1966 (prior to the publication of *Falconhurst Fancy* and *The Black Sun*), the seventy-nine-year-old Onstott died of heart failure in San Francisco, where he had spent his final years. A tiny funeral notice in the *San Francisco Chronicle* noted that he was "a member of the Authors Guild and an international all breed judge for the American Kennel Club," but made no mention of the fact that he had written an international best-selling novel that had spawned an entire publishing genre or that his "brand name" was on millions of paperbacks.

Not mentioned in the funeral notice as a survivor was the author's adopted and estranged son, Philip Onstott, who had helped with the research and editing of *Mandingo*. Shortly after *Mandingo* was published, Philip married his second wife while his first wife, Vicky, became Kyle's live-in caretaker.

Dust jacket of first edition.

When Kyle died, his entire estate was left to Vicky, who died of cancer less than a month later, leaving Vicky's sister as the lone recipient of Kyle's estate and his future book royalties. A $10,000 out-of-court settlement was eventually awarded to Philip's son. During the 1960s and 70s, Philip taught anthropology at Sacramento City College in California. He died in 1992 at age eighty.

Decades after Kyle Onstott's death, *Mandingo* and the half-dozen other novels credited to him would still be in print worldwide, and "Kyle Onstott" was an ubiquitous pulp fiction brand name of the 1960s and 70s. Unlike other best-selling writers, very little was ever written about Onstott before or after his death, and there was no author photo on *Mandingo* or any of his other books. Because of this, some odd myths about the writer would arise over the years. Many felt that "Kyle Onstott" was a false name used on *Mandingo* (and the sequels) by a prolific paperback hack. Some fans believed that he was a black descendant of slaves who was recounting the true stories of his ancestors. Noted cult film and pop culture historian Michael Weldon once described Onstott as "supposedly a pseudonym for a black French Quarter queen." [3]

Although Onstott was dead and had been retired from writing for quite some time, the tireless Horner—who had moved from Boston to St. Petersburg, Florida, by this point—was not slowing down and was by no means finished with Falconhurst. His next entry, *The Mustee*, was not a direct follow-up to *Falconhurst Fancy*, but an immediate sequel to *Mandingo*. It was set about two years after the original novel and about ten years before the Falconhurst section of *Drum*.

Horner explained the new novel's title in his foreword:

> ...we go back to Spanish for the word *mestizo*, which was used to signify a person whose colored blood was so considerably attenuated that in some cases it was scarcely discernible. Although the word *mulatto* remained unchanged in its journey from Cuba to the United States, the word *mestizo* was anglicized to *mustee* and, during slave times in the southern United States, it came to signify a white or nearly white Negro, such as an octoroon.

In *The Mustee*, Charles Woodford, the sadistic, cross-eyed, thieving cousin from *Mandingo*, comes to Falconhurst to cheat money out of the lonely Warren Maxwell. (Hammond, shamed that his wife gave birth to a black baby, is away on the self-imposed exile that he left for at the end of the first novel.) Charles is accompanied by his handsome and well-educated mustee slave, Bras d'Or, who is physically and sexually abused by his owner. After Charles fatally beats the ailing patriarch, he is brutally clawed and bitten to death by the enraged Falconhurst house slaves. ("Both eyes were hanging from their sockets, one ear had been bitten off, and the body under the tatters of clothing was a mass of bleeding meat.") The blonde-haired mustee poses as a white man named Herman Hengst and successfully handles the Maxwell family slave trade for several years until Hammond returns at the novel's end and immediately sees that Bas d'Or is part-black. The mustee is given his freedom and sails to Havana to start a new life.

The Mustee is a fast, solid read and the best of the Horner-written entries besides *Drum*. The Falconhurst history and breeding rituals are repeated again for those who did not read or had forgotten the earlier entries. A number of characters make welcome return appearances, including house slave Lucretia Borgia ("She was a born boss"); the spoiled little heir Sophie; Drumson, the slave fighter from *Drum*; Madame Alix, the whorehouse ruler from *Drum*; Roche, the elderly pedophile slave owner from *Mandingo*; Dovie Verder from *Falconhurst Fancy*, now a successful slave breeder who collects male slaves for her own amusement; and Ellen, Hammond's true love from the first novel, who, now fat and unattractive to Hammond, becomes Bras d'Or's lover and the mother of one of his children. Mede, the fighting slave who was boiled alive in *Mandingo*, does not appear of course, but his skull and bones rest on a mantelpiece, and his presence hangs over the Falconhurst gang.

An interesting new character, who appears too briefly, is Hambone, a fighting slave with a tendency to bite off his opponent's testicles. Literary figure (and octoroon) Alexandre Dumas also pops up.

Fawcett/Gold Medal released *The Mustee* in 1967 as "The new novel in the continuing saga of *Mandingo*." Horner received his first sole author credit on a Falconhurst book. While this was the only early entry that did not have a slave market vignette, the cover art showed a white man auctioning off a cleavage-spilling black woman. The Springfield, Illinois *Journal-Register* called *The Mustee* "The *Peyton Place* of the South."

The constant intercourse among the fertile characters insured that Falconhurst's population would be constantly growing and that Horner would have plenty of new and old figures to write about. As the series went on, plot threads from previous entries were often cleverly incorporated into new books, leading one to wonder if Horner had extensively mapped out the chronology in advance. Because of the constantly repeated back history, it was always possible for a first-time Falconhurst reader to pick up a random entry and not be lost.

The insatiable paperback readers wanted more Falconhurst stories and Horner and Fawcett were happy to oblige. *Heir to Falconhurst* was published in 1968, a year after *The Mustee*. But it was not a direct sequel to the previous entry. The story takes place in 1886–1887, after *Master of Falconhurst*, and is the only book in the series set entirely after the Civil War.

Falconhurst has become a cotton plantation and no longer breeds or trades slaves. As the orphaned son of Sophie Maxwell and Drummage, the now-grown Drum is heir to the estate. Drum is a sexually insatiable narcissist with dark olive-colored skin which he finds, "far more attractive than the milk white skin of his friends, which always reminded him of the underbelly of dead fish." At Falconhurst, the supposedly free black servants are mistreated by Narcisse, the light-skinned, sadistic overseer who moonlights as the organizer of the Big Ten—a group of hooded, towering, pure-black rapists and thieves. After a bizarre twist ending, where it is revealed that Narcisse led a double life as a mask-wearing sex performer named Harlequin, the book closes with Drum and his biracial lover Claire planning their future together. But all further entries were prequels, and this couple was never written about again.

Heir to Falconhurst is the only entry without Hammond Maxwell or Lucretia Borgia, both of whom died in *Master of Falconhurst.* A character that does appear is Drum's personal servant, Mede, the son of Big Pearl and her brother—the late, original Mede from *Mandingo.* Big Pearl has more to do here than in earlier entries, but dies late in the book.

In addition to the usual brutal torture, threatened castration, eye-gouging, and gay incest, *Heir to Falconhurst* still had enough vignettes to shock loyal readers, including a disturbing episode where the Big Ten gang-rapes a white "widder" and her two young daughters, one of whom sobs constantly during the attack while the second begs for more. *Heir to Falconhurst* is a fair entry with some good atmospheric writing in a cemetery scene that reveals the Maxwell family history, and in Drum/Claire's love scene, which ranks as one of the more erotic of the series. ("The tip of his tongue touched and teased the hard, upstanding nipples.")

The *Heir to Falconhurst* cover art depicted a blonde curly haired man and a high-class black woman standing in front of a canopy-covered bed. The man could be imagined as Drum, but the female is too dark to be Claire, and it's obvious that this painting was not created specifically for this novel. Fawcett's publicity boasted: "Grass-roots critical reactions reflect the fascination that the theme of the Kyle Onstott-Lance Horner books holds for modern Americans."

Fawcett's huge Gold Medal line of paperback originals (which included the "Matt Helm" series by Donald Hamilton and the "Travis McGee" series by John D. MacDonald) sold extremely well during this era. Top paperbacks, like the Falconhursts, would have print runs of several hundred thousand copies and could be found in upscale bookstores as well as in the spinning wire racks at drug stores, smoke shops and bus stations.

The phenomenal, perpetual sales of *Mandingo* and its follow-ups spawned a new pulp genre known alternately as "slave fiction," "slaver novels," "slave gothics," "plantation novels" and "bodice-rippers." Throughout the 1960s and

70s dozens of these sleazy, hastily written paperback originals were stuffed into the racks and devoured by readers. With titles like *Machismo*, *Muscavado*, *Flamingo*, *Voodoo Slave*, *Dark Master*, *Ratoon*, *Chane*, *Slaver*, *The Slave Stealer*, *Slave Queen*, *Quadroon*, *Plantation Breed*, *Chains*, *Black Brute*, *The Stonehedge Slaves* and *The Long Whip*, these knockoffs made no pretense about their inspiration. The covers were splashed with blurbs like "In the Brutally Honest Tradition of *Mandingo*," "Even More Explosive Than *Mandingo*," "As Savage and Lusty as *Mandingo*," "More Terrible, More Wonderful Than *Mandingo*" and "Harder Than *Mandingo*! Louder than *Drum*!" The copycats that came from Fawcett proudly boasted "From the Publishers of *Mandingo*."[4] Several Falconhurst-inspired titles like *Sabrehill* and *Dragonard* led to their own successful series.

All of these paperback clones tried to outdo *Mandingo* in terms of sex, sadism, incest and punishment, but perhaps the most extreme of the "slaver novels" was *Mistress of the Bayou Labelle* by the prolific Lou Cameron, published by Lancer in 1968. In this potboiler's ghastly climax, the evil white title character is thrown through a glass window, brutally beaten and gang raped by drunken, vengeful slaves, and—after being covered with bodily fluids and having her nipple torn off—is finally raped to death by a drugged horse. Cameron didn't let up in his sequel, *Ashanti* (Lancer, 1969), which features a starving escaped slave who is partially devoured by an alligator before killing and eating a fellow runaway. The readers of these two epics certainly got their ninety-five cents worth.[5]

In the late 1960s, the Midwest was known as the major market for American paperbacks. Around 200 new paperbacks were released each month when a typical store rack could only hold eighty titles. Many books went unsold and were sent back to the publisher after one month to be replaced with a new lurid title. But *Mandingo*—a decade after its first paperback appearance—was constantly restocked along with other ubiquitous shockers like *Peyton Place*, *Candy*, *The Carpetbaggers*, *The Adventurers* and *Valley of the Dolls*. A bookseller in Muncie, Indiana, referred to these hot paperbacks as "thrill books," which "give you a thrill while you read them but don't leave you with anything." A librarian in the same town said paperbacks were used for "escape reading."

The Falconhurst novels and the imitators were also stocked (wrapped in plastic) in the notorious adult book stores of the East Coast. Mail order forms could be found among the book's final pages so readers who could not find a title on a local rack—and those who didn't want to be seen purchasing racy material—could have them delivered to their home in a plain brown wrapper.

While the original *Mandingo* paperback featured artwork of a white master leering at a submissive black female, many of the knockoff covers presented a fragile blonde Southern belle succumbing to a shirtless, powerfully built male slave. Publishers soon determined that covers with a white man and a black girl didn't sell as well, so in the early 1970s Fawcett followed the successful formula and changed the *Mandingo* cover art. New oil paintings by veteran artist Stan Borack depicting shirtless slaves with adoring blondes were used on re-releases of *Mandingo*, *Master of Falconhurst* and *Falconhurst Fancy*. (Borack's earlier work included realistic covers for numerous paperbacks and adventure magazines including *Stag* and *Zane Grey's Western Magazine*.)

The "slaver novels" were grabbed by men and women of both races looking for lurid reads. In a 1968 *New York Times* article about readers in the city's black ghettos, Mel Watkins discovered: "Older [black] people, according to book dealers, have reacted to the accessibility of paperbacks with increased purchasing of best sellers and potboilers with heavy concentrations of sex and sensationalism…[including] *Mandingo* or other titles from the fictional series on slavery by Kyle Onstott….Basically these people seem to approach reading purely for entertainment." The study found that "potboilers" were read in the black community by "the better educated older people…the less educated of the older people and, moreover, many of the less educated young adults."

George Panton in a 1970 piece for the *Gleaner* (Kingstree, Jamaica): "Among the luridly-illustrated book covers that pry the new Jamaica dollar from many pockets are those that feature lusty black bucks being clasped by blonde wenches, or the reverse side of the same coin—randy Anglo-Saxon men cuddling half-caste gals who are obviously attractive, but clearly not the official or approved consorts of these blonde gallants….The [books] arouse visceral re-actions of one sort or another and one guesses that the authors know that they are writing near-pornography….It must be admitted that Lance Horner and Kyle Onstott seem to have done a deal of research on certain aspects of slavery in the Deep South."

In the classic 1973 study *Black Players: The Secret World of Black Pimps*, Christina Milner (a white anthropology student who befriended pimps while working as a San Francisco stripper in the late 1960s) and husband Richard Milner noted: "Pulp novels in which Black male slaves conquer and win the affections of White Southern belles are devoured by some White hos [sic] with Black pimps. Shannon [a white prostitute] expressed her fascination with one such novel called *Black Love* [1969], in which the wife of a cruel plantation owner runs way with a black slave into a swamp freedom village…. Shannon said she identified strongly with the White girl in the book. We have seen much of this type of reading matter in the homes of players,

Dust jacket of first edition.

and have often heard pimps make reference to the sexual relations between the races during the slavery period."

In the late 1960s, Maleno Malenotti and Dino De Laurentiis—two powerful film producers based in Italy, where *Mandingo* was a huge seller—purchased the movie rights to the Falconhurst books and hired Horner to be "technical advisor" for a lavish adaptation of *Mandingo* and *Drum* to be shot in 1969. The producers expected to follow their *Mandingo* movie with a *Master of Falconhurst* film, to be co-scripted by Horner, but the productions were soon aborted. De Laurentiis (without Malenotti) would produce (separate) popular movie versions of *Mandingo* (1975) and *Drum*

(1976), but not until after Horner's death. *Master of Falconhurst* never became a movie.

Horner never became a screenwriter, but he never slowed down as a novelist. In 1969 Fawcett put out the author's *The Mahound*, which told of Rory Mahound, a white slave trader in Africa, and his affair with a black harem girl. By this time, Horner was a top-selling "brand name" himself in the genre and Fawcett didn't use "Kyle Onstott" or "*Mandingo*" to promote *The Mahound*, which was heralded on the cover as "A New Novel of the Slave Trade" from the "author of *Falconhurst Fancy* and *The Mustee*."

In England, *The Mahound* was a hardcover from Allen & Unwin. A Pan paperback followed in 1972, with art of a crouching, bare-breasted dark girl and a stern, whip-clutching white man. Because of the author, the *Mandingo*-like title, and the Fawcett and Pan publishing, *The Mahound* is often erroneously considered part of the Falconhurst series.

Horner was back for an official entry with *Flight to Falconhurst*, a ten-years-later sequel to *Falconhurst Fancy*, that takes place at the same time as *Mandingo*. In a convoluted flashback, we learn that Tommy Verder (a.k.a. "The Dummy"), Dovie Verder's mute son and the heir to Dove Cote plantation, died of pneumonia shortly after being sent to a Boston college. Tommy's look-alike, mustee servant/half-brother Calico, assumed the dead heir's identity and stayed up North to become a sexually insatiable pimp. After killing a rival, Tommy/Calico flees to Dove Cote (despite the novel's title), announces himself as Dovie's son, and claims that his muteness was cured by a surgeon. Dovie (who still sleeps with Colt, her *Falconhurst Fancy* slave lover, as well as her new purchase, Pollux) learns and agrees to keep Tommy/Calico's secret. (They call each other "son" and "Sweet Mama" in a disturbing love scene.)

Tommy/Calico tries to increase his fortune by marrying the wealthy white woman Missie Acker, but his plans are thwarted when he passes out drunk at his wedding party and is undressed in the daylight by his horrified fiancée. His dark stomach splotches had been revealed earlier when his shirt was torn off by the whip of Ransom Lightfoot (Dovie's husband), but Tommy/Calico protected his secret by killing Lightfoot. Pursued by a betrayed, enraged mob of white men, Tommy/Calico escapes to New Orleans.

Hammond Maxwell appears prominently in the book's latter half, when he accompanies Tommy/Calico to a slave auction. Once again reiterated is Hammond's fear of white women, including his cousin/fiancée Blanche. At one point, he becomes physically ill during a failed encounter with a white whore. ("When I looked up in that mirror over the bed 'n' saw that woman all white like unbaked bread dough, jes' couldn't make myself do anything' for her…Puked up my whole supper.") The twenty-something Lucretia Borgia is first bought by the Maxwells in this entry, while Mem, Alph, Mede (in a fighting scene), and Warren Maxwell also make scant appearances. The old man gets the "chance to finger a real white mustee" as Calico feels "the coarse skin of the gnarled rheumatic hands going over his body."

New characters who turn up briefly to liven things up are Moe the Magimp, a sadistic New York pimp; an unnamed dwarf hunchbacked tavern owner; and Beulah, a one-legged whorehouse madam.

Released by Fawcett in April 1971, *Flight to Falconhurst* is a dull entry that rehashes so much material from *Mandingo* that it reads like a Falconhurst rip-off instead of an official entry. "Falconhurst Slave Breeding 101" is once again re-explained, and there is the usual auction block scene where the slaves "shuck down" and are "fingered and admired" while their testicles are weighed and their foreskins examined. By this point, the strong Southern dialect and regional atmosphere created by Onstott had mostly disappeared from the books. The storytelling is less verbose, suggesting that more trimming was being done by the Fawcett editors than in the past.

Flight to Falconhurst's cover had a painting of a grimacing, whip-wielding overseer leering at a dark-skinned male slave who undresses a light-skinned female slave. Like the book's title, the artwork has nothing to do with the story.

Horner's *Mistress of Falconhurst*, the eighth novel of the series, was out in 1973. Beginning in the same era as *Falconhurst Fancy* and around two decades before *Mandingo*, the loose story focused on Lucretia Borgia, introduced as an "eighteen or so…tall girl, about five feet ten [with] light tobacco-brown skin." She belongs to Elm Grove plantation, where she loves the well-built slave Big Jem, until he is kidnapped by a slave trader. (Jem is yet another of the series's potentially interesting characters who disappears immediately and permanently after being introduced.) Some *Falconhurst Fancy* characters are glimpsed early on: octoroon teenager Fronie and Calico, her six-fingered infant, as well as the white trash Ransom Lightfoot, who appears long enough to impregnate Lucretia.

After she is sold at auction to Warren Maxwell and taken to Falconhurst, Lucretia becomes close to Warren's wife, Miz Sophie, who is ashamed of her husband's business, and the five-year-old Hammond, who is already obsessed with slave breeding. (Onstott's *Mandingo* noted that Lucretia had been at Falconhurst since before Hammond was born, while *Flight to Falconhurst* had her being purchased by the Maxwells a decade later, at age twenty-something.)

Ten years later (just prior to the opening events of *Mandingo*), Miz Sophie has passed and the now-stout Lucretia runs the Falconhurst household, has several children of her own (including twins Alph and Meg). The Mandingo-obsessed Warren buys Omar, a half-Arab, half-Mandingo. When Lucretia is discovered bedding the prized slave against Warren's orders, she is stripped (except for her ever-present "turban of red calico") and given twenty lashes of a whip. (This sequence is the most effective beating in the series, due to Lucretia Borgia being the closest thing to a well-developed slave character.)

Warren gives Hammond a stallion as a sixteenth birthday gift, and the boy is thrown and breaks his leg. (*Mandingo* and other previous entries had reported that Hammond limped because a pony threw him when he was six.) Lucretia, still bleeding and in agony from her beating, gets out of bed to nurse the youth. ("She knew that she occupied a unique place in her two masters' hearts. She was more than just a black slave, more than a mere chattel. She was a person.")

Mistress of Falconhurst is a tame, odd entry in the series and certainly the least extreme and perverse novel to be credited to Onstott or Horner. Mostly a character study of Lucretia Borgia, it has the least plot and action of all of the Falconhurst books. The violence is diluted and sparse and the sex scenes try to be sensuous and erotic rather than vulgar.

There are a few memorably shocking vignettes, however: Lucretia first making love to Agamemnon (Mem) while they are chained together; Lucretia discovering that Hammond has been having sex with his "far too pretty to be a boy" slave "playboy" Audrey; and Hammond losing his virginity with Aphrodite, his first "bed wench." But almost all of the lurid elements—goose grease and bacon rind used for sex lubricant, slave genitals being examined, the paddling of bare, upside-down backsides—were recycled from earlier books.

Fawcett's cover art showed a domineering, turban-clad black woman standing on a rotted plantation porch while watching a white male firmly grasping a submissive, frightened slave girl. (The cowering girl bore no relation to anyone in the story.) The front matter gave a helpful chronological order in which the books should be read, while the back cover declared: "A story of tragedy and ultimate triumph as only Lance Horner could tell it."

On the night of June 21, 1973, Horner was in a Florida restaurant with his bisexual lover and the lover's girlfriend when he suddenly got severe stomach pains. His two companions drove him to the hospital that was the farthest one from the restaurant, and took their time getting him there. The seventy-year-old author was pronounced dead-on-arrival at 9:30 a.m. on

June 22 at St. Anthony's Hospital in St. Petersburg. Before an autopsy could be performed, Horner's companions had the body shipped immediately to Mountain View Cemetery in West Pawlet, Vermont, for cremation. A number of people, including some of Horner's relatives, suspected that the writer had been poisoned during his last meal.

Horner's lover expected to inherit the author's estate, but the collateral heirs listed in the will turned out to be some young female relatives, aged ten to twenty, who lived in New England. The Kenric L. Horner Trust was set up by a Florida bank to oversee the estate. Horner had spent most of his money on frequent trips to exotic places and had lived modestly in a small house in St. Petersburg, which was sold after his death to provide money for his young heirs. The author left behind some unfinished novels and outlines. The heirs would collect the future royalties from Horner's already-published books as well as from the many later Falconhurst-set books that were written by another author.

Like Kyle Onstott, almost nothing had been written about Horner during his rein as a top-selling author, and many readers assumed that "Lance Horner" was a pen name. The obscure, forgotten 1956 hardcover printing of *The Street of the Sun* was the only Horner novel that included an author photo.

By 1975 there were 16 million Falconhurst books in print in North America, with *Mandingo* accounting for 4.5 million of those copies. *Mandingo* had been reprinted thirty-eight times in paperback and was thirty-third on a list of top-selling books published in America from 1895 to 1975. The saga sold millions more throughout the rest of the world, including England, where each new entry still debuted in hardcover. At the time, total worldwide sales for the fifteen books credited to Onstott and/or Horner was estimated at over 25 million copies. Reader interest in other "slaver novels" was also as high as ever.[6]

Jeff Millar in *Los Angeles Times*, 1975: "*Mandingo* is the *Baby and Child Care* of bus-station literature. Nearly a whole generation of Americans, in the process of being Greyhounded from Bakersfield to Anaheim, have doubtless acquired some of their most lasting images of Southern culture from Onstott's account."

Rudy Maxa in *Washington Post*, 1975: "The success of the Falconhurst series is a publishing phenomenon: despite the fact that millions of copies of the books are sold each year, they receive little notice....[The series] sells enough copies yearly to make your average bestseller-that-simply-everyone-is-talking-about look like a piker."

Fawcett publicity director Bell Blanchard said in 1977 that "many middle American housewives" were fans of the Falconhurst series, while Fawcett editor Harvey Gardner often saw paperbacks of *Mandingo* and the sequels in the hands of many subway-riding blacks. Blanchard explained that black readers liked the series "because many think they can get some sort of historical references [about slavery] whether accurate or inaccurate. It's debatable whether they can get an accurate picture."

Andy Sawyer, a British librarian and Falconhurst fan: "it was also known for middle-aged women to enter libraries and ask for them as 'something for my husband...with plenty of whippings.'"

Al Tony Gilmore, chairman of the University of Maryland's Afro-American studies program, noted in 1977: "They're escape books that, unfortunately, help perpetuate old stereotypes. I don't think they need to be taken too seriously. After all, you don't have to buy them."

Mary Ellen Perry, *Chicago Tribune*, 1977: "You can't go into a bookstore now without being hit between the eyes with scores of plantation novels, easily identifiable by their titles and covers. Slave gothics...pound home enduring myths about the South and slavery while simultaneously contradicting the myths with an explicitness that borders on softcore pornography....[The books are] immersed in the S & R (sex and race) formula."

In a 2001 posting on Amazon.com, a woman noted: "[*Mandingo*] would never be published in this day and age...this book stands as a mirror into 1970s literature and what we read." A year later, another poster added: "As a 52-year-old Black Man, I read these books in 1969–1970 and found them fascinating."

Naturally, Fawcett was anxious to put out another Falconhurst paperback, and the Horner estate had found another writer who could immediately take over the series. But the business relationship—in regards to rights—between Onstott, Horner and *Mandingo*'s original publisher Bill Denlinger was complicated. Back in 1957, Denlinger had registered himself as *Mandingo*'s lone copyright holder, and he claimed that he was entitled to a financial cut of all books relating to Falconhurst. Horner's heirs retained a law firm in Washington, D.C., that specialized in copyright law. The Onstott estate, unhappy with Denlinger's payment of royalties, hired a San Francisco attorney.

When the attorneys for the Horner estate needed an "expert witness" during the copyright battles, they brought in Earl F. Bargainner. Perhaps the only academic scholar to ever take the Falconhurst books seriously, Bargainner was a Southern literature professor at the all-woman Wesleyan College in Macon, Georgia, where his class curriculum included the reading and study of *Mandingo*. He published a pair of lengthy essays on the Falconhurst series and was quoted in several articles related to the books.

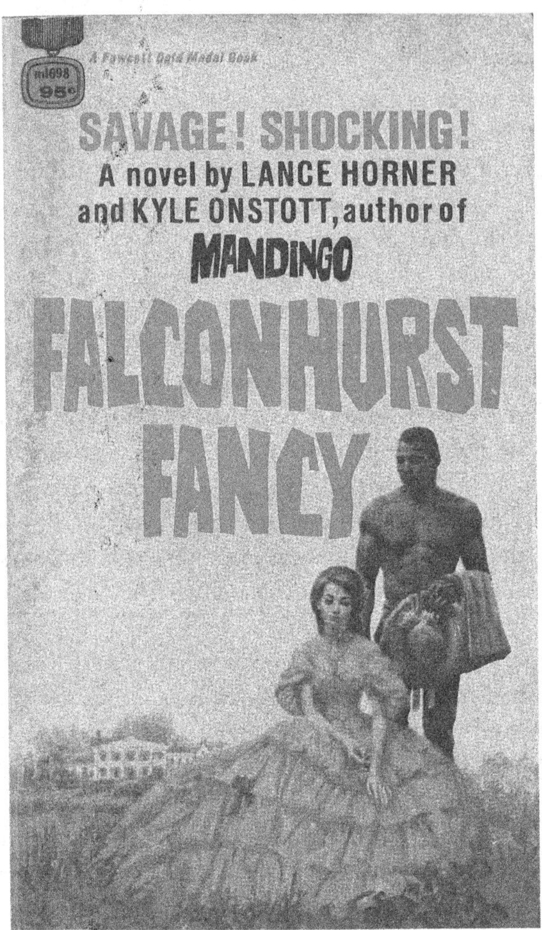

First edition.

Bargainner: "The myth of the Old South was first created after the Civil War. The writers of the 1870s created the happy darkies, the white suits, the white columns. Then came the Uncle Remus stories about the docile slaves. That portrayal continued right up to *Gone with the Wind* which was the apotheosis of the myth....Onstott made sex and violence the big things, replacing the myth of moonlight and magnolia with the mix of sex and sadism....It is easy to ridicule the novels of [Onstott and Horner]. There are errors in chronology and anachronisms; the plots are episodic...and contain massive amounts of coincidence; the characters, both black and white, are stereotypes which are repeated again and again; and sex and violence are so overdone as to become almost parodic. Nevertheless, the novels still sell....It seems likely that, whatever critics may think of the image the novels present of slavery, that image of sex, sadism, and miscegenation will continue to have popular appeal. *Why* is another question."

At hearings related to the Falconhurst copyright battle, Bargainner presented exhaustive timelines of the novels and the characters which were used to show that much of the Falconhurst legend had been created exclusively by Horner. Meanwhile, Denlinger's legal team was trying to prove that almost all of material in the later books had originally appeared in Onstott's *Mandingo*, whose copyright was owned by Denlinger.

In 1975, two years after Lance Horner's death, the author's unfinished Falconhurst manuscript *Six-Fingered Stud* was completed by Fawcett/Gold Medal editor Lawrence Blochman (acknowledged in the American copies for his "invaluable editorial assistance") and the uncredited Harry Whittington, a prolific pulp veteran who would soon be writing regularly for the Horner estate.

Six-Fingered Stud picks up immediately after *Flight to Falconhurst* as Tommy Verder (a.k.a. Calico) flees to New Orleans when his intended marriage to Missy Acker (previously spelt as "Missie") is ruined by the revelation of his secret identity. Verder is pursued by Hammond (oddly called Hamilton in the British text) Maxwell, falls in love with the octoroon slave Chloe and becomes a slave dealer after joining pirate Jean Lafitte on a smuggling expedition to Havana. (A shipmate advises, "Every slave sold today must be a potential breeder....Always be sure that a boy has two balls.") In the end, Hammond confronts Verder, Chloe is killed, and the heartbroken mustee escapes to Haiti to continue his slave-smuggling career.

The enjoyable, if not surprisingly far-fetched, adventure story is marred by having the annoying, self-centered Tommy "Calico" Verder as its hero. Despite—or because of—his convoluted history, Verder is the dullest major character of the series. (An asterisk instructs the reader to "see *Flight to Falconhurst*" for clarification of the character's confusing background.)

A vignette with Verder witnessing the anal and genital inspection of a male slave is the single most graphic and nauseating of the series's many examination scenes. At different points, Verder and Hammond each visit Madame Alix's whorehouse and encounter the original Drum. (The story takes place at the same time as the middle section of *Drum*.) Interesting new slave characters are: Koko, a feisty, statuesque Songhai princess, who bites Verder's buttocks during foreplay; and Panchita, "a hot little number" who chews off a testicle of the Cuban vice-governor.

In England, *Six-Fingered Stud* was published in hard and soft covers as "the latest mighty epic of Falconhurst." But in America, the ongoing copyright battles with Denlinger caused the book to be renamed *Golden Stud* and rewritten as an unofficial Falconhurst clone.

Golden Stud turned Tommy Verder (a.k.a. Calico)—the six-fingered mustee with dark splotches on his torso that reveal his biracial pedigree—into the light-skinned Jeff Carson (a.k.a. Bricktop, because of his red hair), who has "a sixth sense about women" and a brand on his back that identifies his secret slave background. Hammond Maxwell of Falconhurst became Baxter Simon of Willow Oaks, while Missy Acker was changed to Minnie George, Madame Alix to Madame Hortense, and Drum to Lancer. The brief mentions of Warren Maxwell, Dovie Verder and her slave/lover Colt as well as Verder's flashbacks of Falconhurst were removed from the American edition. Baxter Simon was rewritten to be more evil and sadistic than Hammond Maxwell. The character would become even more reprehensible when Whittington brought Simon back for the books *Master of Blackoaks* (1976) and *Sword of the Golden Stud* (1977).

Despite not being able to promote their new Lance Horner novel as a much-anticipated *Mandingo* prequel, Fawcett/Gold Medal still gave a huge promotional push to *Golden Stud*, which was the house's major release for July 1975. The Falconhurst name was deleted from the text, but the *Golden Stud* cover and ads still boasted: "The New Bestseller by the Author of *Mistress of Falconhurst*." Less than six months after publication, 1,075,000 copies were in print.

Pan's British paperback of *Six-Fingered Stud* was out in 1977. The cover artist supplied Tommy Verder with an attractive physique but an especially haggard and homely face.

Denlinger made more money off of his Falconhurst properties when he sold the movie rights to Italian mogul Dino De Laurentiis—who produced big-budget, hit film versions of *Mandingo* and *Drum* in 1975 and 1976, respectively. Onstott's estate received a cut of Denlinger's movie money. But even though *Drum* had been ghostwritten by Horner, his heirs got nothing from the film sale. (Paperback "movie tie-ins" of the *Mandingo* and *Drum* novels were released in America and England to cash in on the controversial films and led to more royalties for the estates of both authors.)

In January of 1976, a brief mention of *Mandingo* and the successful "plantation novel" genre in the "Paper Back Talk" column of the *New York Times* prompted reader E.W. Leoni of New York City to write to the paper: "I'm delighted, as an admirer who feels that the work of Kyle Onstott and Lance Horner should eventually earn a place parallel to that of Scott in England and Dumas in France, to note some Literary Establishment acknowledgment, however left-handed." Although he doubted that Onstott actually wrote *Mandingo* because the author "was too old and literarily inexperienced to have provided more than the initial idea," Leoni noted the cult following for Horner's books and added that "it would be more sensible to have a craze of Horneries instead of Trekkies."[7]

First edition.

Notes:

1 Other publishers also felt that Onstott's name on the cover of a slave-related novel would help sales. A positive endorsement by the *Mandingo* creator was prominent on the cover of the 1960 Ace Books paperback of Edgar Mittelholzer's *Kaywana Blood,* which dealt with the slave trade in Guyana. Mittelholzer was a British Guiana native. His epic Kaywana trilogy—*Children of Kaywana* (1952), *Kaywana Stock* (1954) and *Kaywana Blood* (1958)—was about the descendents of a child born to a Guyanese woman and an English sailor. The author committed suicide in 1965 at age fifty-six by setting himself on fire.

2 Onstott described the theatre ejaculation episode as "certainly revolting, albeit substantiated by historical records....Although events such as this would certainly have to be deleted if *Rogue Roman* is ever made into a moving picture, I do feel that the story lends itself to such a medium and anxiously anticipate seeing it on the screen." *Rogue Roman* never became a film. Had Onstott lived to see them, he probably would have been surprised by the graphic accuracy of the *Mandingo* and *Drum* movies.

3 When I asked Weldon about this rumor, reported in his book *The Psychotronic Video Guide* (1996), he couldn't recall where he had heard or read this intriguing myth.

4 *The Street of the Sun*, Horner's initially unsuccessful debut novel, was reissued several times in paperback in the late 60s by Fawcett as a "novel of men and women sold into slavery" by "Lance Horner, who, with the author of *Mandingo*, wrote *Falconhurst Fancy* and *The Tattooed Rood*." In Britain, *The Street of the Sun* became a Pan paperback called *Santiago Blood*.

5 Not all of the "slaver novels" released during this era were fly-by-night paperback originals. Back in 1941 British author Marguerite Steen's *The Sun Is My Undoing*—about an 18th-century slave-trading family and the torrid romance between one of the sons and a female slave—had sold a million copies. In 1967 Avon trimmed the 1,015-page hardback to an "Authorized, Unexpurgated Abridgment" paperback with cover art of a topless slave girl and a leering master. MacKinlay Kantor was a Civil War specialist best known for his Pulitzer Prize-winning *Andersonville* (1955) about the notorious Confederate prisoner-of-war camp. His *Beauty Beast*, despite being called "the antebellum sex novel to end all antebellum sex novels," failed as a 1968 Putnam hardcover but quickly reemerged "from the publishers of *Mandingo*" as a Fawcett paperback with a slave buck/southern belle cover and the generic copy: "brings to life the passion, the decadence, the savagery of the Old South." Frances Gaither's major slavery-themed novels of the 1940s—*Follow the Drinking Gourd*, *Double Muscatine* and *The Red Cock Crows*—were each released post-*Mandingo* with Falconhurst-like cover art and

lurid blurbs. ("In the smoldering tradition of *Mandingo*—a novel of human lust, inhuman bondage and a crime of many passions.") The most popular (after *Mandingo*) and prestigious slave fiction entry of the late-1960s was William Styron's *The Confessions of Nat Turner* (1967), an embellishment of the famous true slave revolt of 1831. After debuting in hardcover and becoming a ubiquitous paperback, the novel earned its white author a Pulitzer Prize and a great deal of controversy, mainly due to the graphic descriptions of Turner's "remorseless desire" for a blonde teenage girl, who he ultimately stabs and bludgeons to death. Shortly after the novel's publication, a major film version starring James Earl Jones was announced, but aborted.

6 One of the "classier" successful Falconhurst clones of the early 1970s was Lonnie Coleman's *Beulah Land* (1973). Promoted as "Bolder than *Mandingo,*" the epic about the slave-breeding Kendricks family of Georgia sold 1.8 million paperback copies and led to the sequels *Look Away, Beulah Land* (1977) and *Legacy of Beulah Land* (1980) as well as a highly rated, all-star TV miniseries in 1980. The *Beulah Land* TV presentation was postponed and edited when the NAACP complained about the portrayal of blacks in numerous scenes, including one that was a staple of the Falconhurst books: an affluent white baby being breast-fed by a slave. *The Plantation*, a paperback original by George McNeill, was given a massive promotional push by Bantam Books in June 1975. ("Bolder than *Beulah Land.* More sensational than *Mandingo*...a world half free, half slave...ruled by uncontrolled passions between master and slave.") At 945,000 copies, it was another huge seller in the "slaver" genre.

7 No Falconhurst book, including *Mandingo*, was ever reviewed in the *New York Times*, but one of the paper's critics, Eliot Fremont-Smith, once reviewed another novel as "the absolute worst, most regurgitory new-and-advertised book that I've read in 1975, the one most deserving of the Kyle Onstott Memorial Award."

Chapter 3:
The Ashley Carter Entries

In 1975, while waiting for the rights to the Falconhurst name to be sorted out, the Lance Horner estate commissioned the tireless pulp author Harry Whittington to write (under the deliberately androgynous pen name "Ashley Carter") the novel *Master of Blackoaks*—a blatant *Mandingo* clone which centered on the sexy, violent, and lurid lives of the Baynards, a Maxwell-like dysfunctional family of pre-Civil War slave owners. "My writing life has been a blast," Whittington would write shortly before his death. "It's been a wonderful life and I've met some wonderful people. It's been one hell of a roller-coaster ride."

Harry Whittington was born on February 4, 1915, in Ocala, Florida, where he grew up on a farm and became an avid reader and moviegoer. He had careers in the 1930s as a advertising copywriter, newspaper reporter and postman before he started writing fiction. He wrote in 1986: "I spent at least seven years writing seriously and steadily before I sold anything. [In] 1943, I sold a short-short story to United Features for $15....Phoenix Press bought my first western novel, *Vengeance Valley*, [in] 1946....For the next 20 years I sold everything I wrote."

During the 1950s, he sold more paperbacks than any other author. Many were published by Fawcett, later home of the Falconhursts. Most were published under one of the almost twenty pseudonyms that he wrote under, including Whit Harrison, Kel Holland, Clay Stuart, Hondo Wells, Hallam Whitney, Blaine Stevens, and Tabor Evans. For the "nurse romance" market, he used Harriet Kathryn Myers, the real name of his daughter.

Crime/mystery author Ed Gorman recalled on his blog in 2006: "Back in the 1950s you could run but you couldn't hide from Harry Whittington... Harry told me that he'd once seen five books of his displayed on the same rack, all published that month."

Among Whittington's fine (and still-revered) suspense novels were *You'll Die Next* (Ace Books, 1954), *The Humming Box* (Ace Books, 1956), *A Night*

For Screaming (Ace Books, 1960), and *Any Woman He Wanted* (Beacon Books, 1961). He also banged out radio plays, non-fiction books on real estate, novelizations for movies like *Man in the Shadow* (1958) and *The Fall of the Roman Empire* (1964), and over one hundred short stories and novellas for magazines like *Stag*, *Male*, *Dime Detective* and *True Romance*.

Whittington recalled: "I worked hard; nobody ever wrote and sold 150-odd novels in 20 years without working hard, but I loved what I was doing. I gave my level best on absolutely every piece of my published work, for one simple reason: I knew of no other way to sell what I wrote....I needed a fast-reporting, fast-paying market; the paperbacks provided this. I wrote 8, 10, 12 hours a day. Paperback editors bought and paid swiftly. We were good for each other. The reason why I wrote and sold more than almost everybody else was that I was living on the edge of ruin, and I was naive....I wrote suspense novels, contemporary romances, westerns, regional 'backwoods' tales. People who wonder such things, wondered how I could crossover in these genres with such ease."

Whittington was signed in 1957 by Warner Brothers to write a Western feature for Gary Cooper, but the premise was turned into the TV series *The Lawman* (1958–1962) with John Russell. Several Whittington novels became movies including the sweaty Southern drama *Desire in the Dust* (1960) with

Harry Whittington (a.k.a. Ashley Carter), 1980 (Collection of David L. Wilson)

Raymond Burr and the fine spaghetti Western *Adios, Gringo* (1965) with Giuliano Gemma. He also wrote original scripts for the major (but weak) Warner Brothers Western *Black Gold* (1962) and the insane, shoestring-budget, race car epic *Fireball Jungle* (1965) featuring the ailing Lon Chaney, Jr. The latter picture was shot in Whittington's home state of Florida where, also in 1965, he wrote, produced, directed, and partially-financed a horror film called *Face of the Phantom*. The now-lost feature failed to find distribution and its auteur failed to recoup his investment. (Whittington used his real name on all of his film and television scripts.)

In 1966 Whittington's new agent foolishly encouraged him to accept a $1,500 flat fee from Ace Books to write the TV tie-in novel *The Man From U.N.C.L.E. Number 2: The Doomsday Affair*. "I saw it on the Chicago *Tribune* paperback best seller list for one full year," lamented the author, who would have collected $15,000 if he had signed a royalty deal.

In debt from his failed film venture and disgruntled by his recent dealings with publishers, Whittington took a steady-paying job in Washington, D.C. in 1968. He explained, "I threw away every unsold script, put my books in storage. I quit. I asked for a job as an editor in the U.S. Dept. of Agriculture, and they hired me for Rural Electrification Administration. I had reached the low place where writing lost its delight, the place where I refused to go on."

During his self-imposed, seven-year hiatus—which he called an "exile from the Eden of writing"—Whittington "sold only three books" including his top-selling novelization of the Elvis Presley Western *Charro* (1969). "I felt *guilty* when I wasn't at my typewriter," he recalled.

Whittington returned to paperbacks after meeting Lance Horner's last agent. He explained, "In 1974, my wife [Kathryn]...got the name and address of literary agent Anita Diamant.[1] Mrs. Diamant arranged for me to become Ashley Carter. Since 1975, I've written the Falconhurst and Blackoaks novels, the antebellum slave stories of the Mandingo slaves done by Kyle Onstott and then Lance Horner." Whittington was then living in St. Petersburg, Florida—where Horner spent his final days—but he had never met the prior Falconhurst author.

The Ashley Carter pseudonym was created by Whittington and the Fawcett staff and was inspired by two Southern icons: *Gone with the Wind* character Ashley Wilkes and Georgia governor and then-presidential candidate Jimmy Carter.

Whittington/Carter's *Master of Blackoaks* begins by focusing on Baxter "Bax" Simon of the legendary Willow Oaks slave-breeding farm. (The Simon moniker had been created for 1975's *Golden Stud* after copyright issues forced the Hammond "Ham" Maxwell name to be deleted from that book.) Baxter Simon is an exact physical copy of Hammond Maxwell and has the same viewpoints toward slaves ("I'm interested in top-grade black animals") and white women ("anything lighter of skin than a submissive mustee rendered him ill at ease"). But instead of seeking Mandingos, Simon is obsessed with owning members of the virile Fulah tribe. The novel seems to be developing Simon as the sympathetic (if flawed) protagonist, but he is banished from the Blackoaks plantation (and the book) after an early vignette when he decapitates a female runaway slave with one snap of his bullwhip and dumps her body into a pen of hungry hogs.

The lead villain of *Master of Blackoaks* is Styles Kenric, a name apparently derived from the first names of Kyle Onstott and Kenric Lance Horner. Styles Kenric is impotent with his heiress wife and secretly gay and is featured in the novel's most shocking moments—he orally rapes a teenage slave boy and becomes aroused while examining a male slave's genitals.

When published in 1976, both the Fawcett/Gold Medal and Pan paperback covers billed *Master of Blackoaks* as "A Lance Horner Novel by Ashley Carter," and the copyright page insinuated that the story was derived from unfinished material written by Horner. (*Sword of the Golden Stud*, Whittington's next assignment for the Horner estate, would be promoted the same way.) Whittington (as Ashley Carter) continued the Baynard family history in *Secret of Blackoaks* (1978) and *Heritage of Blackoaks* (1981). Yet another chapter, *A Farewell to Blackoaks* (1985), appeared only in Britain. Tamer and less crude than the books by Onstott and Horner (or the later Falconhurst entries from Whittington), the "Blackoaks" novels come across as "Falconhurst Light"—most notably in the scenes depicting the Baynard's subdued treatment of slaves.[2]

By 1977, Fawcett had printed more than 14.5 million paperbacks in the "slave fiction" genre. "Fawcett has published these novels very successfully," said Bell Blanchard, the house's publicity director. Editor Harvey Gardner added, "We'll continue to publish them as long as they sell." Fawcett didn't disclose actual monetary figures to the press, but outside estimates claimed that the Falconhurst series had made around $16 million. (The same year, Fawcett Publications was purchased for $50 million and became a division of the CBS, Inc. conglomerate.)

At the time, the Horner estate still wasn't able to commission a new Falconhurst entry, but a deal was made with Whittington to write another clone to be released in August of 1977. "It's called *Sword of the Golden Stud*, a Lance Horner Novel by Ashley Carter," Fawcett publicist Bell Blanchard announced. "We're going to do a lot of heavy advertising on it." The publisher spent an impressive $50,000 to promote the book and ordered a first printing of 725,000 copies.

To American readers, *Sword of the Golden Stud* was a direct sequel to

Golden Stud and continued the adventures of runaway mustee slave Jeff "Bricktop" Carson. But in England—where *Golden Stud* had been released in alternate form as the Falconhurst entry *Six-Fingered Stud*, with Tommy "Calico" Verder as the light-skinned protagonist—*Sword of the Golden Stud* became a stand-alone title with no relation to any earlier book. To further baffle British fans, Tommy Verder's companions from *Six-Fingered Stud* are—under the same names—now Jeff Carson's friends in *Sword of the Golden Stud.*

The plot had Jeff "Bricktop" Carson still involved with Jean Lafitte's slave trading expeditions while still pursued by Baxter Simon. After numerous adventures (including our hero's stint as a whorehouse sex performer), Carson's new lover—the rich, white and mentally-unstable Margarith (with "creamy, cherry-tipped" breasts)—is fatally shot at the climax by Simon before Carson impales his ex-master with a sword. Superior to *Six-Fingered Stud/Golden Stud*, the sequel is a solid yarn, but it is fatally marred by having an unsympathetic, uninteresting Tommy Verder clone as its lead character.

Ed Hirshberg, *Florida Accent*: "Well written, richly laced with good, lusty sex and soundly plotted to keep you reading all 415 pages....a fine example of a...'slave gothic.'"

The lawyers for Bill Denlinger, copyright owner and original publisher of *Mandingo*, apparently didn't notice that *Sword of the Golden Stud* included Don Cesar, a character from the official Falconhurst entry *Drum*. Whittington's new creation Julien Jacques-Gischairn, trainer of quadroon brides in New Orleans, would later turn up in *Scandal of Falconhurst* (1980).

Fawcett announced that "Ashley Carter" would continue the "Golden Stud" series over the next several years, but for some reason, despite the success of the first two entries, Jeff "Bricktop" Carson had no further adventures.

In 1977 the battle over the Falconhurst copyright, name and characters was finally resolved when the parties agreed that royalties from all future books in the series would be divided among the Onstott and Horner estates, Bill Denlinger, and the author of the new entries. (Today, Bill Denlinger is still with the Denlinger's publishing company, which is now based in Florida.) Whittington's contract with the Horner estate required him to write (as Ashley Carter) one Falconhurst entry every eighteen months for a fee of $5,000 plus royalties, per book. He retained the copyrights to his Falconhurst novels, which were registered under his real name.

Five years after *Mistress of Falconhurst*, the anxious and loyal legion of *Mandingo* readers finally got a new chapter when *Taproots of Falconhurst* was stocked in 1978. The timeline is shortly after *Mandingo* and runs parallel to much of *The Mustee.*

After a Falconhurst-set prologue—where the lonely Warren Maxwell and Lucretia Borgia deal with Hammond's self-imposed exile—we catch up with "about thirty-two years old" Hammond Maxwell in Texas almost a decade later. He now raises cattle (instead of slaves) on a ranch with a sexy, feisty Mexican named Lydia and their three children. Teenage runaway slave Tige (called Tiger in *Mandingo*), the result of Hammond's first mating with a slave girl, arrives at the ranch with his pregnant fifteen-year-old white lover, Nell. Lonely for Falconhurst and unable to accept Tige as a son, Hammond abandons his Texas brood, shackles Tige, and takes the boy South, where he plans to turn him over to authorities before returning home. But Tige turns out to be craftier that his father realized.

Pulp veteran Whittington adapted easily to his Falconhurst duties and filled *Taproots* with the requisite sleazy sex ("She bent forward, her smooth breasts hanging like mammoth clusters of dark grapes") and brutality. There is a gruesome sequence with a stillborn baby ("It died right in her hole. Looks like it strangled on its cord"); a new rheumatism cure for Warren that involves soaking his feet in a stinking, simmering pot of hog blood and entrails; and a graphic, extremely creepy vignette where the fifty-year-old Warren beds Missy, a slave virgin of "nine or ten." *Taproots* contains the standard Falconhurst back history that serves as both a refresher and an introduction.

Also accounted for are the classic, ubiquitous descriptions of food, body stenches, biblical references, ejaculations, torture ("The whip dripped blood and flicked huge globules when it cracked") and Hammond's fear of white women ("My stomach turns at the sight of that white, dead-fish flesh"). Conspicuously missing are homosexual characters and gay sex, but these Onstott/Horner staples would be back in all of Whittington's later entries.

Taproots brought back many regulars briefly: Maxwell family members Cousin Charles and Sophie; slaves Mem, Ellen, Lucy and Big Pearl; and Brass Door (a.k.a. Herman Hengst), title character of *The Mustee*. Doc Redfield, a bland character in the earlier books, was re-imagined by Whittington as a "horny old satyr" who finger-rapes young female slaves during forced "examinations." Jingo Jim, the new "prize stud at Falconhurst," is a memorable new addition. Whittington was a fine storyteller, and his first Falconhurst novel is an exciting, well-plotted page turner. Less downbeat than most previous entries, *Taproots of Falconhurst* has good moments of bawdy dark humor and a surprisingly touching conclusion.

The Ashley Carter pseudonym was originally meant to be androgynous and ambiguous, but a brief biography in the *Taproots of Falconhurst* front matter revealed: "Ashley Carter traces his Deep South ancestry back at least nine generations….His great-great-great uncle…was one of Lee's generals."

Also in the initial pages was an "Author's Note" explaining the series's convoluted pedigree: "The eight [previous] Falconhurst novels are based on themes, settings, character, atmosphere and situations created by Kyle Onstott in his novel *Mandingo*....In the sense that Mr. Horner extended and expanded ideas originally created by Mr. Onstott in *Mandingo*, these books were collaborations, though most of the writing was done by Mr. Horner. In this present novel, the writing is entirely mine. However, in the same way Mr. Horner extended and expanded ideas created by Mr. Onstott, I am continuing and developing the work, ideas and situations carried forward by Mr. Horner. In this sense, this book is a collaboration, and Mr. Horner a full partner in its development."

In addition to a $2.25 price and a title embossed in metallic lettering (a then-popular marketing trend), Fawcett/Gold Medal's *Taproots of Falconhurst* cover featured a beautiful painting depicting a rumpled, barefoot Warren Maxwell (with the "fading red hair" described in the book) as he sits barefoot in a wicker chair while holding a hot toddy. His child bedwench Missy sits, topless, at his feet. In England, the W.H. Allen hardcovers and Pan paperbacks touted the entry as "A Lance Horner Novel by Ashley Carter." Fawcett billed the book as "A Turbulent Tale of Passion In The Lusty Falconhurst Saga" and apparently felt that the plantation's brand name negated the need for a "Lance Horner" banner. The new entry sold well to old fans and new readers in both countries.

At this point, Whittington was living (and writing) comfortably near the Gulf of Mexico in a Florida beach community called Indian Rocks Beach. According to an old legend, a Native American medicine man had used the area's sulfur spring water to cure sick tribe members.

Each morning at 9:00, Whittington would enter his cluttered, but tidy, home office to start typing new pages and continue until his 2:00 p.m. lunch break, after which he would do revisions until early evening. "It's my business. I have to write for a living," he told the paper *Florida Accent* in 1978. "When things are going right, I can keep it up all day. Sometimes I'd just go all night, when it's going particularly well or when I'm in a hurry, though I rarely skip a meal."

The embossed metallic title *Scandal of Falconhurst* appeared on bookshelves in 1980, touted as "the biggest, boldest addition to the bestselling Falconhurst series that began with the sizzling *Mandingo*." This direct sequel to both *Taproots of Falconhurst* and *The Mustee* spans over seventeen years and begins at Falconhurst in 1844, when Ellen (Hammond's favorite *Mandingo* bed wench) has her first child, a near-white girl fathered by Herman Hengst (a.k.a. Brass Door) of *The Mustee*. The baby is described as "seven pounds of scandal," by Doc Redfield and named Scandal by her mother. ("Ashley Carter" had previously written about a light-skinned slave baby called Scandal in *Master of Blackoaks*.)

Although enraged that she took another lover during his long Texas exile, Hammond sets Ellen and her child free and purchases a nearby farm for them. In a vignette as gruesome as any in the series, returning white trash villain Ransom Lightfoot and his equally repulsive brother, Jonas, rape ("Bloody mess, ain't she? Looks like your big ole tool just 'bout whopped her to death") and slaughter ("The knife was driven upward to the hilt into her vagina and ripped upward") Ellen in her home. (In *Master of Falconhurst*, Ellen had died unceremoniously at a much later time while still living at Falconhurst.) Raised by a poor white couple, Scandal grows into a stunning teenager and a hater of white men.

Blonde horse breeder Wade Cameroon has a roll in the hay with Scandal (in the image depicted on the book's cover) and is forced to marry her in a shotgun wedding. Pursued by Albert Le Blanc, whose brother was killed by Wade, the new lovers go to New Orleans. Le Blanc claims that Wade is a light-skinned fugitive slave and has him arrested and sent to a horrid prison for blacks where Wade is tortured before being purchased by Le Blanc and forced to work in the cane fields. Meanwhile, Scandal has become a prominent society member of plague-infested New Orleans. At the happy conclusion, Scandal and Wade are reunited and escape on a cargo ship to the Caribbean.

The final chapters of *Scandal* take place in the same timeframe as the last part of *Drum* and include Scandal's brief encounter with Hammond, Miss Augusta and Lucretia Borgia at a New Orleans party—but less than a third of this entry takes place at Falconhurst or involves any of the original characters.

In addition to the customary sex, Whittington added some effective fight scenes. ("When Cameron's knee battered into Le Blanc's gonads, everything inside Le Blanc's mind and body instantly short-circuited. He lost control of his bodily functions.") In 1986, the author explained, "I was in two fights. In one, I got my front teeth smashed loose. In the other, overmatched, I was struck sharply in each temple by fists with third knuckle raised like a knot. When I wrote about pain, I knew what I was talking about."

There are strong physical descriptions of the Falconhurst regulars, including Doc Redfield ("His hands were gnarled, liver-spotted. A thin line of black edged his fingernails....Tobacco stains discolored the sparse, gray-streaked, red whiskers about his mouth. His few teeth were blackened stubs.")

A notable new character is Tupelo, a massive, raging black overseer who enjoys whipping his fellow slaves. Returning from Whittington's Falconhurst black sheep book *Sword of the Golden Stud* is Julien-Jacques Gischairn—an aging, silk-clad, opium-smoking queen who enjoys watching his adolescent slave boys, Ymir and Aditi, writhing naked on his Persian carpet. ("Ymir repeated his gulping of Aditi's gonads and his nipping of them, this time more savagely, until Aditi yelped in pleasurable anguish.")

Scandal is an intriguing young woman and probably the best female character in the entire series—the main reason why this book is a particular favorite among women Falconhurst readers. *Scandal of Falconhurst* is occasionally slow-moving, but this good entry is almost the best of the Falconhursts by Whittington.[3]

The series continued to sell for Fawcett, which was acquired by Ballentine Books (part of Random House) in 1982, and the house released *Rogue of Falconhurst* in May 1983. *Rogue of Falconhurst* is the heaviest-plotted of Whittington's entries as well as his Falconhurst with the most major characters. Set in 1831, the book takes place right after *Flight to Falconhurst* and begins as Hammond Maxwell desperately tracks Tommy "Calico" Verder—apparently the "rogue" of the title, although he spends little time at Falconhurst in this story. (Hammond: "a white man can't be friends with a black no matter how much he might like him….I got to hang him when I gets my hands on him.") To the confusion of British readers, this entry replaces *Six-Fingered Stud* as the immediate *Flight to Falconhurst* sequel and negates all of Verder's adventures in that book.

Teenage Yankee Dighton Hawley travels with and learns the business from slave trader Brownlee (from *Mandingo*). (Brownlee: "Until you've seen a nigger that's reverted to the bush, you ain't seen no mindless, violent, brutal, and irreclaimable animal. They say the bite of one of them rabid blacks is deadlier than any rattler." Unfortunately, no rabid slaves show up.) During a stop at a white-trash fish camp, Hawley meets and becomes infatuated with incest victim Myra Belle Stark. Hawley and Brownlee's slave inventory includes the teenage lovers Cairo and Leve, who are separated when Warren and Hammond Maxwell add Cairo to Falconhurst. Warren changes Cairo's name to Anger "cause he act like he's out of his mind half the time."

Verder and Myra Belle begin traveling together and end up as actors on a showboat. At a performance, Hammond recognizes and shoots Verder, who escapes once again. Verder's wounds are treated by the boat's medicine man, Doc Cardell, who reveals his own biracial pedigree by showing his dark fingernails. ("As clear a sign of black ancestry as any.")

Hawley gets a severe fever and is nursed by and reunited with Myra Belle. Cairo/Anger and Leve are reunited when they both become property at Dove Cote. Verder rescues rich white widow Anne-Jeanne Casale from a rapist and becomes a guest at her Meadow Leas Plantation. Naturally, Anne-Jeanne is unable to resist Verder and tells him, "I feel this irresistible urge to throw my head in your lap and show you—how grateful I am."

Notable excerpt: "Dighton winced at the naked beauty, the full, firm, high-standing globes tipped with pink. He tried to nurse from her, grabbing at her....He had torn her dress down to the dark triangle of femininity at her thighs." Effective action scenes include: Cairo/Anger escaping from Falconhurst, only to run in circles and be easily recaptured; a tavern brawl with Verder defeating a knife-wielding hunchbacked dwarf; and the bloody battle between Big Pearl and another hefty Falconhurst girl. There's also a well-written, concise recap of the bizarre Tommy Verder/Calico backstory—far less confusing than the similar flashbacks in Horner's books.

The showboat is a refreshing change of location, even if the sequences with the acting troupe seem jarringly out of place in a Falconhurst book. Included are Whittington's first mention of Hammond's limp and the author's first scene at one of Onstott and Horner's constant settings: the slave auction block.

There's plenty of expected sleaze. Cairo/Anger is forced to mate in front of Hammond and Lucretia Borgia and is later branded with an "R" (for "Runner") on his shoulder. (Hammond: "It smell kinely bad, nigra flesh burnin'.") In a queasy scene that ranks with the creepiest in the series, Hawley beds Lavinia, "a lovely caramel-colored little doll" of thirteen who is sent to him at Falconhurst. (Hammond to Hawley: "I like 'em old enough to have boobs, at least, an' a little hair around it.")

Fortunately, Verder is only one of the many major characters in this book, making it better reading than the entries that focus entirely on this dull, annoying figure. Hammond's cruelty and hostility toward his slaves and his vicious, cold way of speaking to Lucretia Borgia is out of character from the other books. (Although he once again vomits in shame and confusion after ordering a slave whipping.) The regular characters are around for atmosphere, but as usual, very few have anything to do with the plot. Warren Maxwell has some good moments with speeches written in the extreme dialect not seen since *Mandingo* ("Mem, they ain't no fiah in this heah front room fireplace again this mawnin'."), and the vulgar Brownlee is an amusing secondary character. Although Miss Dovie's lover Colt was the prominent title character of *Falconhurst Fancy*, his token appearance here—like all subsequent books with scenes at Dove Cote—is extremely brief and uneventful.

Interesting new characters: Captain Andy Stone, the stocky, bald, pink-faced star of the showboat; Earcel Hoggs, a gay white-trash thug; Falconhurst slave Big Phallus (!), who possesses a "rigid fourteen inch maulstick;" and Cairo/Anger and Leve, two of the more well-written, pure-black characters in the series. (This is the only entry with a love story about separated slaves.)

The Fawcett/Crest *Rogue of Falconhurst* cover promised that "The Seething Passions of the South's Greatest Stud Farm Explode Again" and the art showed a pensive, red-haired white man sitting in a soft chair while a black beauty (wearing a brief pink frock and bandana) rests in his lap. The couple could only be imagined as Hammond and (his *Mandingo* bedwench) Dite, although they don't appear together in this book, and the elegant chair is in too good of condition to be part of the Falconhurst décor.

Whittington said at the time, "You can have all the beautiful descriptions and inspiring thoughts and great characters and heavenly thoughts that you want to. But in fiction, if you don't have a plot, you don't have anything." While simultaneously continuing the Falconhurst and Blackoaks sagas, he also worked on *The Pillagers*, an original novel about racial tensions among black and white musicians in the modern-day rock scene that was apparently never published.

Three years after *Rogue of Falconhurst*, the wrapper for *Miz Lucretia of Falconhurst* screamed, "Here Is The Most Sizzling Chapter Yet In The Great Falconhurst Saga!" when it was released by Fawcett/Gold Medal in April 1986. This direct sequel to *Mandingo* begins at Falconhurst (six months after the original book) while Hammond is in Texas. (This is one of only three entries without Hammond.) Decrepit Warren Maxwell ("He plodded on his bare feet, liver-colored, disfigured by pain, with jagged, malformed toenails") purchases Satyr ("this slave somehow recalled Mede") and sells off Tige, Hammond's octoroon son—setting up the events in *Taproots of Falconhurst*. (In *Mandingo*, the boy's mother was named Sukey, here she is called Ophelia.)

An elegant white woman arrives at Falconhurst claiming to be Vesta Hammond, cousin of Warren's late wife. She is accompanied by Bowen Ledbetter, her gaunt, wax-mustached husband. After Warren becomes deathly ill and bedridden, the suspicious Lucretia Borgia discovers a pouch of dark powder in Vesta's room. Meanwhile, a bevy of teen wenches fail to arouse Satyr. Lucretia discovers that the young slave is merely inexperienced, and cures him. (Satyr: "Minute I sees a lady nekked, my ole tokus, he jump up, hard as iron, and start a-shootin,' all over everything.")

Vesta sells the meddlesome Lucretia to trader Foye Cleavenger. During Lucretia's long journey on foot with the other chained slaves, Cleavenger is excited by a "Nigger Wrestling!" poster, only to be disappointed when the brawl is cancelled after the fighters are injured en route. (Their owner explains: "Careless an Ole Bubba—got to fighting in the cage....Bubba got a choke hold on Careless's throat. When Careless couldn't breathe no more, he bit Old Bubba's testicles...he chewed Ole Bubba's testicles to a pulp. Chewed until he bled, and then kept on chewing.") A substitute battle is held between the hefty slave barmaid, Coffee, and Lucretia—who wins after almost drowning her opponent in a mud puddle.

After seducing Cleavenger while bathing in a creek, Lucretia bludgeons him with a stone, frees his other captives, and returns to Falconhurst to find Maxwell near death after being continuously poisoned by Vesta and Bowen. The devious white couple try to shoot Lucretia, but are strangled by Satyr.

The mid-section of *Miz Lucretia of Falconhurst*—with the title character's captivity—is exciting, but overall the entry is forgettable, with few memorable vignettes or new characters. The Falconhurst segments read like a rehash of *The Mustee*, which also dealt with a murderous plot to get Maxwell's money.

The regulars appear with their repetitive traits, including Mem who, as always, is defined only by his laziness, cowardice and stealing of liquor. Ole Mister Wilson (Mede's sterile young offspring) pops up, but like the other Mandingo characters, has nothing to do with the story. Little Sophie is discussed by Warren as "runnin' 'round the place somewhere," but, unfortunately, the girl isn't seen, and Whittington never employed this offbeat character in any of his entries. A new female slave, intriguingly referred to as "hare lipped little Carrie," is mentioned in one sentence but is given no action.

In *Mistress of Falconhurst*, Horner had rewritten *Mandingo*'s history by having Hammond thrown from his horse at age sixteen, but here Whittington got it right. Warren explains: "[Hammond] got that game leg from a gelded pony when he was a chile of six years old." Whittington also provided *Miz Lucretia of Falconhurst* with a good, concise recap of *Mandingo*'s notorious, gruesome climax. ("It was as if a cesspool had exploded and the corruption would not stop spewing, inundating them in depravity.")

In the least-accurate cover art of the series, a gorgeous, long-haired black female (with Native American-like features) embraces a curly-haired, mustached blonde man in front of a creek. The image is apparently a loose depiction of Lucretia Borgia (described in the text as having "short, wiry hair") with a thin, handsome, clean-shaven version of the chunky, bearded, repulsive Cleavenger. (The sexy Lucretia Borgia that was presented in these later novels was far removed from the stout, elderly "Mammy" depiction of the character in the *Mandingo* movie, which took place at the same time as this book.) *Miz Lucretia of Falconhurst* would be the last entry released in paperback by England's Pan.

The front matter of *Mandingo Master*, the next entry, had an "Author's Note" explaining: "The Mandingan king of this novel was…called by his subjects 'mansa,' the Mandingan word for 'supreme ruler'….Ironically, 'mansa' is pronounced 'massa,' the slave word for the southern plantation owner." (In England, the novel was retitled *Mandingo Mansa*.)

A week after *Mandingo*'s conclusion, Ham is tormented by nightmares of Mede's boiled corpse rising from the grave. Ham hears an anti-slavery speech by Reverend Merrill Hallwell, is moved by the Yankee's rant, and agrees to finance a trip to Africa, where the preacher can find an educated, regal black to help convince American whites about the evils of slavery. The party encounters Cheikh Obed, a legendary, seven-foot-tall Mandingo ruler, who lives in an opulent palace with hundreds of his own slaves. The Mandingo king is convinced to visit America. But Ham, having reverted back to his white supremacist ways, secretly plans to take Obed to Falconhurst to be trained as a brawler.

At Falconhurst, the disobedient king is chained in a tack room and whipped. (His wounds are treated with the famous "pimentade" introduced in *Mandingo*.) Lucretia Borgia is reluctant to betray her masters (she tells Obed, "You belong body and soul to a white man and that means all your body. Even your asshole, do he want to ream it out in any way that pleases him"), but she mates with the king and helps him to escape. After breaking Ham's jaw and chaining him, Obed flees to a scummy swamp, where he strangles a pair of slave patrollers and impales some bloodhounds on tree branches before joining a colony of runaway slaves and Native Americans in Spanish Florida run by an arrogant, power-hungry black named Garcia.

Obed pairs up with teenage runaway house slave Elicia and lives on a secluded farm. When a group sent by General Andrew Jackson to take over Garcia's colony are "attacked and abused and driven back, one of them with an American flag shoved up his asshole with a flagstaff," a war breaks out and Obed joins the Native Americans in their battle against the American army. Obed returns to his farm to find Elicia dead ("Her head had been severed from her body and stared down at him from one of the poles"), then travels to New Orleans, where he encounters Ham Maxwell. Obed robs Ham of his clothes and money, leaves the Falconhurst heir bound and naked in an ash bin, and buys passage back to Africa.

Mandingo Master is Whittington's best Falconhurst entry, an exciting pulp epic with an interesting lead character and no dull spots. A great early vignette has Ham watching a slave bout between the appropriately named Tall Boy and Tiny. ("[Tiny] suddenly twisted his head and closed his teeth on Tall Boy's scrotum….'That boy eatin' good fer the first time in his life,' somebody yelled.") The brawl ends when one of the owners splits Tiny's skull with an axe and shoots Tall Boy in the face.

The African scenes have some especially nice work: "Finally the currents released the boats, like a cat tired of toying with its victims….Up there, black people stirred like ants in a disturbed hill….A Negro howled, tortured or imprisoned by his fellows in some unseen hut or pit outside the reach of a central bonfire." The book works as a jungle thriller, a brutal slave novel, and a semi-historical action adventure. It's also a solid, atypical Falconhurst entry (with not much time at the plantation) and it's unfortunate that there were no further stories with Hammond venturing to strange lands.

Except for his brief, odd conversion, Ham is reprehensible and completely unsympathetic throughout this story. It's even insinuated that he's responsible for the death of an innocent white man that befriends him. The other regulars provide no surprises: Warren is constantly drunk and in pain and insists on giving Obed a rectal exam; Ellen is nothing more than Ham's "high-yeller bedwench;" Doc Redfield has "obscene" breath; "worthless" Mem sneaks hot toddy sips; and the Mandingos Lucy, Big Pearl, and "the mentally retarded giant Ole Mr. Wilson" do nothing but tower over the other slaves. Sophie ("cross-eyed and ugly as a scrawny little weed") appears very briefly clutching a slave-made cornshuck doll, which she named after her dead mother. (The version of Mem in all of the novels is completely contradictory to the character's presentation in the *Mandingo* film, where the non-drinking Mem is enraged by the slavery system, encourages other blacks to revolt, and ultimately murders one of his masters.)

Fawcett/Gold Medal released *Mandingo Master* on November 12, 1986. The cover image had a shirtless, perfectly-formed, short-haired black man whose knee and thigh were clutched by a gorgeous black girl wearing a flimsy antebellum gown, while a pensive, whip-clutching white man (with a fluffy 1980s-style hairdo) looks on. The trio could be taken as Obed, Elicia and Hammond, although the latter's hair is described in the text as "straight and long, swept like a mane." (Black-on-black couplings were unusual for the genre's paperback covers. The *Drum* paperback and *Flight to Falconhurst* were the only other entries with black-on-black artwork.) The *Mandingo Master* painting was by John Solie, an exceptional portrait artist responsible for hundreds of book and magazine covers, print ads and movie posters, including 1973's *Soylent Green* (directed by Richard Fleischer of the *Mandingo* film).

Although, for one of the few times in the series's history, "Falconhurst" wasn't in the book's title, the famous plantation's name appeared five times on the cover. ("Not since *Mandingo* has such a brave, proud stud threatened the very foundations of Falconhurst"; "In the sizzling Falconhurst tradition, a gripping and shocking saga"; "Who Is The Master?" Who Is The Slave?") The front cover screamed, "First Time In Print!" so readers wouldn't confuse it with the original or later books in the series, all of which were still in print. Starting with this entry, the British Falconhurst softcovers were handled by W. H. Allen's paperback division, Star.

Two decades after his death, Kyle Onstott was billed as the author of a brand-new novel. In 1985 the tireless Whittington was given the assignment of completing the post-*Mandingo* novel that Onstott had started but abandoned in 1960. Onstott's handwritten, twenty-five-year-old chapters and notes were compiled by Whittington into *Strange Harvest*—an epic that spanned the first thirty years of the 1900s and dealt with aging honey farmer Manuel O'Brien and his infant son, Jesus, who grows up to becomes a Catholic priest involved with striking farm workers. (Like *Mandingo*, this novel begins with the words "The old man.")

Almost as long as the American *Mandingo* paperback (and even longer than the British softcover version), *Strange Harvest* is plodding, dreary and endless, with none of the sensationalism found in the other books that bore Onstott's name. (The "strange harvest" of the title refers to honey, not human slaves.) It's an odd, subdued novel with almost no violence or sleaze and only one explicit love scene. ("God knew he wanted her, and yet he remained as limp as the dough of a tortilla.") *Strange Harvest* was released in England by W. H. Allen as a 1986 hardcover (and a 1987 Star paperback) as "The final masterpiece from Kyle Onstott author of *Mandingo* completed by Ashley Carter," but the Onstott and *Mandingo* names weren't enough to get the dull novel published in America.

Falconhurst Fugitive, the fourteenth and final entry, was published on September 12, 1988—thirty-one years after *Mandingo* had first stunned readers. (This is the fifteenth entry if we include *Six-Fingered Stud.*) Set in 1825, the story picks up immediately where *Rogue of Falconhurst* ended—with Tommy Verder living an opulent life with widow Anne-Jean Casale at her Meadow Leas Plantation. (He still makes love only in darkness to hide his spots.) Tommy is tormented by nightmares of Hammond Maxwell, who plans to "cut out his tongue, brand him with a white-hot *R* across his forehead, weld a ring through his manhood, or hang him from a rope-scarred tree." When a duel between Tommy and Anne-Jeanne's suspicious cousin, Paul Lavedon, leaves the cousin dead, Tommy assumes the Lavedon name and relocates to the French Quarter to study law.

While traveling, Tommy comes across a dilapidated farmhouse ("Loathsome decay ground into the very plaster and putty") inhabited by white dwarfs Hobart and Junior Cobb and their lovely teenage octoroon half-sister Lily, whom Tommy purchases. (Junior: "You bought yourself some sweet black flesh, young enough to be the eatin' kind an' all, I tell you. And I know for a fact it plumb tastes *good*....You part her legs and spank her good down there, till she turns fiery red, and she goes wild for you.") Naturally, the girl sleeps with and becomes enamored with Tommy. ("Her small breasts—taut, hard-nippled, incendiary—impaled him.")

Passing Lily off as his boy servant, Tommy sails to Haiti to serve as lawyer to a mulatto sugar lord. Haiti is chaotically run by blacks—after a bloody revolt has left the white rulers dead—and Tommy is thrown in jail by black soldiers who believe him to be white. In the fetid prison, Tommy meets the eerie old black voodoo priest Carbe, and is soon released when a strip search reveals his splotched belly and true race.

At the plantation of his new employer, Tommy encounters the ceramic-skinned Marie-Verlaine and her green-eyed, biracial daughter, Jade—a pair of satanic priestesses who turn the black field workers into tireless zombie slaves. After being scratched by Jade's poisoned fingernails, Tommy is turned into a paralyzed zombie and briefly buried alive.[4] The outrageous story keeps getting more bizarre and delirious as it goes on and features a pirate attack at sea, a "march of zombis," secret passages, and a white dwarf getting roasted on a spit by hungry voodoo practitioners. (For some reason, Tommy's six-fingered left hand never seems to get noticed by anyone.) Tommy finally escapes and returns to New Orleans, where a lawyer informs him that Anne-Jean Casale has died and left him her entire estate. Fearful of Hammond's relentless vengeance, Tommy tells the lawyer, "My name is not Tommy Verder. I am a black man. A nigger. My name is Calico."

Falconhurst Fugitive is, by far, the best of the books that feature Tommy Verder. Here the character comes across as surprisingly sympathetic and less selfish than in his earlier adventures. (The four novels that center on the character—*Falconhurst Fancy, Flight to Falconhurst, Rogue of Falconhurst,* and *Falconhurst Fugitive*—are often called the "Tommy Verder" or the "Six-Fingered Stud" books by diehard collectors.)

The fast-paced story has solid action scenes (e.g. a long fight as Tommy is attacked by a gang of masked thugs) as well as some of the better characters created for the series by Whittington, including voodoo priest Carbe and the dwarf Cobb brothers. (Hobart has "a huge head that seemed to grow out of a humped back without any neck at all," while Junior features "protuberant staring eyes that seemed never to blink or to settle on anyone or anything for longer than a few seconds at a time.") Also notable is Don Alfonso Maduro, a gay Cuban sugar lord (with "a mustache carefully combed in the pattern of pubic hair") who drugs and tries to rape Tommy.

But *Falconhurst Fugitive* is a disappointing finale to the *Mandingo* saga, since nothing takes place at the notorious title plantation and none of the beloved original characters appear for a final time. (Hammond Maxwell is referred to throughout the book, but is never seen.) Curiously and unfortunately, the early life of Blanche, Hammond's wife, was never revealed in any of the many prequels.

The generic cover art for *Falconhurst Fugitive* could have been used to wrap any gothic romance and was the dullest of the entire series, with a bedroom-set painting of a brunette Caucasian couple. Their skin was apparently tinted darker to suit the book, and the duo could suggest Tommy and Jade, if not for the anachronistic hairstyle of the man and the woman's modern-day nightgown. Cover blurbs: "His skin is white. His soul is black" and "A Blazing and Exotic Adventure In The Sweeping Falconhurst Tradition." The price was $4.50. The original *Mandingo* paperback had set readers back only 60 cents.

Falconhurst Fugitive completed Whittington's contract with the Lance Horner estate. The heirs wanted to sign him to write more books for the series, but Whittington declined when he didn't get the raise he asked for. The later Falconhurst novels were not as widely successful as those by Onstott and Horner, but the new "Ashley Carter" entries and the reprintings of the earlier paperbacks had sold enough copies to earn the Horner estate around $100,000 in yearly royalties.

At one point, the Horner estate negotiated with another writer who was to replace Whittington as the Falconhurst chronicler. But the replacement author decided that he didn't need the brand name and went on to create a similar plantation-set paperback series without having to share royalties with the Horner heirs. An attorney who worked with the estate estimated that a total of $1 million in royalties was collected by Horner and his heirs during the time that the series was in print.

Whittington died on June 11, 1989, at age seventy-four. Late in his career, he recalled: "[I] stuck with paperbacks because I was married and broke and I needed money and wanted it as fast as I could get it. I never considered that I could write for hardcovers and maybe be thought of more highly. It just never bothered me. If I could enjoy what I was doing and make a living at it, that was the important thing. I have done the best I could on every book that I've written. Everybody who has a book from me has got the best I could do at that moment....I'm satisfied with what I've done. I undoubtedly might have wished for more money and more acclaim and all that sort of thing. But I'm satisfied."

Although he was mostly forgotten when he passed, a growing cult has formed for Whittington's mysteries and Westerns, especially in Europe. Original copies of his paperbacks are highly sought after by collectors and several of his hardboiled thrillers have been reprinted and rediscovered. His Falconhurst entries are also fondly remembered.

Collectors of the Falconhurst series can usually find battered, cracked paperbacks on the used-book market, but copies in collectible condition are hard to come by. When first published, the books would be held tightly and forced wide open as the series' eager fans swiftly flipped through the rough pages. When completed, the novel would be stored in an attic or—hard to believe—tossed away by the reader who was ready to start on something else.

All of the "Ashley Carter" Falconhurst entries are faster and easier reads than any of the books by Kyle Onstott or Lance Horner. But no other novel in the "slaver" genre is as fascinating, compelling or memorable as *Mandingo*. Readers attempting to consume the entire lengthy series in chronological order are advised to open *Mandingo* first.

Notes:

1 The late agent is no relation to novelist Anita Diamant, best known for *The Red Tent* (1997).

2 In September 1976, still another Falconhurst-inspired novel appeared. But this hefty, *Mandingo*-sized tale—featuring slave auctions, whippings, maiming, brutal uprisings, interracial rape and cockfighting (instead of bloody slave battles)—did not end up as filler on wobbly wire racks. Alex Haley's *Roots: The Saga of an American Family* was published in hardback by Doubleday, became an instant bestseller and garnered a Pulitzer Prize for its African American author. Haley had previously conducted several classic *Playboy* interviews of the 1960s, compiled *The Autobiography of Malcolm X* (1965), and wrote the screenplay for *Superfly TNT* (a 1973 sequel that was co-billed with the 1975 *Mandingo* movie). *Roots*—labeled as "nonfiction" and allegedly based on Haley's twelve years of research on his ancestors—begins in the late 1700s as Mandingo teenager Kunte Kinte is captured in Africa, transported by ship to Virginia, and auctioned into slavery. Haley worked with several uncredited researchers and collaborators including the white Jewish *Playboy* editor Murray Fisher, who was reportedly heavily involved with the book's writing and completion. "Writing did not come easily to Alex Haley," recalled David L. Wolper, the author's close friend and the producer of the TV miniseries based on *Roots*. "He was a meticulous researcher; his home was filled with boxes and boxes of materials, but it was difficult for him to commit words to paper."

Roots is a fascinating, extremely entertaining book and is far superior to any of the Falconhurst novels, although most of Haley's success came from his *Mandingo*-like depictions of master-on-slave rape, dismembered limbs and castration. The Kyle Onstott estate didn't accuse Haley of plagiarism, but in 1978 the *Roots* author was sued by Harold Courlander, who claimed that Haley's bestseller included elements cribbed from his 1967 novel *The African*. Haley admitted that some passages in *Roots* were taken from Courlander's earlier book and paid $650,000 as an out-of-court settlement. More controversy came later when several genealogists questioned the accuracy of Haley's *Roots* research.

3 Other Falconhurst-like novels continued to appear. Antebellum interracial sex and whip-cracking slave abuse was prominent in John Jakes's *North and South* (1982), a best-selling hardcover (from Harcourt) and paperback (from Dell). Jakes is a superb storyteller, but his characters—particularly the villains—are no more defined than those in the Falconhurst books. The *New York Times* said, "the shadows of Kyle Onstott and Margaret Mitchell loom large over the story." Jakes followed *North and South* with his sequel novels *Love and War* (1984) and *Heaven and Hell* (1987). All three books became TV miniseries.

4 A number of the copycat pulp slave novels—notably *Black Vengeance* (1968) and *Ashanti* (1969)—had dealt with voodoo, but the first section of *Drum* was the only other Falconhurst entry with supernatural elements.

Book II:
The "Falconhurst" Play

Chapter 4:
Mandingo on Broadway

Shortly after Kyle Onstott's 1957 novel *Mandingo* became a best-seller, entrepreneur Billy Baxter purchased the stage and screen rights from publisher William Denlinger. Seeing great commercial potential in *Mandingo*, Baxter planned a major Broadway production of the popular book and hoped to follow it with a movie version. In the pre-1968 years before the creation of the MPAA ratings system, all movies had to be suitable for a general audience and a mainstream film based on *Mandingo* would have to be heavily altered from the source material in order to be shown in American cinemas. But since live theater catered to a more elite and permissive audience than movies, a faithful stage adaptation of Onstott's novel was possible.

In late 1959, Baxter hired playwright and screenwriter Jack Kirkland to turn *Mandingo* into a play script. Kirkland's films included the Shirley Temple vehicle *Now and Forever* (1934), *The Gilded Lily* (1935) with Claudette Colbert, and Jean Renoir's *Carrosse d'or* (a.k.a. *The Golden Coach*, 1953), but he was best known for writing and producing the notorious Broadway play *Tobacco Road*, based on Erskine Caldwell's best-selling 1932 social protest/dark comedy novel about the dismal lifestyle of a grotesque white-trash family in rural Georgia. The *Tobacco Road* play received mostly-poor reviews and modest attendance when it opened in New York in 1933. The New York *Sun* called it "a play that achieves the repulsive and seldom falls below the faintly sickening." But word-of-mouth soon turned the unforgettable stage shocker about failed farmer Jeeter Lester and his ignorant kin (including a sexy, but hare-lipped daughter) into the longest-running drama in Broadway history. Promoted as "The Most Discussed Play in the History of the American Theatre," it ran for seven-and-a-half years with 3,182 consecutive performances.

Kirkland's personally-supervised hit touring productions of *Tobacco Road* began in 1934, but the sleazy characters and lurid plot elements (including implied incest and a twelve-year-old bride) got the show banned in many cities, including Chicago, where the mayor shut the show down after finding it "obscene." Twentieth Century-Fox produced a sanitized, heavily-altered movie version in 1941. Despite being directed by John Ford and scripted by Nunnally Johnson, it was extremely weak and a box-office disappointment. The play had three Broadway revivals, was an international road show perennial for decades (including an all-black cast version that played London after being banned in Chicago and Detroit), and was an ubiquitous staple of regional, college and community theaters into the 1970s. The Kirkland script was even released as a luridly-covered "Complete and Unabridged" 1952 Signet paperback. But while Caldwell's novel is still being read and studied, Kirkland's once-famous play (which made him a millionaire) is now rarely-revived and mostly forgotten.

But in the early sixties, the *Tobacco Road* play and Kirkland's name still had value and gave credibility (if not prestige) to first-time producer Baxter. *Mandingo* was a sleazy, sex-and violence-filled drama with dark comedy about a dysfunctional family of low-life Southern entrepreneurs, and Kirkland was the perfect choice to write a stage version. (Kirkland's description of the setting: "Falconhurst is not a Tara, magnificent and gracious...Rather, it is a well disciplined, middle class, successfully managed operation that, called by its proper name is nothing more nor less than a prosperous nigger farm.")

Franchot Tone and Brooke Haywood during a dress rehearsal. (Photo by Fred Fehl)

In May 1960, while writing the *Mandingo* adaptation, Kirkland supervised a fourth New York revival of *Tobacco Road*, this time at the off-Broadway Cricket Theatre on Second Avenue. Working in his Central Park West apartment, Kirkland attempted to turn Onstott's lurid potboiler into a serious dramatic social commentary, while still retaining the novel's shock value. Like Onstott, Kirkland did all of his writing by hand, and the first draft of the *Mandingo* play was created with lead and charcoal pencils in cursive longhand on unlined paper. The playwright did a fine job of condensing the rambling, 659-page epic novel into a tight, well-structured, three-act play that could be performed in two hours.

Kirkland kept the flavor of Onstott's writing but, naturally, had to alter the narrative and discard dozens of characters, subplots and vignettes. Among the book's prominent characters that were deleted (but still referred to) for the play were Colonel Wilson, Aphrodite, and Charles (the brother/lover of Blanche).

Like most play scripts, *Mandingo* had very little action and told most of the story through dialogue. Using very little of Onstott's dialect, Kirkland chose instead to recreate the exaggerated, low-life slang of *Tobacco Road.* ("Great cats and little fishes, what in the hell git into that gal?;" "Holy sufferin' little catfish;" "Holy Jumpin' Jahasophat!")

The first scene consists mainly of Warren Maxwell conversing with visiting slave trader Brownlee, as they discuss the Falconhurst stock. (Maxwell: "Began breedin' an' buyin' em young—feedin' an' sellin' 'em growed.") Some slaves are "fingered" (i.e. examined) by the two men, and Lucy and Big Pearl start to disrobe while on display, but on-stage nudity is prevented when other characters interrupt the scene. As in the book, there is much talk about body odors as well as graphic discussion of punishment:

> MAXWELL: Hang the nigger up—just by the ankles, mind you, never by the toes lessen you twist 'em—give the paddle to a strong buck—an in no time at all the skin peel right off. Then we rubs the cuts with pimentade an' you can hear 'em yell clear into the next county.
> BROWNLEE: Heard of them paddles. Never saw one. They do say a strong buck kin make the blood squirt right through the holes an' it must be purty to watch.

In the novel, Hammond—although physically repulsed when slaves were beaten—was fascinated by the Falconhurst trade and proudly followed in his father's footsteps. But the play's main conflict was the son's rejection of his father's legacy:

> HAM: Papa, Mede not a dog or a horse. Niggers not animals.
> MAXWELL: Hell they ain't, or durn close to it.
> HAM: Papa, Ellen died today—and it no animal I held there in my arms, suh. It was no animal.

[The whipping Ellen receives from Blanche is fatal in the play, unlike in the novel.]

Kirkland made Blanche far more aggressive and hateful than in the novel. (On slaves: "I hates big black ones. They the kind rapes you. Wants 'em all snaked.") She even ridicules Hammond's limp at one point. (Ham to his father: "She jest a bitch, suh. Don't like her.") The script had some memorable drunken spiels for Blanche. ("Wishin' my brother Charles here. He pleasure me—he pleasure me all right...Don't care who hear me. Want Charles—Want Charles!...But it jest cause I got to have somebody all the time. Don't you understand? Cain't help myself. Jest took Charles cause he there.")

Hammond's slave lover, Ellen—Onstott's weakest, least-developed character—was a major role in the play. (Kirkland's description: "Her voice is musical and warm and has its southern accent. But her diction is good and her English almost perfect. Only now and then does she slip into the vernacular.") The loves scenes between the interracial couple were non-exploitive, but contained some of the play's weakest dialogue. (Ham: "You like a summer rain, Lovie, washin' the dirty leaves all clean again. You don't know.") In the novel, Ellen is purchased by Hammond from another plantation, but Kirkland rewrote the girl as a lifelong resident of Falconhurst who, like Blanche, was a cousin of Hammond due to numerous master-and-slave trysts.

The script contained a stylized depiction of the bloody punishment of slovenly house slave Agamemnon (a.k.a. Mem):

> *By back lighting, the figure of a MAN—or what could be a MAN— is seen in shadow outline against the upstage wall, hanging, ankles up, from a cross-piece. Then the figure of ANOTHER MAN is seen wielding a paddle about four feet long and six inches wide. As the paddle strikes the victim, the sound comes to us as a rather quiet slap, but the distant, piecing scream of the HANGING MAN that follows is shrill, sharp and terrifying.*

> *With the scream, BLANCHE'S face comes alive with masochistic delight.*BLANCHE: Listen. Just listen to that nigger yell. Just listen. ...[Blanche is] *trembling with the drive of her sexual aberration...she begins silently counting off the seconds between the rythmic* [sic] *striking of the paddle... The blow falls again in its rythmic* [sic] *pattern and BLANCHE's body reacts again with a shudder of delight—perhaps sprawling back, glazed eyes raised to the ceiling, legs stretched out and spread—or perhaps tensed and tight, bent over, huddled. Now the door opens and HAM steps inside, tense, white, sick.*

Kirkland kept the Maxwell men's fascination with Mandingos and created his own myths about the breed. (Maxwell: "A pure Mandingo playful as a kitten, brave as a lion an' strong as an elephant. A half Mandingo a viper—a killer even.")

The brutal tavern fight between slaves Mede and Topaz appeared several hundred pages before the end of the book, but it is the climax of the play's final act:

> *There is nothing of modern style in their method of fighting. We must suggest, rather, that it is, in a sense, much like a dog fight, just as savage and as lethal... Perhaps this encounter can be staged which not only will indicate the brutality of this kind of fighting, but will also exhibit the beautiful bodies and muscular development of the two massive contestants....*TOPAZ *uses, if the actor is capable of it, the French kicking method and such other blows we in this day would consider foul and brutal.*
>
> [After Mede and Topaz are separated at the conclusion of the fight:]
>
> REMICK [looking at Topaz]: My God, his throat chewed clean open.
> HAM *lifts* MEDE'S *head. The mouth and chin are red with blood.*

Also recreated from the novel were the drunken Blanche brutally whipping Ellen and causing a miscarriage (Blanche: "I goin' to whup that pup of Hammond's right out of you...Peel down, you slut—peel you down nekid. Goin' to lambaste that belly of yourin—goin' to lambaste that yaller sucker right out'n it. I goin' to cut you up so bad with this snake no white man ever goin' to look at you, letting' alone pleasure you.") and the elder Maxwell trying to cure his rheumatism by planting his feet on slave boy Alph's bare stomach. (Maxwell: "An scoot off of yo' shirt. Won't rest easy 'til I has my feet on yo' back an' a drink in my hand.") Some dialogue included the novel's references to homosexuality between masters and slaves.

Kirkland also dramatized the novel's most infamous plot point—the frustrated Blanche's seduction of Mede:

BLANCHE: Nigger.
MEDE: Yes'm, mistress?
BLANCHE: Come here.
MEDE: Yes'm.
He comes to her and stands waiting as she surveys his bulk appraisingly.
BLANCHE: God, you a ugly, dirty black ape.
MEDE'S fists clinch. He would willingly kill her. But he restrains himself.
MEDE: Yes'm. I go now, Mist'ess?
BLANCHE: No, you don't go now.
She takes up one of the toddies and drinks deeply.
BLANCHE: You know what you goin' to do, nigger?
BLANCHE: No, Mist'ess.
BLANCHE: I goin' upstairs to my room an' you goin' with me. Let yo' Masta have his yella slut in his room, he wants her. I have you in mine. Understand, don't you? You goin' to come with me now an' you goin' to come back again an' again—often as I wants you. Understand now?
MEDE: Yes'm, I understand.
BLANCHE: Well? Comin'?
MEDE: No, ma'am.
BLANCHE: No? Want me to scream out you try to rape me an' have Masta Ham come an' kill you? Burn you alive? Know he will, don't you? Has to. See this whip? Know what I just done with it? Whupped a sucker out of yo' masta's yella wench. Want me to go down to your cabin an' whup <u>your</u> bastards out of <u>your</u> wenches?

They exit the stage. (End Act II)

As in the novel, Warren is desperate for Hammond and Blanche to produce a male heir. But unlike in the book, the patriarch turns to Lucretia Borgia for help:

> MAXWELL: Conjure, Lucretia. It the only way.
> LUCRETIA: Masta, please, suh, don't looks to me. Cain't conjure. Ain't got the power.
> MAXWELL: Knows that. Find somebody has. Some crazy old woman. Always one around some place. Tell her I say put the sign on Miz
> Blanche to have a child. Tell her I say give her the eye.
> LUCRETIA: Masta, suh, please, it dangerous. It nigger carry in's on. Not for white folks.

In the novel, Blanche accuses one of the male Falconhurst slaves of being "a conjure" several times. But nothing supernatural ended up happening in Onstott's book or in Kirkland's first draft, and the playwright deleted the black magic discussion during revisions. Kirkland also created an exchange between Warren and Lucretia indicating that they had sexual relations years earlier. (It's odd that Onstott didn't think of mating this pair.)

For comic relief, Kirkland kept some humor from the book (adolescent slave twin Alph always sneaking Maxwell's "corn") and added some of his own (Doc Redfield: "Only lady I ever around' much these days my wife—an' God knows with that mustache she don't look like no lady.")

The major discrepancy between novel and play was the ending. In the book's climax, the enraged Hammond, after discovering that Mede fornicated with Blanche, fatally stabs and boils the slave. Both Hammond and his father survive the novel. At the play's conclusion in the tavern, Ham doesn't hold Mede responsible for the affair with his wife and doesn't want to kill Blanche or Mede. He plans to leave the area with Mede, prompting his disgusted father to rave, "Why you nigger lovin' son-of-a-bitch…What kind of a white man is you? What kind of a son and spawn?" Maxwell takes Hammond's pistol from the boy's holster and demands to know which slave went to bed with Blanche. Mede steps in front of the gun and admits it was him. Maxwell aims at Mede, but Hammond tries to disarm his father and is shot dead. Maxwell then shoots Mede, whose body sprawls over Hammond's. Maxwell announces, "Had to kill me a nigger an' my son try to stand in the way of it. That's all. Anybody here do different? I'm goin' back to Falconhurst now. The sheriff or anybody want me that's where I'll be." The unrepentant father leaves the tavern accompanied by loyal slave Agamemnon. End of play. (In the 1975 film version, it is the elder Maxwell who gets shot dead—by Agamemnon.)

Kirkland worked on his *Mandingo* script throughout 1960. In February 1961 his handwritten first draft was given to a secretary to be typed onto onion paper. The playwright was a heavy reviser and editor of his own material and worked on additional drafts of *Mandingo* as production approached.

Baxter and his coproducer, Edward Friedman—another entrepreneur who, like Baxter, had no experience in New York theater—set up their *Mandingo* production office in a suite at the Hotel Astor on Broadway and 45th Street.

Franchot Tone and Dennis Hopper during a dress rehearsal. (Photo by Fred Fehl)

Mandingo was a daring attempt for the novice producers. The subject matter, the characters, and the dialogue was certain to shock theater audiences. If handled poorly, the play would be unintentionally funny or campy, if the audiences even dared to laugh.

The producers had originally hoped to open *Mandingo* in the fall of 1960, but finally arranged for the play to open in May of 1961 at the Lyceum Theatre at 149 West 45th Street. Built in 1903, the elaborate theater had room for 922 patrons, a small number of seats by Broadway standards. Theatre legends John Barrymore, Ethel Barrymore, Leslie Howard, Maurice Evans, and Billie Burke had all appeared at the Lyceum.

Rehearsals began early in the year under the direction of Louis Macmillan, who had extensive experience as a producer and director of regional and off-Broadway productions, including Kirkland's adaptation of Nelson Algren's novel *The Man With The Golden Arm* at the Cherry Lane Theatre in 1956. *Mandingo* would be Macmillan's first (and last) Broadway credit.

The *Mandingo* novel took place in numerous poverty-stricken and prosperous locations throughout the South, but the play's settings were limited to the decaying Falconhurst and the rough tavern where the climactic fight takes place. The two sets and the lighting were designed by Frederick Fox, a veteran of dozens of major New York productions.

Headlining the cast as Falconhurst patriarch Warren Maxwell (and adding prestige to the marquee) was the fifty-two-year-old stage, screen, and television star Franchot Tone. An early student of legendary acting coach Lee Strasberg, Tone had been appearing on Broadway since 1927, including the original productions of Irwin Shaw's *The Gentle People* (1939), Ernest Hemingway's *The Fifth Column* (1940), and Eugene O'Neill's *A Moon for the Misbegotten* (1957). The actor made his movie debut in 1932 and starred in many Hollywood films, including *Dangerous* (1935) with Bette Davis, *Mutiny on the Bounty* (1935) (which earned him an Oscar nomination), and *Five Graves to Cairo* (1943). He performed live on numerous TV anthologies in the early 1950s and had guest roles on many shows like *Bonanza* (1961 season), *The Twilight Zone* (1961 season), and *Alfred Hitchcock Presents* (1959 and 1965 seasons). The actor had been a regular in fan magazines and scandal sheets due to his marriages to the glamorous Joan Crawford and the unfortunate Barbara Payton.

Tone—who had been attached to *Mandingo* since May of the previous year, when the script was still being written—began rehearsing with Macmillan and Kirkland on Monday, March 27, 1961, before most of the other roles were filled. In the *Mandingo* program and advertising, Tone received billing above, and in the same size lettering as, the title.

Originally hired to play Hammond Maxwell—the young, troubled, limping Falconhurst heir—was an edgy unknown named James Caan, a twenty-one-year-old Bronx-born actor who was studying in the city and had performed for nine months in an off-Broadway show called *I Roam*. But Tone and Caan didn't get along, and the young actor was out of *Mandingo* after only four rehearsals. Later the same year, Caan was Peter Fonda's understudy for the Broadway play *Blood, Sweat and Stanley Poole*, then started appearing in movies. He went on to a legendary screen career that included *Brian's Song* (TV, 1971), *The Godfather* (1972), and *Thief* (1981).

Replacing Caan was the more-experienced, but also-moody Dennis Hopper, who had a promising film career—with roles in the hits *Rebel without a Cause* (1955) and *Giant* (1956)—until his unpredictable, self destructive personality made him unpopular in Hollywood. In 1961 the twenty-five-year-old was heavily involved with the New York art scene and was continuing his training at the famous Actors Studio with Strasberg, Tone's former instructor. Tone and Hopper had appeared together on a 1958 episode of the live TV anthology show *Studio One* and apparently got along while playing father and son in *Mandingo*. Throughout the rehearsals and the (brief) run of the play, Hopper resided at Tone's apartment on East 62nd Street. The young actor was billed last, but prominently, in the program. His credit "and Dennis Hopper" was set in smaller letters than Tone's name but larger than those of the other players.

Cast as Hammond's neurotic, drunk, unsatisfied wife/cousin was Brooke Hayward who, unlike the blonde Blanche in the novel, was brunette. (One appalled theater critic would accurately describe the character as "incestuous, sadistic and degenerate. As if that wasn't enough, she's a dipsomaniac and a nymphomaniac.") Thin and strikingly pretty, the twenty-two-year-old actress/model had recently appeared on the cover of *Vogue*. Hayward was a divorced single mother and the daughter of Margaret Sullavan, the Broadway and screen legend (*Three Comrades*, 1938) who had committed suicide a year earlier. Like Dennis Hopper, Hayward had an intense personality, and the two began dating during rehearsals of *Mandingo*, which would be the only Broadway credit for both actors.

Falconhurst family friend Doc Redfield was played by Philip Huston from the original 1939 production of *Journey's End* and the 1943 *Othello* revival starring Paul Robeson.

The stage production of *Mandingo* employed many black actors, a rarity for a Broadway show, especially for a non-musical.

Originally announced to play Mede, the pugilist Mandingo slave, was the tall, well-built John McCurry. But the actor was already employed in (and receiving good notices for) the off-Broadway production *The Death of Bessie Smith*, the top half of a double feature of Edward Albee one-acts that had opened on March 1. Since McCurry's nightly role in *The Death of Bessie Smith* at York Playhouse on 64th Street would be over before he was needed in *Mandingo* at the Lyceum on 45th Street, it was originally hoped that the actor could commit to both plays.

Rockne Tarkington ended up as Mede. (As in the novel, the role had very little dialogue and most of the performance required physical acting. Unlike in the book, Mede is already part of the Falconhurst inventory and is already a trained fighter when the play starts.) The towering, six-foot-five Tarkington had been in Los Angeles theater productions and had uncredited bits in several major films and TV shows. *Mandingo* was the young actor's only Broadway play, but he went on to a long career on TV shows like *The Andy Griffith Show* (1967 season) and *The Man from U.N.C.L.E.* (1966 season) and popular movies like *Clarence, the Cross-Eyed Lion* (1965), *The Great White Hope* (1970), and the title role in the outrageous blaxploitation entry *Black Samson* (1974). From 1968 to 1969 he starred in the *Danger Island* segments of the Saturday morning show *The Banana Splits Adventure Hour.*

Onstott had described Lucretia Borgia, the most powerful and respected of the Falconhurst slaves, as being in her thirties and still producing babies, but Kirkland rewrote the character as an older, matronly figure, and the role was played by eighty-one-year-old Georgia Burke. Her prior Broadway credits included the original 1940 production of *Cabin in the Sky* and a 1953 revival of *Porgy and Bess.*

Hammond's slave/lover Ellen was played by gorgeous actress/dancer Mauriska Ferro, who was light-skinned (as the character was described by Onstott). Ferro was a nightclub performer and had danced in the movie versions of *The King and I* (1956), *South Pacific* (1958), and *Porgy and Bess* (1959).

Among the other black cast members were stage and television veterans Clark Morgan as Memnon (a.k.a. Agamemnon), Vinie Burrows as Tense, and Fran Bennett as Lucy. Twelve-year-old twins Arnold and Ronald Moore made their only Broadway appearances as Meg and Alpha. (These sexually-deviant slave brothers were completely sanitized in Kirkland's adaptation.)

Heavyweight boxer Coley Wilson played Topaz, the vicious fighter who battles Mede in the climactic bout. (Kirkland's description: "Topaz is tall... and of formidable appearance. He is a mulatto and should be frighteningly ugly, made up so that his eyes appear unmatched, a cheek caved in and many of his front teeth missing. There are welts on his oiled body and back and streaks of discolored skin that look to have been seared.") As a young fighter, Wilson had defeated Rocky Marciano by decision at the 1948 New York Golden Gloves tournament before starting a decent professional career in the ring. Wilson's boxing skills and impressive physique had been put to good use when he played the title role in the movie *The Joe Louis Story* (1953). *Mandingo* was Wilson's only play, but he had been on stage before for road show boxing demonstrations. At the time of *Mandingo,* the former fighter was a barber at his own shop in Brooklyn.

As in the novel, the play script had the Topaz character being given a pre-fight snort of cocaine by his owner. (Topaz [referring to his burns]: "Oh,

Masta Henry do that when I 'fuse to fight a long time back—'fore I didn't have no powder. I feared then. Not no more. Masta Henry give me powder now.")

Among the *Mandingo* understudies—none of whom ever got to appear during the short run—was white actress Lane Bradbury (the original productions of *J. B.*, 1958; *Gypsy*, 1959; and *Night of the Iguana*, 1961), who was on standby to fill in for either Hayward or Ferro.

During rehearsals, Kirkland made numerous revisions to his script and gave suggestion to MacMillian regarding the blocking of the actors. The final script was heavily altered from Kirkland's early drafts and contained more dialogue taken directly from the novel. Added, then deleted, during the rehearsal process were a love scene between Hammond and the beaten Ellen where she dies in his arms; Hammond learning of Blanche and Mede's affair and planning to kill the slave; and a scene of Lucretia Borgia taking a poisoned hot toddy to euthanize Blanche. (Blanche is alive at the end of the produced play.) The tavern scene in Kirkland's first draft retained several minor characters from the book: slave fighters Trinket and Sweetness; teen slave boys Star and Kit; slave barmaid Daisy; and Kyle, one of the fighter's owners. But these superfluous roles were cut during revisions. The final version of the script ran 140 pages.

In April, the New York *Daily Mirror* reported: "Insiders say that the talk in Jack Kirkland's *Mandingo*, now in rehearsal, makes *Tobacco Road* sound like *The Girl of the Limberlost*." (*Girl of the Limberlost* was a syrupy, popular 1909 novel by Gene Stratton-Porter about poor white folk.)

The producers' lackluster, ambiguous promotional campaign included a print ad with a crude drawing of a dark-haired, tanned young woman in a tattered, skimpy garment—apparently meant to depict Ellen.

After five days of previews that started on Wednesday, May 17, *Mandingo* had its opening night premiere performance on Monday, May 22, 1961—four years after the publication of the novel. John Chapman raved in the *Daily News*: "a taunt and colorful narrative....Director Louis Macmillan keeps *Mandingo* tingling, and Franchot Tone is giving a remarkably resourceful and technically splendid performance....Another exciting performance is being given by Brooke Hayward...And Hopper does a fine job....The play winds up with an incredibly realistic fight to the death between two 'buck niggers'....*Mandingo* is strong meat and absorbing theatre."

Every other reviewer despised the production. Howard Taubman, the *New York Times*: "To a world painfully aware of the anguish of racial tension, a play like *Mandingo* can only seem like a crude, sensationalized effort to capitalize on a newsworthy theme....[The play] parades the brutalities and decadence of the old South with a savor that has less to do with drama than unceasing shock effects....It may well be that [Kirkland] wishes to say something compassionate and purging about the misery of the slaves and the malevolence of the slave owners. But what emerges is a group of stereotyped characters taking part in noisome affairs and speaking a lush dialect that must have gone out of literary fashion a century ago.... *Mandingo* takes an inexhaustible interest in the varieties of matings that have taken place around Falconhurst....It throws in a bit of incest for good measure....Franchot Tone, who has an honorable record of worthier things, snorts, wheezes and blusters his accomplished way through the role of Mr. Maxwell. There are other actors, white and Negro, with whom one can only sympathize....In a time when insight and wisdom are desperately wanted, *Mandingo* offers only a shabby, coarse, surface treatment of an agonizing theme."

Walter Kerr, *Herald Tribune*: "Let me say at once that *Mandingo* is dreadful, but not dull....Between times there are discreet offstage screams, forced rapes, hints of sodomy and drug addiction and—oh, I don't know, all sorts of things....If it were conceivable that a good performance could be given in such an extravaganza, Mr. Tone would give it. One must admire the earnestness with which he keeps pretending to be plausible. Brooke Hayward is certainly pretty as the girl with the blacksnake whip, though she does not yet phrase or project on a Broadway scale."

Robert Coleman, *Mirror*: "It's not exactly a lengthy offering; it just seems so....We can only wonder how Franchot Tone got trapped in this one. And we regret that such promising players as Brooke Hayward and Dennis Hopper had to make their first important appearances in such a sorry vehicle.... Other good actors [in the cast are] working against overwhelming odds. They all deserve better. Louis Macmillan's direction isn't of much help. After all, you can't expect a megaphoner to be so gifted a magician as to turn doss into gold....*Mandingo* has taken a serious subject and treated it with a cheap theatricality that we think is self-defeating. Oh, well, we didn't like Kirkland's *Tobacco Road* either."

Frank Aston, *World-Telegram*: "[*Mandingo*] has scenes that drip like blood-raw meat....The language is profane....*Mandingo* is a weirdly wallowing melodrama of hatred, lust, incest, miscegenation, brutality, love, vengeance and corn."

Richard Watts Jr., the *Post*: "[*Mandingo*] contemplates sex, sadism and decadence on a slave plantation in violent detail and with a mixture of indignation and relish. Its catalogue of lust and cruelty is explicit, but its lurid melodramatics keep it from being either convincing or moving....The plantation owner...is played with gusto by Franchot Tone. The beautiful

Newspaper advertisement.

Brooke Hayward achieves the feat of retaining her appeal in the impossible role of the horrible girl neurotic, and clearly has the instincts of an actress. Dennis Hopper is remarkably good as the son….But *Mandingo* is lost in its own luridness."

John McCarten, *The New Yorker*: "Toward the conclusion of [the novel] *Mandingo*,…[a slave] is put in a pot and boiled to death because he has had congress with the wife of his master. This scene…has been eliminated in Jack Kirkland's adaptation…But if Mr. Kirkland has been charitable in refusing to expose us to the simmering down of a fellow human being, he has not hesitated to follow the Onstott lead in presenting for our entertainment a full set of samples of incest, nymphomania, dipsomania, sadism, miscegenation, flagellation, homosexuality, and other deviations from the social norm. When he gets his characters into high gear, Mr. Kirkland establishes the fact that he, with the help of Onstott, can make other students of Southern decadence look like a passel of sissies....As directed by Louis Macmillan, *Mandingo* is as agitated an affair as you've ever laid eyes on, and when, to wind things up, the male Mandingo is entered in a fight against a New Orleans battler, there ensues the damnedest rumpus I've ever seen on the stage. Among those trying to make sense of the drama are Franchot Tone, whose Southern accent is laced with some Down East effects."

Time magazine: "*Mandingo* makes mere plot seem an anachronism, it has so much erupting at such lurid levels, so much more belching forth when nothing more seems possible. Except for its blatant treatment of sex, *Mandingo* would itself seem an anachronism, written in 1832 as well as taking place then....Conceivably, over this orgy of miscegenation, incest, torture and carnage can be draped some kind of indictment or protest. But in invading the Alabama of *Mandingo*, the Kirkland who portrayed the Georgia of *Tobacco Road* seems, steadily and shamelessly, to purvey sensationalism. The result may not be boring, but it is everywhere bad and, in more than one place, backfiringly [sic] ludicrous."

Jack Gaver, United Press International: "As a novel, *Mandingo* is fascinating for its mounting shock values, but the drama that Jack Kirkland fashioned from it at the Lyceum theater is a mild distillation that badly misses the goal of stirring melodrama that must have been the playwright's aim. Franchot Tone, Brooke Hayward and Dennis Hopper are not able to bring it to life as the leading players, under the direction of Louis Macmillan, and it is unlikely anyone could....Kirkland has been able to get only a few of [the novel's] highlights onto the stage and compromise has had to be made with some of those....*Mandingo* just wasn't meant for the stage."

Thomasina Norford, *Amsterdam News* (a popular and influential black newspaper): "Slavery was not a beautiful story, nor is the play *Mandingo*.... William Faulkner and Tennessee Williams combined in all their plays and novels never combined as much depravity and decadence of the old South as Kirkland does in *Mandingo*....It wallows in the evils of this in-human institution and comments harshly on the nature of the southern whites who perpetuated and profited from it....Kirkland relies on the shock value to hold the audience."

John McClain, *Journal American*: "*Mandingo*...is pretty heady stuff...and apparently clings to life in the hope that it will shock a number of people into buying tickets. This I doubt....However raw and searing [the play is] supposed to be, it caught me on the verge of the sort of giggles one sometimes gets in church....Even the final shooting had its humorous side: It was just too neat and complete....Of the pleasant things to be said about *Mandingo*: There are good performances by Dennis Hopper and Brooke Hayward...And there is a whale of a realistic fight between Rockne Tarkington and Coley Wallace.

It is legend that *Tobacco Road* got poor notices when it opened on Broadway, yet survived to make a fortune for Mr. Kirkland. I doubt that *Mandingo* will stage any such happy upset."

This reviewer was right. Broadway patrons had no more interest in *Mandingo* than the critics did, and the production closed on Saturday, May 27 after only eight regular performances.

Two months later, in *Theatre Arts*, Julian Mitchell recalled: "Jack Kirkland based this insultingly unintelligent play on a novel by one Kyle Onstott, but it seemed more like a television producer's ignorant idea of a Faulkner novel. Its bad taste almost defies description....Franchot Tone...spent most of the time...swilling toddies in an obvious attempt to forget the whole preposterous melodrama. Brooke Hayward...did her best, which was really quite good. I'm not at all sure that she deserves praise for that; the play is so offensively ill-written, wantonly violent, pointless and immoral that everyone connected with it should be ashamed.....I was of a mind to suggest the NAACP send pickets quickly, but an early and merciful closing made that unnecessary."

It isn't known if Kyle Onstott attended the show or what he thought of seeing his book on stage. But Kirkland was apparently distraught over the reviews and only kept the positive clipping from *Daily News* in his archives.

On August 9, 1961, three months after the play closed, Hopper and Hayward were married in New York, then moved to Hollywood. They both spent the next few years doing guest spots on TV episodes and had a daughter in 1962. Hopper's extreme drug use and violent personality soon drove Hayward to request a divorce and a restraining order. Their divorce was finalized in 1969, the same year that Hopper directed, co-wrote, and costarred in the smash *Easy Rider* and continued his long, up-and-down Hollywood film career. In 1977, Hayward exposed her dysfunctional childhood in the memoir *Haywire*, which became a best-seller.

A year after *Mandingo*, Macmillan directed *Sweet Miani*, a short-lived, off-Broadway musical.

Although New York rejected it, the *Mandingo* play could possibly have become a successful touring production in less sophisticated markets, but after the Broadway disaster, producers Billy Baxter and Edward Friedman gave up entirely on theatre. Baxter did move forward with his plans to make a movie version of the still-hot book. In 1966 he put together a proposal for a *Mandingo* film, which included a treatment written by Kirkland and newspaper editor Donald Feitel. Unable to attract investors, Baxter never produced *Mandingo* or any other films. He later became a partner in the Steinmann-Baxter Company, which handled American distribution for foreign films like the Israeli production *Abu el Banat* (a.k.a. *Daughters, Daughters*, 1973).

Kirkland died in 1969, shortly after writing the book for *Jeeter*, a never-completed *Tobacco Road* musical. (A different, unsuccessful musical adaptation played in Westport, Connecticut in 1974.) Kirkland's obscure *Mandingo* play was never revived and was never published. The playwright's brittle and crumbling handwritten manuscript and his typescript drafts of *Mandingo* are among the items in the Jack Kirkland Papers, which are housed at the Billy Rose Theatre Division of The New York Public Library for the Performing Arts.

Book III:
The "Falconhurst" Films

Chapter 5:
Mandingo: The Movie

By the late 1960s, Kyle Onstott's lurid novel *Mandingo* was a perpetual, international paperback sensation, had sold five million copies, and had spawned a whole series of official sequels and prequels as well as dozens of pulp imitators with sensational covers of frail Southern belles succumbing to shirtless, muscular male slaves. The creation of the MPAA rating system in November of 1968 allowed filmmakers to explore previously taboo themes and social issues. Contemporary mainstream films could contain explicit nudity, language and violence, and it was now possible for a no-holds-barred movie adaptation of *Mandingo* to be made.

In America the reviews for *Mandingo* had been scathing, but in Italy the translated novel was not only a popular sensation, but was taken seriously by that country's critics and literary scholars. In early 1968 Italian producer Maleno Malenotti, hoping for an international hit, obtained the film rights to *Mandingo* and the book's four popular sequels from William Denlinger, the original publisher and the copyright holder of *Mandingo*. Malenotti had produced a number of major European films, including *La Legge* (a.k.a. *Where the Hot Wind Blows!*, 1959), Nicholas Ray's *The Savage Innocents* (1960) with Anthony Quinn, and *Arabella* (1967), and had directed the popular "shockumentary" *Slave Trade in the World Today* (1964). (The American ads screamed "Never before seen on the screen...The truth about slavery—today!") With Carlo Ponti, another top Italian movie mogul, Malenotti was co-owner of the huge studio facility Cosmopolitan Film.

To produce *Mandingo*, Malenotti teamed with fellow Italian Dino De Laurentiis, the famed mogul responsible for more than sixty features including the international hits *La Strada* (1954), *Barabbas* (1961), *The Bible* (1966), and *Barbarella* (1968).

Malenotti assigned his son Roberto Malenotti and Damiano Damiani to turn the massive *Mandingo* novel into a screenplay. Roberto Malenotti had written and co-directed (with his father) *Slave Trade in the World Today* (1964), while the prolific Damiani's credits included the spaghetti Western classic *Bullet for the General* (1966) and the baffling horror film *The Witch* (1966). The screenwriters' previous work contained plenty of sex and violence, making them well-suited to handle *Mandingo*'s subject matter. (Much later, Damiani would direct 1982's *Amityville II: The Possession* for De Laurentiis.) When the Italian-written *Mandingo* screenplay—which also contained material from the hefty sequel book *Drum*—was completed, translator Beverly Bennet prepared an English-language version to present to English-speaking actors and distributors.

Mandingo was to be directed by Alberto Lattuada, a renowned European director and screenwriter since 1943 who was known for handling multiple genres and had already directed films for Malenotti and De Laurentiis. Much of his work is very hard to locate today, especially outside of Italy, but many of Lattuada's films are considered classics, including the controversial *I Dolci inganni* (a.k.a. *Sweet Deceptions*, 1960) about a teenage girl's sexual awakening; the comedies *Il Capotto* (a.k.a. *The Overcoat*, 1952) and *Mafioso* (1962); *La Steppa* (1962), from an Anton Chekhov novel; and the World War II espionage thriller *Fräulein Doktor* (1969).

Malenotti and Lattuada began extensive preproduction on *Mandingo* in late 1968 and chose locations in Brazil to substitute for the book's Alabama and Louisiana settings. Lance Horner, the (sometimes uncredited) author of the *Mandingo* sequel books, was hired to serve as the film's "technical advisor." If the *Mandingo* movie turned out to be a hit, the producers planned to have Horner co-write a screenplay of *Master of Falconhurst* (the third novel of the series) to be produced in 1970.

At a January 1969 press conference in Rome, Lattuada announced the film and defended the controversial subject matter: "The breeding process is humanely degrading, but it was practiced as an economic expedient by plantation owners who found cotton a risky staple for survival."

The prominent role of Mede, the pugilistic Mandingo slave, was offered to one of the most famous African Americans in the world: heavyweight champion Muhammad Ali. But the iconic boxer turned down the part, reportedly because the subject matter was at odds with his Muslim faith. Already cast in a major part was Lionel Stander, who had been a top Hollywood character actor (*Mr. Deeds Goes to Town*, 1937; *A Star Is Born*, 1937) before being blacklisted during the McCartney era. In the late 1960s, Stander was working steadily in European hits like *Once Upon a Time in the West* (1968), *Al di la della legge* (a.k.a. *Beyond the Law*, 1968), and *La Collina degli stivali* (a.k.a. *Boot Hill*, 1969) and was a semi-bankable name on the international market.

It would have been interesting to see how the gravel-voiced, Bronx-born actor handled a Southern accent for *Mandingo*. Incredibly, Malenotti and Lattuada hoped to lure Hollywood legend James Cagney (*Yankee Doodle Dandy*, 1942; *White Heat*, 1949) out of retirement to star in *Mandingo*. (De Laurentiis did get Cagney to return to movies, but not until 1981's *Ragtime*.)

Malenotti and Lattuada went back to Brazil in February to finalize the locations and to audition local blacks to serve as bit players and extras. Screen tests for the major black and whites roles were to be held in Hollywood and New York. While in New York, Malenotti and Lattuada planned to meet with "major Negro organizations" to discuss the screenplay and possibly tone down some of the more offensive material adapted from the novels. *Mandingo* was to begin shooting in mid-March in Brazil to be followed by a short period of filming in New Orleans and was to be released at the end of the year or in early 1970.

But in mid-1969 Maleno Malenotti became disillusioned with the film industry—mainly due to the lack of activity at his stagnant Cosmopolitan studio—and cancelled *Mandingo* and the other films he had in preproduction. He retired from the business after selling his share of Cosmopolitan to Carlo Ponti. Alberto Lattuada continued to direct films until 1989. He died in 2005.

The film rights to *Mandingo* and the other books in the series went to De Laurentiis. In 1971, the aggressive, high-rolling fifty-two-year-old mogul moved his operation from Rome to New York, where he took over a floor in the Gulf + Western Building on Central Park South to begin shooting his movies in America.

Despite the lowbrow source material, De Laurentiis wanted *Mandingo* to be a major production with a multi-million dollar budget, lengthy shooting schedule, and prestigious cast and crew. He began shopping the English-language version of the five-year-old *Mandingo* screenplay to American directors.

In 1973 partial financing for *Mandingo*, as well as North American distribution, was secured from Paramount Pictures, the major film studio that had already co-financed and/or released several De Laurentiis projects, including *The Valachi Papers* (1972), *Serpico* (1973), and the upcoming *Death Wish* (1974). Charles Bludhorn, the extremely powerful and wealthy Austrian businessman who had taken over Paramount in the mid-1960s, was a neighbor of De Laurentiis, and the two moguls would often meet at the Italian's home for a breakfast of fried spaghetti, and then walk together to their offices at the Gulf + Western Building. De Laurentiis explained in the book *Dino: The Life and Films of Dino De Laurentiis*: "It was a way of exchanging ideas and potential projects in private, before we were both sucked into the quotidian whirlwind at work."

James Mason and Paul Benedict examine Ji-Tu Cumbuka and other slaves.

Despite rumors that De Laurentiis received financing from the Mafia and oil sheiks, the mogul raised the multi-million dollar *Mandingo* budget through his traditional method of pre-selling the distribution rights. "Generally speaking," he explained, "the funds for a film come from two primary sources: the American distribution (which is financed by a big studio) and the foreign distribution (meaning the advance sale of the rights to various territories overseas)...While we were waiting for the cash from foreign-rights sales, we needed a line of credit to cover that portion of the production costs... My problem, then, was to find a financial institution that would extend me a line of credit. It wasn't an easy task, because the intrinsic risks of the film industry terrified all the major American banks and they were very reluctant to go out on a limb." De Laurentiis arranged the financing for *Mandingo,* his fifth American production, through an extensive line of credit from a European bank.

To direct *Mandingo*, De Laurentiis sought Richard Fleischer, the prolific American filmmaker who had helmed the producer's successful 1960 biblical epic *Barabbas*, which had also dealt with slave labor (albeit in a different era and location). Fleischer was the son of pioneering animator Max Fleischer

(Betty Boop, Popeye), and had been directing since 1944. After *Barabbas*, Fleischer began pre-production on several aborted De Laurenttis productions before the mogul and the director had a major falling out and sued each other. (Both suits were later dropped.)

In his 1993 memoir *Just Tell Me When to Cry*, Fleischer described De Laurentiis: "An impeccably tailored bundle of raw energy and volatile emotions, he is not only a legend, but also a character. The impact of meeting him for the first time is something akin to sticking your finger into an electric light socket....His personality is the same as his speech: curt, abrupt, brusque."

"I've done every kind of movie and I put the same energy into all the pictures, it didn't make any difference to me [what the genre was,]" Fleischer says.[1] By 1973, the fifty-seven-year-old director's long resume included the classics *The Narrow Margin* (1952), *20,000 Leagues Under the Sea* (1954), *The Vikings* (1958), *Compulsion* (1959), *Barabbas* (1962), *Fantastic Voyage* (1966), *The Boston Strangler* (1968), *Tora! Tora! Tora!* (1970), and *10 Rillington Place* (1971). Fleischer hadn't handled a black-themed film before, but in the late 1960s he was under consideration to direct 20th Century Fox's (aborted) biopic on Malcolm X. Fleischer was highly regarded within the industry, but his huge output was vastly underrated by critics. Pauline Kael of *The New Yorker* once wrote: "A glorified mechanic, Richard Fleischer pleases movie executives because he has no particular interests and no discernible style."

Despite their earlier falling out, De Laurentiis was insistent that Fleischer direct *Mandingo*. In 1973, while Fleischer was making the Charles Bronson vehicle *Mr. Majestyk*, he received the *Mandingo* screenplay. The director said, "It was absolutely the worst thing I've ever read, a translation from Italian into English. I was not interested....Dino seemed to have a staff of truly terrible Italian hack writers under contract....My mother, who's 80, read [the book] and told me it would make a wonderful movie. [After reading the script] I turned the picture down, then read the book. It was worse than the screenplay."

Several other filmmakers, including Michael Campus, the white director of the popular black-themed films *The Mack* (1973) and *The Education of Sonny Carson* (1974), were briefly involved with rewriting and prepping *Mandingo* before De Laurentiis hired Norman Wexler to write a new first draft in late 1973.

Wexler recalled, "I was a reporter for the Boston *Herald*, the San Francisco *Chronicle* and other newspapers after college. Then I worked for ad agencies like Bates and D'Arcy, writing copy on Navy and Air Force missile weapons systems for General Dynamics. In 1961 I quit work and started playwriting." The Harvard graduate and struggling playwright penned the low-budget 1970 film *Joe*, which became a critical and financial hit and earned the first-time screenwriter an Academy Award nomination. Wexler got another Oscar nomination for rewriting Waldo Salt's script for De Laurentiis's production *Serpico* (1973). "What I tried to do [with *Mandingo*] was dispel all the racist myths," the writer explained. Wexler's *Mandingo* paycheck was $100,000.

To make the 659-page novel filmable, Wexler removed many of Onstott's flavorful, but often pointless, subplots and vignettes. Many of the book's numerous characters were omitted or altered, including the cousin, Charles, who popped up throughout the book but only appears for the first part of the movie. The slave trader Brownlee, a sinister and reprehensible character (and a pedophile) in the book, was rewritten to be a friend of the Maxwells. The screenplay took much of Doc Redfield's material from the novel and gave it to Brownlee. Also deleted was the child that Blanche gives birth to before spawning Mede's baby: Sophy, a cross-eyed girl whose father is apparently her uncle Charles.

The screenwriter also gave more definition to Onstott's characters—both black and white. The abused slave Agamemnon (a.k.a. Mem) was cowardly and submissive in the book, but Wexler rewrote the character as an enlightened, proud black man who secretly learns to read and ultimately rebels violently against his enslavement. (In the book, Mem was whipped not for reading, but for being lazy and for stealing his master's liquor.)

The new *Mandingo* screenplay was sent to Fleischer. "Dino desperately wanted me to do *Mandingo*," Fleischer says. "I turned the picture down about four or five times, but he kept coming back. I realized that the book did have something very important to say. I was captivated by it, but repelled at the same time. I could see the commercial value in that kind of story if anyone were brave enough to do it. Finally, I decided to go ahead with it under some conditions. [De Laurentiis agreed] that I would make the picture that I wanted to make without interference and to not be exploitative, but be accurate." *Mandingo* would be the director's thirty-eighth feature. Fleischer didn't know why De Laurentiis saw him as the appropriate director for the film, but he knew that the producer saw the subject as a money maker. "[De Laurentiis] would never make a picture that he didn't think had commercial potential. But I don't know anybody who would."

Despite the shocking subject matter, Fleischer was not concerned about potential censorship problems. "That's not my problem, that's the producer's problem," he says. "I don't worry about that. If the producer wants to make the picture and I want to do it, I don't care about the other end of it."

"My intention always was to make primarily a Gothic horror story with a very big social point," the director told *Movie* magazine. "It would have been a mistake to pull the punches and not direct as forcefully as I could. The subject is too serious and has been mistreated so long in films. The whole slavery story has been lied about, covered up and romanticized so much that I thought it

Perry King and Susan George between takes of the proposal scene.

really had to stop. The only way to stop was to be as brutal as I could possibly be to show how these people suffered."

Fleischer continued, "The white people in the film are corrupt without knowing they are corrupt. They weren't being deliberately cruel and brutal. They did what was perfectly normal to them. If you swatted a fly on the table, none of us would wince, but a Hindu would fall over in shock. I wasn't portraying the whites as being great villains; to these people, whipping was the very proper way to discipline a slave—there was no other way to do it. You were considered a very dangerous white man if you didn't do it. I tried to show the whites as just practicing the behavior of the time—they didn't originate it."

Fleischer recalled that he worked "very, very closely" with Wexler on the final *Mandingo* draft. "We worked at the Plaza Hotel [in New York] in a suite and locked ourselves up," the director says. "The structure wasn't quite right. We worked on not only the dialogue, but restructuring each scene and analyzing constantly whether it was the right way to go and what we were trying to say in this scene or that scene. We would bounce ideas off each other. It was a challenge all the way because my intent was not to be sensational, but to tell a good story. I kept [the novel] as kind of a bible while we were shooting and while we were writing the script. I don't think we had any problems selecting the best scenes in the book that we would dramatize. We left what we thought was good and changed what we didn't like." The screenplay ignores the entire plodding middle section of the novel and focuses mainly on the final 187 pages, which contained most of the book's plot.

"I did a lot of research," Fleischer explains. "Research is one of my pet things, one of my joys of making films. I found every book I could get from the libraries about slavery and what happened in the South. I read everything I could get my hands on about the South—novels, documentary things." (*The Vikings* and *Barabbas* are two of the director's earlier classics that show the results of extensive historical research.) The spoken lines in the *Mandingo* script, like those in the novel, were written in a grammatically-poor Old South dialect. The screenplay and the final film contain a great deal of dialogue and slang that had been created by Onstott.

"I liked him very much," Fleischer says about Wexler. "[He was a] really bizarre guy. [Laughs] He was fun to be with, but he could be an embarrassment, too. He was a hell-raiser and tying him down to work was part of the job. I think he's kind of crazy. [Laughs] We'd go out to lunch and he'd order a lunch of soups; three or four different kinds of soups. Strange things like that."

Wexler's odd behavior and reported manic depression and substance abuse problems often led to trouble. During a 1972 plane flight, Wexler pointed to a Richard Nixon magazine cover and declared that he was going to assassinate the then-President. The writer was arrested by the FBI and given a brief jail term. In March of 1975, shortly before *Mandingo* was released, the writer was arrested for insulting a fellow airline passenger and biting a stewardess's arm. Immediately after being released on bail, Wexler got into a confrontation in a coffee shop and verbally assaulted an escort service employee before he was arrested once again. *Time* magazine noted: "The skies seem to grow less friendly when Norman Wexler is airborne."

While the screenplay was being finalized, executive producer Ralph Serpe began putting together the rest of the $3 million show, which was to begin shooting in August, 1974. The muscular, no-nonsense Serpe had been a member of the United States Army Special Services during World War II. After meeting De Laurentiis in Europe in the late 1940s, Serpe became involved with the European film industry in both production and distribution. At the time of *Mandingo*, Serpe had dozens of films on his resume, including the action hit *Across 110th Street* (1972) and many De Laurentiis productions.

During the months of pre-production in early 1974, Serpe scouted the antebellum plantations that still stood near the Mississippi River region of Baton Rouge and New Orleans, Louisiana. The newly-formed Louisiana State Film Commission was pleased that *Mandingo* would be bringing money into the state and hiring several hundred locals to work on both sides of the cameras. Fleischer once said, "I want to do as many interiors on location as possible. You get a better feeling, a better sense of place. If we have an interior where there's a lot of people, which means a lot of staging and a lot of camera movements, we'll do it [in a studio]. You can get more control on a stage. Otherwise, if there's just a small group of people, I'd rather use the real thing on location."

The location chosen for Falconhurst was found thirty miles south of Baton Rouge. "People from the Louisiana State Film Commission showed us several plantations," Serpe recalled. "We saw Belle Helene, and decided to use the mansion part to represent the Falconhurst main house." The privately-owned Belle Helene, one of the largest plantations ever built in Louisiana, was built in 1841 for a sugar merchant and had housed many slaves. The three-story, Spanish Moss-surrounded mansion had eight pillars on each side and had been seen previously in *Band of Angels* (1957), *The Beguiled* (1971), and *The Autobiography of Miss Jane Pittman* (TV, 1974). The well-maintained plantation had to be "aged" by the *Mandingo* art department to look like it was uncared for by the Maxwell men.

The state-owned plantations The Oaks, Oakley House (a former home of famous painter James Audubon), Houmas House (which was used for Blanche's home, Crowfoot), as well as the privately-owned Hermitage and the two-hundred-year-old Evergreen, were other mansions used in *Mandingo*.

De Laurentiis and Serpe didn't insist that Fleischer use any particular actors in *Mandingo*—"They wouldn't dare try that with me," the director says—but casting the film was extremely difficult.

Serpe recalled, "It took a long time to persuade Fleischer to take this picture, and we got turned down by an awful lot of actors. Charlton Heston turned us down for the father part." (Heston had starred in Fleischer's *Soylent Green*, 1973.)

Several other names passed on the role of Warren Maxwell, the aging and ailing patriarch of Falconhurst. Fleischer explains, "There was one actor who I knew pretty well, socially. He and his wife were a famous couple. We were pretty good friends and I approached him with the script and he vehemently turned it down."[2]

Finally cast in the part was James Mason, the highly-respected British actor who had worked with Fleischer two decades earlier on the Walt Disney classic *20,000 Leagues Under the Sea*. Mason had been a major film star in England during the 1940s before he came to America and became a top character actor, a Golden Globe winner, and an Oscar nominee after starring in numerous pictures including *Julius Caesar* (1953), *A Star is Born* (1954), *North by Northwest* (1959), *Journey to the Center of the Earth* (1959), and *Lolita* (1962). By the 1970s, the prolific Mason lived in Switzerland and appeared mainly in European movies that never played American theaters. The sixty-five-year-old actor said at the time: "I'm really only pleased with a few of my performances. The majority of my films were crummy." His wife, Clarissa Kaye, said that during that period she and Mason were "a couple of gypsies, living from film to film, but James was always worried about money and where the next job would be coming from."

Fleischer says about Mason: "I thought he would be very good for [the role]. He was a superb actor. He could do anything. And he wanted to do it. Virtually everybody that we offered it to turned it down. I expected that they would. A lot of actors turned the part down, but James saw something in the part that he wanted to do and he enjoyed making the picture. We were very good friends."

Mason said, "When I first read the screenplay of *Mandingo*, I saw horror piled on horror and I was worried that there might be too much over emotionalizing of the issues raised by the film. Then on re-reading it I saw the script was saying that what happened at Falconhurst was not the exception, but was common at all plantations which based their operations on slave breeding. Maxwell is a business man, having one of those dubious careers, like being a professional soldier. In fact, Maxwell is a fairly decent chap, again in the context of his time. He maintains reasonably decent standards of living for his slaves and he does pursue domestic tranquility at Falconhurst. In this sense he is a man of integrity who has a code of living handed down to him by his father. He doesn't think about the rights or wrongs of it."

In *Biography News*, Mason said: "It's not a sadistic part. This man just has different standards from the ones we adhere to nowadays. He thinks he is very fair and he treats his slaves extremely well. But in fact, of course, the behavior judged by present standards is absolutely horrendous. And I think it draws our attention to the fact that some of the standards we now apply will horrify our grandchildren in a couple of generations."

Mason began preparing for *Mandingo* while shooting the British TV movie *Great Expectations* (1974). To develop his accent for *Mandingo*, the actor listened to recorded speeches by elderly North Carolina senator Sam J. Ervin Jr. (chairman of the Senate Watergate committee.) Mason explained: "For a Britisher, the Southern accent is much easier to do than those in other parts of the United States. What you do to get it right is eliminate such letters as 'r' from your words and get a sing-song rhythm going. It's essential to listen very carefully to the vowel sounds. In the film I don't do the traditional 'honey chile' accent."

After a long search, twenty-six-year-old Perry King was cast as young Hammond Maxwell. Serpe said, "We really got the business for the Hammond role. That Bottoms kid—Timothy?—turned us down. Jeff Bridges. Jan-Michael Vincent. Beau Bridges."

Fleischer recalls, "I remembered [Perry King] from something that I'd seen with him: Sylvester Stallone's movie, *The Lords of Flatbush* (1974). I saw him in that and I thought that he was great and I interviewed him and met him and thought that he would be just right for the part."

The tall, blue-eyed, handsome King had studied at Yale University and Julliard before starting a film career and gaining attention for his fine performances in the offbeat films *The Possession of Joel Delaney* (1972), *Slaughterhouse-Five* (1972), and *The Wild Party* (1975). "The main reason I've enjoyed my career," King told *After Dark* magazine, "is that everything I've done has been a departure from what has come before." The actor's striking facial features were given additional character by the slight gap in his front teeth and the chipped tooth (from a street fight) which he refused to cap.

King said: "When I first saw the [*Mandingo*] script, I thought it was gratuitous junk, but if you research the period you will find that it's pretty accurate. It's upsetting as hell...One of the disturbing facts I discovered was that whites in that region who owned slaves really believed that blacks were suspended somewhere between the animal world and people. That is the way whites could justify their treatment of them and that is what's reflected in that film...It was a diseased society...When you study the [*Mandingo*] script you see that every important white character in the film is crippled, which is probably how the author saw what slavery did to those who imposed the evil system on the blacks. Blanche, my wife in the film, is a drunk; my father, Maxwell, is rheumatic, and I have a permanent limp that resulted from a horse accident when I was a child. I'm sympathetic towards Hammond without playing him sympathetically."

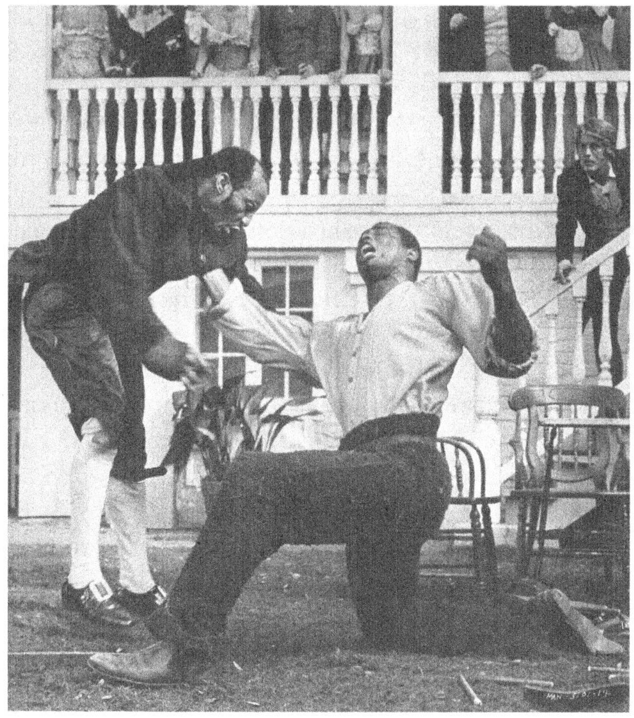

Babouin (Earl Maynard) and Mede (Ken Norton) fight.

Shortly after completing *The Wild Party* in June 1974, King, who had never been to the American South, went to Louisiana several weeks prior to shooting his first scenes for *Mandingo* and spent time with the locals to work on his accent for the film. He also read extensively on slavery and Southern history. "I had to place Hammond in a particular time and place in American history," the actor explained, "so that I could play him without asking what he would do in any given situation. I had to respond instinctively to situations." To limp believably and consistently throughout the film, King would bind his knee with a tight surgical bandage before shooting each scene. "I live with the character," the actor once explained about his approach. "It's like having a roommate. Some roles changed my life…When I finish something, I almost feel like I've taken a person and buried him." (Surprisingly, King bears a very strong resemblance to the artist's rendition of the character that appeared on the original 1958 *Mandingo* paperback.)

For the role of the drunken, unsatisfied Southern belle Blanche, Fleischer chose the slender, twenty-four-year-old blonde, tanned British actress Susan George. Born in London to a saxophone player/hotel manager and a former showgirl, George began acting as a child. "I was a child prodigy," she told the *New York Times*. "I made my first film when I was four. I don't remember what it was called, but it was one of those special features they show at kiddie matinees. I just remember that in it I had long hair and big pink bows, and I walked down the street eating an ice cream cone."

The young actress received her education at a school for child performers and at age twelve was starring in the West End production of *The Sound of Music*. "[I was] a child star at thirteen, which is something I don't advise anyone to do. I was very much ahead of myself and missed a lot of my childhood," she told *Women's Wear Daily*. After a dozen television plays, she made her feature debut at age seventeen in Ken Russell's *Billion Dollar Brain*. ("I played a Russian girl. I had two lines.") Her career gained momentum with lead roles in the British features *The Strange Affair* (1967), as a sixteen-year-old dating a young policeman (Michael York); *Twinky* (a.k.a *Lola*, 1969), as the teenage bride of a middle-aged writer (Charles Bronson); and *Spring and Port Wine* (1970) as James Mason's rebellious daughter. "I just like working and took anything that came along," she said. "All I care about is the work—good, bad, hopefully never indifferent." (*Mandingo* executive producer Serpe was one of the *Twinky* producers.)

By the early 1970s, George was one of the more stunning, magnetic and underrated film actresses and was best-known for playing Dustin Hoffman's wife in Sam Peckinpah's controversial *Straw Dogs* (1971)—which featured George in a notoriously brutal gang rape scene. She later explained in *Telegraph*: "[Peckinpah] wanted it to be utterly explicit and to tell the story by flesh, and as much flesh as could be exposed. And he would have loved the real action. He really got into this rape scene, and it terrified me. One day I will tell the whole story." Prior to *Mandingo*, George had recently given memorable, offbeat performances in the Euro-Western *Sonny and Jed* (1973) and the car chase drive-in hit *Dirty Mary Crazy Larry* (1974). She recalled, "It was a fantastic time, the real heyday of Hollywood. You would go to a party and Grace Kelly and Cary Grant would be standing in the same room. It was wildly glamorous. But it's also a fickle town."

Fleischer says, "I always liked her work and I interviewed her. I think we might have [screen] tested her as well. We did quite a bit of testing on the picture, lots of testing. She came through with a dynamite performance."

Like most actors who were approached about doing *Mandingo*, George was reluctant to do the film. "I distrusted the initial intent of the film," she said at the time. "I thought it was trying to be solely sensational, putting things up on the screen only for shock value." But after doing some historical research and discussing the screenplay with her father, George decided to do the film. "I realized the movie script was based on historical fact. I don't often make pictures to get across important messages to an audience, but I saw how important this picture was for me. The public in America and Europe should know how badly the blacks were treated."

"Blanche was meant to be a grotesque character," Fleischer explained. "To me, she is the most tragic figure in the story and she, more than anybody, is the victim of herself. Basically she's just a regular Southern belle who is a brainless, uneducated girl. Most of the young people in the South never had any education. They were brought up by their illiterate parents or they were sent to England. Here's a girl who, because she isn't a virgin, is rejected completely, for life, and dies virtually because of that. The double standard of the time comes into play. The women are working with one moral attitude and the men are completely different."

George said, "[Blanche] finds herself rejected by a man, the most awful thing that can happen to a woman. There is no way a woman can go through life without having a man, if not physically, at least mentally. It's really a more mental than physical thing, needing to know someone is there when you need him. Blanche is really a cow, and a bad cow, too. Her upbringing in such a bizarre Southern family doomed her from the start. She turned out to be such an extremely calculating person. Because of...her alcoholism, I found her the most challenging role of my career." George found the role of Blanche to have similarities with Scarlett O'Hara, the heroine of *Gone with the Wind* [1939] and the most famous Southern belle in movie history. "After all," George asked, "aren't they both bitches?"

None of the primary or supporting actors cast in *Mandingo* were authentic Southerners. Fleischer said, "It seems that many British people do have a knack of picking up the Southern dialect as easily as any American actor. As far as I was concerned, [Mason and George] were the best casting for the roles. The fact that they both turned out to be English was truly a coincidence."

Scarlett O'Hara had been played by Vivien Leigh, who, like George, was British. But George did not study Leigh's performance to capture a Southern accent. "I've never seen *Gone with the Wind*," George said at the time. "I didn't want to imitate Vivian Leigh's accent as Scarlett O'Hara, so I didn't go now. It's far easier for me to do a straight American accent than it is to do an authentic Southern dialect...I have a terrific ear, although when I do American my voice goes up an octave." [The actress had recently done an impressive California accent for *Dirty Mary Crazy Larry*.] Mason was using audio tapes to prepare for the film and Fleischer suggested that George also listen to recordings of authentic Southerners, but the actress turned down

James Mason with twins Durwyn and Kerwin Robinson

his request. "The first time on the set was the first time I used a Southern accent," she explained. "There is a way of doing a stagey one, which is much easier, drawling words and saying 'you all.' But I'm a very good imitator. All I had to do was hear a real Southern accent. It's the rhythm of the speech, rather than drawling or cutting off words, that makes the accent so distinct. So I listened and I imitated. Once I'm in front of the camera I respond by pure instinct. And when the day is done I don't take my work home with me…I'm a very instinctive actress, and I don't in any way knock it. I'm not a Method actor…The only thing that one learns in one's trade is to be instinctive ten times over if that's necessary. In other words, to make it new every time."

Cast as Ellen, the slave girl who becomes emotionally and intimately involved with the younger Maxwell, was the petite and stunning Brenda Sykes. Ellen was a submissive, undefined character in the novel, but Wexler recreated the role as a woman who was unhappy with the institution of slavery. Sykes had been a political science major at UCLA in the late 1960s before she dropped out of college to pursue an acting career after appearing as a contestant on the TV game shows *The Dating Game* and *Dream Girl of '67*. "In the late 1960s all the agents wanted a black client," Sykes recalled. "I guess fate was propelling me towards acting even if I wasn't consciously aware of it."

After bit roles in TV shows and major movies like *The Liberation of L. B. Jones* (1970), *Pretty Maids All in a Row* (1971), and *Skin Game* (1971) (as a slave), she got her first lead in the offbeat low-budget feature *Honky* (1971), which dealt with an interracial high school romance. She then costarred in the movies *Black Gunn* (1972) and *Cleopatra Jones* (1973) and the short-lived syndicated TV sitcom *Ozzie's Girls* (1973) with Ozzie and Harriet Nelson. *Black Gunn* starred football legend Jim Brown, the top black movie icon of the late 1960s and early 70s. Sykes's off-screen relationship with Brown lasted two years but ended when she took an overdose of barbiturates to get his attention. *Mandingo* was the most-important screen role to date for the twenty-five-year-old actress.

While almost all of the actors cast in the film fit the physical description of their characters in the *Mandingo* novel, Sykes was an exception. In a 1975 article for the magazine *Sepia*, writer Ted Stewart called Sykes "the most beautiful of all the new black cinema stars.... If ever there was need for undisputed, ultimate proof that black is beautiful, Brenda Sykes is it....Her blackness [is] so dark it is almost certainly untouched by any interracial mixture in the past..." The description of Ellen in the *Mandingo* novel read: "...only the slight fullness of her lips hinted her Negro origin, for she was lighter than many white women, lighter." The screenplay described Ellen as "a bit plump," which the rail-thin Sykes was certainly not.

"When I first read the script, I didn't want to do *Mandingo*," Sykes said. "I was turned off by the violence and sex inherent in the material. Then I read the script again and I saw it could be educational for all Americans. It's about a terrible period of history. The film is necessary. The point of the film is that blacks would still be what they were in the antebellum South if they hadn't been fighters." To prepare for *Mandingo*, the actress read slave narratives. "Though my great-grandmother was alive when I was a child, and though she had been born a slave, I really didn't know anything about that part of American history other than what I was told in school."

At the time, Sykes was a follower of the Buddhist religion and explained, "Buddhism is a practical, everyday life philosophy; it is not a strict moral code. It is based on positive fact and says that whatever you do must have a result. If you steal from someone, you must be prepared to have someone steal from you. Heaven and hell are here on earth. You make your own moral code."

Mandingo's title character was the most difficult role to cast. Mede, the pugilist slave, had a powerful physique that was envied by men and desired by women, and whoever played the role would spend much of the film with his shirt off. Fleischer and Wexler had greatly embellished the undeveloped character from the novel, most notably strengthening the friendship between Mede and Hammond. The character had few lines in the screenplay, but the role required a great deal of physical and facial acting. Early in the planning stages, De Laurentiis had offered the role to and was rejected by stars Sidney Poitier and Harry Belefonte, as well as boxing icon Muhammad Ali.

Fleischer wanted an unknown to play Mede and began screen testing a large number of handsome, pumped-up actors and athletes. Sports heroes crossing over into acting was a popular trend at the time. Major athletes like Jim Brown, Fred Williamson, Joe Namath, and Rosey Grier were all appearing on movie screens with varying degrees of success. Serpe contacted Madison Square Garden fight promoter Teddy Brenner. "They wanted a black fighter for the slave part in *Mandingo*," Brenner told the *New York Times*. "[Serpe] mentioned Muhammad Ali and Joe Frazier, but I told him, 'If you want the most beautiful physical specimen in boxing, Ken Norton is the guy.'"

Born in Jacksonville, Illinois in 1943, Ken Norton first started boxing while in the Marines Corps and fought his first professional match in 1967. At the San Diego Sports Arena on March 31, 1973 Norton stepped into the ring with Ali. Norton's manager, Bob Biron, recalled, "Right up to fight time, nobody believed in Ken's chances but those of us in his corner. Four days before the fight, Howard Cosell said it was the greatest mismatch in history and [that] it should have been barred by the State Athletic Commission." On national television, underdog Norton broke Ali's jaw and was named the North American Boxing Federation (NABF) heavyweight champion on a split decision. It was only the second time that Ali had been defeated. Cosell apologized to Norton. Six months later, Ali beat Norton in a rematch that ended in another split decision.

Norton's high-profile fight career and photogenic features kept his picture in the papers and established him as an international sports celebrity. Prior to *Mandingo*, his only acting experience was a small, unbilled, non-speaking part in the 1972 low-budget movie *Top of the Heap*, in which he and fellow boxer Hedgemon Lewis are featured in a barroom scuffle. He can also be spotted hitting a punching bag in the Jon Voight boxing drama *The All-American Boy* (1973). "To be honest," Norton explained in his autobiography, *Going the Distance*, "I never had any acting ambitions, never thought of it in any respect and, in fact, never went to the movies much. I was too busy playing sports and chasing the girls. Back in those days, acting was for sissies."

Norton filmed a *Mandingo* screen test in mid-1974. "It was not much of audition," Norton recalls. "I met Dino and the director, Richard Fleischer. They liked my look and my body, so I was kind of a shoo-in. Fleischer said that I had the look and the personality. He saw the character in me."

Fleischer says, "[Norton] was a complete non-actor, had never acted. I made a test with him and nobody liked the test. But I saw something in him. I just had a hunch that Ken was going to be very good in the role. Everybody thought I was crazy when I cast him in it. Dino had seen the test and said 'How can you make this guy into an actor?' I said, 'I'm sure I can and I think he's perfect for the role in every way.'"

Norton remembers that football star O. J. Simpson, who was then starting an acting career, tested for Mede. "He and also a body builder of that time. I can't think of his name," Norton says. (Simpson missed out on *Mandingo*, but he soon made his movie debut in 1974's *The Klansman*, another Paramount release that dealt frankly with racism in the American South. In 1978 Simpson played Norton's role on *Saturday Night Live* in a skit called *Mandingo II* which featured Simpson in a tryst with Laraine Newman while Bill Murray got intimate not only with Garrett Morris in drag, but also with a cow.)

Prior to meeting the filmmakers, Norton was not familiar with the *Mandingo* novel. He explains, "Once I heard that they were thinking of casting me, I bought the book and read the book. I read it about ten times." Norton refused the role twice "because the way blacks were treated in the book was offensive to me. I couldn't deal with it." But he soon changed his mind. "I felt that I could portray the part. I felt that it was something that needed to be told, that was never told before. And the love scene, between black and white, had not been done before. So, I wanted to be the one to do it." (During his brief reign as the number-one black action star, Jim Brown had fairly explicit onscreen trysts with Raquel Welch in *100 Rifles* (1969) and Stella Stevens in *Slaughter (*1972), but neither film attracted much mainstream attention and neither of those interracial love scenes were as explicit as the Ken Norton-Susan George coupling in *Mandingo.*)

After finishing another boxing match in June 1974, Norton quickly started a new kind of workout. To help the inexperienced Norton hold his own with the highly trained actors who surrounded him, Fleischer assigned New York acting instructor Robert Modica to serve as the boxer's on-set instructor. Norton explained, "I worked with Bob [Modica] for six weeks

Hammond (Perry King) and Mede (Ken Norton) watch Cicero (Ji-Tu Cumbuka) hang

going over technique, delivery, acting for the camera, hitting my marks, speech, and inflection. I found that with acting, you have to psyche yourself up just as you would for a boxing match." The role required Norton to shave off his trademark mustache.

"Ken Norton we got because of his stature," Serpe said. "He's a handsome guy, too, that's important. He couldn't act, but we got him a coach, and he's developing into a pretty good actor. The scenes aren't too demanding. He passed up a quarter-million-dollar gate to fight Jerry Quarry to make this picture."

"I spent a lot of time with Ken and I think he came through beautifully," Fleischer remembers. "He understood what he was doing. Ken is very intelligent and understood what I wanted in the picture and he surprised everybody except me. Of course, I was a little surprised that he came out as well as he did."

Among the African Americans in the featured cast were gravel-voiced Richard Ward (*The Learning Tree,* 1969; Serpe's production *Across 110*th *Street*) as the embittered Agamemnon (a.k.a. Mem); husky, Tony-winner Lillian Hayman (*The Night They Raided Minsky's*, 1968; TV's *One Life to*

Live, 1968–1986 seasons) as Falconhurst ruler Lucretia Borgia; and Tony nominee Beatrice Winde (*The Autobiography of Miss Jane Pittman*, TV 1974) as Lucy. The dark-skinned Ward and the stout Hayman were fifty-nine and fifty-two, respectively, at the time and their roles were presented differently than in the novel where Mem was around thirty years of age and possibly the son of a white man while Lucretia Borgia was in her early thirties, voluptuous, and still producing babies for Falconhurst. (The obscure 1961 stage version of *Mandingo* had also presented Lucretia Borgia as older and matronly.)

The angry, rebellious slave Cicero (a creation of Wexler's not in the book) was played by Ji-Tu Cumbuka, a towering thirty-two-year-old who stood 6' 5" (1.96 m). The actor, whose appropriate first name meant "giant man" in Swahili, had been in a number of features including *Change of Habit* (1969) and *Blacula* (1972) and TV shows like *Night Gallery* (1973 season) and *Kojak* (1973 and 1974 seasons). Norton and Cumbuka each had a scene in *Top of the Heap* (1972), but did not appear together. Cumbuka says, "They wanted to see me for a film concerning slavery, for the role of Mandingo [Mede], along with several other people. There was Fred Williamson, Jim Brown, and Bernie Casey. [Cumbuka also recalled O. J. Simpson auditioning.] The guys that looked like a Mandingo. They were big, powerful-looking guys. Those football players were hot at that time. They already had the name, plus it didn't matter if they could act or not, they were making exploitation films."

Cumbuka continues, "After the audition, they said they'd like to see me for a recall. I nailed it. They strongly considered me for the role of Mandingo, but I said I had my reservations about that. There were no redeeming factors in the role of Mandingo. I couldn't see a black man letting a little crippled white boy make him jump in a pot of boiling water. I couldn't wrap my head around that. I wanted them to change the scene. Instead of jumping in that boiling water, shoot him, hang him, anything. They'd have to kill me with a bullet rather than boil my ass. So, I [said] to Dick Fleischer—we had met before, we hit it off, and I liked him—'I know I can't come in here and tell you how to do your business. But if you want me to play the role, I can't play it. However, I'd like to play the role of Cicero. I'd like to be considered for that.' He said he'd like to think about it and as soon I got home, my agent called saying I had the role."

Cumbuka recalls his preparation: "I read the book. I had already done research on slavery. I tried to make Cicero intelligent. I was a militant dude, anyway. I had a chip on my shoulder. I'm a warrior-type of dude. I served in the paratroopers and the combat infantrymen. I liked all that gung-ho stuff.

I wanted to fight. I didn't want to sit back and just take it. That was the type of dude I was and the type of dude I am now."

Wexler and Fleischer continued to make major revisions in the screenplay throughout June and July as the start date of August 1974 approached. Among the late screenplay alterations was the complete removal of Hammond's "Cousin Dick," another brother of Blanche. The twin slave boys, Meg and Alph, are nameless in the film and have much smaller roles than they did in the book. Also cut from the final draft was Meg's gay attraction towards Hammond. (In fact, none of the novel's unsubtle homosexual themes appeared in the film.) The screenplay had Blanche's mother, Beatrix, appearing during the climax and spouting darkly humorous dialogue about childbirth, but the final draft limited the character to only one early scene. (In the novel, Blanche's newborn dark baby is killed not by bleeding from its untied umbilical cord, but by getting its skull smashed on the commode by the appalled Beatrix.)

Serpe told the *Los Angeles Times*, "We're faithful to the story of the book, but not the spirit. I mean the book's hackwork, isn't it? It's almost repulsive. A lot of people have read it, but they read it for the wrong reasons. It's really a story of love. We had the script rewritten three times. Norman Wexler, who's a fine constructionist, wrote it. But we had to rewrite and rewrite to get to the warmth."

Fleischer recalls, "One of our big discussions was who would be killed at the end—Hammond or the father or both. We argued that point for weeks. The father doesn't die in the book. But I felt very strongly that an audience would be left very dissatisfied if we didn't kill one white person."

Mandingo began shooting in August 1974 and continued throughout the fall on location in Baton Rouge and New Orleans, Louisiana. "You must go where the story requires to be shot," De Laurentiis once told the *New York Times*. Paramount's publicity materials boasted that *Mandingo* was shot "on locations were the actual story took place."

The director of photography was Richard Kline, who recalled in a 2005 interview for the American Society of Cinematographers: "Richard Fleischer is another very gifted director and a very hard worker. He has never received the recognition that he deserves....We had worked together on *The Boston Strangler* and on *Mr. Majestyk* [1974] after *Soylent Green* [and *The Don Is Dead*, 1973]. He called me about another picture a few years later and sent me the script. The film was called *Mandingo.* The truth is that I hated that script. It just rubbed me wrong. I told him that I would do it if he let me do one thing. I said that I'll let you have the final word, but give me the privilege of arguing with you. He agreed. It was set in a hateful time and place in the 1840s, where

Ken Norton and Susan George in the notorious love scene.

a slave owner was training a slave to make money for him as a bare-knuckle fighter....We decided not to show cruelty and oppression blatantly, but to make the audience sense it more than visually dwell on it. That was the reason why I was able to work on it comfortably."

Fleischer says, "[Kline] was a great cameraman. We got along great, we were real good friends."

The exceptional costumes were designed by Ann Roth, whose credits included *Midnight Cowboy* (1969), *The Owl and the Pussycat* (1970), and De Laurentiis's mafia epics *The Valachi Papers* (1972) and *Crazy Joe* (1974). Roth did extensive research and examined antique Southern dresses prior to creating the many outfits needed for *Mandingo.* Unlike many period films, where the costumes look unbelievably fresh and pristine, all of the *Mandingo* wardrobe appears sweaty and lived-in. The accuracy is lessened at one point in the New Orleans hotel sequence when Susan George's bikini-cut underpants are visible beneath her antebellum nightgown.

"You're really like a detective," the costumer explained. "On every film, regardless of the period, you have to do painstaking research. You start with a character and begin by imagining what he or she would wear, how much it would cost, where would they buy it, when would they wear it and where in the house would they keep it. The clothes for *Mandingo* are the late 1840s, a period never really done before in film. There are no photographs of those days, as there would be two decades later during the Civil War, so books and paintings were invaluable. *Gone with the Wind* is in a later period, one much closer to the Civil War. If *Gone with the Wind* is the hoop-skirt period in fashion, then *Mandingo* is the crinoline. It's a very romantic period. Women wore vanilla on their breasts and cinnamon behind the ears to make themselves attractive for lovemaking. It was a lusty period in fashion when clothes were meant to last." (At least two of the attractive costumes created for Susan George went unseen by audiences when some scenes were deleted during editing.)

The first six weeks of production were in Baton Rouge. Oscar-winning production designer Boris Leven had previously worked on the classics *Giant* (1956), *West Side Story* (1961), and *The Sound of Music* (1965). According to cinematographer Kline, "[Leven] painted the streets so they looked like cobblestones, authenticating the look of the period." Much of the furnishings used by Leven's crew for *Mandingo*, including a one-hundred-year-old harp, were real antique pieces provided by the State of Louisiana. These valuable props would later be shipped to the Paramount studio in California where some interior scenes were shot.

Novice actor Norton learned how complicated filmmaking was. He told *Black Sports* magazine, "In fighting, you train two hours in a gym, then you relax. But this stuff goes on twelve hours a day. It's very tedious." Looking back, he says, "I was surprised that there was so much rehearsal [and that] there were so many takes. I was surprised at how much it took for each individual to do one movie. I wasn't expecting it."

Looking like he just stepped off the cover of a Falconhurst paperback, the 6' 3" (1.91 m), two-hundred-pound fighter was perfectly cast in *Mandingo* and displayed one of the most impressive male physiques in the history of cinema. Amazingly, the boxing champ didn't exercise or diet while shooting the film. "I didn't do any work-out routine," Norton explains. "I stopped running, I stopped working out, and I started feasting on that New Orleans food. I did not work out at all. In fact, I got bigger by not working out. Because I was eating so much and I put on weight, I was a little plump, which is unusual for me."

The boxer-turned-actor took the project seriously and worked on his role even on his days off. "I'd go over my lines, I'd practice, I'd rehearse," Norton says. "I was engrossed in the movie making. I'd watch how the actors got into the character. For me, it was on-the-job training. When I wasn't working, I was watching. I didn't want to look like a bimbo."

Fleischer was known in the industry as a soft-spoken, patient director with a dry sense of humor. "Beautiful, excellent director and a real nice human being," Cumbuka recalls. "Quiet spoken. We all respected him."

"He was a good man, a good director," Norton says. "I can say nothing negative about him. He never was difficult for me at all. He was a very intelligent man. He knew what he wanted. That was the first time I had been on a set and everything to me was Greek. I watched his direction. He explained it to me and showed me how to do things and would tell me why I should do it that way. I would incorporate what he felt into my performance or at least I would try to."

Norton continues, "The reason I started boxing wasn't because I wanted to be the best in the world or the champion. It was to open doors that ordinarily wouldn't be open. And boxing at that time was starting to open the doors to movie land. Everyone on the set helped me. Perry [King] was good. I can say nothing negative about anybody. I had no complications with anyone. They knew I was an amateur and they helped me as much as they could. Because the better the movie looked and the better I looked in the movie, the better it was for them. Everyone on the set was helpful, everyone on the set was friendly, and I don't know how most sets are, but during the filming of *Mandingo*, everyone got along. It was a good thing for me to be doing because I enjoyed doing it."

In an interview for *In Touch* magazine, King remembered, "One of the things that fascinated me about [acting in *Mandingo*] was that you really had to find in yourself the consciousness of treating a person as other than a person—as an animal. As a loved animal, a worshipped animal, a valued animal, but not as human. Because that was part of the depiction in that film, part of the thing we were exposing and investigating. And consequently, I used to make Kenny Norton very nervous doing it. On that film, in rehearsals, doing it, I would find myself touching him, stroking him, the way you would a beautiful horse. And on that level I found him extraordinary, because he is, physically, such a perfect specimen. And Kenny never quite got comfortable with me doing it!"

Norton is first introduced in *Mandingo* in a notorious scene where he is displayed half-naked on an auction block and keeps a stoic, distant look on his face while a fat German widow examines his private attributes. "During rehearsals, you got your laughs out," Norton explains. "By the time you get to the point where you're shooting, it was numbing. For the first three or four times, you giggle. But after doing it so many times, it's like brushing your teeth. You forget it. Plus, she was a nice lady. She was more embarrassed than me." The widow was played by New Orleans resident Rosemary Tichenor. Her voice was dubbed by another actress.

Some other locals had minor roles. Fleischer says, "If you remember the sequence where the two young men are traveling from Falconhurst to New Orleans and they stop overnight and their host provides them with... [Laughs]... entertainment. That actor [Ray Spruell as Wallace], who was quite good, was a local talent." Spruell appeared briefly in other regionally-shot movies including *The Toy* (1982). Blanche's parents were played by locals Stanley J. Reyes—who had a bit in *Panic in the Streets* (1950) and other Louisiana-shot movies including *Obsession* (1976)—and Evelyn Hendrickson, from the exploitation classic *Bayou* (a.k.a. *Poor White Trash*, 1957). Louisiana actor John Barber was Le Toscan (a wealthy customer seen at the New Orleans whorehouse) and had previously been in the locally-filmed drive-in staple *Night of Bloody Horror* (1969). (Le Toscan was played by a different actor in the *Mandingo* sequel *Drum*.)

Several hundred black and white locals were used as extras in the crowd scenes. Norton recalled, "For one scene, [when] we were shooting in Baton Rouge, they needed a mulatto. So they painted a white extra to look like a

Producer Ralph Serpe, Playboy model Laura Misch and director Richard Fleischer behind the scenes in New Orleans. (Photo by Richard Fegley)

mulatto. That was one thing I complained about. I mean, in *Baton Rouge* they couldn't find a real mulatto! But after I complained they went right out on the street and found somebody."

Fleischer followed the shooting script closely and used much of the blocking that had been described on the pages. All of the director's films have an elegant visual style in terms of composition and camera movement. He explained, "I always look for two things, for style and for a way of doing something that I haven't done before, that I haven't seen before. The style of [*Mandingo*] is very Gothic, and I wanted the camera movement to be very elaborate." *Mandingo* was one of the very few Fleischer films to be shot in a 1:78 screen ratio instead of the wider 2:35 image. "All my films are in a wide ratio," the director says. "I'm one of the pioneers of wide screen. *20,000 Leagues Under the Sea* was the second movie made in Cinemascope."

Fleischer used a great deal of hand-held shots in *Mandingo.* "It gives an honesty, a newsreel feel to it," the director explains. "[In *Mandingo*] I do a lot of playing with the camera that you're probably not aware of. I decided, right from the beginning, the mood that I wanted and I decided to keep the camera in motion constantly. And you're not aware of some of that movement, but it's there. Even close-ups would have a camera that's moving very, very slightly. I wanted to have that feeling of unrest. Also, the camera was not on a level, it was off-center, it was unbalanced, like the [characters] that we were photographing. So the photography becomes a comment on what you're looking at. It's called 'cocking the camera,' tilting it one degree. I've used it on many, many films. It works. Outside the house I didn't use it, but on every shot in the house, inside Falconhurst, where I felt there was an air of insanity, I wanted a slight tilt to the camera." (The "tilted camera" technique was also used effectively in the scenes set in Dean Stockwell's bedroom in the director's *Compulsion.*)

Many of the interior scenes have an orange glow to simulate candlelight or sunlight. Fleischer said, "We had filters on the lights, not on the lens, to give it this very earthy tone, which brought a very strange kind of contrast. I told the cameraman that [Falconhurst] should have a certain look to it and that the image we should keep in mind always was a beautiful wedding cake that's filled with maggots, so that when you're a distance away from it, it's very beautiful and romantic, but when you get up close, it's horrible. As you go closer and finally get inside, you see there's no furniture. It's completely barren, the walls are strained and cracked. I even tried to get ants and beetles into some shots, but I couldn't keep them there long enough to shoot."

"I try not to preplan too much," the director says. "I get very familiar with the scenes. I direct it without looking at the script because I know what the scene is about and what it has to say. I used to block way ahead of time and try to get the actors to do what I had visualized, but I became more confident as a director.

I know that if I can get people on the set, that we'll work it out there. So actors were always very comfortable doing what they have to do in my films."

Fleischer's extraordinary visual style is most evident in *Mandingo* in the late scene where several dozen Falconhurst slaves are being readied for auction. In a shot lasting for two minutes, the crane-mounted camera and the actors are in constant motion as Warren takes inventory, Hammond secures the human stock to a wagon, and the frightened, departing slaves ponder their fate.

This image is almost immediately followed by a shorter (forty-five second) but equally-impressive traveling shot: on the mansion's balcony the camera dollies quickly towards the furious Blanche, then turns into her point of view as she watches her husband drive off with Ellen sitting in a privileged spot behind the master while the lesser slaves follow on foot. "I like to do scenes that hang together [in one shot] for a long time," the director explains.

The frank depiction of forbidden interracial sex between male slaves and blonde Southern belles was a key reason for the popularity and notoriety of the *Mandingo* novel and its many paperback imitators. While the love scene between slave Mede and mistress Blanche took place off-stage in the novel and in Wexler's screenplay, Fleischer decided to actually show the act on-screen in a stylish, erotic, and explicit nude sequence. "Because it was, at the time, shocking and daring," the director explains. "It was something that we all wanted to see and not see at the same time. I discussed with Dino De Laurentiis several times before shooting, how far to go with that scene. Dino said, 'Use your judgment. Just go ahead and do it the way you want.' So I went as far as I thought was within the bounds of taste. I think it's quite an effective scene. It was a day's work. I was after a contrast between the white skin and the black skin, almost like a work of art." A number of Fleischer's earlier films had love scenes, and his *Soylent Green* and *The New Centurions* (1972) included interracial couples, but the Norton-George encounter in *Mandingo* would be the most explicit sexual tryst in the director's filmography.

Norton could not recall how long it took to shoot the intimate scene. "I don't remember," he says. "But the longer the better. [Laughs] It was the first time for black and white and it was not seen [as] negative. The way it was done was very good, I thought. [George] was a very nice lady. Most of the crew was kept out. For me, it wasn't embarrassing and I felt that she felt comfortable. If you didn't feel comfortable, you couldn't do it. We worked into it. I had met her before. In fact, we talked about it. Once you become comfortable with the person, you're not as frigid in the scenes. There are things they do so you're not completely nude. They cover you in the front because it was only shot from the back. It was not a thing where I was walking around the set in my birthday suit. Years after the movie, I was invited to go to England for [the 1986 TV special] *This Is Your Life, Susan George* and I think she was pleased that I came."

More interracial nude lovemaking was provided in intimate scenes featuring King and Sykes. "I'm a black person, and without being an extreme nationalist about it, I identify with being black," the actress said. "That doesn't mean I'm incapable of falling in love with a white man, but I'm not interested in crossing the line."

During the shooting of the many scenes involving explicit nudity, alternate camera angles that obscured breasts and genitals as well as alternate takes in which the actors were clothed were filmed to insure that *Mandingo* would get an R rating, could be released in conservative foreign territories, and could possibly be shown on television.

Fleischer did delete some nudity that was called for in the script. A vignette of Hammond watching Ellen taking a bath was scripted but unfilmed and a written scene that described a tipsy Blanche as being nude was shot with George wearing underclothes. Also not filmed was an incident in the screenplay where a staggeringly drunk and topless Blanche asks one of the twin slave boys, "You ain't never seen a white lady's breasties? You like 'em? Ellen's titties any better'n mine?" (In the novel, the twins are several years older than they are in the film and Blanche is blackmailed into sleeping with both of them.)

King found working with the legendary Mason to be one of the highlights of his career. "He was wonderful to me," the younger actor recalled in a 1998 interview for *Hollywood Spotlight*. "I was mid-twenties and he took me under his wing, treated me like a son and taught me wonderful things....I asked his advice about how to play a scene and he said, 'People make it too complicated, acting. Particularly the method form. What we're paid to do is to believe that what's happening is really happening and has never happened before. Not easy. But never let it get too complicated.' In that film, I was finding myself having to compete. Some actors are competitive, they try to take over every scene. And I found myself doing that with someone in the film. I asked James what I should do. He said, 'Don't compete. If your work is good, it will be good. You can have your back twenty feet away from the camera and it'll still be good. But the other person will spend their energy on competing and their work will suffer. He was absolutely right. I've never been competitive since then. It's worked well, helped my acting, kept me sane." King also mentioned this conflict in a 1984 interview: "I was having trouble with somebody else in *Mandingo* being very competitive for screen space. It was irritating me because I don't like to compete, but Mr. Mason didn't seem perturbed about it at all....I won't tell you who the person was because it wouldn't be fair."

Cumbuka says, "Some of the actors had their problems. They were mostly between the female lead and Perry, the young male lead. But I wasn't involved in it, and I didn't even try to find out what the difficulties were." Cumbuka recalls Mason as "a very nice guy. Very aristocratic dude. Very English."

Norton was also impressed with Mason. "He was an accomplished actor," Norton says. "The way he could look, the way he could make a move, and the smallest utter of a word could mean so much. On the set, he kept to himself. He was never around me much. I'm not saying he wasn't friendly or didn't socialize at any time, but on the main part of the film, I never saw him. And that was because I was out playing. [Laughs] My first time in New Orleans. Boy, can you imagine that? At that time of my life, I was happy-go-lucky and full of energy. I was a very virile, young human being. At that time there was no disease. You could have fun."

The *Mandingo* promotional materials reported that Norton and Brenda Sykes were involved off-screen. The actress said at the time, "It surprised both of us that we got together since after we met for the first time in Hollywood just before going on location for *Mandingo*, we spent most of the time running away from each other. And then we started to talk...We seem to fight every time we're together. He's always clowning around to hide the real person while

American newspaper advertisement with offensive images removed.

I'm relatively quiet and serious to compensate for my natural shyness. This difference was overcome when we discovered we had something very much in common. We are both spoiled and very much independent people." Intimate photos of the couple taken on the set appeared in the magazines *Black Sports* and *Sepia.*

"During the movie, Brenda and I became good friends," Norton recalls, looking back. "I'm not going to say anything negative about her and make me seem like an individual that takes advantage of his relations. Brenda Sykes, to me, was a very nice person. She helped me during the movie and we went over our parts together because I was an amateur and she was an actress. We did rehearse together quite a bit."

The mood on the set was the complete opposite of the grim tone of the story. George said that it was the only film of hers for which she enjoyed coming to the set each day.

"The atmosphere was wonderful," Fleischer says. "Everybody got along just great. There was very good humor on the set and no problems with black or white. Everybody co-mingled beautifully and became friends. One thing happened on the set which was hilariously funny that Ken Norton did. [Laughs] We were shooting the sequence with Susan George giving birth to his baby. We shot that scene and she did all her screaming and moaning while the baby is being born. Ken Norton was on the set, and when I cut, Ken went around with a box of cigars, handing out cigars at the birth of his child. [Laughs] We all thought that was hilariously funny. It gives an idea of what the atmosphere on the set was. Everybody was having a good time making what we all felt was a very important film."

During the Baton Rouge shoot, Norton spent time with his visiting parents and his then-eight-year-old son, Ken, Jr., who later became a successful pro football player. Also visiting the set was George's then-boyfriend Jack Jones, the pop crooner who was performing in a New Orleans supper club at the time. (George had sung a duet with Jones on his recent album and TV special.) King was accompanied during the shoot by his wife and their little daughter. He threw a pool party for the cast and crew when the humidity began making some of them testy.

"It was a hard film to work on," Cumbuka says. "It was really hard for me because we filmed at Belle Helene Plantation and this plantation had actually been used as a breeding plantation for slaves. It also had a hanging tree that slaves were hanged on. The tree that I got hanged on was a [real] hanging tree. When I was on the back of that cart with a rope around my neck and running my last lines, I interjected words that weren't in the script." [After reciting the scripted words that Cicero says to the lynch mob, Cumbuka added, 'Kiss my ass!'] "And everybody got real quiet because nobody was expecting that. And I was just looking over the crowd with a mean look on my face and the director just let the scene run for about two minutes. And I happened to zero in on this little white boy and I just stared at his eyes until he said, 'Don't look at me! I didn't do nothing!' [Laughs] And the director said, 'Cut.' [Laughs] And Richard [Fleischer] came over to me and said, 'I loved it. I loved that last line. Can you do it again?' I said, 'Yes, Richard, I can do it all day!' [Laughs] We all got a big laugh on that."

Cumbuka remembers veteran Richard Ward as "[an] excellent actor. He and I became friends. We tried to be role models for the younger people there. Everybody looked up to Richard, including me. He gave me pointers on how to play my role."

Of George, Cumbuka recalls, "She was real feisty and kind of flirty. A really good actress and she did a fine job. She was always nice to me. We had no problems. I didn't have any problems with anybody except Ken."

"I didn't like his attitude," Cumbuka says of Norton. "He was a boxer. It was his first film and he started off playing a lead and a title role. He was a big distraction on the set. We almost got into a fight because of his playing around with all the chicks and acting like a lover boy and causing me to have to do five and six retakes. He was just reciting lines and looking at me. I didn't see no feeling. We had a little friction and I told him one day, 'Hey, man, I know you're having a nice time and all this is new to you, but quit screwing the rest of us up. You don't know your lines. You have to take the same scene five, six, seven, eight times to get it right. And actors like me, we do our best work on the second take. So if you can't get serious, you better get your ass on back to that boxing ring, but don't be disrespecting the rest of us.' I was the only one that had enough balls to talk to that big fool. Man, this was the dude that broke Muhammad Ali's jaw. At the time, that was big. I wasn't scared of him. Where I come from, we weren't scared of nobody."

Cumbuka continues, "They starting breaking us up and finding out what's wrong. I told the director, 'Richard, you gotta' talk to this fool. He's messing everybody up and everybody's scared to say something. Man, shooting is over schedule. He's supposed to be here at 1:00, he's coming in at 1:30.' So we had a meeting. His manager [said,] 'We can't have these actors complaining about you.' He came up the next day and apologized. After that, we became friends and shooting went a lot better. I started working with him and helping him with some of his scenes, which was Richard's suggestion. [Norton's performance] was really doctored up. They did a lot of shots to cover him to get a performance out of him because he didn't know what he was doing. One of the first things an actor works on is projection, enunciation. And he had never studied that. That was one of the first things that would have allowed him to give a good performance. Originally, he did [his character's voice], but he needed help. Roger Mosley did the voice over." Mosley was an actor who had starred in the urban hits *Terminal Island* (1973), *The Mack* (1973), and *Darktown Strutters* (1975) and would play a major role as Norton's father in the *Mandingo* sequel, *Drum* (1976).

Norton needed no help when it came to performing the physical scenes. Hand-held cameras were used extensively during his two bare-fisted fight scenes, which were extensively planned and blocked. The first fight takes place in a courtyard and is between Mede and Babouin, a high-class valet. (This battle was actually taken not from the *Mandingo* novel, but from the sequel book *Drum*, where the fight was between brothel bartender Drum and a valet named Pompey.) Babouin was played by former Mr. Universe Earl Maynard, a champion wrestler and bodybuilder of the 1960s and 70s who was originally from Barbados. Maynard's exceptional build was featured in numerous physique magazines and in the movies *Melinda* (1972), *Black Belt Jones* (1974), *Truck Turner* (1974), and *Circle of Iron* (1978).

Norton's second battle in *Mandingo* is extremely brutal and bloody and pairs him with ex-L. A. Rams receiver Duane Allen as Topaz. The imposing Allen bore a remarkable resemblance to the book's description of the brute: "Topaz's skull was long and lean, like the other parts of him. It rose to a pinnacle which was accentuated by his high, retreating forehead...a sunken cheeked lantern-jaw, small, amber, feral eyes...narrowly together under scant but meeting brows." In the novel and in the final draft screenplay, Topaz snorts a white powder just before the fight, but in the film the character is drug-free. In the book, both opponents are completely naked for the battle and Topaz has no ears because they were torn off in a previous fight. Naturally, alterations were made for the film due to censorship and special makeup restrictions.

Norton had to learn different stances and moves than the ones he used in the real-life rings. "For one thing, I had to try to look awkward for my fights in the film," he said. "We made the movie fights a lot more physical. In fact, they became almost wrestling matches. I guess the hardest thing for me was to have to stop trying to punch through an individual as you would in the fight. Before the camera, I had to throw a punch convincingly, then stop before hitting my opponent. The first fight I have in the film is with Earl and it's more like a brawl. The second fight with Duane, since in the film I have been training for it, is much more professional. Duane really worked me over in the fight....I took more of a beating in this film than I did in some of my earlier bouts."

Fleischer explains about the fights, "You have to choreograph, it's too dangerous otherwise. Particularly when you're working with someone like Ken Norton, a world champion. You don't want to get hit by *that*! We had to teach him how to pull punches and how to miss, which he found difficult.

But he caught on. You have to do a general blocking and then you have to get with the actors and the stunt men and make up the sequence. [Stuntman Joe Canutt] was very, very valuable because none of us were fighters and he knew a lot about what would look good and what wouldn't look good on the screen. He was a very valuable stunt man to have." (The novel had Hammond entering Mede in a number of successful fights, but the film limited Mede to one major prize battle.)

Norton performed all of his own stunts for the fights. "I did everything," he says. "I wanted to learn as much as I could about filmmaking. There was quite a bit of rehearsal. We had no problems."

Norton also refused a stuntman for the gruesome climax when King forces him into a pot of boiling water and stabs him with a pitchfork. "The boiling water was comfortable water and at the bottom of the bowl there were holes with hoses, which made it bubble," Norton explains. "The pitchfork gave way like a [retractable] knife that goes back into the handle. When Perry went to jab me, he did it a little too hard. I told him he did and that it should not happen again. To make it look real, he had to move it around and by doing that you can very easily get scratched."

Norton received a large bruise on his shoulder when he hit the ground acting like he had been struck by a gun blast. (The climax in the novel was even more repulsive: Hammond leaves Mede's body to simmer in the pot for two days, then pours the resulting broth in the open coffin containing the bodies of Blanche and the baby. Serpe said, "I hated that ending in the book, where the guy boils his slave down and pours the soup over his wife's grave.")

While filming the many exterior scenes, the snake-hating Fleischer expected to come in contact with reptiles at some point, but never did.

During the six weeks that the production shot in the Baton Rouge area, Hurricane Carmen headed towards Louisiana and forced the cast and crew to break from filming to stock up on supplies and board up windows.

But despite the rainy weather, the film stayed on schedule and in October, the *Mandingo* company moved on to New Orleans for three weeks of filming. The slave market sequence was shot at the famous French Market area. For the auction block shots that revealed topless female extras, a "modesty curtain" was hung to prevent onlookers from seeing the bare breasts. The sumptuous interior and garden of the Beauregard-Keyes House, which was built in 1826 in the French Quarter, was used for the whorehouse segments.

During the New Orleans shoot, Fleischer told a visiting *Los Angeles Times* writer, "[*Mandingo* is] the first honest representation of slavery I've ever seen. Everything else I've seen in movies gilds the image: happy darkies strumming banjos….It's shocking to think that [slavery] existed in our country as late as 115 years ago….I'm not interested in making white people feel guilty about

Alternate American newspaper advertisement.

slavery but just to show what black people had to go through to arrive where they are today."

"I'd never been to New Orleans before," Mason told the paper. "[*Mandingo*] has the nature of a classic. Classic Greek tragedy, you see....My character thinks he's extremely fair and reasonable to his slaves, even though he attempts to cure his rheumatism by sleeping with a black infant at his feet, hoping the poisons will be drawn out into the child's body. It's racism carried to its limits. It will make, I feel, not only a successful film but a worthwhile film, quite different from the book." He added, "One mustn't be too inquisitive as to why one takes certain parts in certain films. There is such a thing as alimony." The actor described his recent films as "approved by computers on the basis of combinations of certain superstars, or perhaps a single superstar and a best-selling notorious novel, or other more dubious mixtures."

In the same article, Serpe said, "It's only now that blacks and whites have changed their ways of thinking so that they could work together on something like this. Can you imagine Paramount coming here [New Orleans] or into the Baton Rouge area, where we did the plantation scenes, five years ago to shoot this picture? We wouldn't have lasted one day. Now, the cooperation has been fantastic. The governor of the state is going to be in the whorehouse scene."

Louisiana's then-governor was Edwin W. Edwards, a legendary politician whose outgoing persona, ability to speak Cajun, and alleged fondness for gambling and extramarital affairs made him well-suited for his bit role as a gambler at a New Orleans brothel. In January 1975, the *Washington Post* reported that Edwards "has asked that his part in the movie *Mandingo* be deleted. The governor decided that the part he played in the film about slavery in the Old South was too small to appease his fans." Edwards told the paper, "It was also an ego-saving measure because I didn't think I had done a very good job in the picture," and claimed that his appearance was cut "at great expense" to the production. A different report claimed that the politician, who had the support of many African American voters and had won praise for appointing blacks in his administration, asked to be edited from the scene when he became leery of the film's racial and sexual content and the notoriety of the source novel.[3]

Serpe wasn't lying when he boasted, "In the whorehouse scene…we're going to have some of the most beautiful girls in some of the most beautiful costumes you've ever seen." Playing Madame Caroline was Simon (a.k.a. Simone) McQueen, a former showgirl at the renowned Latin Quarter nightclub in Miami Beach, Florida and a model for several American and British men's magazines of the 1950s, including the October 1957 *Playboy*.

Laura Misch, a mesmerizing brunette *Playboy* centerfold model, is featured in the *Mandingo* bordello sequence for one brief, but unforgettable, full-frontal nude shot. In *Playboy*, she explained her cameo: "A door opens and through the doorway you see me standing there, clutching my underwear. Then I blow a sensuous kiss to a satisfied customer. I thought it would be awful with all those people watching me. But they were good about it and kept their eyes on my face." (An alternate, non-nude take was used in some foreign prints.) Misch can also be seen watching Mede's first battle in the bordello courtyard.

At the time, Misch was a twenty-year-old model who had worked as a "Bunny" at the New Orleans Playboy Club. Looking back, she explains, "I was in print ads for various local companies. *Mandingo* was fun because it was my first movie. I was shooting for [*Playboy*] at the same time I was an extra in this film. I shot my centerfold in the summer of '74. I was in the film in the fall. I didn't audition for *Mandingo*. I had no acting experience. I'm sure somebody probably said, 'Put her in because she's in *Playboy*.' [Laughs]"

Misch's appearance is at the beginning of one of Fleischer's trademark long dolly shots, which in this case tracks through the New Orleans whorehouse. Misch recalls: "It was many, many takes. Movies take forever. It was at least three or four days of shooting. You had to show up at five or six in the morning for makeup and then wait around for hours. The weather was nice for *Mandingo*. We were shooting down in the French Quarter, up in some old houses. Wherever we were shooting, [it] would draw a crowd. It would be in the paper, there would be a lot of press around. New Orleans was not Hollywood. It was not usual to have film stars walking around everywhere. Plus, the French Quarter is not very big—it was twelve blocks by four or five blocks. We'd be down there blocking off huge areas."

"It was interesting, but not glamorous, except for meeting James Mason," Misch continues. "I'm a movie buff and a massive James Mason fan. One of my all-time favorite films is the second *A Star Is Born*. Somebody brought me over and introduced us and told him something like, 'And she's in *Playboy*.' He didn't react to that, he was warm and gracious and took my hand and said, 'Very nice to meet you, Laura.' I was really nervous and very tongue-tied. We were both in costume. He was very handsome and tall. I remember thinking, 'He's being so nice to me and I'd like to tell him how much I really like him and that I've followed his career,' but it was over in ten seconds and I just mumbled something and was really embarrassed. I remember thinking, 'I'm sure he thinks I'm just this little nitwit.'"

"Dick Fleischer was very nice and patient and not nasty to me because I didn't know what I was doing. I never saw anybody who acted like a jerk. I did talk to Brenda Sykes a little bit. I thought, 'I wonder how I could be like her. She really looks like she knows what she's doing and I don't know anything.' The makeup guy [Gerald O'Dell] seemed more interesting than anybody because he was telling me all this gossip." Top *Playboy* photographer Richard Fegley was on set to take photos of the young model.

Playboy's February 1975 issued featured Misch's centerfold (37C"-24"-36") and pictorial. The on-the-set *Mandingo* stills included one of her conversing with director Fleischer and producer Serpe. She was also the cover model, clad in the lace bonnet and top that she wears in the film. (The hidden "Bunny Head" was on her right breast.)

Misch recalls, "When my issue was on the stands, I kept waiting to be recognized, because I was on the cover. I was going to a 7-11, where they kept [*Playboy*] behind the counter, and I thought, 'I wonder if any of these guys in here know I'm standing right here?' [Laughs] But no one ever did. In every single photo I ever did, I always had huge wigs and hairpieces on and gigantic false eyelashes and lots of makeup. I looked pretty different in person. If I was walking around, I was sort of like a little hippie chick in bellbottom jeans and my hair just kind of streaming down my back and no makeup. People never recognized me." She also wore a wig for *Mandingo*. "My part [in *Mandingo*] is so tiny. *Playboy* played up my role, but it really wasn't much of a film credit." (*Mandingo* got more *Playboy* coverage when steamy publicity stills of Norton with George and of King with Sykes were later included in the magazine's annual "Sex in Cinema" feature.)

"I was in, pretty much, every movie that came through New Orleans from '74 to '78," Misch says. She provided eye candy for the 1975 TV movie *A Shadow in the Streets* ("I had lines with Tony Lo Bianco in that one"); 1975's *Hard Times* ("James Coburn goes to a whorehouse and there's all these sleazy women lounging around and I'm one of them"); 1977's *French Quarter* with Virginia Mayo ("She was a little bit cool and remote, probably a little bit mortified to be in the film"); and 1978's *Mardi Gras Massacre* ("That has to be the worst film ever made"). "Once I got into newspaper work, I left all of that behind completely." Now known as Laura Watt, she is a reporter and the author of the 1997 novel *Carry Me Back*.

De Laurentiis visited the *Mandingo* location only briefly. He later wrote, "I could no longer personally supervise every film....After putting together the story, screenplay, director, actors, and budget, I would limit myself to the occasional visits to the set, and one of my trusted right-hand men would oversee the production on a daily basis." The mogul explained to the *New York Times*: "Making a good picture is a mixture—like a barman mixes a good drink. You have to hire a good writer, a good director, a good cast and so on. And once I hire them, I leave them alone to make the picture.... A good producer can make all the difference—if he knows his business. Above all, I consider myself a showman. The point is to make happy the guy who spends three dollars to see your movie. With a good story, if you make happy that guy, you have a hit in your hand."

During the production of *Mandingo*, De Laurentiis relocated his New York office to Cannon Drive in Hollywood, partly because of disagreements with the East Coast unions. While De Laurentiis has often been described as difficult and temperamental, Norton had a good relationship with him. "I liked him," the boxer-actor says. "He was a very nice man. He wasn't really demanding. He didn't say a lot. And to me he was friendly. I can't speak for anybody else, but I enjoyed the man."

The Italian mogul kept his agreement with Fleischer and gave the director no interference during the production of *Mandingo*. "We've always gotten along very well," Fleischer says about the mogul. "[He was] a very exciting person to work with because he tells you exactly what's on his mind. [Laughs] He doesn't spare anything, and I liked that."

The director also got along with executive producer Serpe, who was on the *Mandingo* set constantly. "He was involved with the business and the budget and scheduling," Fleischer explains. "He was a good guy to be with and had the best interest of the picture at heart and he was a good personal friend. I liked Ralph."

Fleischer had no trouble shooting *Mandingo* on the lengthy schedule and substantial budget and says, "I didn't have to cut corners or pinch pennies. I

German lobby card: Blanche (Susan George) arrives at Falconhurst.

just did it economically, but correctly." Serpe said during production, "When Dino started seeing [Fleischer's] rushes, he increased the budget."

Among the crew members was De Laurentiis's nineteen-year-old son

Federico. "[Federico] came to the United States for the first time in the summer of 1974, to work as a lowly production assistant on *Mandingo*," explained the elder De Laurentiis. The teenager had just been named vice-president of The Dino De Laurentiis Corporation and would be involved the next year on the *Mandingo* sequel, *Drum*.

"Working in that [Louisiana] heat, we were all grimy and smelled terrible," Sykes recalled. "It was a real challenge filming in those conditions. I worked harder on this film than anything I ever worked on."

The Paramount publicity department reported that the set was plagued by a bomb threat and that Serpe received complaints from white supremacists and black militants. De Laurentiis quipped, "All it means is that we won't be showing the film in Harlem." (*Mandingo* ended up being extremely popular with blacks in urban New York theaters.)

After the location work, the cast and crew relocated to Hollywood in October 1974, where some interiors were shot in the Paramount studio.

While Fleischer went into post-production, the *Mandingo* cast and crew moved on to other projects. Several days after shooting her final scene for *Mandingo*, George flew to England to begin shooting her first scenes for the dark drama *Out of Season* (1975). Norton went back to throwing real punches and resumed his fighting career with several bouts in 1975. Kline followed *Mandingo* with his Oscar nominated photography for De Laurentiis's 1976 *King Kong* remake.

Oscar nominee Frank Bracht (*Hud*, 1963; *Nevada Smith*, 1966) was hired to edit the film. During that process, Fleischer decided to reshuffle several scenes from the order they appeared in the script. For example, the escape and lynching of Cicero took place very late in the screenplay, but were inserted in the middle of the film. Post dubbing and looping had to be done for some of the scenes that had been shot on location, most notably for the scenes shot in New Orleans that were ruined by the sounds of automobiles.

Based on a massive novel, *Mandingo* had become a massive film. "My first cut was about four hours," Fleischer explains. "We had to bring it down. I took the most spectacular tracking shot out of the picture, unfortunately. I regret it now, but the picture was very long. I'll never forget it. It took a big part of the day to set it up. It starts in the slave market in New Orleans in the basement where the slaves were kept before they were brought outside. Down below they were dressing and undressing the slaves and oiling their bodies so that they would glisten and their muscles would shine. [The shot followed] one of the slaves who was taken outside into the arena where the slaves were being auctioned off. It's a shot that starts deep underground and goes out into daylight and picks up our principals as we got outside and followed them. It was a hell of a shot. If they ever do a director's version, that's the first thing that would go in, if it still survives. I think that all that stuff was destroyed, but, I'm not sure. I had it researched by a friend of mine. I think they destroyed the negative."

"We had to bring the picture down and tighten it up," Fleischer says. "That brings me to another point about the film. I felt, and still feel, that the four-hour version was much better than the picture that was released. It gave a different kind of flow to the picture, a leisurely flow. There are several really melodramatic scenes in this film and several emotional high points and they come too close together for my taste. One's right after the other. [De Laurentiis and Paramount] were anxious that it not run over two hours. Because when you go over two hours, you're cutting into the number of times that you can run the picture in a day in a theater. I was pleased with [the final cut]. I just felt it could have been improved. I was proud of what we had accomplished."

Each of the major actors lost numerous scenes during the final edit, and a young actor named Sylvester Stallone had his entire bit role deleted. Among the cut scenes were more dialogue between Blanche and her brother, Charles; the primitive, hasty wedding of Hammond and Blanche; a white abolitionist receiving a bloody flogging at the slave auction; Blanche's initial dislike of, and increasing dependency on, alcohol; Mede being massaged by Lucretia Borgia with snake oil; Blanche and the elder Maxwell choosing land to build her new home; Hammond and his father arguing over whether they should raise slaves or crops; a drunken Blanche demanding that Hammond let her go with him on one of his trips; two scenes showing the growing friendship between Hammond and Mede; Mede feeling intense shame after his encounter with Blanche; the elder Maxwell smelling snake oil and asking if "that Mandingo" had been in the house; and Blanche fearing that her baby may be black. (Images from some of the deleted vignettes turned up on foreign publicity stills and lobby cards.)

Also cut was a kitchen scene with Mede and several other Falconhurst slaves that shows his suppressed resentment towards slavery:

MEDE:
I alluz git good treatin' from my white
mastas.

AGAMEMNON:
Cuz you bigger and blacker an' all Mandingo.

> But you still a slave...doin' they work, a-takin' they orders, a-carryin' they shit...an' goin' to an early grave the white man done dig fer you when you was born. That thinking' never come into yo' haid?
>
> MEDE: (slowly)
>
> It come...I don't let it stay there.

The lush orchestral score was written by Maurice Jarre, the Oscar-winning French composer and conductor whose 100 scores included *Lawrence of Arabia* (1962), *Doctor Zhivago* (1965), *The Train* (1964), *The Longest Day* (1962), *Grand Prix* (1966), and *Topaz* (1969). The *Mandingo* score included a sparse, percussion-based tribal-like piece that was played during several of the slave scenes.

Jarre collaborated with blues artist Hi Tide Harris for a song called "Born In This Time" which played over the opening and closing credits. Performing the track (which was produced by Harris) was Muddy Waters, the legendary electric blues artist best known for his 1950s hits like "She Moves Me" and "Mannish Boy" for the Chess record label. The music style of "Born In This Time" may not match the time period of *Mandingo*, but the lyrics and the tortured vocals of ex-Mississippi sharecropper Waters are a perfect fit for the film's tone. ("I was born in this time to never be free. Waiting on my time for freedom, it's too far up ahead of me.")

At the time, movie soundtrack albums were popular and ubiquitous and Jarre's *Doctor Zhivago* score had been a best-selling record, but surprisingly there was no vinyl release of the *Mandingo* music. Nor was the Muddy Waters song released as a single, despite the fact that, due to an auto accident, the popular artist had not recorded since 1972. (A foreign bootleg record with Jarre's work for *Mandingo* and *Topaz* has surfaced among collectors.)

In early March of 1975, *Mandingo* was given several sneak previews in New York City. That same month, a lawsuit was filed in the New York State Supreme Court against De Laurentiis by Billy Baxter, one of the producers of the flop 1961 Broadway adaptation of *Mandingo* and the would-be producer of an unsuccessful attempt to make a movie version in 1966. Baxter's suit alleged that he alone owned the *Mandingo* film rights. Baxter, who at the time was distributing foreign films, demanded a percentage of the profits from the De Laurentiis production. As part of an agreement, the *Mandingo* screen and advertising credits were altered to read: "based on the novel by Kyle Onstott and upon the play based thereon by Jack Kirkland," even though none of the filmmakers had read or seen the play nor did the screenplay contain anything created by Kirkland for the stage version.

When *Mandingo* was submitted to the Motion Picture Association of America (MPAA) to secure a rating, there was surprisingly little objection to the frequent nudity. Fleischer says, "There's a scene in the picture that has never really been commented on. It was a scene with Perry King when he is going to bed and his slave girl is waiting for him and he's completely nude and it's frontal nudity. He was willing to shoot it that way and I wanted to bring total realism to the screen. I thought, 'We're going to really raise hell with the shot of his frontal nudity.' [Laughs] And I never heard it mentioned or talked about when the picture came out. I was really surprised. That shocked me more than anything else." This was one of the first examples of full-frontal male nudity in an American mainstream film. Some foreign versions included a less explicit version of the scene in which King wore pajama bottoms while alternate camera angles masked the slave girl's breasts.

Mandingo press kits reported that "King is becoming the king of male nudity in films," and noted that the actor had previously appeared unclothed in *The Possession of Joel Delaney* and *The Wild Party*. "I'm not self-conscious," the actor said at the time. "I have a perfectly alright body. There are plenty of situations in a film when I wouldn't appear nude, but what I really hate to see in a movie is an unnatural coyness. It's so false. If the logic of the scene has a man going to bed with a girl and he is getting undressed, then he should be naked in bed. If the director wants it and can justify it from the script, then I do it. Men are fascinated by a woman's body, so we get plenty of scenes of frontal female nudity. But male producers and directors believe women are not supposed to be interested in the nude male, so until recently we have had very little of it in film. I would think everyone's interested in another person's body, regardless of sex. I don't really see why a man is unable to look at another man's body without it being homosexual."

A graphic moment when Norton bites into an opponent's neck during a fight was too much for the MPAA and had to be trimmed before the film could get a R rating. "They let me get away with the frontal nudity, they didn't comment on that," Fleischer says. "The only thing they did object to was in the fight, the jugular vein. That had to be manipulated so it wasn't as graphic as when I shot it. I was very unhappy about that. I felt that was a compromise that I didn't want to make. This film more than any other, I wanted to appear real and actual." The regrettable deletion of the spurting neck image lessened the emotional impact and made the action technically awkward. Reaction shots of the spectators were clumsily used to cover the edit.

Spanish lobby card: The German Widow (Rosemary Tichenor) inspects Mede (Ken Norton).

"They cut it because it was too bloody," Norton recalls. "I was biting him and they shot it real close. There was more blood coming out. They cut part of the love scene [with Susan George]. For that time, it was a little too long and had too much nudity." Norton laughed when he recalled his mother's reaction to his on-screen nudity: "Mom just couldn't handle it. When I told her about the scene she just threw up her hands and cried, 'Oh, my God! How can I ever go to church now?'"

Paramount opened *Mandingo* in New York on Wednesday, May 7, 1975 at the Criterion on Broadway (a venue for many black action hits) and at the RKO 86th Street Twin. Huge ads in the *New York Times* promoted the engagements. "There was a special screening for it in a huge theater in New York," Fleischer says. "It was a big Broadway movie theater. It was a huge crowd. The first screening was tremendous, the audience reactions were so great. The black audiences were very much for it. They loved it and they let you know when they like it. There was a lot of yelling, 'Go get 'em!' and a big hand when James Mason gets killed. The audience really applauded that. I know it offended some people. I was in the lobby taking a break during the picture and a couple walked out and said, 'Are you connected with this film?' I said, 'Yes.' They said, 'You should be ashamed of yourself,' and they walked out of the theater."

Fleischer recalls, "After the performance, [De Laurentiis] and I were walking down the street in New York on Broadway and he put his arm around my shoulder and said, 'You know why this picture works?' and I said 'The nudity?' [Laughs] and he said 'No, because you took it seriously.' I was very flattered with that observation."

The New York premiere was exciting for Norton. "It was fairly large and it was fairly crowded," he remembers. "Seeing me in the cinema—I'm from a small town in the Midwest—it was a big thing. I was pleased with the way I looked, but I was sitting there with my friends on either side and I asked them, 'Well, what do you think? Do you believe it? Do I look real?' I really meant that. I was full of questions and that feedback helped me."

Paramount's promotional campaign for the film was exceptional. Paperback covers for *Mandingo* and the sequels and rip-off books would either have artwork of a white master ogling a submissive black female or a painting of a bare-chested black male being admired by a frail, white woman. Not taking any chances, the studio prepared promo art for the film that featured both a black man/white woman embrace *and* a white man/black woman clinch. The sexy poster painting of interracial couples parodied the ubiquitous artwork from the 1967 re-release of *Gone with the Wind.* (Press materials described *Mandingo* as "a severe jolt to those whose ideas of the South in the days prior to the Civil War were formed by the romantic sentimentalism of *Gone with the Wind*...behind every Tara there was a Falconhurst...")

Under the poster's blurb "Expect all that the motion picture screen has never dared to show before," was more artwork depicting some of the film's more notorious moments: the naked, upside down Mem being paddled on the backside; Mede getting pitch-forked in the boiling pot; and Mason resting his decrepit feet on a black boy's belly. These extreme images were often cropped or airbrushed out of the newspaper ads by cautious theater managers and newspaper editors. In the *New York Times*, the risqué ads were stuck on the same page as promos for a hardcore double bill of *Deep Throat* and *The Devil in Miss Jones* (both 1972) and the gay porno *Behind the Greek Door* (1975).

The *Mandingo* posters and ads featured an image of the novel's most recent paperback cover. Copies of this edition that were still in circulation had a "Now A Major Motion Picture" sticker hastily slapped on them. Fawcett/Crest also issued a movie tie-in paperback with a cover featuring the movie artwork under the text "Now A Sensational Motion Picture." Unlike many movie tie-ins, this edition of *Mandingo* contained no promotional stills inside. (Cross-promotion between book publishers and movie studios became big in the 1970s and the blurb "Now A Major Motion Picture" was inescapable in bookstores.)

The gripping trailer for the film (which contains alternate takes not seen in the movie) featured glimpses of the elegant mansions, gunfire, whippings, passionate interracial kissing, drunkenness, Norton's physique, bloody fistfights, the lynching, and the boiling pot, accompanied by a deep-voiced narrator promising "All the shocking realism, the magnificence, and depravity! All the passion of the explosive novel that sold over nine-and-a-half million copies has now been brought to the screen! *Mandingo* is the first *true* motion picture epic of the Old South!" Filmmaker Nelson Lyon, editor of the trailer, recalled, "I couldn't believe my eyes! The scene where he boils the guy in the pot! Even in black-and-white, because you're using a work print to cut the trailer from, it was still shocking. A Hollywood movie never went so far! *My God*!" One shot in the trailer (and on a lobby card) had an alternate take with Perry King and Brenda Sykes wearing nightclothes, although the scene in the actual film has them both fully nude.

A radio spot made from sound bites from diverse audience members had quotes like: "Gory, but good;" "That's the way they really treated women in the South;" "It was alright for a white man to get a black woman, but it was wrong for a black man to touch a white woman;" "I can't get over it;" "It was horrible;" "I don't think that, five years ago, they could have presented this without having a riot;" "Ken Norton was beautiful;" and "It's an education to the young and a reminder to the old."

An alternate advertising campaign for the movie centered on a smiling, whip-wielding King standing behind a sweaty, shirtless Norton. Ironically, this unintentionally homo-erotic image was designed for communities that would be offended by the original campaign's images of interracial male-female couples. (From the pressbook: "These Ads Are Only To Be Used If The Original Set Is Not Acceptable To A Particular Newspaper.") While there were no gay themes or characters in the *Mandingo* film, there was plenty of graphic homosexuality in all of the Falconhurst books, and gays were among the loyal readers of the series. Promo stills of King and a topless Norton were featured on the cover of the New York underground paper *Gay Scene*.

Every New York critic hated the film, and *Mandingo* received more scathing reviews than any other film of the year. Vincent Canby of the *New York Times*: "the *Mandingo* ads show two pairs of lovers, and both are what the pornography trade calls 'mixed combos,' a black man with a white woman, and a white man with a black woman.…*Mandingo* is steamily melodramatic nonsense that purports to tell what life on the old plantation was really like, though its serious intentions are constantly denied by the camera's erotic interest in the techniques of humiliation, mostly with sex and violence.... Perry King...talks like a Bryn Mawr graduate to his neurotic white wife (Susan George), who talks a thick, movie-Southern dialect....[The film] is acted with ludicrous intensity."

Canby hated the film so much that he panned it again a few weeks later in a piece called "What Makes a Movie Immoral?" and wrote "the camerawork [in *Mandingo*] is not at all bad, but what the camera sees is enough to make you long for the most high-handed, narrow-minded film censorship. *Mandingo* has less interest in slavery than *Deep Throat* has in sexual therapy. It is as silly as *The Little Colonel* [a 1935 Old South/Shirley Temple vehicle] but much more vicious. While the poor darkies are singing on the soundtrack, they are being beaten, humiliated, denied, raped and murdered on-screen, with the kind of fond attention to specific details one more often finds in the close-ups employed in pornographic films. This one is strictly for bondage enthusiasts."

Some *New York Times* readers weren't happy with the film either and wrote to the paper. A Harlem schoolteacher: "I am constantly aghast when I see lines of blacks waiting to go into the latest Blaxploitation film that costs $4 and certainly the pride and good sense of the black viewer: *Mandingo*, *Cleopatra Jones*, *Bucktown*, not to mention such past denigrations of the black race as *Shaft* and its sequel *Sweet Badass* [sic]. Why doesn't CORE [Congress for Racial Equality] fight these cheap and unscrupulous ventures and their stars of little talent and even less racial integrity...[?]" A gay white poet from Brooklyn: "*Mandingo*...as book and movie has probably done more to perpetuate the sordid and violent Old-South nigger-myth in this country than any other fiction."

In his *Village Voice* review headlined "*Othello* It Ain't," Andrew Sarris wrote, "On the scale of stinkiness [sic] *Mandingo* rates somewhere between garbage and sewage. Let the buyer beware of any admission price above three pennies....For a critic to go on and on about how awful something is supposed to be runs the risk of arousing the reader's suspicions....Unfortunately, a senior editor has decided that *Mandingo* is too significant as a 'popular phenomenon' to be dismissed with concise disgust....I may be performing a public service for readers of *The Voice* by doing my own stink-piece on *Mandingo* rather than letting a more charitable soul do a trendy think-piece. As it happens, several viewers have already designated *Mandingo* as the worst picture of the year..."

"What I find particularly appalling about *Mandingo*," Sarris continued, "is not the grisly spectacle of blacks biting big chunks out of each other as they battle each other like gamecocks, nor the denouement in which a black is boiled alive in brine for poaching on his master's sexual preserves, but rather the relentless racism and sexism of the narrative as a whole....I am puzzled by the fact that blacks are even patronizing *Mandingo*, much less enjoying it....

German lobby card: Deleted image of an abolitionist getting publicly whipped.

Fleischer's landscaping lenses drag these cartoon characters across a social canvas as if they were real human beings. The result is boredom amid the barfing. At this point, I should be angrier than I am for wasting so much time and space on such a tedious crowd-puller. But anger is wasted on mere mediocrity. Under the unfortunate circumstances, Ken Norton's dignified incarnation of the Mandingo takes some of the bad taste out of the stereotyped role of the black stud...But enough. We are getting in way over our heads for such a little mud puddle of a picture." (The review was accompanied by stills of the Norton-George love scene and of Norton in the boiling pot.)

Angela E. Smith of the African American paper New York *Amsterdam News*: "*Mandingo* is the kind of film that makes Black History courses worthwhile, for if one had to wait for filmmakers to tell the real truth about slavery, Black folks might still be walking around, singing the praises of the Emancipation Proclamation....The film is a brutal and sadistic piece of violence which leaves you numb....*Mandingo* is filled with many cliches that hit too close to home, and when you're not laughing you're sitting back clinching your teeth in disgust."

Pauline Kael of *The New Yorker* did not review *Mandingo* but later referred to it as a "swacked [sic] paranoid fantasy."

The New York audiences didn't care about the bad reviews. In its first day at only two of the city's theaters *Mandingo* collected $20,717. After the sixth day, the gross was up to $100,248.00 and the film had broken the Criterion theater's first-day and six-day house records. The New York first week gross of $126,638 prompted Paramount to take out a full-page ad in *Variety* that screamed "*Mandingo* Means Money!" Later trade ads gave updated grosses and boasted "*Mandingo* Means More Money!" and "*Mandingo* Means Millions!"

"It's the best movie I've seen since *Gone with the Wind*," raved pop artist Andy Warhol who arranged a private showing of *Mandingo* at Paramount's New York screening room for a group of his friends. "As one of Andy's non-camp followers, I am hardly impressed by this latter manifestation of upchuck chic," wrote critic Andrew Sarris.

Cumbuka saw a screening in the city: "I was in New York at the time promoting something. I put on my cowboy hat and some sunglasses and I went to the theater to see it. It was packed and after I said my line, 'Kiss my ass,' everybody jumped up and gave the 'high-five' and laughed and what not. And when I came out of the theater, somebody recognized me. 'There's Cicero!' And then there was a mad rush and here they come and I had to take off. I ran down the streets of New York with a mob chasing me for the first time in my life! [Laughs] I went to a drive-in theater to see it. And after I delivered my line, all of the people starting turning on their lights and honking their horn. They liked the role I played. That Nat Turner type of thing."

Grindhouse historian Bill Landis reported a New York *Mandingo* screening where a black patron screamed, "All you white people outta this here audience!" The film played in the same two New York theaters for nine weeks before being replaced by another black action hit: *Cleopatra Jones and the Casino of Gold* (1975).

As the film started to play outside of New York, *Mandingo* got a few fair reviews. Richard Basch, *The Living Arts*: "For once, I agree with the ad campaign for a movie. *Mandingo* is 'sensual, shameful, savage, shocking,' but mostly just disgusting....It lacks the subtlety to make it more than memorable for anything other than its utter brutality....It fails to show the complexity of its central character, Mede, played by boxer Ken Norton—sluggishly....Norton is huge and physically awesome, but he fails to give the role inner dimension....However, there are some wonderful performances. Richard Ward as Agamemnon, the chief slave of the plantation, gleams with dignity and strength. Susan George, as Blanche, the young mistress of the manor, is perfectly teasing and coquettish. James Mason…is masterful in his portrayal….Provocative and dispassionate, *Mandingo* provides food for thought; it is engrossing and repellent. The audience was moved and excited. Catcalls filled the theater. If you like to be shocked, shamed, aroused, and brutalized, you will like *Mandingo*. If you don't, you won't."

Charles Shebe, *Oakland* (California) *Tribune*: "The critics, most of whom are incidentally white, have been denouncing *Mandingo* as a thoroughly offensive movie designed to exploit a black audience….*Mandingo* is a Gothic movie reeking of sex and violence and built on a compulsively symmetrical, almost formal plot…Well, maybe the movie is exploitive—but certainly far less than the system it describes. And certainly no more than Tudor drama, even Shakespeare and Marlowe, exploited the bloodthirsty tastes of its audience. And the parallel is well drawn, for *Mandingo*, believe it or not, sustains an emotional power and tone which recalls Elizabethan (and earlier) tragedy….The screenplay, the dialogue, the directing, the settings are carefully thought out."

"Perry King's performance is well paced, thoughtful, sympathetic much of the time: the role is complex, and he enters it believably. As his wife, Susan George is fatiguing, combining the qualities of too many Tennessee Williams slatterns into one part, but the drama requires it. Brenda Sykes is perhaps too virtuous as Ellen, but she's unusually beautiful and her chaste good-heartedness wins you over immediately. Ken Norton, the prizefighter, is sleek, warm, gorgeous as the Mandingo, but be can't really act vocally very well….There's nothing coy about the sex or the violence: frontal nudity and bloody fighting are depicted more than once. But the plot needs them, and they're shown naturally, inoffensively….The film isn't hopeless or hateful. It records history unblinkingly, dramatically, and does a good job of it."

But most American critics were repulsed by the movie. *Variety*: "a ludicrous film….Schoolboys of all ages used to get off on Kyle Onstott's novel of sexploitation sociology, *Mandingo*, and now, thanks to Paramount and producer Dino De Laurentiis, they still can. This embarrassing and crude film…wallows in every cliché of the slave-based white society in the pre-Civil War South, where you-know-what went on….Norman Wexler's cornball adaptation…is exceeded in banality only by the performances…. Lots of cardboard tragedy ensues." (This reviewer incorrectly predicted that the film's box-office potential was "Doubtful even in lesser exploitation markets.")

Richard Schickel, *Time*: "Writer Wexler and director Fleischer treat us to gaudy depictions of all the evils in the Old South that we have learned to know and loathe….Floggings, hangings, slave auctions and gory combats follow in quick succession....If *Mandingo*'s makers had permitted themselves even a moment of genuine feeling, a single honest insight into the historical conditions they pretend to examine, they might have destroyed the distance their hack mentalities place between film and audience. As it is, derision finally gives way to numbness. There is not the slightest danger that this animated comic book can do anyone, of any race, any harm—unless Mel Brooks is looking to the Old South for his next subject."

Paul D. Zimmerman, *Newsweek*: "*Mandingo* is calculated to appeal to the broadest possible audience—sadists, masochists, bigots, sex fiends and historians."

The Independent Film Journal: "[O]ne of the most concentrated doses of sex, sadism and lovingly detailed violence to hit the wide screen....[A]n incendiary melodrama, updated enough to qualify as blaxploitation with an added spicing of soft-core and offbeat sexuality to cover that market as well.... [T]he film's emotional appeal will be to the lowest common denominator of any audience and may even provoke some harsh backlash....As grisly as *Mandingo* sounds in bare synopsis, its execution is even more graphic than might be imagined. Protracted beatings, multiple shootings and immersions in boiling water are all given extended time on screen, but none of these turn out to be as stomach-churning as a savage hand-to-hand fight between Norton and another massive black....The camera records each eruption of flesh, blood and bone in intimate detail. The R rating should not be taken as a valid index of the film's violence since several minor exploitation films recently received X ratings for considerably less savagery. *Mandingo* does have its moments of comedy, most of them unintentionally contained in screenwriter Norman Wexler's over-jargoned plantation dialogue....The only dignity ever really conveyed comes from Brenda Sykes, who actually underplays her sympathetic role..."

Jacqueline Trescott, *Washington Post*: "the tasteless movie that glorifies, with every gory and sado-masochistic trick known, the unglorious [sic] period of slave breeding."

Michael Buckley, *Films in Review*: "A potpourri of racism, violence ad nauseam, nudity, incest and sex....Norton is forced to engage in a no-holds-barred fight to the death (perhaps the most sadistic ever filmed) with another slave....Mason comes across as half-baked Virginia ham....Miss George at her best seems a poor imitation of Bette Davis at her worst....*Mandingo* is a potboiler and probably the worst film this reviewer has ever seen."

Christene Meyers, *Billings* (Montana) *Gazette*: "If you were to call *Mandingo* a pot boiler, you'd be right for two reasons. First, it's put together so hastily and with such a bent for clichés that it certainly can't be meant to be taken seriously; except perhaps by the box-office. And secondly, well, they actually do boil a guy in a pot—complete with a pitchfork for a spoon....Richard Fleischer assembles a cast that, but for James Mason, who must need the money, no one's ever heard of....The Mandingos are considered a new breed of slave, but everything offered up in this movie is old and inbred....There's sex and violence galore....To tell how the film ends, well, it would just kill the suspense potential for those of you in the mood for this kind of tripe....It's the kind of messy movie that could have been used to apply for a federal grant back in the early days of the Civil Rights Movement. Director Fleischer and writer Norman Wexler may have gone into hiding after they laid this egg because their names aren't used on any of the advertising. [sic] And as for producer Dino De Laurentiis—he should take his name and go to some remote island to design clothes no one will ever see."

Manny Weltman, *The News* (Van Nuys, California): "Kyle Onstott took all that was decadent about the South prior to the Civil War and wrote a sick saga....Dino De Laurentiis produced a film that graphically depicts almost every sadistic, masochistic and perverted detail of the book, tastelessly shoving the misdeeds of its characters in our faces with far more vivid brutality than necessary....The film as a whole is repugnant [and] completely degenerates to unendurable depravity."

Motion Picture Product Digest: "a sensationalized, heavy-breathing melodrama of the Old South....Its melodramatic excesses are so flamboyantly carried out they are funny. It is not persuasive—just ludicrous. The biggest hope for *Mandingo* commercially is that it may be taken as camp. On that level it is not without its vagrant amusements....The audience we saw the film with howled with laughter. The absurdly lenient 'R' rating is already causing considerable talk."

Catholic Film Newsletter: "Nudity, graphic sex, violence, sadism—all this and more is laid on with a cynical disregard for the demands of either mortality or art. The sole concern seems to be the box office. Ordinarily, it would be best to all but ignore this grossly offensive film...but the meretricious justification offered by Paramount makes extended comment necessary. All this 'uncompromising honesty and realism,' we are told, is intended 'to show the true brutalizing nature of slavery, which makes victims of both owner and slave.' *Mandingo*, indeed, leaves the field strewn with victims, one of them being the MPAA Code, which let it get by with an R rating." (The Church gave the film its "condemned" rating, meaning it was morally objectionable for Roman Catholics in America.)

Kevin Thomas, *Los Angeles Times*: "may well prove to be this year's trash masterpiece....[A]n excuse to project the most salacious miscegenation-inspired sex fantasies ever seen this side of an X rating. It is also, mercifully,

Japanese poster.

hilarious in its sheer excessiveness....Alternately titillating and inflammatory (to say the least), *Mandingo* is all the more explosive for having been made so well. Lush, authentic Louisiana locales have been luminously photographed. There's superior production design, sumptuous period costumes and a richly evocative score by Maurice Jarre, no less....There's no denying that *Mandingo* is entertaining or that director Richard Fleischer has had the courage of his sizzling material. He's stuck to it with straightforwardness through each and every progressively sensational and prurient turn. To describe Mason, King, and especially Miss George as melodramatic is to indulge in severest understatement....Perhaps—hopefully—there's some therapeutic value in such extravagant and uninhibited exploitation."

Gene Siskel, *Chicago Tribune*: "½ * To the best of my knowledge,

Mandingo is the first film to offer a mayhem sequence that can only be described as human fondue. A black slave is tossed by his rabid white owner into a pot of boiling oil [sic]….That may be the most tasteless moment in the utterly trashy *Mandingo*, and then again, it may not. I was more repulsed by (and was forced to look away from) a scene in which the same slave wins a boxing match by biting the jugular vein out of his black opponent. My apologies if you're reading this during a meal. But graphic description of *Mandingo* is the best argument against its attendance. This nasty little movie uses a pre-Civil War southern setting as an excuse to serve up some steamy helpings of interracial sex….A car accident would be more subtle than *Mandingo*."

Boxoffice: "After *The Klansman*, it seems only natural that Paramount should be releasing a similar type of film in a period setting….With a wealth of violence, including a savage, no-holds-barred brawl, and a large amount of nudity, mostly male but including frontal views of both sexes, the film is the kind which gives the R rating a bad name. Those expecting to see a faithful visualization of a trashy novel should not be disappointed and initial word-of-mouth may help."

A few years later, in 1978, Frank Rich of *New York Post* included *Mandingo* on his list of the five worst films of all time, explaining, "For me, a worst film can't be any mediocre movie, but must be a movie that is *both* atrociously made and philosophically ridiculous—a merging of form and content, as it were."

Fleischer was stunned by the reviews and said shortly after the release, "The thing that is infuriating to me is that the critics become blinded by their own dislike of the subject. They may loathe the story, but then they say that the photography was bad, the sets were lousy, the costumes stank and that the writing was rotten. I can defend all of that. I can defend the direction, and everybody said the direction was terrible, inept. I really don't think you can criticize a lot of things in the film as being badly done. You may hate what it is or what it says, but you can't say it's all rotten. It's just not true."

Looking back, the director says, "I was very surprised and very hurt. I felt that so many of the reviews were inaccurate if not outright lying and criticizing scenes that weren't even in the picture. [Laughs] I've never seen such bad reviews. I think those reviews could have been career ruining and I might have been damaged somewhat, but I pretty much keep working. I can only remember two reviews that were good. Very good. They both were magazine reviews and the whole issue of the magazine, I believe in both cases, was devoted to the review of the picture and an analysis of it. And both of the reviews said 'this is a masterpiece,' which [Laughs] was nice but late, too late." (One of the magazines was the British publication *Movie.*) *Che!* (1969), the biopic about the controversial revolutionary Ernesto "Che" Guevara, was the only previous Fleischer film to receive such devastating reviews.

King was also surprised by the bad reviews. "I loved *Mandingo,*" the actor said in 1977. "What fascinates me is that it received such angry, carping, incensed reviews, and yet it's an incredible success and going to make [millions] in this country alone. Obviously, there's a schism between the critics and what the American people seem to want to see. Most of the reviewers were northern white liberals, and it seemed to me they were judging the film subjectively. Those who were incensed by the film didn't want to know about what it describes....People resented the fact that [De Laurentiis] has been successful and that his films, coming from an Italian, have been fairly violent attacks on American society."

In a 2003 interview, King still spoke highly of *Mandingo*: "I love that film but there aren't very many people who do. James Mason and I are really two of the only people on the planet who really think highly of that film, or at least he did when he was alive....That film was released as a piece of pulp and created its reputation. It really deserves a much better reputation....The film is so much more interesting than it ever got credit for being. It's a wonderful screenplay."

Norton said at the time, "I don't think [*Mandingo* is] derogatory to black people. If I did, I wouldn't have taken the part. I don't need the money. [Black-oriented films] usually deal with pimps and junkies, low budget films that cost two, maybe three thousand dollars. But we have a good budget and some good talent. There's a lot of sex and violence but I think it has a message: we must be a hell of a race to have lived through all that...I just hope people won't take the film the wrong way. I'd hate for some kid to see me on the street somewhere and say, 'Hey, Mede, you mother—'"

Today, Norton recalls, "You either liked it or you didn't like it. It was different because it was a black and white thing. I don't think it was a negative film and people didn't see it that way. Except the Klan."

Surprisingly, one group that did not see the film as negative was the National Association for the Advancement of Colored People, which gave their 1975 Image Award to Wexler for his work on *Mandingo.*

Despite the vicious reviews, the controversial *Mandingo* was one of the most talked-about films of the year and a huge box office hit. 1970s audiences were drawn to the compelling, uncompromising depiction of slavery. With its gorgeous production values, unusual story, graphic violence, fisticuffs, and the attractive young stars exposing their breasts and genitals, the film had something for everyone.

In its first month of national release, *Mandingo* grossed $10 million. (A re-issue of *Gone with the Wind* was also doing good business.) By early June, *Mandingo* had climbed to second place (behind *Shampoo*) on *Variety*'s "50 Top-Grossing Films" chart and was a staple on that list until September.

As the hit film went into smaller markets in the country, Paramount added new text to the newspaper ads: "Over 6 ½ million people have already experienced the savage, the sad, the powerful, the shameful. It is the motion picture that is shocking everyone, everywhere! Now is your time to experience *Mandingo*."

In the summer of 1975, Paramount paired *Mandingo* with the trashy *The Klansman* for an effective drive-in double feature. *Superfly T.N.T.* (1973) was *Mandingo*'s co-feature for some engagements. During a screening at a low-class theater on the West Coast, one black patron got so enraged at Norton's death scene that he stood up, screamed "You can't do that!," and fired a pistol into the screen. There were no injuries, but the theater was shut down for the rest of that day.

Mandingo was a moneymaker in all regions of the country, including New Orleans, where part of the film was shot and where it had a long run at the Saenger, a huge, historic movie palace on Canal Street. *Mandingo*'s final domestic gross of $17.2 million made it the 18th highest-grossing film of the year in American theaters. (The top hit of 1975 was *Jaws*, which also became the highest-grossing movie up to that time. Other popular black-themed films released that year were *Mahogany*, *Cooley High* and *Let's Do It Again*.)

In early fall of 1975 *Mandingo* was released in England, where the British Board of Film Classification (BBFC) cut three minutes from the film, including the hemorrhoid inspection, the images of bloody buttocks in the slave whipping scene, and the climactic shots of King stabbing Norton with the pitchfork. The Mede/Blanche encounter was cut in half and that scene's shots of George's breasts and Norton's buttocks were deleted. All images of nudity were cut or replaced with angles that hid the private parts. Even with these extensive edits, the film still received an "X" (Adults-Only) certificate from the BBFC.

The British critical response was mixed. David McGillivray, *Films and Filming*: "The word from America is that *Mandingo* is generally considered to be a load of old rubbish....Perhaps the truth of the matter is that guilt-ridden America just cannot bear to have her sins finding her out yet again, particularly in a manner as ruthlessly harsh as this....The settings, the crowd scenes, even the finer details of décor and costume appear authentic enough for one almost to smell the aroma of sweat and mint juleps hanging on the air….Perry King and Brenda Sykes as his pathetic, abused mistress are outstanding in a fine cast. There were sniggers from the press show audience when Susan George was introduced as a Southern belle but by the end of the film she had fully justified her presence by giving one of the most moving, unaffected performances of her career…One [fault] lies in the casting of James Mason. This great and learned actor has shown quite recently (in *Cold Sweat* [1971]) that his Achilles' heel is an ability to affect an American characterization: *Mandingo* rams this point home rather cruelly."

"Richard Fleischer seems to veer towards [the] view that social injustices are best portrayed in graphic detail if audiences are to appreciate their significance. He regularly strips the younger members of his cast naked in order that we may study every detail of the pleasurin' and whappin.' The unfortunate result is titillation, which is hardly conducive to the mood. For all its excesses, however, *Mandingo* unquestionably has its heart in the right place."

David Pirie, Time Out magazine: "Fleischer utilizes the real sexuality and violence behind slavery to mount a compelling slice of American Gothic which analyses, in appropriately lurid terms, the twists and turns of a distorted society….The story is basically Victorian melodrama with more than an echo of the Brontes, but it is acted with enormous gusto….Good to see Fleischer returning to the kind of psychopathological thriller that he can handle so well."

Geoff Brown, *Monthly Film Bulletin*: "two full hours of racist brutality, in which little sympathy is allowed for any character, white or black….all events are seen from the lords and masters' perspective….Fleischer's direction studiously avoids tasteful restraint: his cameras hover lovingly over every assault and beating, and the finale…provides an effective display of bludgeoning bravura. In the original book, Maxwell survived to stomp and rave in other Falconhurst novels, but Fleischer's ending is much to be preferred, if only because it lessens the possibility of sequels."

For the spring 1976 issue of *Movie* magazine, Andrew Britton wrote an intense, twenty-page review/analysis/defense of *Mandingo* and called the film "a masterpiece of Hollywood cinema." Britton wrote, "The arbiters of taste have spoken. The critics have indicated their…unanimous antipathy to Richard Fleischer's *Mandingo*….Yet it is remarkable how many critics apologise [sic] for taking so much time over such a 'farrago.' They profess to be nauseated but are still unwilling to leave the film alone until they have expressed their superiority to it….I neither know nor care whether James Mason sounds exactly like a real plantation-owner in 1840….Any work of art presents

Yugoslavian poster.

one with a set of conventions which one can either accept or refuse.... Susan George's beautiful performance expresses superbly the tension in Blanche between what she knows as a white lady must be and do, and the desire which she must consequently repress....[The first scene between King and Sykes] must surely be one of the most beautiful and moving love scenes in the cinema—moving in the complexity, depth and honesty of its emotions, superbly realized by Fleischer and his actors....*Mandingo* is a great and achieved work of art....One feels it continuously, in its assurance, fluidity, economy, and its formal conservatism, as a supreme example of a conventional art-form." (The magazine also included an extensive interview with Fleischer.)

De Laurentiis later said, "*Mandingo* was a critical disaster but a huge success at the box office. And not only in America: throughout the world."

In some London cinemas, black audiences gave the film standing ovations. The film appeared in most foreign territories in late 1975 and throughout 1976. (It didn't appear in the Philippines until 1978.) Distribution in some countries, including Mexico, was handled by Twentieth Century Fox. In Italy, the film was released by Titanus, who distributed most of De Laurentiis's productions in the mogul's homeland. Fleischer says, "It was very popular in Europe. They liked the picture enormously. It was a successful movie, no question about that." (A condensed Super 8mm version of *Mandingo* was later released to the German home movie market.)[4]

The controversial promotional artwork originally created for America was used in many other territories. In Australia, the offensive images were cropped out and the film was billed as "In the tradition of *Gone with the Wind*." The artwork was also altered for Germany and England while France, Turkey, and Mexico had no problems with the promo image in its original form. The Yugoslavian poster featured a new painting centered almost entirely on Mason pressing his feet on the boy. Alternate artwork was also created for Italy, Spain, Poland, Germany, and Japan.

New editions of the *Mandingo* novel were put on store shelves throughout the world to tie in with the movie's release. The London-based Pan Books, which had been successfully publishing *Mandingo* in England since 1961, issued a new paperback version featuring several color movie stills on the front and back cover. The photos included a shot of the obese widow holding Norton's genitals (a vignette that was edited from Pan's edition) and a still of Mason stepping on the slave boy (an image censored from the British movie ads). Pan used this cover design on numerous reprints for years. In Italy, the publisher Euroclub released a hardcover edition with a photo of King and Sykes on the dust jacket. The Danish publisher Lademann issued a new hardcover with a Norton and George image.

Although Norton's face and physique were already known throughout the world, starring in a hit movie increased the boxer's fame. "I became more of a sex symbol because of the movie," he recalls. "It helped me with the females a lot more than boxing. You'd be surprised at the females that show up at the fights and the cards you get. But after the movie, with the black and white thing, more white females came up and talked to me about that scene. 'Did this happen? Did that happen? Did you relate to it? How did you feel doing it?' Because she [George] was white. It was good for me, it was good for race relations, and it helped me get a little 'poontang.' [Laughs] Oh, boy. I'm sick."

Unfortunately, Norton's costar George, whose fine performance was inexplicably ridiculed in many of the reviews, did not benefit from

Mandingo. Fleischer says, "Why [her *Mandingo* performance] wasn't recognized, I don't know. Certainly, it was Academy [Award] stature, the work that she did on the picture." Although she was a presenter at that year's Academy Award ceremony, George was never able to break into the Hollywood mainstream and was soon being wasted in exploitation features like *Tintorera* (1977), *Enter the Ninja* (1981) and *The House Where Evil Dwells* (1982).

Today, the still-lovely George lives with her husband, actor Simon MacCorkindale, in England and continues to act (mostly in television). She also runs a world-class horse farm and has gained a reputation as a photographer. "Acting has never been everything for me," she said in 2007. "My life is for living. I don't eat, sleep and breathe this business. I'm not knocking anyone who has given the industry commitment, but my zest for life is so huge that it never was just about acting. I always wanted a new challenge."

Mandingo led to more work for Cumbuka. The film's casting director, Lynn Stallmaster, found him a similar role in the 1977 TV miniseries *Roots*. "*Mandingo* [got me] the role of 'The Wrestler' in *Roots*," the actor says. "Eddie Murphy hired me for [*Harlem Nights*, 1989]. When we got ready to shoot my scene as the toothless gambler, he told me, 'I've been watching you ever since I was twelve years old. I saw you in *Mandingo*, and then every time I'd see you on TV or a movie, I'd go, 'There's Cicero!'"

Mandingo was not one of the movies mentioned in Fleischer's amusing memoir *Just Tell Me When To Cry* (1993), but not because the director is not proud of the film. "There really was no place for it," he explains. "I wasn't trying to do a 'and then I directed' book. [I was] showing the craziness of Hollywood and there wasn't that much about *Mandingo* that I thought could be entertaining reading."

Paramount released *Mandingo* on VHS and Beta videocassette in 1979 and on laserdisc in 1982. *Mandingo* attracted more viewers in 1982 when it was shown numerous times on the pay-TV service Home Box Office (HBO) and was also available on RCA's short-lived VideoDisc format in 1983. *Mandingo* videotapes became a staple of video rental shops and were also available in many public libraries. Paramount re-released the movie on VHS in 1991. (The covers for all of Paramount's video releases of *Mandingo* reproduced the notorious theatrical artwork with the "footstool" uncensored.) There were at least three video releases of *Mandingo* in England.

In the mid-2000s, official, but censored, DVDs of *Mandingo* were released in several non-America territories and bootleg DVD-Rs of the film were popular in the States until an official release from Legend Films (who licensed the film from Paramount) finally happened in 2008. Unfortunately, but not

Mede (Ken Norton) and Topaz (Duane Allen) battle on the cover of reel 2 of the German Super 8 edition.

surprisingly, none of the official DVDs contained "special features," although Legend's release was the complete R-rated cut nicely presented in the original 1:78 image, while the back cover featured some lovely, rarely-seen color publicity stills.

Mandingo is still shown frequently on pay-TV stations, but the content has prevented it from ever being shown on network or syndicated television. "I think I got a residual for $2.20," Fleischer recalls with a laugh.

Decades after its release, the cult following for *Mandingo* continues to grow, and many believe that it is one of the more underrated and important films of the 1970s.

Norton doesn't agree with the criticism that the film is politically incorrect and exploits slavery. "It happened," the actor-boxer says. "How can it be politically incorrect if it happened? It's part of life. It's part of things that happened in life in the building of America. In getting to where we are now, we had to pass so many hurdles. The blacks, whites, Mexicans, Puerto Ricans, Italians, anybody. That goes for any race. I think at that time in life [the 1970s], at that time in the period of the century, that [*Mandingo*'s release] was good. It changed the minds of a lot of people. Whether it be good or bad, it changed their minds. And I think at that time of the century, [*Mandingo*] was right on time."

Cumbuka notes, "It brings back those unpleasant memories of the doo-doo we had to go through. Through no fault of our own, just being born black and in that place at that time. I didn't like the subject, but it was history that did take place and people need to know that. Somebody needed to portray it as realistically as possible. A lot of people don't like to watch it because it reminds them, but all that shit went down. That's what happened."

Fleischer remained very proud of *Mandingo*. "I saw it a couple of months ago and I thought it was great," he recalled in 2003. "I ran it at home and the people that I ran it for were knocked out. They just thought it was terrific and so did I. I'd forgotten how really, really wonderful that picture is. I'm very proud of that movie. I'm proud of what it looks like and the way it plays, the performances, and what it has to say. In spite of its reviews, I have complete faith in the picture. I'm very proud that I made it and I would like to see a revival today."[5]

Notes:

1 All quotations that were taken from interviews conducted exclusively for this book are introduced in the present tense (i.e. "Fleischer recalls") to distinguish them from excerpts from previously-published interviews, which are introduced in the past tense. This includes the quotes from Richard Fleischer, who died in 2006.

2 Fleischer may have been referring to George C. Scott, who worked with the director on the then-recent *The Last Run* (1971) and *The New Centurions* and the later *Crossed Swords* (a.k.a. *The Prince and the Pauper*, 1977). Scott and spouse Trish Van Devere costarred in a number of films including *The Last Run*.

3 Edwards had worse public relations problems in 2000 when the then-seventy-three-year-old was sentenced to ten years in federal prison after being convicted of fraud and racketeering for his involvement in a scheme involving casino licenses.

4 During the 1970s—prior to the advent of consumer video cassette recorders or pay-TV channels like Home Box Office—many movie buffs owned Super 8mm film projectors and collected officially-licensed small-format prints containing scenes from major features.

These digests were edited—often quite skillfully—to run on 200-foot (approximately eight minutes) or 400-foot (around seventeen minutes) Super 8 reels with sound and full, vivid color. A number of the decade's bigger films (including *The Godfather*, *The Exorcist,* and *Jaws*) were released in longer digests that filled two or three 400-foot reels (running thirty-five to fifty minutes) and allowed fans to project huge chunks from Hollywood hits on their own walls.
Some American features (like the DeLaurentiis productions *Death Wish* and *Lipstick*) were condensed and released on Super 8 only in Germany. Shortly after *Mandingo*'s international theatrical distribution, Marketing Film Club released a well-done digest on three 400-foot Super 8 reels, to be purchased separately. The fifty-one-minute, German-dubbed digest of dramatic, violent and sexual highlights included some of Fleischer's more picturesque shots—although the hanging of Cicero and the Blanche/Mede love scene were among the missing scenes. The first two reels ended on a cliffhanger: reel one concluded when Blanche demanded that Ellen be brought before her; the second reel closed as Blanche summoned Mede to her bedroom. To own all three reels of the Super 8 *Mandingo* digest in the mid-1970s, a collector would have had to pay around $180.00. (In 2009, a new DVD of the entire film could be had for less than $10.00.) Today, the Super 8 *Mandingo* reels are rare and highly-sought by collectors, even though the colors on the prints have faded mercilessly.
Reel One: *Mandingo: Sklavenzucht* (*Slave Breeders*) (Catalog number 869)
Reel Two: *Mandingo: Todeskampf der schwarzen Sklaven* (*Death Struggle of the Black Slaves*) (Catalog number 870)
Reel Three: *Mandingo: Die schwarzen Brut der weiben Herrin* (*The White Lady's Black Brood*) (Catalog number 871)
Distributed by Marketing Film Club, Bochum, Germany. Super 8mm. Magnetic Sound. Color (OptiColor). 24 frames per second.

5 A 19-film Richard Fleischer retrospective, sponsored by the American Cinematheque, was held at the Egyptian Theater in Hollywood in August, 1999. A 35mm print (unfortunately from England and slightly cut for violence) was screened and introduced by Fleischer, Perry King and Brenda Sykes.

Chapter 6:
Drum: The Movie

In late 1975, shortly after the release of his hit film version of *Mandingo*, producer Dino De Laurentiis had $60 million in working capital and over a dozen films in various stages of development. Top directors Ingmar Bergman, Martin Scorsese, Robert Altman, and Peter Bogdanovich where among those attached to the mogul's announced films. At the time, Thomas Meehan of the *New York Times* wrote, "[De Laurentiis] is in roughly the equivalent position of a Las Vegas high roller who has been making pass after pass.... De Laurentiis seems to posses an uncanny knack, especially for a foreigner, for sensing what American audiences want in the way of entertainment." The producer told *Variety*, "I no longer feel European, I consider myself an American," and later explained, "A producer can operate with so much more freedom in America."

Even before *Mandingo* became a financial success, De Laurentiis and his producing associate Ralph Serpe were already preparing a movie based on *Drum*, the 1962 novel that was the first of the many follow-ups to the *Mandingo* novel. De Laurentiis formed Drum Productions Limited and set up offices at MGM Studios in Culver City, California to create the sequel, which, like *Mandingo*, had a multi-million dollar budget and was to be distributed in North America by Paramount Pictures.

"Personally, I dislike sequels," De Laurentiis said. "I always prefer to turn to new areas." Movie sequels were a big trend at the time. *The Godfather Part II* (1974), *The Trial of Billy Jack* (1974), *Airport 1975* (1974), *The Return of the Pink Panther* (1975), *Funny Lady* (1975), and *Part 2, Walking Tall* (1975) were recent hits while *Part 2, Sounder* (1976), *That's Entertainment, Part 2* (1976), *Exorcist II: The Heretic* (1977), *Jaws 2* (1978), *Earthquake II*, *Chinatown II*, *The Sting II*, and *The Continuation of Gone with the Wind* were about to hit theaters or had been announced. (*Earthquake* was never revisited and the latter three pictures weren't made until years later with different scripts.)

In the book *Dino: The Life and Films of Dino De Laurentiis*, the mogul explained: "[*Mandingo*] was such a big success that many people asked me to make a sequel. In general I'm opposed to number two, number three, and so forth. That's why I turned down the idea of continuing *Death Wish* [1974] and sold the rights to somebody else. I did the same thing with *Serpico* [1973], when suddenly everybody wanted to make it into a TV-movie or an entire miniseries. But with *Mandingo*, for some reason, I ended up making a sequel—a mistake I repeated much later with *King Kong Lives* [1986]." *Drum* was the producer's first sequel and he would make very few in his sixty-year filmmaking career.

Mandingo screenwriter Norman Wexler was hired to turn Kyle Onstott and (the uncredited) Lance Horner's *Drum* into a script. At 502 pages, *Drum* was a slimmer novel than the 659-page *Mandingo*, but its epic three-book structure, multi-decade chronology, and dozens of characters made for a challenging adaptation for Wexler, who merged "Book II" with "Book III" of the novel and combined several characters into single roles. Most notably, Drum, the protagonist of the book's middle section, and Drumson, the main character of the novel's "Book III," were molded into one character called Drum. As he did when adapting the Mede role for *Mandingo*, Wexler made the Drum character more intelligent and aware than the one-dimensional character in the novel.

Ellen, the slave whose relationship with Hammond was a major plot point in the *Mandingo* movie and who appeared in most of the books, was ignored in the *Drum* movie and her absence is unexplained. The twin slave boys, Meg and Alph, were major (and perverse) characters in *Drum* and in other novels in the series, but were ignored by Wexler. (The twins were briefly seen, without names, in the *Mandingo* movie.) Other slave characters who had appeared in the first film and the *Drum* book, but were deleted from the movie sequel were Agamemnon (a.k.a. Mem), Lucy, and the prized female Mandingo, Big Pearl. (Lucy is mentioned in the film's dialogue, but is not seen.) The characters of veterinarian Doc Redfield and his wife, featured in the *Mandingo* movie and most of the Falconhurst books, appear in the *Drum* climax played by different actors.

A "Revised Final Draft" credited to Wexler and dated November 17, 1975 ran a tight and brisk 118-pages and, while not as sprawling as the novel, was packed with numerous locations, characters, and events and spanned twenty years. The first act focused on Tamboura, a captured African who becomes an ill-fated Cuban slave, and opened in Central Africa as Tamboura hunts among numerous rhinoceros, elephants, giraffes, gazelles, and exotic birds before being captured along with several hundred other blacks by a dozen horse-riding Arab slave traders. One gruesome passage read like it was lifted from a lurid Falconhurst rip-off:

> One of the women in the slave caravan, her swollen belly indicating the final days of pregnancy, stands tottering on her feet. An Arab whips her twice to get her moving. She collapses, lies on the ground moaning, her body shuddering with labor contractions. An Arab dismounts, takes out a knife, leans over the woman and slashes her belly. Then he sinks his hand inside her abdomen and pulls out the baby. He cuts her umbilical cord—then hands the baby to one of the slave women.

None of the African sequences were ever shot. The film would ultimately begin with the captured Tamboura's adventures in Havana and his forbidden affair with the mistress of his owner. Wexler's *Mandingo* screenplay had the love scene between slave Mede and white mistress Blanche take place off-screen, but in his *Drum* script the writer describes the first encounter between Tamboura and Alix as explicitly as the filmed version of the Ken Norton-Susan George tryst:

> Almost dazed, Tamboura takes his clothes off, his eyes fixed on Alix. When he is naked, she walks to him until she stands close enough for her nipples to touch him. Then she twists her torso back and forth so her nipples brush against him. Then she puts her arms around his neck, lifts herself off the ground and wraps her legs around Tamboura. Holding her, Tamboura walks to the bed. Without disengaging, he lies down on top of her. A moment later she straddles him and begins to ride him violently, wildly, her hair flying, her breasts shaking, her head whipping from side to side. Her orgasm is intense, prolonged, a crescendo of cries and convulsive shudders.

The script's second half dealt with Drum, Tamboura's racially-mixed son, who is raised in New Orleans, gets sold to Hammond Maxwell, and becomes involved in a bloody slave uprising at Falconhurst. Wexler used much dialogue from the novel and, while having to delete many characters and incidents, was faithful to the book's plot and tone.

Wexler once again had Hammond Maxwell develop a strong respect for a male slave and become disillusioned with the institution of slavery. Hammond's tragic, confused relationship with Mede was referenced when he warns Drum, "Don't you stand up to me, now. Best nigger I ever had did that. He made that mistake. He made another one, too. He let his pecker get him in trouble. I don't want nothing like that happening to you. So don't you go running off wherever your pecker points."

The dialogue in the *Drum* script was more bawdy and vulgar than what Wexler had created for *Mandingo*, such as this exchange that was unfortunately not used:

DRUM

Blaise, Master Hammond says he's going to castrate you. Tomorrow morning."

BLAISE

Why don' he cut off his bitch daughter's pussy?"

Mandingo director Richard Fleischer remembers: "[De Laurentiis] offered me *Drum*. I read the screenplay and I said, 'Dino, [Laughs] we got away with one. Let's not press our luck.' And I turned it down." (When *Drum* was completed, Fleischer never watched it.) Fleischer followed *Mandingo* with *The Incredible Sarah* (1976), a biopic about actress Sarah Bernhardt. *Mandingo* was his last great film, although he directed another nine movies including *Ashanti* (1979), which dealt with the modern-day slave trade in Africa, and four more De Laurentiis productions including *Conan the Destroyer* (1984). He died in 2006 at age eighty-nine.

When Fleischer turned down *Drum*, De Laurentiis hired another underrated Hollywood veteran, fifty-four-year-old Burt Kennedy. Kennedy was a World War II officer, a stuntman, and a radio writer before he penned the 1956 Western *Seven Men from Now*, directed by Budd Boetticher and starring Randolph Scott. After scripting more entries in the now-classic Boetticher-Scott series, Kennedy began directing television episodes. "I went and did *Combat!* [1962 season] and *Lawman* [1958 season] to find out physically how you shoot pictures," he told *Movie Maker*. "And when I got that behind me, I could go ahead and do movies."

Kennedy began directing stars like John Wayne, Kirk Douglas, and James Garner in the Western hits *Return of the Magnificent Seven* (1966), *The War Wagon* (1967), *Support Your Local Sheriff!* (1969), and *The Train Robbers* (1973) and worked for De Laurentiis and Serpe on the cavalry western *The Deserter* (1971). His movies were known for their action, eccentric characters, and bawdy humor and he was well-suited to the *Drum* material. He had been the

Isela Vega (as Marianna), Roger E. Mosley (as Tamboura), and John Vernon (as Don Cesar) in a scene cut from the prologue.

original director of the slavery-themed comedy *Skin Game* (1971) before he quit during preproduction, but he returned to the material when *Skin Game* was remade as the TV movie/unsold pilot *Sidekicks* (1974). Just before getting the *Drum* gig, Kennedy directed an interesting, low-budget film of Jim Thompson's 1952 paperback classic *The Killer Inside Me* (released 1976). In late 1975, he began working with Wexler on revising the *Drum* script.

De Laurentiis and Serpe planned *Drum* as a starring vehicle for Ken Norton, the boxer-turned-actor who had effectively played Mede in *Mandingo*. Mede had died a brutal death in *Mandingo* and, naturally, did not appear in *Drum*, but the producers wanted Norton to play a new part: the sequel's title role. Norton says, "During the shooting of *Mandingo*, they were discussing *Drum* and they wanted to know if I would play the part." While *Mandingo* was collecting big bucks at the box-office and *Drum* was being prepped for production, Norton's fighting career was in full force throughout 1975. At the time, the World Boxing Council and World Boxing Association both rated Norton as the number-one boxer in the world.

In early 1976, Bob Biron, the fighter's manager, said, "[Norton] is an absolutely engaging personality, which you already know if you saw *Mandingo*.

Dino De Laurentiis wants him for the sequel this winter for six or eight weeks, but I don't know how it can be fit around his boxing schedule. The movie people are so enthused they have several other properties lined up for him, too." A deal was worked out for Norton to play Drum between matches. A nervous Serpe took out a $5 million dollar policy insuring Norton's face. The producer didn't collect; the fighter's movie star looks were undamaged when he returned to Hollywood.

Production design for *Drum* was handled by Stan Jolley, a veteran of numerous TV Westerns including *Gunsmoke* (1955 season). He had previously worked with Kennedy on the features *Mail Order Bride* (1964), *Young Billy Young*, and *The Good Guys and the Bad Guys* (both 1969). In his memoir *Hollywood Trail Boss*, Kennedy wrote, "On the trip we took to find the locations for *Drum*, we went to New York, then Jamaica and Cartagena, and ended up shooting ten minutes from my house down here on Coldwater Canyon [in California]. On that one, we must have traveled a good twenty-five thousand miles, at least, to find something ten minutes from my house."

When preparing for *Mandingo*, Norton had read the novel, and he got ready for the sequel by studying the *Drum* book. Norton says, "I felt that the only way to learn about the character and think about becoming the character was to read up on him." Norton fought a match in early January 1976 and reported to the set the same month.

Norton's character in *Drum* was not related to Mede (his role in the previous film) and Drum and was not even a Mandingo. But the casting could be justified by Hammond Maxwell's dialogue in the novel (not spoken in the film): "You look like him. Jesus Christ! You the spittin' image of that Mede. Never saw two niggers look so much alike."

Perry King, who had starred in and was proud of *Mandingo*, was asked to reprise his Hammond Maxwell role in *Drum*, although the character was twenty years older than in the first film. In late 1975, after the first Falconhurst movie, King starred in the off-Broadway play *Knuckle* at the Phoenix Theatre and in the TV-movie *Foster and Laurie*. The actor recalled in a 1978 interview in *After Dark*, "[De Laurentiis] asked me to star in *Drum* and I was very happy. But then I came in contact with a project—the most wonderful screenplay I've ever read in my life—called *A Different Story*. The dates of the two films overlapped and he did everything possible to work it out so that I could be in both. He was wonderful. Then he said, 'In return, do me a favor—a part in *Lipstick*.' A somewhat dry, dead, functional part that at this point I wouldn't normally have taken." (*A Different Story* (1978) was about a gay man (King) and a lesbian (Meg

Foster) who fall in love. De Laurentiis's production *Lipstick* (1976) was a rape-and-revenge story.)

King told a different story in a 1978 interview for *Blueboy*. "I did *Lipstick* to get out of the sequel to *Mandingo*, which Dino had. He was, I must say, very kind to me. I loved the first one; up until now it was the only film I liked. And *Mandingo* had integrity, no one believes it, no one sees it that way, but I did. But the script of *Drum* had no integrity and I just couldn't stand it. So Dino was very kind and let me get out of it. But he said, 'All right, I'll do you a favor if you do me one. Do *Lipstick* for a couple of weeks.'" (*Lipstick* began shooting in November 1975, two months prior to *Drum*'s production start.)

Director Steve Carver says, "I was friends with Perry. I remember him saying 'I'm not gonna do that.' He was against doing it; he did not accept the role. That I know for sure. As for him having a [scheduling] conflict, conflicts are always worked out in Hollywood. Agents always find some way to move the schedules around. His agent was afraid that if he did *Drum*, he would be typecast and never work in Hollywood again."

King went on to star in the offbeat features *Andy Warhol's Bad* (1977), *The Choirboys* (1977), and *Class of 1984* (1982) as well as numerous TV projects including the short-lived action series *Riptide* (1984). In a 2003 interview, the underused and underrated actor said, "There are only two films I've ever been in that I think are good movies, *Mandingo* and *A Different Story*."

It would have been interesting to see how King would have interpreted the aging Hammond Maxwell in *Drum*, but when the young actor turned down the role, it allowed one of the all-time great character actors to step in. Warren Oates was raised in Kentucky during the Depression, and after a stint in the Marines he studied drama at the University of Kentucky. Oates appeared in live TV shows in the 1950s before heading to Hollywood where his accent was put to use in featured roles on an endless list of TV episodes and in classics like *Ride the High Country* (1962), *Major Dundee* (1965), *In the Heat of the Night* (1967), and *The Wild Bunch* (1969). By the early 1970s, he was playing leads in the offbeat movies *The Hired Hand* (1971), *Two-Lane Blacktop* (1971), *Bring Me the Head of Alfredo Garcia* (1974), and *Cockfight* (1974). Oates had been in several features directed by Kennedy, who explained, "When I do a script and some actor changes his lines, I get furious. The late great Warren Oates used to say to me, 'Why don't I say this instead of the way it's written?' I used to say, 'Warren, say anything you can remember.'"

Time accurately described Oates as a "Paul Muni, John Garfield, Humphrey Bogart combination." The actor told the *Los Angeles Times*: "[I have] a face like two miles of country road. Every night I've stayed up, every woman I ever chased, every drink I've ever taken—shows. I don't work in spite of my face—I work because of it—and I know that for a fact. Anyway I wouldn't trade one of these lines or scars for the memory it carries." He explained in another interview: "I want to do it all. I want to get into the dirt, the classics, the filth, the pornos, the historical dramas. In other words, I would like to star in every possible type of film in the future. I can think of nothing better for an actor to do than to portray every type of role. How else can one satisfy an actor's ideals and ideas?"

Several of Oates starring vehicles, including *The Hired Hand* (1971), *Two-Lane Blacktop*, and *92 in the Shade* (1975), flopped in U.S. theaters but were acclaimed by European critics and young American movie buffs. He described his acting process in *Honey* magazine: "I try to be as precise as possible if it's a fictional character. I read the script five or six times to the end. I think about it as long as possible. I draw on my own experience. I imagine the character's physique from head to toe. I try to find a small, relevant detail, then I draw that detail from someone I know, someone I observe or a detail that comes to me."

The forty-eight-year-old Oates was gangly, grizzled, bearded, and deep-voiced. He was nothing like the handsome Perry King and made no attempt to recreate the younger actor's *Mandingo* performance. Unlike King, who did extensive research to obtain the Southern accent needed to play Hammond Maxwell, Oates had no trouble with an authentic dialect. "I was a total hick with a mountain accent," he recalled. "I didn't even talk like the city boys from the same area."

The female lead character of Alix begins *Drum* as a pampered mistress in Cuba. But after her scandalous relationship with Tamboura, she becomes a New Orleans whorehouse madam and the secret mother of Drum. Described in the script as "a beautiful, arrogant, French woman," Alix was a challenging role that aged two decades during the story and required an attractive actress who could handle drama, action, and nude love scenes. Voluptuous, thirty-six-year-old Isela Vega was already a hugely-popular model and movie star in her native Mexico before she costarred in the brutal American films *The Deadly Trackers* (1973) and *Bring Me the Head of Alfredo Garcia* (with Oates), both of which had been shot in her home country. *Drum* would be her first role filmed in the States.

In Mexico, Vega had received the Diosa de Plata, two Ariels, and the Heraldo—each of which were Hispanic versions of the Academy Awards. She was also a singer and photographer and claimed that she was often turned down for Hispanic roles in non-Mexican films, "For the simple reason, I didn't look Mexican enough." Midway through the production of *Drum*, since Vega was obviously not French, it was decided to change her character's name from Alix to Marianna.

Tamboura was played by the charismatic Roger E. Mosley, who had been in the grindhouse hits *Terminal Island* (1973), *The Mack* (1973), and *Darktown Strutters* (1975) and had reportedly re-dubbed Norton's voice in *Mandingo.* Tamboura dominated the first part of the *Drum* screenplay and was to be Mosley's best role to date.

Blaise, the angry, violent, rebellious slave who leads a bloody uprising, was a composite of three characters from the novel: one with the same name from "Book II" as well as Brutus and Clees from "Book III." The role went to Yaphet Kotto, one of the most accomplished African American actors of his generation, who was often referred to as "the black Marlon Brando." After off-Broadway and TV episode roles, Kotto was in Hollywood features like *The Thomas Crown Affair* (1968), *The Liberation of L.B. Jones* (1970), and Ralph Serpe's production *Across 110th Street* (1972), then played the villain in the James Bond entry *Live and Let Die* (1973). He was also the bad guy in the blaxploitation hits *Truck Turner* (1974) and *Friday Foster* (1975).

In late 1975, Kotto told *Sepia* magazine, "Producers don't even send black scripts to my agent anymore. They finally realize I won't do them. I could have made a fortune doing black movies. But I'm not going to toss aside the integrity I've been able to build just to cash in on a few dollars.... Many [black-themed films] are rip-offs. They say they're telling it like it is, but they're pandering mainly to violence and sex....My scripts don't designate whether the part is for a black man or a white. That's progress. I want to be in a class with James Caan, Dustin Hoffman, or Jack Nicholson for example." He told another interviewer, "I want to maintain a certain artistic level. Artistry and integrity are a lot more important to me than how much money I make." Just before signing on for *Drum*, Kotto had starred in *Report to the Commissioner* (1975), for which he was expected to receive an Oscar nomination and the lead in a spin-off TV series. He got neither.

Kotto's role in *Drum* was a step back for the actor, but he did feel a personal connection to his role. He believed in reincarnation, claimed to have been a slave in a previous life, and said of his *Sharks' Treasure* (1975) costar Cornel Wilde: "Cornel was a slaveholder in a previous life, and I had to escape from his bondage. Working on the movie dissolved my karmic tie to him." Off-screen, Kotto was a reclusive student of East Indian metaphysics who meditated five hours daily and claimed to not own a television or radio. He was thirty-nine at the time of *Drum*, but his official bios shaved four to five years off his age.

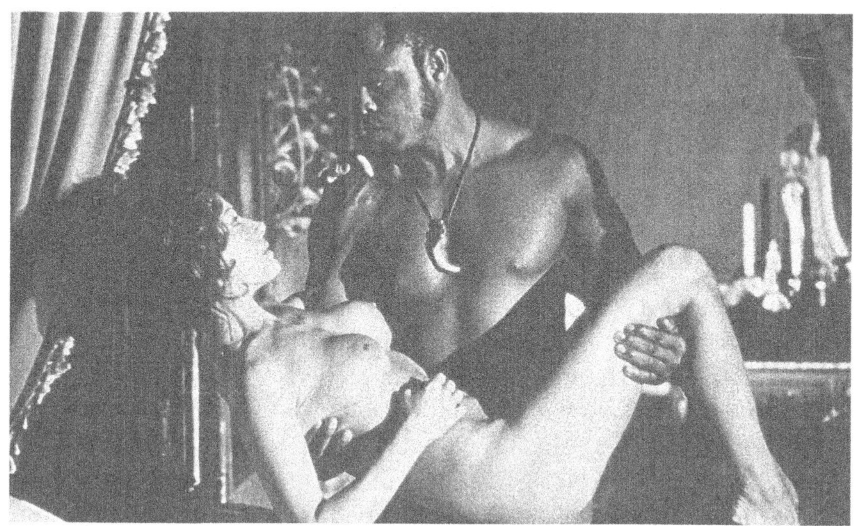

Roger E. Mosley (as Tamboura) and Isela Vega (as Marianna) were completely nude during the filming of this love scene, which was almost completely deleted in the final cut.

John Vernon was hired to play the first-act character of Don Cesar, the aristocrat owner of Tamboura who has the slave killed when he discovers Marianna's interracial affair. Vernon was a top supporting actors with credits including *Point Blank* (1967), *Topaz* (1969), and *The Outlaw Josey Wales* (1976), which he had just finished before being cast in *Drum*.

Thirty-year-old British actress Fiona Lewis, of *Joanna* (1968) and *Lisztmania* (1975), made her American movie debut as Miss Augusta Chauvet, the refined woman recruited by Hammond to domesticate Sophie, his teenage daughter. Lewis was a brunette, unlike the blonde Augusta in the script where Hammond expressed his desire for a whore with "yella hair."

Sophie is described in the novel as "plump" with "her pale blue eyes so badly crossed" and the script called the teenager "rather plain." But the casting department ignored these descriptions and the role went to the petite and very pretty Jane Actman, who had been in a 1968 production of *The Prime of Miss Jean Brodie* on Broadway. Her TV roles included David Cassidy's girlfriend on a 1970 segment of *The Partridge Family*, the star's daughter on *The Paul Lynde Show* (1972–1973), and a blind chimpanzee on *Planet of the Apes* (1974). *Drum* was to be the twenty-six-year-old actress's first feature.

Returning from *Mandingo* were Lillian Hayman (who got a hiatus from her soap opera *One Life to Live* to once again play head house slave Lucretia Borgia) and Brenda Sykes, who had done some TV guest appearances in between the Falconhurst movies.

Like Norton, Sykes didn't recreate her *Mandingo* role for *Drum*, which doesn't mention Ellen, her character from the first film. In the sequel, the young actress (wearing a wig) played Calinda, a feisty slave who briefly becomes Drum's woman in the New Orleans act. (In the novel, Calinda was Drummond's mate and gave birth to Drum.) Sykes received special screen credit on *Drum*, as she had on *Mandingo*.

Director of photography was Emmy nominee Robert Hauser, a specialist in exterior location shooting, who had worked with Kennedy on the *Combat!* TV series in 1962 and on three back-to-back TV movies in 1974. Hauser's features included *A Man Called Horse* (1970) and *Soldier Blue* (1970).

Mandingo costume designer Ann Roth returned for *Drum*. Roth's garments for the sequel included eighteen gowns for Vega (many of which ended up not being seen in the final film) and twelve dresses for Lewis.

Drum was given a $5 million budget and a three-month shooting schedule that started on January 12, 1976. (Two other De Laurentiis projects, *King Kong* and *The Shootist*, also began production on that date.) *Drum* began with three weeks of exteriors in San Juan, Puerto Rico and New Orleans (mainly in the French Quarter), to be followed with exteriors and interiors in California.

In San Juan, an eighty-six-foot, twin-master ship was hired for three days and painted black to serve as the slave vessel that transports Tamboura from Africa. For the planned title sequence, Kennedy shot extensive footage of the chained Tamboura and his fellow slaves being transported by rowboat to the stone steps at the 250-year-old El Morro Fort. Several hundred local blacks were hired to play background slaves. A shocked English female tourist, unaware that a movie was being filmed, saw the extras being whipped (with soft cotton lashes) and exclaimed, "The police ought to prevent that sort of thing."

One visitor to the San Juan set was Norton's former and future ring opponent Muhammad Ali, the iconic boxing champion who had turned down the lead role in *Mandingo*. The champ was in Puerto Rico to train for an upcoming bout with Belgian boxer Jean-Pierre Coopman. During a break in shooting, Ali told the *Drum* extras, "Work hard and you'll find success. We're all slaves to work. So don't feel badly about being chained to do your roles in this here picture. I'm a slave to my business just like you. So long as you enjoy what you're doing, that's the main thing. And, as for Ken Norton, who stars in this picture, I'm going to whup him again. Norton and Jim Brown and I are the best in our business, but I got to whup Norton again to show him who's the greatest."

Other Puerto Rico locations were Fort Cristobal and La Casa Rosa, former location of the governor's mansion. Rain machines were shipped in from the special department of Paramount Pictures at great cost for the scenes of Roger E. Mosley as Tamboura getting whipped at the post and dragged through the streets during a storm. Producer Serpe quipped, "It was the first time in Hollywood history that a producer spent water like money."

The shooting of the New Orleans act was also elaborate. While filming at a Louisiana plantations, Oates said, "You don't realize such places exist anymore. That main mansion building is something out of a storybook." Hundreds of white and black locals, many of whom had appeared in the background of *Mandingo*, were hired as extras. Norton was often approached not only by sports fans, but by many moviegoers who had recently seen him in one of 1975's big hits. On one night, Serpe treated his major cast members to a French Quarter performance by legendary Jazz trumpeter Al Hirt.

Slave market scenes were filmed at the New Orleans Mint, a large red brick National Landmark where gold and silver coins were made from 1838 to 1961 and from 1897 to 1910. (It closed during the Civil War and reconstruction.) Serpe explained, "The trouble with most buildings in the French Quarter is they have been renovated, making them unacceptable for a period film like *Drum*. The old Mint Building has that ancient look, with its steel doors and barred windows, giving the appearance of being a place where slaves were kept, sold and traded."

While the film was being shot, the completed scenes were being edited by Harold F. Kress and his son Carl Kress, who had recently shared an Oscar for their work on *The Towering Inferno* (1974). The elder Kress was one of the industry's most sought-after cutters. The classics *Mrs. Miniver* (1942), *The Yearling* (1946), *Silk Stockings* (1957), and *The Poseidon Adventure* (1972) were among his fifty-plus credits. The younger Kress's movies included *The Liberation of L. B. Jones* (1970) and *Rape Squad* (a.k.a. *Act of Vengeance*, 1974).

Kennedy was an efficient, well-prepared director who always made his decisions before he came to the set and often finished ahead of schedule. On previous movies, he was often the producer as well as the director. Confrontations with producers on some earlier films had caused him to walk off the set. He said, "You have to create an atmosphere on the set where everyone can do his best job and not worry about failure. Once in awhile, you have to put your foot down." But when *Drum* became a troubled production—like *The Deserter*, Kennedy's previous movie for De Laurentiis and Serpe—it was De Laurentiis who put his foot down.

When De Laurentiis watched the early *Drum* footage, he complained about the lighting, specifically in the interiors, and fired cinematographer Robert Hauser and the entire camera department. Ironically, a few years earlier Hauser had replaced the original directory of photography on *Soldier Blue* when that film's first week of rushes were deemed unacceptable. Kennedy later wrote, "[Hauser] was actually great, but he had a little problem with the actors, because he treated them kind of like cattle. When he was ready for the actors, he'd say things like, "Open the cage and let 'em out.' He didn't play the game too well, and consequently, he never became a very successful cameraman." Hauser, whose later work included Kennedy's 1979 TV movie *The Wild Wild West Revisited*, died in 1994.

Hauser was replaced by the renowned Lucien Ballard. The then-sixty-eight-year-old Oscar-nominee had been shooting films in Hollywood for fifty-five-years. He was best-known for his use of color and widescreen in the 1960s and for several Peckinpah collaborations including *The Wild Bunch*. Other credits were Three Stooges shorts, *The Devil Is a Woman* (1935), *The Lodger* (1944), *The Killing* (1956), *The Rise and Fall of Legs Diamond* (1960), *The Parent Trap* (1961), *Nevada Smith* (1966), *True Grit* (1969), and *Breakheart Pass* (1975).

On Friday, February 13, Kennedy and the *Drum* company returned from Louisiana to complete the filming in California. The production was on schedule, but De Laurentiis abruptly decided to replace the veteran director with thirty-year-old Steve Carver. Kennedy wrote in his journal: "A man would be a fool to challenge Dino De Laurentiis at this time, when he's considered a giant in the movie industry. I'll wait until they find out what he *really* is—a short Italian." He recalled later, "I never finished *Drum*, due to a knock-down, drag-out fight with Dino...About three weeks into the picture I got fired."

De Laurentiis recalled, "It's my old conviction that creative freedom *must* be accorded to the producer, who's the only one with both an artistic and financial vision of the film...[On *Drum*] I signed up one director and fired him a week later, since I wanted to try out a young guy, Steve Carver. I always have a tendency to seek out new talent. But new talents are like watermelons: you never know if they're red until you open them up."

Carver was a photojournalist and a director of educational films before being accepted into the prestigious American Film Institute in 1970. At the institute, Carver made the acclaimed short film *The Tell-Tale Heart* (1971), which was viewed by numerous industry insiders, including the legendary and prolific low-budget filmmaker Roger Corman (*House of Usher*, 1960; *The Wild Angels*, 1966). Corman had just formed New World Pictures and hired Carver to edit some trailers. The young director was soon sent to Italy to direct *The Arena* (1973), a period New World action film about female gladiators.

Next, Corman had Carver direct *Big Bad Mama* (1974), a huge drive-in hit starring (a naked) Angie Dickinson as a prohibition-era gangster, and *Capone* (1975), a Twentieth Century Fox co-production with Ben Gazzara as the famous mobster. Carver was going to follow *Capone* with *Billy Jack Goes to Washington* (1977) until Tom Laughlin, that film's star-writer-producer-distributor, decided to direct. (Laughlin had already directed the three previous "Billy Jack" entries.)

Carver recalls, "I came off of *Capone* and then, like a week later, I went to do *Drum*. Dino called me in. I walked into his office—this great big office in Beverly Hills. Pretty office, pretty impressive place. Bodyguards and all that stuff. Great atmosphere, smells. [Dino] had his own barber there. He had his own theater. I sat opposite Dino at his big, old desk. He was very mogul-like. He had these Coke-bottle glasses on and he's looking and just analyzing me. It was very awkward. Very few words. And he took the [*Drum*] script, which was on his desk, and threw it across the desk. He could have thrown it twenty feet and it would still be on his desk. I remember him saying, 'Alright, kid, go and make this picture for me,' in his Italian accent. Dino didn't speak English very well. He mostly interpreted through Ralph [Serpe]. I met Ralph and I liked him right away. Good guy. Cigar smoking, tough Italian. I looked at the script. I remember picking it up and thinking, 'My God, it's a phone book!' That was not the script I shot. I was given a say, not necessary final say, as to what I could cut down. Quite a bit of things were cut down. [De Laurentiis] says, 'You are my director.' I remember him slapping me in the face—an Italian slap—when I was leaving and I was, sort of, wanting to hit him. I didn't know if I liked him or not."

"For some reason, in those days I had no fear of taking over a big picture and replacing a great director. [Laughs] Unbelievable. I remember I was at Dino's house—he was cooking spaghetti—and he went over the picture with me scene-by-scene. *Mandingo* was a different flavor, a different picture. [De Laurentiis] told us that he wanted something else. He'd slap me on the side of the face—an Italian thing. It's almost like a caricature, but that's how Dino actually was."

"I knew Burt [Kennedy] very well because when I was at the American Film Institute, he came by a few times and chatted with us and with me in particular because I always liked his stuff. He was a good guy. I thought he made good pictures. The day that Burt was taken off the show was the day that I was put on the show. It was 'Fire one director, get the other one going.' Burt was working the day that he was going to be fired and I was in the wings. I was at [De Laurentiis's] office and Dino was asking, 'Is he finished? Is he finished?' When [Kennedy] finished, I was told that I was the [new] director. I couldn't do anything until the other director was out. That was a [Directors] Guild rule. Two directors can not work on the same [film]. So when Burt left the set, I was able to go onto the set. The same set that he was working on was the same set that I started on. That's how weird it was. I remember that Ralph Serpe felt bad about Burt [getting fired]. Burt had the problem with Dino."

Pam Grier as Regine

"I had to go to Burt's house to talk to him about something that was set up [for the shooting]. Burt was very cordial and not resentful at all. He told me about Dino, who didn't sound like a nice guy. It had to be really hard on Burt. I remember him bad-mouthing Dino. You don't bad-mouth Dino without fearing for your life."

According to a mid-1976 article in the British paper *Screen International*, several crew members and "directorial personnel" lost their *Drum* jobs when "alcohol induced errors" caused numerous re-shoots. Carver was never told why Kennedy was dismissed, but he doesn't believe that alcohol could be the reason. "If it was alcohol, I'd be very surprised," Carver says. "I can't see it. He didn't have a drinking problem. Burt was [on schedule]. He was a seasoned pro. You cannot fire somebody without having probable cause. I just can't imagine what the reason was."

Carver adds, "I've replaced a million directors since. It's horrible because the whole crew goes against you. Actors won't listen to you, they ridicule you. The problem with replacing a director is [that] you don't want to just thumb your nose because someday they'll be replacing you." (Among Carver's later movies was 1988's *Bulletproof*, for which he replaced Fred Olen Ray. In 1993, Carver was the original director of *Death Wish V: The Face of Death*, but was replaced by Allan A. Goldstein.)

Kennedy was not the first or last director to be dismissed from a De Laurentiis production. During the filming of *A Man Called Sledge* (1970), director Vic Morrow had a major quarrel with De Laurentiis and was replaced by first assistant director Giorgio Gentili. A few months after Kennedy was dismissed from *Drum*, De Laurentiis fired Robert Altman from *Ragtime,* which was then in preproduction. (The long-delayed *Ragtime* finally came out in 1981 under Milos Forman's direction.)

Kennedy later said, "My dear Italian friend Dino De Laurentiis put me out of business for a while, but not forever." Kennedy went on to write Clint Eastwood's *White Hunter, Black Heart* (1990) and direct some minor features and TV movies-of-the-week. "I used to call them 'Mortgages of the Week,'" he quipped. He died in 2001.

Prior to getting the *Drum* gig, Carver had seen *Mandingo*. "I liked it very much," he says. "I thought it was great." He was not familiar with the Falconhurst books, but did read the *Drum* novel when he was hired to direct the movie. "I thought it was pretty accurate because it showed the Southern hypocrisy with slavery. It tried. At the time, the Falconhurst [book] series wasn't a big deal, no one really knew of them." De Laurentiis was adamant that the young director made sure to pack *Drum* with plenty of sex and violence.

After being hired, Carver was given only five days of preparation before he had to start shooting. Carver says, "[I] cast, re-cast, re-looked for locations. I went to all the sets. I was busy for ninety-four hours a day with very little sleep. I went and visited Warren Oates. I spoke with Fiona Lewis. I called Yaphet Kotto, but never made contact with him until [shooting]."

The new director spent a couple of days looking at *Drum* footage shot by the original director. Carver explains, "I really didn't see everything [that Kennedy had shot.] I should have seen everything, but quite frankly I only had five days in which to do pre-production. He shot an exorbitant amount of footage, that's why I couldn't watch all of it. It was tons. I remember watching chained black people, in Puerto Rico, walking up steps. I saw some cut sequences. I looked at Kenny's [Norton's] footage."

Carver recalls, "I was told to re-shoot certain things because the casting was redone. I know that some of the actors that were originally in the picture, fell out because of timing. They couldn't do it. They let them out of the contracts. [De Laurentiis] had to negotiate and renegotiate everybody's contract. It was a fast 'do it quick before any lawsuits get filed.' I had to crew up and re-cast quite a number of people." Most of the script's first forty pages, which made up the Cuba sequences, were discarded at this time.

Among the actors who had been directed by Kennedy for the Havana-set scenes were Robert Alda (*Rhapsody in Blue*, 1945) as plantation lord Don Gregorio; Majel Barrett (TV's *Star Trek*, 1966–1969) as Don Gregorio's wife, Eva; Don "Red" Barry (1940s "B" Western star) as a slave auctioneer; Peter Savage (a New York actor and coauthor of the 1970 Jake La Motta autobiography *Raging Bull*) as wealthy Don Raimundo; Esther Sutherland (*Truck Turner*, 1974) as older slave matriarch Mama Baba; Ann McRae as plantation wife Anita; Ned Wertimer (*Bad Company*, 1972) as an aristocrat; Harry Caesar (*Lady Sings the Blues*, 1972) as Clemente, an abused slave coachman; stuntmen/actors Bob Minor (*Switchblade Sisters*, 1975) and Harold Jones (*Friday Foster*) as Omo and M'Dong, slave friends of Tamboura; Alberto Morin (*Two Mules for Sister Sara*; *Chisum*, both 1970) as the Cuban artist that paints an incriminating portrait of Marianna with Tamboura; and Ann Summerfield, Cynthia J. Mitchell, and Marilyn Joi as Pia, Graciella, and Maria Luz, the teenage slaves who mate with Tamboura and friends. (At the time, Joi was a popular men's magazine model and drive-in movie regular. Her credits include 1972's *Hammer*, 1976's *Ilsa, Harem Keeper of the Oil Sheiks*, and the sleazy 1977 "patch-job" version of *Uncle Tom's Cabin*, which was inspired by the success of *Mandingo* and *Drum*.)

Many of these cast members had already been listed in trade paper announcements, but the already-shot footage of their characters, most of which came from the novel, was discarded. (Minor ended up doing some stunts and can be spotted briefly in the completed film.) Carver says, "Cutting their roles out [gave me a] horrible feeling, but it had to be done and that's what directors that come in and replace other directors have to do."

Characters cut during rewrites of the New Orleans sequences were Maspero, slave trader and original owner of Calinda, and Dominic, a white man who trains Drum as a boxer. Much of the dialogue written for Dominic was given to Kotto's Blaise character. Young, unknown actresses Genji James and Norma Smith were cast as Falconhurst slave girls Edna and Elvira, but their roles were never filmed. The dialogue for Edna, Blaise's love interest, was altered and given to the Lucretia Borgia character. (Edna and Elvira are briefly mentioned during the first Falconhurst dinner scene.)

Under Kennedy's direction, the character of Lazare Le Toscan appeared in one scene and was a platonic friend of villainous gay Cajun aristocrat DeMarigny. In the novel, Le Toscan is twenty-four and described as "the handsomest beau in the city," but Kennedy had cast the role with his poker buddy Gene Evans, a middle-aged, hefty character actor (*The Ballad of Cable Hogue*, 1970; *Walking Tall*, 1973). "I can't imagine Gene Evans playing that," Carver says. "He had a Western drawl and he was playing a Cajun character? That's bad casting if you ask me. Some of [the actors] were right [for their roles], some weren't."

After Kennedy's dismissal, Le Toscan was rewritten as a young, virile lover for DeMarigny and was added to more scenes and given more action. (Although *Drum*, like all Falconhurst novels, had plenty of gay characters, Le Toscan, unlike DeMarigny, was straight in the book.) Carver explains, "Gene bowed out when Burt went and Alain [Patrick] was cast." Patrick was a handsome young French actor whose previous American credits consisted of bits on television. (In *Mandingo*, middle-aged, Louisiana-based actor John Barber briefly played Le Toscan in a New Orleans segment.)

Carver continues, "I brought in a whole bunch of people—Paula Kelly and a lot of the younger black actors that I worked with before. Paula Kelly was a dancer. We went to the same high school, for music and art. [The High School of Music and Arts in Manhattan.] We're the same age and she went the same time I did. She's a beautiful lady."

Kelly danced in the stage and screen versions of Bob Fosse's *Sweet Charity* (1969). Other films were Richard Fleischer's *Soylent Green* (1973) and a number of black-themed urban hits including *Trouble Man* (1972), *The Spook Who Sat by the Door* (1973), *Three Tough Guys* (1974), and *Uptown Saturday Night* (1974). Kelly had been one of the first models to display full-frontal nudity in *Playboy*, but she was the only actress in *Drum* who did not appear naked. Her character in *Drum* spans two decades. When the film was shot Kelly and Norton, who play mother and son, were both thirty-three. (They had both appeared in the obscure *Top of the Heap*, but had no scenes together.)

Carver says, "I brought Pam Grier in, because I worked with her in *The Arena*. I don't know who she replaced [on *Drum*]. I like her a lot. She wasn't a *great* actress at that time. She's gotten really good now."

Grier once told *Ebony*, "When I was a young girl, I never thought of acting. I never thought of television, of fans, movie stars, signing autographs. It never crossed my mind." Like *Drum* costar Brenda Sykes, Grier entered a beauty pageant and was spotted by a Hollywood agent who sent her on auditions. Her extraordinary figure came to the attention of Russ Meyer, who cast her in *Beyond the Valley of the Dolls* (1970), for which she received billing, but can't be spotted in the final film.

Grier got hired as a switchboard operator for the legendary American-

International Pictures and was soon starring in a string of ubiquitous drive-in classics for the company, including *Women in Cages* (1971), *The Big Doll House* (1971), *Black Mama, White Mama* (1972), and *The Big Bird Cage* (1972). Then came the title roles in *Coffy* (1973), *Foxy Brown* (1974), *Sheba, Baby* (1975), and *Friday Foster*, which were all huge urban hits for American-International. *Newsweek* called Grier "Queen of the B movies;" *Ms.* magazine labeled her "Super Sass;" pressbooks referred to her as "the female James Bond."

"They didn't think *Coffy* was going to sell, having the first female black heroine," Grier explained. "*Coffy* was a true story and it shocked a lot of people….I just wanted to show in films what we are doing when everyone says things are getting better. I don't see where. We're still doing the same old thing.

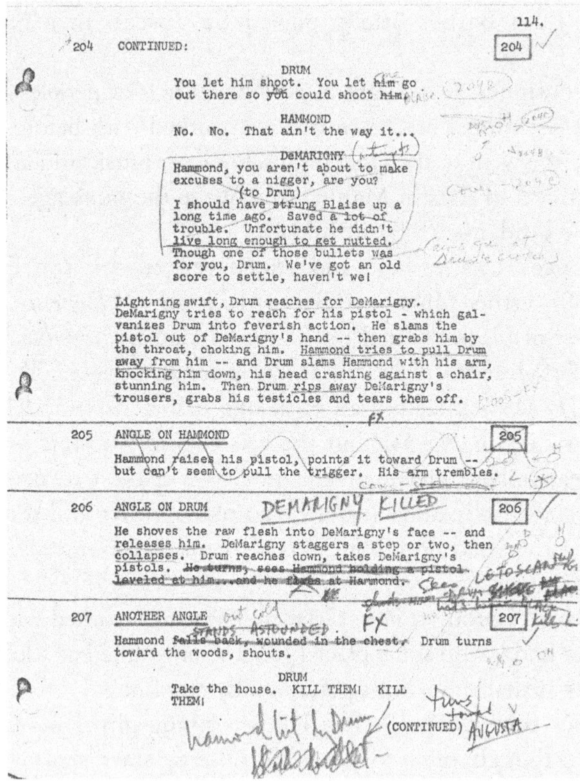

114.

204 CONTINUED: 204

DRUM
You let him shoot. You let him go out there so you could shoot him.

HAMMOND
No. No. That ain't the way it...

DeMARIGNY
Hammond, you aren't about to make excuses to a nigger, are you?
(to Drum)
I should have strung Blaise up a long time ago. Saved a lot of trouble. Unfortunate he didn't live long enough to get nutted. Though one of those bullets was for you, Drum. We've got an old score to settle, haven't we!

Lightning swift, Drum reaches for DeMarigny. DeMarigny tries to reach for his pistol - which galvanizes Drum into feverish action. He slams the pistol out of DeMarigny's hand -- then grabs him by the throat, choking him. Hammond tries to pull Drum away from him -- and Drum slams Hammond with his arm, knocking him down, his head crashing against a chair, stunning him. Then Drum rips away DeMarigny's trousers, grabs his testicles and tears them off.

205 ANGLE ON HAMMOND 205

Hammond raises his pistol, points it toward Drum -- but can't seem to pull the trigger. His arm trembles.

206 ANGLE ON DRUM 206

DEMARIGNY KILLED

He shoves the raw flesh into DeMarigny's face -- and releases him. DeMarigny staggers a step or two, then collapses. Drum reaches down, takes DeMarigny's pistols. ~~He turns, sees Hammond holding a pistol leveled at him...and he fires at Hammond.~~

207 ANOTHER ANGLE 207

FX

Hammond ~~falls back, wounded in the chest.~~ Drum turns toward the woods, shouts.

DRUM
Take the house. KILL THEM! KILL THEM!

(CONTINUED) AUGUSTA

Page from Steve Carver's copy of the script. (Collection of Steve Carver)

We're cutting each other. Half the black men do not respect women. They do not respect their little sisters; they're still using profanity in front of them….I showed this in the pictures and it was just so ugly and people saw it and said, 'Wow! That's really the way it is.'"

The young actress told *Jet,* "I took the parts no other Hollywood starlet would touch because they didn't want to be demeaned or mess up their nails. It was a risk but I didn't know any better and somehow I came out on top. I don't know why. I just played myself and audiences liked me. I am where I am because I took those tough roles. If I had held out for those sweet, pretty, demure parts, I'd still be waiting."

When Grier was offered *Drum*, she was receiving about ten scripts a week from producers of low-budget action movies and saw the multi-million dollar De Laurentiis film as a big step up from her previous credits. The twenty-six-year-old actress had recently enrolled in the prestigious Lee Strasberg Theater Institute and was trying to break into major films. (In the *Drum* screen credits, she was billed as "Pamela" Grier for one of the few times in her career.)

While filming *Drum* Grier said, "It's weird, playing a black maid to a white mistress. And putting myself into the role makes me think of the hardships our people endured, the horrible treatment they received, the atrocities and all. In a way, I have a fear of playing the role, knowing I have to bow down to someone. I've developed a fear of the white mistress. It's really strange, but I guess it comes from inside me through my ancestors, blacks who were slaves, even though I have some Filipino and Indian in my lineage. Having heard about slavery from my parents, I made up my mind to obtain knowledge."

For unknown reasons, Jane Actman was replaced in the role of Sophie. The young actress left the business a few years later after more TV, including a 1977 version of *Last of the Mohicans* and two episodes of *The New Adventures of Wonder Woman* (1978 and 1979 seasons).

Sophie ended up being played by Cheryl "Rainbeaux" Smith, the much-beloved drive-in icon. Smith once recalled how she got into acting: "During my first year at Bancroft Junior High School, I was approached by my classmate's mom, who asked me if I'd be interested in doing a short film called *Birth of Aphrodite* [released 1971]. I did it and it was hard work, balancing on the small of my back and coming in and out of the freezing ocean at dawn. I was about eleven or twelve at the time. I had seen many movies. I fell in love with them and decided then I wanted to act. When I got to Fairfax High in Los Angeles, that's all I could think of—acting. So, when I graduated I went to Theater Arts Drama School for six months. I modeled in L.A. and in New York and for some European magazines. I did a lot of advertisements for films and fashion modeling....I've also done nudes and semi-nudes for *Playboy*, their pictorial article on magic with Bill Bixby, their occult issue and—my favorite—in their "History of Women's Lingerie."

The ethereal blonde got the nickname "Rainbeaux" after spending a lot of time at the Rainbow Club, a popular Sunset Strip rock venue. Billed as "Cheryl Smith" or "Rainbeaux Smith," she starred in the low-budget classics *Lemora: A Child's Tale of the Supernatural* (1973), *The Swinging Cheerleaders* (1974), *Caged Heat* (1974), *The Pom Pom Girls* (1976), *Massacre at Central High* (1976), and *Revenge of the Cheerleaders* (1976). At the time, she called acting "the one great thing in my life. I love it."

Carver says, "Rainbeaux Smith was one of the people that I cast. The casting person came down with a whole bunch of girls. I talked with her and I liked her look. She was cute. She could play a little girl. She looked like the impish little girl that would screw the slaves and get them in trouble. And Warren [Oates] hit it off with her. I remember introducing her to Warren. They spent a little time together and I remember Warren coming to me and saying 'I like her,' so Warren had a lot to do with casting her." Carver had edited the *Caged Heat* trailer, but did not remember the actress from that film when he cast her in *Drum*. Prior to Smith's *Drum* audition, Carver watched footage from one of her earlier films. "I remember seeing something softcore on a Moviola [an editing machine]. There was a scene where she was coming on to somebody and acting very risqué. She was in bed with somebody."

In his autobiography *Out of Bounds*, football legend and movie star Jim Brown (*The Dirty Dozen*, 1967; *100 Rifles*, 1969) recalled, "I was once offered a role in the sequel to *Mandingo*...they wanted me to play Mandingo's father. I said, 'Give me a billion dollars. I'll do it.' Obviously I didn't want the role. For the sake of argument, if they had met my unbeatable price? I would have taken the part." Brown was apparently referring to the role of Tamboura, Drum's father, who appears in the first act. Carver says, "I don't remember that."

Adding to Carver's pre-production stress were his conflicts with screenwriter Wexler. The director explains, "To work with him, you had to be drunk because he was. Always. I would be talking with him and he'd just get up and walk away. [Laughs] He was cantankerous and did not really confer. [I'd ask,] 'Can you cut this down, please, Mr. Wexler?' He did not do half of the things I said. I remember feeling weird because the guy just didn't give me the time of day. In those days, I was humble. Ralph Serpe dealt with him and got whatever it was that we needed done. I remember Wexler bouncing down the steps at Dino's office. He missed a step and almost fell. I laughed and that was the last I saw of him. There's always a drinker. Like on *Capone*, Ben Gazzara was outrageous, he was drunk all the time."

Wexler was soon relieved of his *Drum* duties. The eccentric, paranoid writer often felt that he was being followed. At the time, he told the press, "Occasionally I get requests and get involved in projects for various government military intelligence agencies. It's kind of a leisure-time hobby with me." Years later, he admitted to *Variety*, "I had a few troubles."

After *Drum*, Wexler scripted the huge hit *Saturday Night Fever* (1977) and the sequel *Staying Alive* (1983) and started writing an aborted third entry. He contributed uncredited material to *Night of the Juggler* (1980) and *If You Could See What I Hear* (1982). After writing his final screenplay—for De Laurentiis's Arnold Schwarzenegger vehicle *Raw Deal* (1986)—Wexler left the movie business and returned to playwriting before his natural death in 1999.

Wexler's *Drum* screenplay was extensively re-written on the set by Richard Sale, a prolific pulp fiction writer, screenwriter, and director who had been around since the 1930s and had movie credits like *Suddenly* (1954) and *Gentlemen Marry Brunettes* (1955). Sale had recently joined the De Laurentiis camp when he adapted his 1975 novel *The White Buffalo* for the producer. (The movie version with Charles Bronson came out in 1977.)

Sale adapted well to the *Drum* assignment and created some gruesome material that seemed to be ripped out of a Falconhurst paperback. In a fight scene, Wexler had Blaise smashing a log on the head of the villainous Babouin. But Sale's rewrite replaced the head thumping with a bloody, fatal throat slash. For the blazing climax when the slaves attack the Falconhurst party guests, Sale wrote some outrageously lurid (unfilmed) action:

> Three blacks corner Mrs. Redfield and Mrs. Gassaway and cut their throats with swinging sickles. The blood spouts everywhere. It is an abattoir...Meanwhile, the thin sister has run and is followed by a buck who grabs her. She slashes a slap across his face and in pure fury, he knocks her flat. Then, instead of raping her, he pulls up her skirt and swings the sickle in his hand into her genitals as she screams once and dies...In another part of the parlor, a gang of bucks corners Holcomb and spread eagle him in midair, as a fifth one with a cane cutter chops off his privates and then splits his skull which erupts blood.

Sale also had no problem with rough dialogue. Oates's line, "You knows I like big titties" was conceived by the rewriter, as was this unused dialogue assigned to the perverse DeMarigny:

> Put Blaise in the shed and nail his scrotum to the floor. Spread coal oil all around him and light it. Then we hand him a very dull knife, light the coal oil and let him make up his own mind.

Carver recalls, "[Sale] was a tall, thin guy who was very, very cultured. He was an excellent writer. I enjoyed that guy. He was super. He re-wrote the whole script. I remember him actually coming down to the set. We conferred during lunch hours. [*Drum*] wasn't his pride and joy, he was just doing it quick and dirty. He was a gentleman—unlike Wexler [Laughs]. Literally, I was shooting pages that would be coming in the same day. They were hot. They came to the set right off of Richard's [Sale's] desk and Dino had to approve it. A lot of Sale's writing came from Dino and Ralph Serpe with regard to 'this scene, that scene.'"

Some of Sale's revisions were typed and/or handwritten on tiny scraps of paper. For his work on *Drum*, Sale was paid one thousand dollars. Wexler got sole screen credit. Sale later wrote the Charles Bronson vehicle *Assassination* (1987). He died in 1993.

When Kennedy left *Drum*, fifty percent of the crew either quit or were fired and had to be replaced. Lucien Ballard remained as cinematographer. Carver explains, "Burt was a really good friend of Lucien's. Lucien stayed aboard. I was very humble and told him how honored I'd be to work with him. I remember him saying, 'Oh, kid, don't worry.' We became very close and I used to go out to his beach house almost every weekend during the production. He lived next to Steve McQueen. We used to have dinner and lunches on the beach. It was a really nice, amiable father-son type thing. Lucien was a beautiful guy, very handsome and always wore ascots and carried his riding crop. He was a tough guy. He was a master lighter. His work was gorgeous. The set was run by Lucien." Like *Mandingo, Drum* was shot in the 1:78 widescreen ratio.

Carver began directing *Drum* on Tuesday, February 17—four days after Kennedy was fired. The new director's first two weeks of shooting consisted of soundstage interiors, and the first day involved Oates, Norton, Grier, and Lewis. Carver recalls, "The interior sets were on the MGM lot because Dino pretty much owned MGM at the time." Prior to each day's shooting, Carver filled his script with extensive blocking diagrams, camera angles, and rough storyboards. He explains, "I usually do storyboarding on things. That's how I work. I do all of my own. I get very detailed with them." The first week of shooting under Carver was four days long and was followed by seven weeks of

Steve Carver directs a dinner scene with Pam Grier and Rainbeaux Smith. (Collection of Steve Carver)

shooting Monday-through-Friday. Most days lasted twelve to fourteen hours. After each day's shooting on the soundstage, the crew would pre-light the sets for the following day.

In an article for the *San Diego Union*, Serpe said, "The production is on track and schedule. We've lost some footage but we're going to make the picture we started out to make. It's going full blast and we're excited about it. The kid [Carver]'s marvelous. He keeps me up until midnight every night with work. He's energetic, well-prepared, cost-and-time conscious and sensitive. I'm impressed. He's going to be one of our brightest directors." Serpe refused to discuss *Drum*'s original director in the article, which blamed Kennedy's firing on "artistic differences." In a memo to De Laurentiis, Serpe reported: "Steve is making bigger use of sets, costumes and giving better quality and story than the concept of Burt Kennedy."

During production, Carver told the press, "The bigger the film, the bigger the scope. So you have to adjust, take advantage of all the corners you learned to cut in the lower budgets, and apply them to the big film. At the same time, you realize you have more money to work with, so you make use of this also. Naturally, there is more detail with a bigger film, so you have to concern yourself with more things, you have to keep up with more areas that your crew will become involved in. For example, for a larger picture you generally have more props to deal with. So you decide which way to go, to cut down or go full-bore….Here I have better actors and I get what I want the first time. And better nuances."

De Laurentiis spent a lot of time on the set during Carver's first few days on *Drum*. "But then as it went on, he got busy on other things," says the director, who also recalls other visitors. "We had tons of people observing that had to be accommodated, from the NAACP to the animal rights people. The NAACP was allowed on the set all the time. They could have shut it down by protest. I ignored them. Kenny put up with a lot. You know, 'Why are you doing a picture like that? Why are you putting down blacks?' There was a lot of publicity in the trades about it. I was born in Brooklyn, New York and I didn't grow up with racial overtones. I knew about the black exploitation pictures through Roger Corman and A.I.P. [American International Pictures], but to do a major picture with black stars kissing and screwing white girls was kind of weird. I used to scratch my head like, 'Am I really doing this?'"

Carver says, "I don't remember anybody giving me bad mouth except for the Kresses [The father-son editing team of Harold and Carl Kress]. I went into the editing room to review the footage and I asked one of the Kresses if I could run it on a Moviola. I knew how to use a Moviola, I had cut pictures on it. I remember them saying, 'It's against the union.' One of those nice people called the union and I got fined. It was a $5,000 fine because I touched the Moviola and I ran some footage on it—one reel. I got really pissed. [The Kresses,] of course, denied that they were the ones who called the union and brought me up on charges. I actually had to face my peers at the Directors Guild for touching the Moviola. It was a joke. It's union crap, but they turned me in and it was very, very rude. [Harold Kress] was a real snotty guy."

One or two weeks after he began shooting, Carver had one final confrontation with the editors. The director recalls, "They were putting a sequence together, and I had a few things to say and some notes and they ignored it and I had some words with them. That week they were replaced. Not by me, by Serpe because Serpe was the guy who said 'You want this guy, you want that guy? No? Okay, they're gone.' [Harold Kress] with his son got fired and we got someone else in there."

The Kresses were replaced by another Oscar-winning editor, Thomas

Stanford (*West Side Story*, 1961; *Jeremiah Johnson*, 1972), assisted by David Ramirez (cutting assistant on 1972's *Cabaret* and 1975's *Funny Lady*) and Lorraine Catalano. At one point, Stuart H. Pappe (*The President's Analyst*, 1967; *Alex in Wonderland*, 1970) was also involved with editing *Drum*.

Carver got along with everybody else on *Drum*. He says, "I had a good relation with Kenny [Norton]. Kenny liked working with me. We worked hard with him and he had [acting] coaches. First day of shooting with Kenny, I'm standing next to the camera. We're doing this scene where he was walking toward camera with a horse. Kenny couldn't ride and was afraid of horses. He hated the horse. This gigantic, muscular guy sitting on a horse—scared. Between takes, he was asking me questions. I didn't hear him. I wasn't paying attention. To get my attention, he picked up a brick—a real, heavy brick. He threw this brick at me and it landed two feet from my foot. He was a good hundred feet from me. That's the accuracy he had with a brick. He should have been a ball player. I'll never forget that day and that's how we became friends."

Norton says, "The first director [Kennedy], I have no memory of. I do remember Steve [Carver]. Richard Fleischer was older and more set in his ways. [Carver was] more flexible and a little friendlier. We were more of the same age, so we talked differently. I could pick his brain. We'd go back and forth until we found a happy medium. They'd show us the takes [the dailies] that evening. That to me was very educational. [Carver] liked to show the actors what they did and keep them in the groove."

With one major movie role to his credit, Norton felt more comfortable on the *Drum* set. "I think there was more pressure on *Mandingo* because, number one, I was green. I didn't know anything about the movie world. For *Drum,* I was very relaxed. For *Mandingo*, I was hyper."

In *Mandingo*, an actual plantation home in Louisiana was used to represent Falconhurst, but for *Drum*, which ends with the Maxwell home burning down, the mansion exteriors were shot on a set built at Lake Sherwood Ranch in Ventura, California, near the San Fernando Valley. The set required two months, sixty laborers, and $1 million to complete and was described in press materials as "bigger than renowned Tara in *Gone with the Wind*."

To help create a Southern atmosphere, tons of Spanish moss was delivered from Florida and draped over the California oak trees. Press sheets claimed that the Falconhurst in *Drum* was modeled after Belle Helene, the real mansion used for *Mandingo*, but the sequel's mansion looks nothing like Belle Helene. (The *Drum* novel had explained that Hammond now lived in a new house built in another area of the Maxwell estate, but the movie doesn't make this clear.)

Also constructed at Lake Sherwood was the exterior of Marianna's New

Orleans brothel, on a set that cost $100,000. "I've worked and produced many a film, but I never had sets built like these in *Drum* before," Serpe said. "I've been all over Europe, in some of the nicest and most elegant homes, castles, vistas, what-have-you. I say our bordello set is outstanding and can compare favorably with the fancy places of the wealthy in France, England, Italy, and Spain."

The whorehouse interior, which was shot on a stage, was stocked with antiques including crystal chandeliers, a $20,000 Steinway grand piano, and a Savonari Italian carpet worth $30,000. "They just don't build sets like these anymore," set decorator John McCarthy said. "The fabrics on the wall were especially designed. All the furniture, including those great nudes on canvas, were selected from top antique shops throughout the Los Angeles area... All these decorating pieces cost us about $90,000 in rentals." Fiona Lewis said, "This bordello matches some of the most elegant mansions we have in London. The decoration is marvelous."

Carver recalls that some of the actors who were offered *Drum* turned down the film because of the subject matter. "In fact, I even hesitated at first, but it just felt right and it was a challenge. But Warren [Oates] didn't give a damn. He was a character actor who worked no matter what. I loved Warren. [Before *Drum*,] I got to know Warren through John Cassavettes, who I had worked with [on *Capone*], because they lived right near each other."

During *Drum* Oates, who lived on a ranch in Montana, stayed at the Beverly Hills Hotel, where his dirty station wagon was parked next to flashy vehicles in the lavish hotel's lot.

A major trait of Hammond Maxwell in the books and the *Mandingo* movie is that the character has a pronounced limp, but Oates ignored the ailment. Carver explains, "I remember Warren saying that he's not going to play the limp and Dino was in the meeting and said, 'I don't care. Whatever you think is good.' It was a decision made by *them*. I was silent and wondering, 'What limp?' [Laughs] Warren just felt that it wasn't necessary. Some things were changed on almost all the characters, because it was going to be re-shot. [The actors] decided to change things because everybody tries to second guess what they can do better or what would be better [in a re-shoot]."

Oates and the movie also ignored Hammond Maxwell's aversion to white women—an integral part of the character's psyche in the Falconhurst books and the *Mandingo* movie. In dialogue that was mostly omitted from the shooting script, Hammond told Miss Augusta, "You a white woman all right. Never could stand 'em. But I need one, dammit. Spend a lifetime tryin' to find one thouten that meaness." In *Drum*, the character has a steady sexual relationship with Marianna (Vega) and gleefully gropes several bare-breasted white whores.

Unlike Perry King's sullen interpretation in *Mandingo*, Oates plays the role with plenty of humor. Carver says, "In *The Wild Bunch*, Warren played this lecherous guy. That's what he wanted to play [in *Drum*]. I remember him pinching some girls in the ass as they went by and so on. We played it more cartoonish, more graphic, and less realistic [than *Mandingo*]. The whole vibe was different [than *Mandingo*]. I was following the lead of Dino and the lead of just about all the actors. When you take over a film, you're at [the original actors'] mercy because they're dead set to go a certain way. I remember having lots of chats with [Oates] and liking his ideas and suggestions. [He played the role] google-eyed and bumpkin and broad. [Oates] was faithful to the actual dialogue. I don't remember any ad-lib scenes because this was a technical, surgical operation to save this picture and get it made. [Screenwriter] Sale had humor.

Yaphet Kotto, Steve Carver, and Ken Norton between takes of a fight scene. (Collection of Steve Carver)

He writes with humor. Wexler was a grump—he didn't have humor. I put humor in if it's black humor, but I don't normally like to lighten the character up for fear of getting too cartoonish. These characters were quickly approaching cartoon, so I didn't play up the humor."

Oates told a *Los Angeles Herald-Examiner* reporter who visited the set, "Is it a good time for riots in Boston over busing black and white children to school? How far have we come away from what was going on in 1850, the time of the film? It was called slavery then, one of the ugliest words in human experience. It's called 'rights' today. But the immoral problem is with us more than one hundred years later. All *Drum* asks is that we *remember* how it all started. Is that enticing? It should be inspirational to us to examine our hearts rather than dragging our feet."

Wild Bunch member Bo Hopkins told Oates's biographer Susan Compo that during *Drum*'s production an unhappy Oates said, "If you pass buildings when you're going into town, look over at a few of them, because those are movies that I didn't turn down. I own those buildings....I don't trust any of these sons of bitches. Goddamn it, I wish to hell I hadn't gotten into some of this shit."

Oates and Vega had become close while shooting *Bring Me the Head of Alfredo Garcia*. In 1974, shortly after that film wrapped, the actress told Earl Wilson of the *New York Post*, "[Oates] was one of the ones who said no. He was separating, I was separating at the time of the film. He's my ideal. I love him for his soul, for his sweetness as a man. He's not selfish, he's warm. But he got away."

Decades later, Vega recalled in an interview with Nicanor Loreti, "I have beautiful memories of Warren Oates. I could describe him in a single word—compassion. He was a person very committed with art and with his fellow man. Warren Oates loved it all, he petted everything that came across his path. He turned any situation into an ideal one. He was perfect."

Norton also recalls Oates fondly: "I liked Warren. He was a very friendly man, a good man. Easy to rehearse with, easy to talk to, easy to ask questions. Because I was green, I asked a lot of questions and he was easy to talk to. I asked everybody questions, even the extras. And Warren was very helpful to me and he would tell me why he would do something a certain way. And I watched him do it and I understood why he did it that way."

Drum has a more humorous tone than *Mandingo*, due mainly to Oates' performance. Norton says, "Warren Oates just came off that way. He would say things that were just funny. It was supposed to be serious and whatever, but it came off humorous. And he enjoyed doing it that way and I remember laughing on the set with many others. He made something so serious, funny." Although Oates had a reported fondness for tequila and vodka, Norton insists, "I never saw him drink."

Oates said at the time, "Wait till you see Ken Norton. This big guy is terrific both as an actor and a prize fighter. He's going to take on Muhammad Ali you know—and soon. Ken is the fighter who almost put Ali down for the count and broke his jaw as well. Can you imagine what it will mean for the picture if Norton does beat Ali? I think he will."

During production, Norton said, "I like to be the best in whatever I do. That's why I got into acting—because I know that eventually working with such great stars as James Mason, Warren Oates, Yaphet Kotto, I will learn a lot. In learning, I just have to get better. Unless one is good at what he tries, he better give up. Which means I'm not giving up either acting or boxing....A day goes by and sometimes you rehearse a scene over and over again during the ten or twelve hours you work. The director wants to make it as good as he can, and if the actors don't give a top performance, the director keeps trying until he gets what he wants on film. There are days like these. And when they happen, the going is tedious and monotonous."

Norton added at the time, "I like fighting a whole lot more than I do acting. Acting's so tedious. It's worse than training for a big fight. When I train, I work hard for two or three hours. When I'm physically exhausted, I rest and take it easy. But you're on a movie set from six in the morning until five at night. The hardest part is doing retakes and sitting around waiting. It's just like it was in the Marine Corps—hurry up and wait. In the ring, it's all business. It's just you and the other guy. In acting, you make believe and pretend. I feel more comfortable in front of the cameras now than I did in the ring. I'm glad I can fight and act." He recalled later, "One scene required me to cry. To get in touch with those feelings, I thought of my Aunt Mary and how proud she would have been of me. Thinking of Aunt Mary always brought a tear to my eye." (His late aunt had helped to raise him when he was a boy.)

As in *Mandingo*, Norton spends most of *Drum* bare-chested. But his extraordinary physique was not the result of a strict diet. Carver recalls, "[Norton] was called 'Mr. Donut.' He would eat an entire case [of donuts], like twenty-four or something. That was his breakfast and that's what he got every morning. I mean, those big donuts—with all this icing and jelly-filled. He loved those things. I would say, 'Kenny, you're a fighter. You're gonna' get fat!' He says, 'Nope.' He gave me a whole explanation for it. A couple of times, if [the caterer] was late, [Norton would say,] 'Wait, where's my donuts! I'm not shooting without my donuts!'"

Norton and his friend Sykes did not have any love scenes in *Mandingo*, but they made up for it with a nude romp in *Drum* in which Norton also has an intimate scene with Grier. He recalls, "[On *Drum*,] I was more friendly with Pam Grier. I can't tell a whole bunch. I'm not going to say anything negative towards that relationship. I'm not saying that I could, but if I could, I don't think I would. She was a very nice person. I did talk to Brenda and talked to Pam and a few more, but what you don't know, you can't write. [Laughs] The thing is, I don't want to say anything negative about those individuals. I'm not saying that me seeing them during the movie was negative. I didn't think it was. I enjoyed it. You can think mentally how you would act with Brenda Sykes and Pam Grier. Brenda Sykes was so cute, like one of those little black dolls you buy. And Pam Grier was a very nice lady and very attractive and very healthy. So you can think about and derive something from that without me saying too much."

Carver says, "I knew Kenny was doing all of them. He was dating everybody. Kenny was the man. He was a stud and he didn't have a wife at the time. They all were good-looking ladies and all had relationships with Kenny. Brenda was super. Beautiful girl. She was in great shape. What a body. Interesting girl. She was easy, fun. Nice smile. She held her own. She had a lot of pride in her work. She was an outspoken lady. [Grier] had a large chest—one of Kenny's criteria at the time. [Laughs]"

The well-endowed Grier told *Jet*, "I have a tendency to cover myself up. I'm self-conscious of my body having 39-24-37 [measurements]—you know, people staring at you can get to you after awhile." The 5' 9" actress maintained her stunning physique through rigorous exercise including dance, jogging, skiing, and scuba diving. Grier appears topless in *Drum*, but had just rejected a $10,000 offer to pose nude in a major magazine. "I want to show them I'm not just another body for the camera but a serious actress," she explained.

In *Ebony*, Grier compared the *Drum* production to her low-budget work: "[My early movies] were on such short schedules and low budgets, they worked you almost to death. [I was] so exhausted when I got home I would barely get in and turn on the bath water. I never ate dinner. I was too tired. I would usually fall asleep in the tub. Thank God for my long legs: I didn't drown myself....We've all worked on fifteen-to-twenty day schedules, sixteen hours a day, with such pressure, and now we can take anything. To know that you're working and everyone is professional and there is mutual respect, it's the greatest feeling in the world. But when you get up and you know you're going to be rushed and pushed all day, people cracking the whip over you for an inexpensive movie and no one cares what it really looks like in the end so long as you get it on film, you say, 'What am I doing this for?' Your fingernails are bleeding from climbing the ladder. It's exhausting. But now I'm in heaven."

Carver says, "Warren was a cut-up and Kenny was wild. Kenny used to do wild stuff. Kenny was a champion boxer, but on a movie set he was dealt with when he fooled around. I never yelled at him or had any fights, but I saw it with the other actors. I remember Warren screaming at him. [Norton] used to joke during a scene and ruin it and Isela would snap at him. She just turned and went, in Spanish, 'Fuck off, this is my scene, I'm being serious!' She had to do that a couple of times not only to Kenny, but some other people. Every once in a while, she had that Latin fire. She was a tough lady. I said, 'Whoops, I better not joke too much.'"

Carver continues, "[Vega was] just a wonderful lady. Tough when it came down to it. Uninhibited. Isela was walking around naked, completely naked, between scenes when she was going from her trailer to the caterer. That's what she did in Mexico, I guess. She was used to it and she said to everyone, 'You don't like it? Leave!' That was a woman that had security in knowing her body looked great. Isela was running around naked, Kenny was running around half naked. A professional set on MGM with a professional crew of a hundred and you have all these people running around naked. I couldn't believe it."

The immodest Vega had been featured in a 1974 *Playboy* layout and photos of nude models taken by the actress were often featured in Latin American magazines. She said in *Drum* publicity, "I have nothing to hide. My heart is open, I have no secrets….Nietzsche once said, 'You can't alter anything.' It's the same with me. I am what I am and I can't alter my thinking or the way I desire to live." Vega had recently purchased land on the island of Cozumel in Mexico. "I'm a gypsy—a gitana—and I want an island all to myself," she said. "A free life is what most people want, only most are afraid to admit it. The only problem with being completely free is the work. But one can work and live the free life in between. I intend to spend this year in the United States. It will allow me some time to work, and after that I'm going to Cozumel to build my home and live the free gypsy life I'm talking about."

Rainbeaux Smith, who started filming her *Drum* scenes on March 8, gives the best performance of her career as Oates' horny teenage daughter who can't keep her hands off the male slaves' belts. Norton couldn't recall much about the actress. "I didn't socialize with her too much," he says. "I remember that she was, uh…she was frisky." Norton never saw the troubled actress use drugs or alcohol on the set. "On the sets of both *Drum* and *Mandingo*, I was involved with what I was doing rather than sitting back watching other people."

Carver says, "She was fun to work with. She was wild. I liked her. She was just a fun little girl that looked like one of those little skaters on Venice Beach that everybody likes—an airhead-type. But she was fun and professional and I can't remember anything bad about her."

The *Mandingo* movie had no gay roles, but John Colicos and Alain Patrick played unsubtle queens in *Drum*. Canadian actor Colicos (*Scorpio*, 1973) gives an outrageous performance as the flamboyant Frenchman obsessed with

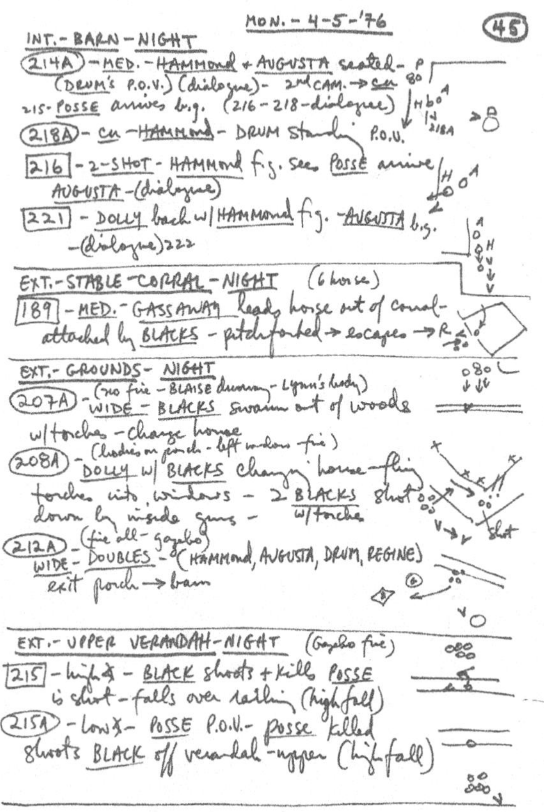

MON. - 4-5-'76 (45)

INT. - BARN - NIGHT

(214A) - MED. - HAMMOND + AUGUSTA seated - (DRUM'S P.O.V.) (dialogue) - 2nd CAM. → CU

215 - POSSE arrives b.g. (216-218-dialogue)

(218A) - CU - HAMMOND - DRUM standing P.O.V.

[216] - 2-SHOT - HAMMOND f.g. sees POSSE arrive AUGUSTA - (dialogue)

[221] - DOLLY back w/ HAMMOND f.g. - AUGUSTA b.g. - (dialogue) 222

EXT. - STABLE - CORRAL - NIGHT (6 horse)

[189] - MED. - GASSAWAY leads horse out of corral - attacked by BLACKS - pitchforked → escapes → R

EXT. - GROUNDS - NIGHT

(207A) - (no fire - BLAISE dummy - Lynn's body) WIDE - BLACKS swarm out of woods w/ torches - charge house

(208A) - (bodies on porch - left window fire) DOLLY w/ BLACKS charging house - fling torches into windows - 2 BLACKS shot down by inside guns - w/ torches

(212A) - (fire all - gazebo) WIDE - DOUBLES - (HAMMOND, AUGUSTA, DRUM, REGINE) exit porch → barn

EXT. - UPPER VERANDAH - NIGHT (Gazebo fire)

[215] - high ∡ - BLACK shoots + kills POSSE is shot - falls over railing (high fall)

(215A) - low ∡ - POSSE P.O.V. - POSSE killed shoots BLACK off verandah - upper (high fall)

Page from Steve Carver's shot list for the April 5, 1976 filming of the slave revolt. (Collection of Steve Carver)

sleeping with and castrating Norton. The prolific Shakespearean stage actor once said, "I've always remained a 19th century, slightly hammy, overblown actor....When you get a really kooky, offbeat villain you can explore all kinds of devious twistings and turnings in the human mind."

Norton says of Colicos, "He was all businesslike on the set. A couple of times he did something that didn't agree with Brenda and she told him so he changed it."

Carver says, "John Colicos [was] temperamental. I had heard he could be a problem, [but] I had no problems with him. At one time Ralph Serpe wanted to get rid of him. But I liked John. Colicos was always in character, playing this piece of shit with the French accent. He looked the part—this warped, lecherous idiot. He looked the part and he just loved it. He had a fey-like quality, which lent well to the part."

One scene called for Colicos to point a pistol at Norton. Carver explains, "I said, 'Okay, roll the cameras,' and John pulls the trigger. He wasn't supposed to. He shot Kenny. I remember looking at Kenny's chest, which was bare and smoking. His skin was on fire. He was shot by a blank. I couldn't believe that. I remember him being rushed off the set. John was apologizing up and down. I remember screaming at the special effects person, 'Who put a blank in it?'" The incident left Norton with a permanent scar on his famous chest.

Carver recalls the late-night shooting of the notorious scene where Norton rips off Colicos' testicles with his bare hands: "We were all freezing. It was one of those distasteful, 'How do you shoot it?' and 'Why are we doing this?' scenes. I remember joking around with it and nobody taking it serious. Props brought a whole bunch of stuff to pick from. [Laughs] It was all latex." From Wexler's script: "He shoves the raw flesh into DeMarigny's face." The special effects checklist for that night's shooting included a request for "bloody balls."

Carver says, "Alain Patrick was French. He was a young kid that was learning and was nervous. I was a little bit hesitant to make [the gay angle as] blatantly as the script said. Colicos wanted to be suggestive. Colicos would carry on with him. When I'd call, 'Cut,' everybody [on the crew would] break out in laughter and Alain would sort of slither away because of embarrassment. He probably didn't know American humor."

Carver recalls, "[Fiona Lewis] was very stately. She had a very nice quality and she was very good for the film. She was in character most of the time. Unfortunately, the writing, the story, and the characters really didn't come up to her level. She took a bath [in one scene]. She had a nice chest."

On the screen, Yaphet Kotto's Blaise character has a love/hate friendship with Norton's Drum. On set, the two actors had a similar relationship. Norton explained in his autobiography, *Going the Distance*: "I was a newcomer, but everyone in the cast was eager to lend a helping hand, except for maybe Yaphet Kotto. He had a reputation for being competitive, especially when another actor got more screen time. Yaphet was a little jealous that I seemed to be getting more attention from the females in the cast."

Carver says, "That rivalry was there. [Kotto] didn't like the idea that Kenny, who wasn't an actor, was getting all the glory. Kotto was having problems with Kenny's motor home. [Kotto thought his own] Winnebago was too small. Ralph went out and bought two gigantic, I mean *gigantic*, motor homes for both of them and shut him up. When Yaphet threw his fits, I remember Kenny mimicking him and Yaphet turned at him. I thought they were going to get into it. [Norton] looked into [Kotto's] eyes, saw that he was not fooling around, and Kenny backed off like a kid seeing a wild dog."

Carver continues, "Yaphet was really a pain on the set. He just did *Report to the Commissioner* and thought he was hot stuff. I'd give him directions, talk with him. We'd be ready to shoot, the whole crew is ready and I'd say, 'Roll cameras," and Yaphet would say, 'Whoa, whoa, whoa, wait, wait, wait,' and he'd walk up to me and say 'What's my motivation?' He was dead serious. That was one of the things that irritated the crew. Everybody kept saying it. They would always mimic him and say, 'What's my motivation?' Actors would joke around right before scenes, [and say,] 'Wait, Steve, what's my motivation?' If [Kotto] didn't like wardrobe or something, he would complain in the middle of a scene, he'd break a scene up by saying, 'Whoa, whoa. Hey, hey, wait. Wait a minute, what's this?' That type of stuff. Yaphet was a pain in the ass to everybody. He was not favored on the set. Unprofessional, but a good actor." When shooting the climactic scene, when Kotto's character is killed, the crew took their frustrations out on a dummy that stood in for the actor. "Everybody who walked by kicked that dummy," Carver says.

While nowhere near as toned as Norton, Kotto had a bulky, 6' 4" frame and was a believable screen opponent for the boxer. In 1972 Kotto had trained under heavyweight boxing icon George Foreman while preparing for the lead in *The Great White Hope* on Broadway. Although nobody had actually gotten hit while shooting the two Norton fights in *Mandingo*, the first battle between Norton and Kotto in *Drum* had some actual contact. Norton recalls, "Yaphet was a true actor and he played his part well, [but] he accidentally hit me. It was one minor mistake. I got hit and it's no fun getting hit when you don't expect it, when you're not rolling with the punch. I told him that I was trained to hit people and hurt people. So if I could miss him, he could miss me."

Carver says, "Yaphet didn't like to do his own stunts. Kenny didn't want a double. Kenny wanted to do his own [stunts] and he did. [Stuntman] Bob Minor did not double Kenny. He was a stand-in for Kenny and we used him as Kenny's camera double for focusing and [rehearsing camera] moves."

The courtyard fight between Norton and Kotto took two-and-a-half nights to shoot. Drum biting into Blaise's torso during their first fight was not in the script and was added while the scene was being blocked. Carver explains, "[De Laurentiis] wanted the fights to be as vicious [as in *Mandingo*] and be handheld, the same style that Fleischer did. Those fights, the bloody ones with Yaphet and Kenny, took days [to shoot]. It was [shot with] many cameras with a lot of cuts and hand-held angles. [Special make-up] appliances had to be put on the actors with Yaphet being bit, and blood and all that crap. Those are latex appliances and it's re-done each time. You can only do eight pages a day, maximum, on one of these large, hundred-crew-member [films]. You can't move too fast."

Make-up artist Bill Turner handled the convincing blood and bruise effects for the *Drum* battles and had done similar good work for the brutal fight scenes in *Emperor of the North Pole* (1973). Turner also applied several hundred wigs, fake beards, and false sideburns to principal actors and extras during the shoot, including the (unconvincing) hairpiece worn by Colicos.

The stunt coordinator was Eddie Smith, co-founder of the Black Stuntmen's Association, whose previous stunt credits included *Earthquake* (1974) and *Blazing Saddles* (1974). Smith also has a brief acting role in *Drum* as Bruno, one of Colicos' henchmen. Carver recalls, "Eddie Smith was a little guy. You can see him in some of the fire scenes, running, as one of the slaves. Eddie was very inexperienced. He brought in a team. Bob [Minor] was helping him, especially with the fights. Bob was a good friend of mine. I worked with him on a lot of shows. Who does the actual choreography? It's hard to say. I worked a lot with action pictures and it's usually a little of everybody."

Eddie Smith died in 2005. Minor's many acting roles included the jealous husband who gets cut up with the switchblade in 1976's *J.D.'s Revenge*. After *Drum*, he played a henchman alongside *Mandingo* veteran Earl Maynard in 1977's *The Deep*. He continued as a stuntman and actor and later became a stunt coordinator and second-unit director.

The best fight scene in *Drum* is between bare-fisted Norton and knife-swinging stuntman S. A. (Scott) Lewis, who helped with the choreography. (Lewis's character is called Babouin, the same name as the Norton adversary played by Earl Maynard in *Mandingo*.) Norton says about the sequence, "It went on very well. There was not a lot of things they had to say to either him or myself to make it look real and it didn't take long to shoot it."

As in *Mandingo*, Norton once again displayed his bare backside for a love scene, but he did request a double for the images where a bare-ass Drum is beaten with a paddle. Norton explains, "That dude hanging upside down who got whipped, that was not me." Carver remembers differently: "Kenny did it all. I hung him upside down. I remember damn well because I remember him talking about blacking out. He was blacking out because all the blood went to his head and he screamed. I actually held his head up for a time between takes when were moving a camera." (Kotto insisted on and did receive a double for that scene.)

Wexler had created an ironic character arc for Don Cesar, the wealthy owner of Tamboura in the Havana sequences. In the climax of Wexler's drafts, Don Cesar had become a lowlife traveling slave trader who visits Falconhurst. For his late-in-production revision, Sale went back to the novel, where the cruel flesh peddler was a previously-unseen character called Zeke Montgomery. The switch diminished John Vernon's Don Cesar role, but gave another credit to veteran character actor Royal Dano. Carver says, "Royal Dano was a friend of mine. I brought Royal on. If you look at my films, I have an ensemble group of actors. R. G. Armstrong, L. Q. Jones, Peckinpah people. Royal was one. He was in *Big Bad Mama* and *Capone*. He was a good guy. You gotta' have Lincoln." (Dano played Abraham Lincoln on stage for decades.)

Dano's endless career included *Johnny Guitar* (1954), *Moby Dick* (1956), *Man of the West* (1958), and dozens of TV Westerns. He was also an old friend of Oates. They met in 1953 when a touring play featuring Dano as Lincoln

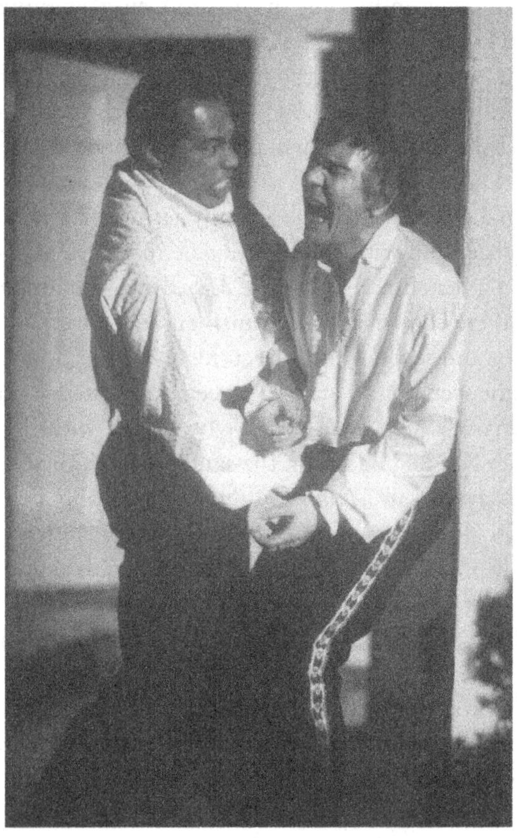

Drum (Ken Norton) takes care of DeMarigny (John Colicos) in the gripping climax. (Collection of Steve Carver)

stopped in Louisville, Kentucky and Dano offered early encouragement to the then-struggling Oates. Dano died in 1994.

Carver recalls producer Serpe: "Great, great man. A gruff Italian—

Sicilian. Carried a .45. I [had been] in Italy for fourteen months, was married at the time to an Italian girl, and I knew what Italians were like. He was real stuff from Sicily and a tough, tough man, yet a sweetheart. He became one of my dearest friends. I knew the [Serpe] family very well. I got to know Ralph very well and he had me in his trust. With Ralph, if you're not in his trust, look out. He was that type of guy."

"I'll tell you two stories, just to give you Ralph's character and his flavor. Some guy was wanting to marry one of his daughters and Ralph found out something negative about this guy. He went to visit this guy in some high rise, hung him out the window by his ankles, told him not to marry the daughter, stay away from her, get out of town. And that was that. Here's the story about *The Brink's Job* [a 1978 De Laurentiis-Serpe project starring Peter Falk]. Peter Falk's chauffer stole two rolls of film that they had shot in Chicago. He was supposed to take the exposed negative to a laboratory. He stole the two rolls and blackmailed Dino. He wanted a half-a-million or a quarter-million [dollars]. The guy turned up dead. I remember saying, 'Whoa, these guys play hardball!' [Laughs] Ralph was called in to take care of that. I remember Ralph talking with some very, very seedy characters."

"Ralph was never that way on the set. I've never seen him physical. He was just a dear, dear man and did a whole bunch of stuff for Dino. Ralph, originally, was Dino's bodyguard and became his producer. He never, ever backed down from Dino. Never. [Dino] was his dear friend, but I never saw him back down from a fight. Dino said, 'Fuck you, don't do this,' and Ralph would always say, 'No, I'm doing it.' Strong. One-hundred-percent behind the director, one-hundred-percent believed in the film, did what was necessary to do whatever it was. He was a true line producer. Always on the set, always ready. He had habits of writing on paper, doodling on paper. He had habits of doing things like cleaning his nails. He had his own chair with his name on it, and he'd sit quietly and just listen, observe, and be there. He was very creative in saving time, money. Never, ever, off playing golf somewhere while the show was going on. He was there. Unfortunately, he died of lung cancer [in 1992.] I went to his funeral."

De Laurentiis later described Serpe as "an Italian-American who had some familiarity with the Mafia. He wasn't personally involved, I should say, but he knew people who were in the thick of it...Serpe (the poor guy, he's dead now) was anything but a mafioso, but sometimes he liked to give that impression."[1]

Serpe's daughter Pamela had a small, uncredited part in *Drum* as a raped guest at the ill-fated Falconhurst dinner party. The attractive actress and model had bits in a few TV shows and low-budget movies and was a memorable cover model for the July 1977 *Playboy*.

De Laurentiis's twenty-one-year-old son, Federico, who had been a *Mandingo* production assistant, was often present on the *Drum* set. He was then serving as executive producer on his father's upcoming *King Kong* remake and would be the producer on the De Laurentiis production *King of the Gypsies* (1978). Federico produced a final film, *She Dances Alone* (1981), before his death in a 1981 airplane crash at age twenty-six. Carver says, "I knew Dino's son very well. I used to go sailing with him. Federico was a great guy. [His death] really was a great loss."

There were minor setbacks, typical of filmmaking, during the eight weeks of California shooting. (Due to overcast skies, it took three attempts on three different days to successfully get the cemetery scene on film.) But the production went remarkably smoothly. Carver says, "It was not a drug-laden set. It was a clean set, that one. I would say the average age of the crew was in the sixties, believe it or not. A mature group of people and I was quite young. It was a great set; it was a great bunch of people."

During the final two weeks of shooting, Norton was training intensely for an upcoming fight and was released from the set each day at 5:00 pm. Norton finished his work on *Drum* on the night of April 2. For the remaining four days of the schedule, which mainly focused on stunts, a double was used for the Drum character. It would be several months before *Drum* would be on the big screen, but Norton was seen on the small screen that same month in a televised fight.

The climax of *Drum*—an action and stunt-packed spectacle where rebellious slaves attack Falconhurst and burn it to the ground—took two days of studio interiors and two nights of exteriors to shoot. The interiors required two stages.

Carver recalls, "The fire scenes were shot at MGM inside the stage. All those burners were butane-controlled, but dangerous. Burt [Kennedy had] set up the sets to be accordant to the fire marshal rules. Burt had [constructed] some move-away stairways for stunts. He designed it to be a certain way and Lucien knew all of it. I remember asking Lucien, 'How was Burt going to do this?' Lucien was the one who actually showed me how to piece the sequence together [and said,] 'Shoot it here, shoot this piece there, and shoot that there.' I brought on a special effects guy named Roger George. [George also did effects for Carver's *Capone*.] He had to hire twenty-five of the best special effects men in Hollywood, and some of them were legends. We had all kinds of stunts. Twenty-five special effects gaffers commanded their own crew, so we had hundreds of special effects people making rain, making fire, making you-name-it. That was pretty impressive."

Oates and Lewis were used briefly during the early filming of the exterior stunts, but for long shots, their characters were played by stunt doubles Bill Hart and Donna Garrett. Tony Brubaker and J.D. Davis doubled for Norton and Grier. *Drum* had daily production costs of $30,000, but since the major actors didn't work and didn't have to be paid for the two final days, those days cost only $22,000 each.

A budget memo from Serpe to De Laurentiis reported, "have replaced expensive bit part players with stunt-acting men and women." Carver explains, "In the [dinner party] scene in the dining room were the greatest stunt people around. The top echelon of stunt people at that time. I had the opportunity, which was a great honor, to work with these people. I really had the choice of the greatest people of the time in Hollywood."

The stunt legends who appeared at the Falconhurst dinner party and the fiery climax were sixty-seven-year-old Lila Finn, Vivien Leigh's *Gone with the Wind* (1939) stunt double and one of the founders of the Stunt Woman's Association; Clay Tanner, whose many physical roles included the devil in *Rosemary's Baby* (1968); Henry Wills, who did many John Wayne films and over two thousand movie stunts; Donna Garrett, Angie Dickinson's stunt double on the *Police Woman* TV series (1974–1978); seventy-six-year-old Harvey Parry, a frequent stunt double for James Cagney and Humphrey Bogart during the 1930s and 40s; May R. Boss, who had done dangerous stunts in many movies including *Earthquake* (1974); and Jeannie Epper, Lynda Carter's stunt double for the TV series *Wonder Woman* (1976–1979).

On April 8, the final night of exteriors, the million-dollar Falconhurst set was burned to ashes as five cameras (including one mounted on a crane) rolled and three fire trucks were parked nearby.

Drum completed filming on Friday, April 9, 1976. The last scene that was shot was the scene in Marianna's bedroom where the madam and Rachel discuss their pasts and have a brief intimate interlude. At the bottom of his notes for that day's shooting, Carver wrote, "T. G. I. O" meaning "Thank God It's Over."

After Kennedy's dismissal, Serpe had prepared a revised budget allowing for $90,000 and three days to be spent re-shooting footage that had been shot in Puerto Rico and New Orleans. The producer made arrangements with some cast members and reported in a memo: "Because of negotiations with Grier [and] others and using statement that additional work covers retakes and new scenes, we have low hold-over charges..." But *Drum* had already run $429,984 over its initial budget and De Laurentiis decided to cut costs by using already-shot footage for the opening act (featuring the Tamboura character).

During his thirty-six shooting days on *Drum*, Carver ended up directing or re-directing the entire completed film. He explains, "I was hired to continue, not to replace and not to re-shoot. It wasn't my real intention at first, but I re-shot just about everything of Burt's, except for the [opening] sequence which shows the two million slaves in chains coming from the boats. Nothing was shot by Kennedy that's in the [final] picture other than that. Lucien said, 'Let's shoot that again.' We never did shoot that again. Everything that was shot [by Kennedy], [Ballard] wanted to shoot again. There were some sequences I was supposed to keep, but then I re-shot them, because little-by-little I started to whittle away at the footage that didn't match. I remember Dino asking me if I could shoot the other half of a scene, [i.e.,] you shoot one way and the actor's not in it and then you shoot the other way to replace him. Lucien said, 'Ah, no it's gonna' be too hard to match the lighting.'"

Principal photography, including the work done by both directors, had taken a total of three months. Altogether, forty-eight sets and nine locations were used. Despite the rocky production start, shooting had completed on schedule. Post-production would not go as smoothly.

On April 14, less than a week after filming ended, *Drum*'s only difficult actor placed a surprising (and costly) full-page ad in both *Variety* and *Hollywood Reporter* reading: "My Best Wishes and Heartfelt Thanks To The Drum Production Co. and Special Thanks to Barry Diller, Chairman of the Board, Paramount Pictures and Dino De Laurentiis. A special and warm thanks to Ralph Serpe whose fair-playing and treatment to all was inspiring to this Black-Jewish performer—Bless You! And to Steve Carver, a director of insight, strength and strong character. Sincerely yours, Yaphet Kotto."

Picture editing and most of the post-production sound work was done at MGM. Since the film was being edited as it was shot, a first cut of *Drum* was completed on April 26, a mere two weeks after the last shot was finished. That same day, Carver started working with the composer. The director wanted jazz icon Grover Washington, who had visited the set during the production. "Grover was going to do the music," Carver recalls. "I thought that Grover was an excellent choice. I said, 'Hey, hire him.' And suddenly, I find another guy on it."

Young African American musician Charlie Smalls was hired to score *Drum*. Smalls had earned a Tony for the music and lyrics in *The Wiz*, the hugely-successful black version of *The Wizard of Oz* that opened on Broadway in 1975. He had also made a memorable appearance on a 1968 episode

During the revolt, Mr. Gassaway (Henry Wills) kills two slaves with a pitchfork. The gory action was cut to avoid an X rating.

of *The Monkees*, in which he explained "soul" to Davy Jones. Carver says, "Smalls wasn't very experienced. He was surrounded by his entourage. I wasn't impressed with the music. I would have preferred Ennio Morricone. Then it would have been a score to reckon with and maybe would have made the picture a lot better. [There was] a hundred-piece orchestra at MGM. There were music unions, so every fifteen minutes they got a five-minute break. I hate working that way."

Carver continues, "Ken Wannberg [was the music editor]. The music editor is actually the arranger—the guy who cuts the music apart, hires the particular musicians, and sets it all up. Ken has incredible credits. Super talented guy. He did a lot more than just music editing. Music editor, basically, just strips the music from mag [magnetic recording tape] to match the picture. He didn't do only that."

Drum was Smalls's first and last film score. Also involved with the *Drum* score was Richard P. Hazard (*Some Call It Loving*, 1973), who wrote additional music, and Charlie Coleman, who conducted and arranged the score. The final mix was handled by Bill Varney. Carver says, "I worked with Varney many times. He's mixed a lot of my pictures."

Drum opens with a moody, effective title sequence montage of old woodcuttings, drawings, and photographs depicting disturbing slavery images. The sequence was created at Pacific Title Company. Carver explains,

"That was one contribution [of mine] that was never in the script. I loved those images. They came from very important pieces of document. They were real. Pacific Title Company—classy guys. The title designer was Don Record. He had lots of taste." (*Drum*'s red-tinted credit sequence is similar to the opening titles in Carver's *Capone*.)

"The whole post-production was a horrible scene," Carver says. "I remember a miserable time in cutting. The editing room was a beehive because we had to get that picture out. I worked with a whole bunch of people. I had a lot of problems with Dino because he wanted to cut the shit out of the picture. That's why some of those scenes are quite truncated. I hated the process because Dino would [say], 'Cut, cut, cut, cut. Put this there, cut there.'"

De Laurentiis once explained in the *New York Times*, "If a picture is a flop, the producer is one-hundred-percent responsible, I am responsible. Because I approve the final cut of all my pictures. A bad picture, a producer can make it a good picture—reshoot, change the order of the scenes, cut, re-cut, fix. I've made more than one hit out of what looked to be flop after the first previews."

The original cut ran close to three hours, but De Laurentiis insisted that the first act be reduced. Deleted completely was John Vernon's featured role as Don Cesar, except for one shot where the horse-riding actor (or his stand-in) drags Tamboura's body through the street. Roger E. Mosley, as Tamboura, ended up with no screen time except for several shots of his bare back. The lone image that represented Tamboura's face was a medium shot not of Mosley, but of Bob Minor, taken from a scene of Minor playing the completely-deleted role of Omo, Tamboura's friend. (If Jim Brown had played Tamboura, more footage would have probably remained.) Cynthia James played Julita, a teenage slave forced to mate with Tamboura, but all of her shots were removed, except for one glimpse of her figure in bed.

Isela Vega and Paula Kelly's roles covered two decades, but since most of their footage in the early scenes was cut, the young actresses spend the majority of *Drum* with their hair sprayed grey. When the first act was extensively condensed during editing, the characters of Marianna and Rachel became more sympathetic. Rachel's vengeful plot against Marianna and Tamboura was omitted, as was Marianna's betrayal of Tamboura. Lost was a scene, cribbed from the book, where Rachel prevents Tamboura from touching her by scaring him with a voodoo-cursed feather. Also gone was dialogue, taken almost verbatim from the novel, where Rachel describes her hatred of men to Marianna:

> They are so brutal. And ugly. Their gross black bodies repel me...Don't make me lie with a stinking nigger. Or any other man. All I ask is to serve you.

The first act of *Drum* was originally intended to run for thirty-to-forty minutes. It became a three-minute, narrated prologue—making the Havana scenes play like a recap of the first night of a TV miniseries. (In the released version, the prologue appears after the opening credits, but trial cuts had the footage appearing as a pre-title sequence and as flashbacks recalled by Marianna and Rachel in the New Orleans brothel.)

Carver explains, "I chose Lonny Chapman [to narrate.] He has a very distinct voice. You've heard it before. He's a character actor that's been on television and a lot of pictures. [Chapman's credits include *Baby Doll* (1956) and *The Cowboys* (1972).] [The] narration didn't make much sense. I didn't like it that much. It made mish-mush of a whole bunch of shots that Burt had shot." (Two minutes of Kennedy-directed footage ended up in the final film.) Most of the costly, elaborate sets and costumes that were created for the Cuban sequences ended up not being seen.

The cuts also left gaps in the New Orleans segments. Drum's dreams of becoming a boxer were completely eliminated from the film. A scene of DeMarigny watching Drum train was deleted. In the final film, DeMarigny simply assumes that Drum can fight and the slave's exceptional pugilistic skills come out of nowhere.

Carl Kress received sole editing credit on *Drum*, although he and his father were fired shortly after Carver joined the production. Carver explains, "Carl Kress got credit because of some contractual thing." Only the first ten shots in the finished movie were cut by the Kress team.

On May 5, the De Laurentiis-approved, whittled-down cut of *Drum* was sent to the MPAA (Motion Picture Association of America) for a desired R rating. MPAA head Jack Valenti had been lenient with *Mandingo*, but threatened *Drum* with an X rating and insisted on many cuts. "The MPAA wouldn't give Dino an R," Carver says. "I used to work for Roger Corman and I used to edit his stuff and I got a relationship with [Valenti]. We used to do all kinds of tricks to get stuff by him." One of Carver's tricks from his Corman days was to show the MPAA a work print that had parts of the frame obscured. The director explains, "With a marking pen, you cover up tits and ass and stuff like that that you don't want to be seen and you get the [R] rating."

But the old tricks didn't work on *Drum*. Carver recalls, "[Valenti] came [into the editing room] and he got all pissed off. I remember this disgusting look on his face. I remember Jack walking out and saying, 'I'll speak to Dino' and Dino calling me late at night saying, 'We have a problem.' And we had to go back and cut the picture again. It's just cut to shit. De Laurentiis put too much of everything in it. Sex, drugs, rock and roll, whatever. Dino wanted me to shoot the nudity blatantly. I mean frontal, everything. And we had to re-cut the thing and re-cut it. I was frustrated because I was watching the picture get chopped. Anytime there was nudity or something that was not acceptable, like a black guy and a white girl, [Valenti] said 'Cut, cut, cut' and Dino would look at me like, 'Don't cut, don't cut.'"

"We should have been careful. We should have shot back-ups, we should have done alternates. We didn't do it that way. We didn't do a TV version. Ask the actors that were bare-breasted, 'Did you do something with your clothes on?' No. Valenti was not crooked, nor is the system. What's crooked about it is that some people could get away with a whole bunch of sex and bad language and some people couldn't. It was a political thing based upon Dino. People, Jack in particular, hated to speak with [De Laurentiis] and would be ruthless."

"I remember knock-down, drag-out fights with Paramount. [*Mandingo*] made money, it was successful. Dino already had *Drum* in place with [Paramount] as a second picture. A lot of the Southern markets refused to play [*Mandingo*] and a lot of establishments and particular groups were up in arms after *Mandingo* came out. The fall-out [from *Mandingo* started] an awkward situation. Paramount wanted to get out of the [*Drum* deal] because *Mandingo* was embarrassing because of the racial stuff. They were embarrassed."[2]

Drum's potential X rating was the final straw for Paramount. Although the studio had successfully released numerous De Laurentiis films in the past and would distribute the producer's *King Kong* and *The Shootist* later in the year, *Drum* was dropped by Paramount in early May. De Laurentiis quickly set up a deal with United Artists. (One year later, De Laurentiis's production *The Serpent's Egg* was distributed by Paramount after United Artists dropped that film.)

Carver explains, "When United Artists came along, they just picked it up as a good deal because it was a buy-out. Paramount and United Artists, at the time, had problems and a lot of it was contractual problems—sharing actors, I don't know which ones. Contractual problems in many ways, even with Dino. United Artists was threatening to drop their offer or their bid based on the fact that Paramount wasn't coming through with a certain amount of money. I don't know what the formula was. I remember Dino worried. He almost blew the deal with United Artists. That was a pretty hairy few days. I saw sparks everywhere. I was, as the director, having to sit in on all that crap and I hate politics. I ignored it mostly. I went into a hornet's nest in every respect. From groups [protesting], to fighting with Paramount, to going to United Artists and having to kowtow to them. Dino used me to, basically, run interference."

Adding to Carver's frustrations was De Laurentiis's insistence that the *Drum* post-production budget be reduced after the fall-out with Paramount.

On May 27, *Drum* was again sent to the MPAA and again was not given an R rating. An unnamed De Laurentiis associate told *Variety*, "If [De Laurentiis] wants to release [*Drum*] as an X he'll do so; if he wants to release it as an R, he'll do that." United Artists had previously released the X-rated hits *Midnight Cowboy* (1969), *Last Tango in Paris* (1972), and *Inserts* (1974), but the studio and the producer knew that the *Drum* grosses would be seriously lessened without an R rating.

Trimmed from *Drum* to secure an R were Blaise graphically slitting Babouin's throat; close shots of Norton biting Kotto's side and ear during their first fight; close-ups of Norton and Kotto's bloody, upside-down buttocks; a white man fatally pitch-forking two slaves during the climactic rebellion; the decapitation of slave trader Montgomery followed by Blaise proudly holding up the severed head; and Norton holding up a pair of bloody white testicles which he has just ripped off with his bare hands. (The 1975 kung fu epic *The Street Fighter* (1975) had also received an X rating partly due to a scene of manual castration.)

The struggles with the MPAA put the *Drum* post-production three-and-a-half weeks behind schedule. Once an R rating was finally obtained, *Drum* had more troubles before it hit theaters. Carver says, "We were having problems with the NAACP. There were talks about how many times you could say 'nigger' and other stuff. It was very strange. It went down to the wire. We had a release [set for] a certain time and I was in the editing room days before [the opening]."

De Laurentiis later said, "[*Drum* is] one more proof of my theory that if something goes wrong with a movie, it's the producer's fault. I screwed up everything on *Drum*....Sometimes you win, sometimes not. With *Drum* I didn't win, and it was a mess. The signature of Dino De Laurentiis is a guarantee for the consumer. If I squander it on second-rate projects, I'm in trouble. In this business, of course, some pratfalls are inevitable, and I don't duck my responsibility for them. But when it's appropriate, and possible, I also don't mind putting some distance between them and myself."

American one-sheet.

As on *Mandingo* and all of the mogul's productions, the first credit of *Drum* was to read "Dino De Laurentiis Presents," but this credit was crossed off the list that was sent to Pacific Title Company. Carver says, "[Dino] didn't even want to be known for it. That surprised me. That shocked me. De Laurentiis [wanted to] make the deal with United Artists, get the money and run, and give up the picture." Because some *Drum* posters that included De Laurentiis's presentation credit had already been printed and distributed, a sticker with the credits minus the mogul's name was slapped on the early one-sheets.

The film was still promoted as a Dino De Laurentiis presentation in non-English speaking territories including Denmark, Germany, the mogul's native Italy, and Mexico where it was billed as "Una Superproduccion de Dino De Laurentiis." (Ralph Serpe, De Laurentiis's close associate and the on-set producer of *Drum*, kept his name on the credits.)

Carver was unsure what the final cost of *Drum* was. He says, "I know that my budget was bigger [than *Mandingo*], but my schedule was smaller. [Laughs] The budget, as we went, grew because we shot more. We added, added, added until Kennedy didn't have anything [that he shot left in the picture]. Expensive as all hell. Ridiculous. In those days, I guess they didn't care. These type of guys [like De Laurentiis] pre-sell pictures. I'm sure he made his money back easily from that picture."

Drum had a "Major Studio Sneak Preview" on July 28 at Mann's Chinese in Hollywood. Carver says, "I remember some black kids sitting in front of us during one of the sneak previews. I was sitting with Kenny. The kids were saying, 'Kenny Norton? He's nothing. I can take Kenny,' all through the whole movie. Kenny waited until the end of the film. Lights went on, kids got up, Kenny got up. And [the kids] turned and they turned white looking at him. [Laughs] Kenny just gave them the eye and just turned and walked away. I'll never forget that. That was cool." Another screening wasn't as funny. "There were some white kids that were saying 'nigger this and that,'" Carver recalls.

A *Variety* critic who saw the first preview: "Dino De Laurentiis has done it again with *Drum*, a grubby follow-up to *Mandingo* which invites its own derisive audience laughter, as evident at public preview. Ham acting like you wouldn't believe, coupled with non-direction by Steve Carver and a correspondence-school script by Norman Wexler, add up to cinematic trash....Film was cut to an R rating, but you can never really clean the Aegean stables....Warren Oates [is] rarely seen to such disadvantage....The worst characterization in the film is that of John Colicos as a New Orleans dandy; got up like a drag act version of Bela Lugosi, and sporting an accent not heard outside of Pepe Le Pew cartoons....Royal Dano manages to keep a straight face as a mean slaver....The film has a ragged look in terms of style and pacing..."

On Friday, July 30, 1976—three months after *Drum* finished production and one year after *Mandingo* hit screens—United Artists opened *Drum* at the Loews State I on Broadway and Loews Orpheum on 86th Street in New York as well as in three New Jersey cinemas.

The previous day, huge ads had appeared in the *New York Times* and the *New York Post* and posters had been plastered on the city's subways. The striking, well-designed artwork for the ads featured the bare-chested Norton surrounded by images depicting the film's sexy and violent highlights. The copy screamed, "*Mandingo* Lit The Fuse—*Drum* Is The Explosion!"

and "It scalds. It shocks. It whips. It bleeds. It lusts. It out-Mandingos *Mandingo*!"

The trailer ("An epic motion picture that penetrates even deeper into the decadence and depravity of the old South") included a dialogue snippet and several images taken from the aborted prologue (including a close-up of Paula Kelly as the younger version of her character). The TV spot was narrated by gruff-voiced black actor Adolph Caesar ("Where *Mandingo* ended, *Drum* begins!"). Fawcett-Crest released the *Drum* novel as a paperback movie tie-in with the movie's advertising artwork on the cover.

Oddly, the American lobby card set contained no images of Norton's face, and half of the eight cards were photos from scenes that didn't appear in the final cut, including a shot with John Vernon and Roger E. Mosley, both of whom were no longer in the movie. The synopsis in some press releases included details of the cut Havana act.

Carver was not impressed with United Artists' promotion. "They didn't spend a lot of money," he says. "United Artists, at the time, was not Paramount. Paramount would have done a classy thing like they did with *Mandingo*. *Mandingo* had a very good campaign."

The press releases made the most of Norton's rematch with Muhammad Ali, which was scheduled for September 28. One ad mat was specially designed for the "Sports" page and informed fight fans that "Ken Norton, the next Heavyweight Champion of the World, stars in *Drum*." The boxer-actor appeared on *The Merv Griffin Show* to promote the film and told the press, "When I made *Mandingo*, people wondered what a fighter was doing on the screen. Curiosity was a factor. They forgot about me as a boxer when they saw me act. This time they know what I can do."

Vincent Canby of the *New York Times*, who had panned *Mandingo* twice, wrote, "There's more hot air than steam in the overwrought melodrama of *Drum*....Life at Falconhurst, the Louisiana [sic] slave-breeding plantation introduced in the first film, is just as riotously unpredictable as it was when *Mandingo* ended with the plantation master being shot and his best slave being boiled in oil [sic]. Some years have now passed and the late master's son, Hammond Maxwell is running the business as usual, sleeping with pretty slave girls, while his teenage daughter skips through the honeysuckle making indecent proposals to the male slaves....Mr. Norton is a fine figure of a man, but no actor. He walks through the film with the gait of a football star coming off the field after a very long game. He can hear the roar of the crowd that we can't. This seeming lack of interest in anyone except himself doesn't help the melodrama, in which Drum is supposed to be a sort of black Joseph Andrews, a young man of such perfection that both men and women (including his white mom

[sic]) can't keep their hands off him. Vanity is a far cry from innocence—a small point that isn't understood by people who make exploitation junk like this....Steve Carver may be a bad director or may simply be defeated by material that could only be contained in grand opera. Life on the old plantation was horrendous, I agree, but movies like this are less interested in information than titillation, which, in turn, reflects contemporary obsessions rather more than historical truths. Not since *Mandingo* have I seen a film so concerned with such methods of humiliation as beating, shooting and castration."

Canby later put *Drum* on his list of the year's ten worst pictures: "I've tried to pick some of the worst films that were also the most successful financially.... [The] sequel to the financially successful *Mandingo* continues in serial style the story of the nasty, lascivious, sadistic, mean, rude, evil, and supposedly erotic goings-on down on the old Louisiana [sic] slave-breeding plantation whose name gave the first film its title [sic]. Steve Carver directed it as if he were making a multi-million-dollar porn film devoted to the activities of what the trade calls 'mixed combos.' It may give you some idea of how bad it is to know that Dino De Laurentiis took his name off it." (Also on Canby's ten-worst list was De Laurentiis's production *Lipstick* and Richard Fleischer's *The Incredible Sarah.*)

On August 6, a two-page spread in *Variety* screamed, "*Drum* is the Explosion at $96,443—First 4 Days, 5 Theaters—New York." Carver says, "That's not a lot of money nowadays, but it was a lot of money then, especially for the first four days in only five theaters."

Drum began its West Coast engagements by opening at Mann's Chinese in Hollywood and two other theaters in the Los Angeles area on August 4. It was promoted with a full-page ad in the *Los Angeles Times.* Carver says, "The first night that *Drum* opened, eighteen chairs were slashed with knives at the Chinese Theater."

Kevin Thomas, *Los Angeles Times*: "*Drum* is more trash from the same barrel *Mandingo* came from....Like *Mandingo, Drum* ostensibly condemns slavery but actually uses it as an excuse for salacious miscegenation-inspired sex fantasies. And like *Mandingo, Drum* has been lavishly produced yet is hilarious—hopefully therapeutically so—because of its unstinting excesses. Only vaguely a sequel to *Mandingo....Drum* is actually but a variation on the first film....If possible, Norman Wexler's script for *Drum* is even more ludicrous than for *Mandingo*, and director Steve Carver...probably had no recourse but to play it for laughs, and at least he keeps things moving at a lively pace....Warren Oates is an engagingly funny villain, and Fiona Lewis... likewise plays for comedy....Norton is likable but stolid, Pam Grier is wasted in a tiny nothing part beneath her, and Colicos is pure Southern fried ham. As a rebelling slave, Yaphet Kotto is such a powerful presence he keeps supplying dimensions to his character never suggested in the writing. *Mandingo* was bad enough, but *Drum*...is one of those pictures that reminds you there can always be worse."

Rainbeaux Smith remembered, "I saw it play on Hollywood Boulevard and I went in one day and I was wearing this shirt with a hood on it. Warren Oates finds out what I'm doing and he kicks my butt because I'm a pretty terrible person. He catches me and he kicks my ass, and the audience stood up and started cheering. I said, 'Oh, fuck!' I put on sunglasses, I put my hood over my head." The actress once called *Drum* a "hysterical experience in which millions of dollars were wasted."

On Friday, August 13, the film hit Chicago at the indoor State-Lake theater and three drive-ins. That night, Kotto appeared onstage at the State-Lake for a "meet and greet" prior to the 7:50 showing. Newspaper ads billed the actor as "the powerful co-star of *Drum*" and touted, "Free Yaphet Kotto star-stills to the first 1,000 patrons." (The theater had 2,649 seats.) *Drum* was the city's biggest hit of the week, with a take of $212,000, and was Chicago's "bellringer" for the week, according to *Variety* where the grosses were called "sizzling," "monstrous," and "robust."

Gene Siskel, *Chicago Tribune*: "*....the sequel to *Mandingo*, which you may recall was last year's grotesque *Gone with the Wind*....As for *Drum* would you believe castration by biting? [sic]....Like *Mandingo*, *Drum* offers much white lust for black bodies, and it is a revolting revenge picture pitched to a black audience..."

By the end of August, *Drum* had already generated $1.2 million in American ticket sales after playing in only eighteen theaters. United Artists began shipping prints to the secondary markets. In September, while still playing at the Loews on Broadway, *Drum* opened in fifty-two theaters throughout New York and New Jersey. *Variety* reported that "a large drum thump was the only noise in the film week" when *Drum* was "a smash $21,500 in first crash" at one indoor theater and a drive-in in San Francisco.

Throughout the country, the *Mandingo* sequel continued to receive even worse reviews than its predecessor. *Independent Film Journal*: "The fact that *Drum*'s original distributor—Paramount—signed the film over to United Artists shortly before release, and the absence of De Laurentiis's name from the final screen and advertising credits, are probably hefty enough clues in themselves as to the film's inherent quality. All of which is amply confirmed in the viewing....*Drum*, while making a play for all of its predecessor's cash-generating components—miscegenation, sexual humiliation, brutal whippings

British lobby card: Hammond Maxwell (Warren Oates) and Sophie (Rainbeaux Smith)

and incendiary racial stereotypes—doesn't even have the bare technical virtues of *Mandingo*, and emerges as a ludicrously written, embarrassingly acted and surprisingly sludge-paced bore….Director Steve Carver, working from another snicker-provoking screenplay by Norman Wexler, can't even tell his story with a semblance of continuity, let alone motivate his actors into anything even resembling a performance. Gross overacting—or, in Norton's case, unsteady catatonic recitation—goes hand in hand with the overblown dialogue. Even the usually crisp and reliable photography of Lucien Ballard is absent here, leaving *Drum* with a visual style as murky and slapdash as its dramatic core."

Gary Arnold, *Washington Post*: "There were two schools of thought about *Mandingo*, last summer's hit potboiler….Some friends insisted the movie was so terrible it was irresistible, while others maintained it was so terrible it was acutely resistible. I was vaguely sorry to have missed *Mandingo*, but never sorry enough to make a special effort to catch it on the second or third run….The cleverest aspect of the production was evidently the advertising, a double take imitation of the poster art for *Gone with the Wind*, which could be appreciated without seeing the picture. The ads for *Drum*, the inevitable ignominious sequel, lack a similar humorous come-on, and while the film may be too cheap, tacky and goofy to fail, it can't be urged upon anyone you like with a clear conscience. Heavyweight prizefighter Ken Norton [is] a monolithic screen presence....John Colicos [is] required to sound French Creole and act viciously homosexual at the same time, a thick assignment played even thicker....Warren Oates struggles with the sort of Southern accent that begins and ends with locutions like 'convarsin' for 'conversing'....At best the plot meanders into a kind of plantation-house variety of bedroom farce....The shooting and burning in the climactic scenes obviously stir some customers up, and one hears shouts of 'Go, Mandingo!' If Dino De Laurentiis runs out of Kyle Onstott books, we can probably expect *Ragtime*, with Norton in the 'Coalhouse' Walker episodes, to become the sequel to *Drum*."

After Dark: "the sleazy sequel to the sleazy *Mandingo*. The movie celebrates what it ostensibly condemns (slavery and decadence in the antebellum South); and its few unambiguous expressions of disapproval are voiced for the wrong reasons. For instance, the villain, a New Orleans dandy, is loathsome not because he deals in slave trade and condones brutality but because he is deviously homosexual. With the exceptions that must be allowed for a sweeping generalization, the black half of the audience became caught up in the movie's considerable bloodlust and appeals for vengeance, while the white half giggled at the picture's camp-promoting crudity. About forty minutes of the film and the audience was all this reviewer could take."

Joan E. Vadeboncoeur, *Syracuse* (New Jersey) *Herald-Journal*: "When *Drum* proclaims itself a sequel to *Mandingo*, very little can be expected other than womanizing and violence. And that's what the movie serves up—in generous doses....Where *Mandingo* was self-conscious and pretentious, *Drum* drops almost all claims to a message and revels in its humor, albeit much of it raunchy."

Dick O'Leary, *Sentinel-Enterprise* (Fitchburg, Massachusetts): "Ken Norton was beaten, battered and boiled in his last movie, so you know he's ready for Ali....*Mandingo* should have prepared him for any indignity Ali could inflict in the ring. But did it prepare him for another movie? *Drum*, his latest film 'triumph,' is a sequel to *Mandingo*....All the action hits hard, below the belt, as the director and writers take over for Norton's more familiar referee and seconds. Granted the institution of slavery itself was often times sadistic, still the re-lay [sic] is not much more than an exploitative yellow brick road straight to the bank....You'll hate practically everybody. Hate oozes through the story and creates many uncomfortable confrontations....The film proceeds on a pseudo-historical path laced with brutality and low humor....Today, many 'historical' pictures are being ruined through sensationalism. Explicit and vulgar, they have limited audiences. The premise of *Mandingo* and *Drum* could be correct, but history can only be witnessed in the re-telling. If that telling disgusts, who will stay around for the lesson?"

Playboy: "This tacky sequel to *Mandingo* doesn't miss a trick that might turn a profit—from miscegenation, lesbianism and castration to interracial homosexual groping....A movie virtually certain to make millions—and every Ten Worst list this year."

The U.S. Catholic Church's Division for Film and Broadcasting: "[an] unsavory stew of sex and brutality that makes a ludicrous attempt to seem an earnest documentary on the evils of slavery." (Like *Mandingo*, *Drum* was given the Church's "condemned" rating, meaning the film was morally objectionable for Roman Catholics.)

In September, Yaphet Kotto appeared on the cover of *Jet*. The accompanying article described the climax of *Drum* and said, "The scene is hardly one of Hollywood's finest." *Drum*-related interviews with the other African American stars appeared in other black-themed magazines. An image of Vega and Mosley (with the latter's full-frontal nudity) from the truncated Havana-set opening was seen in *Playboy*'s annual "Sex in Cinema" retrospective.

With a final domestic take of $5.5 million, *Drum* was a definite (if modest) hit and ended up as number seventy-one on the 1976 list of top-grossing movies. (*Sparkle*, *Car Wash*, and *J. D.'s Revenge* were other popular black-themed movies released that year.) United Artists's other 1976 releases included the major hits *The Pink Panther Strikes Again*, *Gator*, *Carrie*, and *Network* and the phenomenon *Rocky*. It was the studio's most-profitable year up to that time. Besides the drive-in horror/chase smash *Race with the Devil* (1975), *Drum* was the only Warren Oates starring vehicle that made money in American theaters.

In the United Kingdom, *Drum* received an X (Adults Only) certificate and was released in September 1976 by EMI Film Distribution as part of a five-picture distribution deal that De Laurentiis signed with the company in late 1975. (EMI also handled *Drum*'s later distribution in Eastern Africa). In its first week of London release, *Drum* was the city's most popular movie with a $34,556 gross at five theaters. The British publishing house Pan re-released *Drum* in paperback with a still of Norton and Vega on the cover.

In England, where *Mandingo* had received some good reviews, *Drum* was panned. Verina Glaessner of *Monthly Film Bulletin*: "For anyone who has found Steve Carver's energetic career to date even sporadically promising, *Drum* comes as a major disappointment. Some of the blame for its frustrating diffuseness and general lack of thematic focus must be borne by Norman Wexler's clumsy script....In fact, the difference between Wexler's work on *Drum* and his script for *Mandingo* suggests that Carver was much less rigorous than Richard Fleischer in shaping and refining the material....Carver has failed to lend his haphazard selection of key scenes from the novel any kind of perspective....Carver's major tactical error is to elevate Kyle Onstott's deliberately titillating crudities to the status of voice-over narration in the astonishingly incoherent introductory sequence, thereby fatally altering the audience's relationship to what follows....The crude dialogue, and especially the cod French spoken by John Colicos's D'Marigny, simply becomes laughable....The sole convincing performance comes from Rainbeaux Smith as Hammond's willfully perverse daughter Sophie."

Carver says, "It was panned. The trades panned the story and the direction. My agent, Dino, and people at Paramount told me to expect [bad reviews] even prior to taking [the job]. I was prepared. There was nothing I could do and nothing I really cared about. It wasn't career-making. I remember a lot of shit and it was not good. I basically took two steps backwards and tried to stay out of the direct line of fire. The release of it was lukewarm. It just wasn't a picture that people applauded. I was never pleased with anything [about *Drum*]. I came in under very strenuous and weird circumstances. After you finish a picture, you usually fall deeply attached to it and you can't let go. It's like a baby. [After *Drum*,] I immediately said 'Let's get on to something else.' [Laughs] I had a great time with everybody, but [*Drum* was] not something that I nurtured."

In both of the Falconhurst films, Norton's performances were well-received by audiences. He recalls, "There was discussion about Ken Norton, the fighter who did the movies, and how he came off. I think they were surprised that I came off so well without any experience. There was no negativity about the movies or about me making the movies. It was all a big plus. For me, it was a learning experience and it helped me grow up a lot."

At the time, the boxer-actor said, "I'd rather be heavyweight champion than the biggest movie star of all time. There are lots of movie stars...But there is only one heavyweight champion and he's better known all around the world than anybody else....Dino De Laurentiis was trying to talk me out of fighting, telling me that I could act forever, but I just laughed at him. Boxing helps my acting. I've already been offered $1 million for two flicks, but I turned it down. I won't sign for two. One at a time. I'm still a boxer learning how to act. I don't know what I'm doing yet....Eventually, I want to become more involved in the cinema world than I am now."

Norton was planning to study acting in New York with the legendary Lee Strasberg, one of Pam Grier's former coaches. It was rumored that he would be featured in the upcoming biopic *The Greatest*, which was to star Muhammad Ali as himself. But Norton reported, "The chances are one-hundred to one against my accepting a role in it." (When *The Greatest* was released in 1977, it was without Norton as an actor or a character.)

Carver says, "Most of the people that did like [*Drum*] liked it because of Kenny. Certainly he could have gone on into other pictures."

On September 28, 1976, one month after *Drum* opened, Norton collected $1 million for stepping into the ring at Yankee Stadium to fight Ali for a third time. Before the fight, he told the *New York Times*, "The crowd'll be for Ali but I won't hear it. That's what you learn in acting—block out everything around you. When you're making a flick, you block out the cameramen, the watchers, everybody....As far as I'm concerned, acting has made me a better fighter, made me more of a thinking fighter. The discipline is the same—the research, the preparation, the delivery, the concentration." When asked what would happen if Ali damaged his movie star face, he joked, "I can always make horror movies." At the end of the match, Norton lost to Ali by a controversial decision.

Despite having two hit movies under his belt, Norton made the decision to focus on boxing. He explains, "I told my management that my head would get split too many ways. I wouldn't be thinking fully about boxing or fully about the movies. I'd be thinking of both. And I decided that movies took too much time [away] from boxing. So I decided not to do anymore. And at that time, the money [in movies] wasn't that big. I was making more money fighting."

Norton's opponents often taunted him about his movie roles. Ali raged, "I don't want no world champion making no X-rated movies!...We got too much trouble to have a world champion in a movie with his behind out on the screen!;" Larry Holmes bellowed, "Can you imagine me landing seventy or eighty punches...on Norton's beautiful face? The movie studios will be calling me up to make *Mandingo*, and they'll be using Norton for mummy pictures"; and Ron Slander boasted, "I saw that movie, *Mandingo*, where he was in a fight and he bit that guy's jugular vein. I'm gonna' bite his nose off in this one."

Like its predecessor, the *Mandingo* sequel was a big hit in foreign territories. In Italy, it was called *Drum: The Last Mandingo*. The German distributor renamed it *The Blazing Mandingo Slaves*. It became *Black Violence* in Mexico, where the ads gave top billing to Isela Vega and highlighted the native actress's naked form over the tag lines "An explosion of sex and rebellion!" and "Black house slave pleases white women!" In Australia, it was promoted as "The Big Movie Of '76."

Isela Vega and Ken Norton on the cover of the British paperback tie-in.

Carver explains, "*Drum* was illegally [distributed] for European purposes. That's called piracy. I remember it playing in Europe before it opened here and I was surprised. *Drum* was one of the biggest films in Mexico. It did have tremendous value abroad, more so than domestic." Like most American films, *Drum* took years to reach some foreign markets. It didn't hit the Republic of Kenya in Eastern Africa until July, 1983.

Mandingo director Richard Fleischer never heard from any fans of the Falconhurst book series, but the *Drum* director did. Carver says, "I got a lot of mail from [readers of the books saying] how much I screwed it up. I didn't write back and tell them that it was Dino De Laurentiis that screwed it up. They felt [that the movie] didn't do justice to the novel. A lot of [the letters] were from elderly or Southern people."

Drum's continuity as a sequel to the *Mandingo* movie is rather awkward and confusing. Sophie was ignored in the *Mandingo* movie, but she was Blanche and Hammond's child in the novel and was born prior to Blanche's affair with Mede. In the *Drum* movie, Hammond says, "I don't want no wife. I had me two. The first one, Sophie's mother, she was a pretty little thing, but meaner than a plowed-up snake. And the second one ran off with a melodrama actor."

Hammond in Wexler's script:

> Had me two. First one died of drinkin'
> somethin' she shouldn't. Second one run
> off with a Yankee peddler. Way I see it,
> white women is all whores. That's why I
> want a whore. So I won't think she ain't,
> and then discover she is.

Hammond in Sale's revision:

> Had me two. First one were pizen [poison]...
> all prettied outside and rotten inside. Second
> one run off with a Yankee peddler.

De Laurentiis owned the film rights to the next three popular novels in the Falconhurst saga. To set up a planned sequel, Norton's Drum character was still standing at the end of the film. In the book, the character was beheaded with a scythe and his head impaled and paraded on a pitchfork. Discussions about a *Drum* follow-up were held with the agents of Oates and Norton, but De Laurentiis canceled the project.

Carver says, "[De Laurentiis] could have made a third picture, a fourth picture [in the Falconhurst series]. He chose not to, smartly. He really got hit hard by the NAACP. Plus, *Drum* had a lot of problems through Paramount and then United Artists. A lot of it was politics. Those type of pictures created riots and bad, bad relationships."

The then-current projects that De Laurentiis was gladly putting his name on included Ingmar Bergman's $5 million *The Serpent's Egg* (1977) and the $24 million *King Kong* remake, which was one of the heaviest-hyped and highest-budgeted films up to that time and was expected to beat *Jaws* (1975) as the top moneymaker of all time. Paramount and De Laurentiis arranged "the biggest saturation of commercial product ever seen for an American film," which included the "King Kong Cocktail" from Jim Beam. A Paramount publicist boasted, "[*King Kong*] has already generated more audience excitement than any film since *Gone with the Wind*."

The Serpent's Egg ended up becoming one of Bergman's least-acclaimed films and *King Kong* had more production troubles than *Drum* before it was rushed into release for the 1976 Christmas season. *King Kong*'s reviews were as vicious as those for *Mandingo* and *Drum*, but it sold $37 million worth of tickets—enough to make it the third highest-grossing film of that year, but not enough to top the $120 million that *Jaws* had collected.

Notable later movies on De Laurentiis's endless filmography include *King of the Gypsies*, *Flash Gordon* (1980), *Ragtime*, *Conan the Barbarian* (1982), *Dune* (1984), *Blue Velvet* (1986), *Evil Dead II* (1987), *Breakdown* (1997), and *Hannibal* (2001). At the 2001 Academy Awards ceremony, the tireless, still-active producer was presented with the prestigious Irving Thalberg Memorial Award. As he received the statue, a montage of highlights from his films was shown. No clips from *Mandingo* or *Drum* were included.

Carver recalls, "I was supposed to do two other pictures [for De Laurentiis]. I had a three-picture deal with him. I remember him saying, 'We'll do more.' He was always working on projects. He commissioned the telephone book. [Laughs] Someone would come up to him and say an idea. Next thing you know, there's a writer there. [Laughs] He was the typical Hollywood mogul that got things done based on, 'Oh, you liked that? Let's do it!' It was spontaneous. I remember [once] at his house, Anthony Quinn was there, and they wanted to make a [movie] and he was writing on some paper in Italian and an hour later a writer shows up and starts writing it. [Laughs] He was funny."

"Dino became a very good friend. I socialized with him a lot after [*Drum*.] I was just out of step with Dino's thing. He gave me some projects that never got made. Dino had a 'family' and, basically, I was in that family for a while. Even now, I can call him up and still be family. But time goes by and I didn't get to do more for Dino. But now that you reminded me, maybe I'll do *Drum Part 2*. [Laughs] *Drum* definitely wasn't something that either of us were proud of due to the fact that it had so many problems as far as the morality and the ethics and all that crap. I do get residuals [from *Drum*]. DGA [Directors Guild of America] goes out and collects them—with a gun, I think. Dino's still making money off of it, even though he sold it and washed his hands."

The trade papers announced that Carver's follow-up to *Drum* would be *Freestyle*, an action film about skiing, to be released in 1977. It didn't happen. Carver continued as an action specialist, with later credits like *Fast Charlie, the Moonbeam Rider* (1979), *Steel* (1979), *River of Death* (1989), *The*

Wolves (1995), and two of Chuck Norris's best movies: *An Eye for an Eye* (1981) and *Lone Wolf McQuade* (1983). In recent years, he has concentrated on still photography.

Warren Oates continued to work non-stop and give fine performances before dying of a heart attack in 1982, shortly after completing Richard Fleischer's *Tough Enough*, which was released a year after his death. His later pictures included the De Laurentiis production *The Brink's Job* (1978), *1941* (1979) and *Stripes* (1981).

Isela Vega followed *Drum* with another period action film starring a black athlete: Fred Williamson's *Joshua* (a.k.a. *Black Rider*, 1976). The ageless beauty continued her career as one Mexico's top stars with occasional American projects like *Barbarosa* (1982) and *The Alamo: Thirteen Days to Glory* (TV, 1987) which reunited her with original *Drum* director Burt Kennedy.

Yaphet Kotto's long, impressive resume lists roles in *Blue Collar* (1978), *Alien* (1979), *Midnight Run* (1988), and the classic TV series *Homicide* (1993–1999).

After *Drum*, Brenda Sykes appeared in episodes of the TV comedies *The Love Boat* (1977 season) and *Good Times* (1978 season) before leaving acting. She married and divorced the spoken word artist/musician Gil Scott-Heron.

Pam Grier continued to work constantly as a supporting actor in major films like *Greased Lightning* (1977), *Fort Apache The Bronx* (1981), *Tough Enough*, *Something Wicked This Way Comes* (1983) and *Above the Law* (1988) and on TV with recurring roles on *Miami Vice* (1985 and 1990 season) and *Crime Story* (1986 and 1988 seasons). Longtime Grier fan Quentin Tarentino (*Pulp Fiction*, 1994) cast her in the title role of his 1997 film *Jackie Brown*, which led to a revived career as a popular character actress. Today, she doesn't discuss *Drum* or her other early films.

Among Paula Kelly's later credits were *Jo Jo Dancer, Your Life Is Calling* (1986), the TV series *Night Court* (1984 season), and the TV movie *Uncle Tom's Cabin* (1987). The Emmy nominee is also a choreographer and cabaret performer.

Fiona Lewis's later movies included *Tintorera* (1977), with *Mandingo* star Susan George, *The Fury* (1978), and *Innerspace* (1987).

Lillian Hayman left *One Life to Live* in 1986 after spending eighteen years on the soap opera. She passed away in 1994.

John Colicos was in movies like *The Postman Always Rings Twice* (1981) and played memorable regular villains on TV's *Battlestar Galactic* (1978–1979) and *Star Trek: Deep Space Nine* (1994, 1995, 1998 seasons). He died in 2000.

Rainbeaux Smith followed *Drum* with the title role in the soft-core musical *Cinderella* (1977), featured roles in *Slumber Party '57* (1977) and *Laserblast* (1978), and bits in movies like *The Choirboys, Up in Smoke* (1978), *Melvin and Howard* (1980), and *Vice Squad* (1982). Tragically, her drug and alcohol problems ultimately led to prostitution, living on the streets, a prison term, and finally, death by hepatitis in 2002 at age forty-seven. She is fondly-remembered as one of the most-beloved cult movie stars of the 1970s.

Alain Patrick did more television and features including (under the name Alain Chappuis) the Chuck Norris vehicle *The Octagon* (1980).

John Vernon and Roger E. Mosley had their roles cut out of *Drum*, but they both continued their long careers. Vernon appeared in *National Lampoon's Animal House* (1978) and many other movies before his death in 2005. Mosley worked with Carver again on *Steel* and gained TV fame as a regular on *Magnum, P.I.* (1980–1988).

Lucien Ballard shot two more features before retiring at age seventy. He died in 1988.

Ken Norton was named the WBC Heavyweight Champion in 1978 and continued to box and collect hefty paychecks until his retirement from the sport in 1981. During his acting hiatus, his two starring roles were still being enjoyed by movie fans. In 1981 Joseph Brenner Associates, Inc. re-released *Drum* to U. S. drive-ins and grindhouses on a double bill—with *Sacrifice!*, a 1972 Italian jungle/cannibal shocker (a.k.a. *Il Paese del sesso selvaggio* and *Man from Deep River*)—and *Mandingo* was shown in 1982 on the pay-TV cable channel Home Box Office.

Norton explains, "When I went back to fighting, I had totally forgotten the movies. At the end of my fight career, I started acting school. You know Milton Katselas? He's an acting instructor in Beverly Hills. I started going to his class. He's a good instructor and I enjoyed the therapy of going to the class whether I used it or not. It was good for me. It was good therapy." The retired boxer began working in front of the cameras again and had guest roles in TV shows including *The A-Team* (1983 season) and *Knight Rider* (1986 season) and in the comedy feature *Delta Pi* (a.k.a. *Mugsy's Girls*, 1985) with Ruth Gordon. Ten years after *Drum*, he reunited with Carver for the made-for-TV action movie *Oceans of Fire* (1986) where he had a good supporting role alongside Billy Dee Williams, David Carradine, Lyle Alzado, and fellow boxer Ray "Boom Boom" Mancini.

Norton explains, "I went [to acting class for] about three or four years before I got hurt. I had a real bad car accident in '86." On February 23 of that year, Norton got into his limited edition 1978 Clenet Excalibur to visit Carver and watch some of the *Oceans of Fire* rough cut. On the way, the Clenet hit a curb and a tree before flipping upside down and trapping Norton. He spent two years in a wheelchair and had to undergo extensive physical therapy before he could walk again.

Today, Norton works out regularly, still looks great, and has kept busy as a fight trainer and an entrepreneur. In 2000 his autobiography, *Going the Distance,* came out. Norton is an inductee in the International Boxing Hall of Fame and his likeness has been used on several popular video boxing games. His frequent appearances at sports conventions and autograph shows attract numerous boxing fans but not many movie buffs. "It happened once," he recalls. "A man brought a picture of Mede. I asked, 'Where'd you find that?' [Imitates fan's voice] 'Oh, I like that movie!'"

Norton recently returned to acting with a good featured role in *The Man Who Came Back* (2008), a straight-to-DVD Western with Eric Braedon and Armand Assante. "I've come to realize through my recovery that it's mind over matter," he says. "What the mind can conceive, the body can achieve. I feel good. My outlook on life is: Find a challenge to keep you going. And once I complete one thing, I try something else."

Drum was released on VHS and Beta to the booming home video market in 1986 by Vestron Video, one of the then-top players in the field. Vestron's box cover gave an incorrect running time of eighty-nine minutes, but the tapes contained the complete 100-minute theatrical cut. *Drum* videotapes were available in other countries, including England, where it was released on the PAL format by Guild Home Video.

In the early 2000s, DVDs of *Drum* started getting released in several non-American territories. In England, Castle Home Video released a dreadful-quality version (apparently sourced from videotape) in 2001. Prior to the availability of home DVD burners and the official DVD releases, ex-rental VHS copies of *Drum* would fetch high prices on internet auction sites. (Longer versions of *Drum* have not appeared officially or as bootlegs.)

Like *Mandingo*, *Drum* has never been seen on network or syndicated television in America. The complete theatrical version of *Drum* was often shown on late-night slots of pay-TV and cable channels like Cinemax. More recently, the high-definition digital channel MGM-HD has shown the film.[3]

Looking back, Carver has mixed feelings about *Drum*: "The making of the picture was fun and a challenge. It was an achievement to get it done and to get it out there. [Today,] it still has that flavor of being racist and being a thing that is unpleasant. People have always liked and hated facets about it and always wanted to talk to me about it. If somebody asked me, 'Name two of your films with a lot of black actors in it,' I wouldn't name that one. [Laughs]"

This Japanese poster tried to connect Drum with the international best seller Roots.

Notes:

1 In the book *Dino: The Life and Films of Dino De Laurentiis*, De Laurentiis explained that his distribution deal with Paramount for *The Valachi Papers* (1972) (based on a true story about a notorious mob informer) was cancelled when the studio received a bomb threat from the Mafia. Serpe set up a meeting between De Laurentiis and a Miami-based boss referred to in the book as "Jimmy Blue Eyes," who assured the producer that he would have no further trouble. Columbia Pictures picked up American rights to *The Valachi Papers* and successfully distributed it without incident. (Some industry insiders suggested that Paramount dropped *The Valachi Papers* because it was too similar to the studio's *The Godfather*, released the same year.)

2 *Mandingo* wasn't the only 1975 film that had embarrassed Paramount because of racial content. The studio's *Coonskin* was a live action-

animated satire featuring Uncle Remus-like fables set in a New York ghetto. Loaded with profanity, violence, and repulsive, mostly-black characters, *Coonskin* was the creation of white filmmaker Ralph Bakshi, best known for the acclaimed, X-rated animated hits *Fritz the Cat* (1972) and *Heavy Traffic* (1973).

After a pre-release screening, Congress for Racial Equality (CORE) officer Elaine Parker complained that *Coonskin* "depicts blacks as slaves, hustlers and whores. It is a racist film to me and very insulting." *Coonskin*'s characters were voiced by notable black artists, including musician Barry White, playwright Charles Gordone, and actor Scatman Crothers. Gene Garvin, another CORE officer, said, "We consider the black actors who appeared in this film as traitors to their race." Members of CORE were soon picketing the Gulf + Western offices in New York. CORE representative Charles Cook told the press, "We had several discussions with the people from Paramount and we were able to reach an agreement....We call it self-defense, not censorship. We're not going to give these filmmakers license to exploit black people."

Albert S. Ruddy, producer of *Coonskin* (as well as Paramount's all-time biggest hit, *The Godfather*) told the *New York Times*, "There was enormous pressure from CORE. You have to remember that Paramount is only one small branch of a huge conglomerate—Gulf and Western. In fact, people don't realize it, but Paramount Pictures represents only about three or four percent of the total income of Gulf and Western. The company is very concerned about its public image and maintaining a good relationship with minority groups."

The film's title was one of CORE's biggest complaints. An angry Bakshi complained, "Paramount wanted the title changed to *Coonskin*; they thought it was catchier. That was before they decided not to release the movie....*Coonskin* is a tough, angry film, but it's not racist. I love black people. I love the guys I grew up with." (The filmmaker was raised in Brooklyn, New York.)

Paramount dropped *Coonskin* and an altered version of the film was unsuccessfully distributed by Bryanston Pictures, a shady, struggling, short-lived outfit best-known for releasing *The Texas Chain Saw Massacre* (1974). Protestors set off a smoke bomb during a screening at a New York cinema.

One African American supporter of *Coonskin* was Eddie Smith, an executive board member of the Hollywood branch of the NAACP as well as the stunt coordinator for *Drum*. After arranging a *Coonskin* screening for the NAACP and the Black Stuntman's Association, Smith said, "We thought the movie was very good. It is not a putdown of blacks. It is very positive."

Like *Mandingo*, *Coonskin* (reissued as *Bustin' Out* and *Street Fight*) developed a cult following among some African Americans. Fans of Bakshi's film included Richard Pryor and filmmaker Spike Lee (*Do the Right Thing*, 1989).

3 All VHS, DVD, and cable/pay-TV presentations of *Drum* have been full-frame and open matte. The version shown on Cinemax revealed a sliver of more picture information at the top of the screen. (At one point during the first Falconhurst dinner scene, a camera flag is visible.) The MGM-HD presentation was in the original theatrical aspect ratio.

Chapter 7: Slavesploitation and Spaghetti Mandingos: Additional Slavery-Themed Films from the Falconhurst Era

Onkel Toms Huette/Uncle Tom's Cabin (1965)

Onkel Toms Huette/Uncle Tom's Cabin is a lavish, multi-million dollar, widescreen, stereophonic, epic film adaptation of the classic novel. The movie is almost completely forgotten and unavailable now, but in its day it was a huge hit and was seen by millions of moviegoers throughout the world—including in the United States.

Harriet Beecher Stowe, a matronly abolitionist from Connecticut, wrote her anti-slavery protest saga *Uncle Tom's Cabin (or Life Among the Lowly)* after receiving "visions" of abused blacks and hearing tales from escaped slaves. First published in 1852, the episodic, syrupy, irresistible melodrama became an immediate international bestseller, was translated into forty-two languages, and became the second best-selling book of the nineteenth century—after the Bible. But not everybody appreciated the exposé —diehard abolitionists thought the book was too tame and one enraged Southern reader sent Stowe a severed black human ear.

The novel's vivid characters became some of the best-known in American literature: Uncle Tom, the noble, loyal, God-fearing slave; Little Eva, the angelic, blonde white child; Topsy, the nappy-headed, mischievous slave girl; Eliza, the gorgeous biracial slave desired by lecherous white men; and Simon Legree, the drunken, sadistic, racist, whip-cracking plantation lord.

Millions more people were exposed to Stowe's story when numerous unauthorized stage versions began playing throughout the world. These ubiquitous, loosely-adapted, often comedic live shows starring droopy-mustached Legrees and blackfaced whites were popular well into the twentieth century.

One of the first narrative motion pictures ever made was Edwin S. Porter's 1903 adaptation of *Uncle Tom's Cabin* for the Thomas Edison Company. The 14-minute silent film recorded one of the more elaborate stage versions featuring an energetic, charming troupe. Later that year, Edison rival Sigmund Lubin released his (now-lost) hastily-produced cash-in with a lower-rent touring cast. Several later silent shorts were produced, but Uncle Tom wasn't played by a black actor until Sam Lucas starred in the admirable 1914 version, which made good use of actual locations.

In 1927 Universal Pictures spent $2 million to produce an outstanding, action-packed (i.e. unfaithful), feature-length spectacle directed by Harry Pollard (who had "blacked up" to play Uncle Tom in a 1913 version). African American James B. Lowe was Uncle Tom. Also featured were blackfaced whites and some real African Americans—including a 104-year-old former slave.

Hollywood never produced another *Uncle Tom's Cabin* feature, but over the next two decades vignettes with Stowe's characters would appear in movies starring Judy Garland, Betty Grable, June Haver, Frank Morgan, Joe Cobb (the fat white boy of "Our Gang"), and Mickey Mouse—each in blackface. A sumptuous, faithful adaptation of the book with an all-star cast (none in blackface) was in development at Metro-Goldwyn-Mayer in 1946 until an NAACP protest caused the studio to reconsider. In 1958 Universal Pictures' 1927 silent version was a surprise hit when a newly-narrated and scored (and often-pirated) edition played small-town theaters and drive-ins.

By the early 1960s, Stowe's novel was mostly ignored by American literary scholars and teachers and the plays were never revived and long forgotten. But throughout Europe and Eurasia, *Uncle Tom's Cabin* was a constantly read, highly-regarded classic, and producer Artur Brauner saw it as an ideal source for a new, epic film.

Brauner, a Polish-born, Berlin-based producer with dozens of credits, raised the financing for *Onkel Toms Huette* from sources in West Germany, France, Italy, and Yugoslavia. It was to be the first version of the book with sound and color and the first to have all of the slave roles played by actual blacks. Sixty-one-year-old Geza von Radvany, best known for the 1949 children's film *Somewhere in Europe*, was hired to direct. The acclaimed Hungarian director had made films throughout Europe and was operating out of Germany at the time.

The *Onkel Toms Huette* script was a loose adaptation of the episodic book and was written by von Radvany with Fred Denger (author of some German Westerns of the 1960s and an entry in the notorious *Schulmadchen-Report/*

Schoolgirl Report softcore series of the 1970s). Augustine St. Clare, the kindly plantation owner, was renamed "Pierre" and was rewritten to have more drama—including adulterous affairs with two new female characters. Simon Legree, the villain for only the last fourth of the book, was merged with Mr. Haley (Stowe's other evil slave trader) to become the antagonist for the entire film. Legree is even more loathsome than in the novel: He lusts after slave girl Eliza, repeatedly rapes Cassy, fatally shoots St. Clare, and frames and hangs an innocent black man for the murder. (In the book, St. Clare was knifed to death while trying to stop a drunken brawl.) Topsy became a well-groomed adolescent boy slave, instead of the impish, nattily-clad little black girl of the book. (Topsy-like kids with nappy pigtails and sack dresses were seen in the background.) To add musical interludes, Uncle Tom became a singer of classic "Negro spirituals." New action sequences were created featuring a slave-eating alligator; a comic barroom fight; and a climactic slave revolt with a burning plantation, flooded cotton fields, and a shootout between Legree's men and some slave-aiding Catholic monks.

The dreary, bare tree-infested landscapes of Yugoslavia stood in for the American South when *Onkel Toms Huette* was shot in 1964 on a budget comparable to three-million American dollars. The exterior set used for the town's "Independance [sic] Day" celebration can be seen in numerous European Westerns of the 1960s and 70s.

Leading the marketable cast as St. Clare was top-billed O. W. Fischer (*Helden*, 1958), at the time one of the more popular and well-paid stars of German cinema. Hungarian actor Herbert Lom (*A Shot in the Dark*, 1964) played Simon Legree, wearing a dapper wardrobe (unlike the slovenly attire described in the book) as well as a large, unconvincing facial scar. Uncle Tom was played by John Kitzmiller (*Dr. No*, 1962), a former American soldier who stayed in Italy after World War II and became a European film star. He died shortly after completing his Uncle Tom role. Slave girl Cassy was played by lovely African American singer Olive Moorefield (*Monpti*, 1957), who had starred on Broadway before launching a successful stage and recording career in Germany. George Goodman, another black American relocated to Europe, appeared onscreen as the henchman Sambo, and provided the baritone singing voice that Kitzmiller lip-synched to. In cameo roles were Italian sex goddess Eleonora Rossi Drago (*Le Amiche*, 1955), popular French singer Juliette Greco, and the mesmerizing French sexpot Mylene Decongest (*Fantomas*, 1964).

To give *Onkel Toms Huette* the look of an American-made blockbuster, the financiers decided to use a widescreen process called MCS 70-Superpanorama.

Norwegian technician Jan Jacobsen had designed the system in the late 1950s for Modern Cinema Systems (MCS), a partnership of European showmen. Jacobsen's surprisingly compact and mobile 65mm cameras were ideal for exterior use and were first used on *Flying Clipper* (a.k.a. *Mediterranean Holiday*), a feature-length travelogue that was blown up to 70mm and played worldwide in 1962. Prior to *Onkel Toms Hutte*, MCS 70-Superpanorama was used for several other films including the German Western *Old Shatterhand* (1964) and the opening shot of *The Sound of Music* (1965).

Flying Clipper veteran Heinz Hölscher shot the *Onkel Toms Hutte* exteriors with the existing MCS-70 cameras while Jacobsen created two new units specifically for the studio interiors. The advanced new cameras were "blimped" (i.e. muffled to silence the grinding motor), which meant nothing to the *Onkel Toms Hutte* crew since the film was shot without sync sound. Jacobsen's many later achievements included creating the first IMAX camera in 1969. (When Modern Cinema Systems went out of business around 1970, one of the Superpanorama field cameras ended up being used for NASA technical films.)

The completed *Onkel Toms Huette* is a well-mounted, entertaining show with an effective cast, attractive costumes, nice compositions, impressive scenes like the recreation of Eliza's famous escape on floating ice, and embarrassing moments like the garden sequence with Uncle Tom and Little Eva, which plays cornier than the similar vignettes in the silent versions. The unfortunate lack of a death scene for the reprehensible Legree gives the film a frustrating, unsatisfying conclusion.

On April 14, 1965 the film was premiered in 70mm with a six-track stereo soundtrack on the enormous curbed screen at the Matthäser-Palast in Munich, Germany. The epic ran 170 minutes and was presented with an intermission. It was then released throughout Europe and was a box-office hit in much of the world. (Italian prints were cut to 141 minutes; French prints ran 125 minutes.)

A *Variety* reviewer who saw the Munich screening: "Europeans may take this version of *Uncle Tom's Cabin* as it stands, which is full of anachronisms and liberties with the Harriet Beecher Stowe hardy perennial melodrama. But for playoff in the U.S. itself, there must be the wonder about audience reaction....Coproduction retains nominal Dixie locale but the tone of the production is closer to the 'westerns' which currently fascinate German film showman....Serbian farm workers [are not] very convincing in their switch from redskins to blackface. They may just possibly push American audiences out of their cottonpicking minds with unintended amusement....Director Von Radvany could not cope with the mass agitation and fighting scenes. Chases and barroom brawls come off, at best, as stereotypes from some American Western."

An English-dubbed print—with a voice cast that included American stars Jeffrey Hunter (*The Searchers*, 1956) and (a non-singing) Ella Fitzgerald, both of whom were working in Europe at the time—was shown to major studio reps and independent distributors at screenings in New York and Los Angeles.

Independent producer-distributor David F. Friedman (*Blood Feast*, 1963) recalled in his memoirs: "I screened it—it looked almost as good as *Gone with the Wind*. It had been dubbed into what the Italians thought passed as English. Instead of using American voices, the producers had employed some of their fellow nationals, with limited abilities in the King's English, to deliver the lines of two or three of the principal characters....There were another half-dozen independent film distributors in the screening room. We were holding our sides in laughter....I thought this 'Uncla Tomsa Cabin' could be released with the fractured English sound track intact, and played for high camp. But the asking price for the U.S. distribution rights to the film was too steep to gamble on a gimmick. I, along with my fellow distributors, passed....Everyone in the trade who saw it got a laugh and walked out, until one day, a retired exploitation-film living legend, Kroger Babb, attended a showing and made a deal."

Kroger Babb was a successful showman and promoter best-known for the "unwed mother" shocker *Mom and Dad* (1944)—which featured graphic, full-color footage of a real-life child birth—and the marijuana expose *The Devil's Weed* (1949). Babb would use aggressive marketing tactics and garish publicity campaigns to turn low-budget, obscure movies into blockbuster hits at theaters and drive-ins in small towns. In early 1968, after ten years of semi-retirement as an exploitation consultant, Babb returned to the picture business in full force after seeing *Onkel Toms Huette/Uncle Tom's Cabin*.

Sam Sherman, the president of Independent-International Pictures (responsible for drive-in hits like 1969's *Satan's Sadists* and 1971's *Dracula vs. Frankenstein*), explains, "The U.S. rights were sold outright, in perpetuity, to Kroger Babb. He paid a lot of money for the U.S. rights. Babb thought this picture would be very successful. Nobody believed him. He had been inactive for awhile, so he started a new company called KBA—Kroger Babb and Associates. He had some other, rather meaningless, pictures from KBA, but the big one was *Uncle Tom's Cabin*."

Friedman recalled, "I knew Babb had been having IRS problems, and where he got the front money to pay the Italians I never knew, or asked.... He dubbed the picture, using good, southern-accented dramatic voices, and created a campaign proving that old showmen never die."

Babb and editor Will Williams cut the film down to 118 minutes, deleting almost an hour including a modern-day prologue with an aerial view of New

York City and the Statue of Liberty; a title sequence with the main credits revealed on a leather-bound book; a recreation of Lincoln's assassination; at least one musical number; and a closing credit sequence with the singing face of Eartha Kitt superimposed over the waters of contemporary New York. The classic Jerome Kern/Oscar Hammerstein II show tune "Ol' Man River" was cut from the soundtrack for copyright reasons. Babb's newly-created prologue featured images from the fire-filled climax accompanied by music from a stock library. The now-abbreviated ending was dubbed with inane philosophical narration. ("Only God understands these United States...")

Babb spent three months with a major ad agency preparing the promotion, including an epic trailer that ran four minutes. A gorgeous, full-color painting was created for the key art. Unfortunately, most of the artwork's impact was lost when the posters were cheaply printed in only two colors. "Kroger Babb Presents" was the only credit that appeared on the posters. Director Geza von Radvany was the lone European crew member billed on screen.

Flyer for 1969 American release.

Babb's revision of *Uncle Tom's Cabin* and his ad campaign had a test run in late June, 1968 at the Park-Aire Drive-In in Santa Maria, California. "We always test our films and campaigns in the smaller situations," the showman explained.

Uncle Tom's Cabin officially opened in the States on New Year's Day, 1969 in Savannah, Georgia. Weeks before, the area was saturated with six different TV ads, twenty radio spots, and garish printed flyers loaded with Babb's customary hyperbole: "A Great Timeless Classic In The Tradition Of *Gone With the Wind*!" "You'll Scream, Laugh and Sing!" "The Story of Blacks & Whites in Color!" "As Big As Our Nation!" "It Explains What No Teacher Can!" "Hear Uncle Tom Sing Those Haunting Negro Spirituals!" "See The Bull-Whipping of Black Females!" "See The Negro Slaves Whipped/Chained!" "See The Hanging Of Innocent Andy!" "See Harris Dragged Behind A Horse!" "See The Big 'Gaitor [sic] Swallow Napoleon!"

The posters boasted: "Cast of Thousands—33 International Stars!," but no specific actors were listed, since none of the names meant anything to American moviegoers. Also promised was a "Panorama Screen" process, but Babb's prints were made from a 35mm reduction negative, and the original 2.20:1 image was considerably cropped to 2.35:l. (The film was never shown in 70mm in the United States.)

Although the film contained some strong violence and a few mildly risqué moments between Simon Legree and his slave concubine Cassy, it received a G rating in 1969 from the newly-created MPAA rating system.

Boxoffice: "this lavish European-made offering...is both exciting and historically enlightening. Approached with the artistry of Kroger Babb's exploitation ideas, the film can pull record grosses, as was done in its American premiere in Savannah, Georgia....[S]cenic highlights are numerous."

By mid-March 1969, *Uncle Tom's Cabin* was booked to play in over 400 theaters in twenty-two states and the laboratory was having trouble keeping up with KBA's increasing orders for more prints. The KBA headquarters in Hollywood hired more employees and added two more offices to handle the distribution and promotion of the picture. Babb proudly told *Boxoffice* that the film was "breaking records in both large and small cities," including the Albany Theatre in Albany, Georgia and the elegant Plaza Theatre in El Paso, Texas. Some of the bigger indoor houses received prints in four-track (optical) stereo. Babb's earlier, overly-hyped movies often left the audience feeling ripped-off, but most viewers of *Uncle Tom's Cabin* were highly entertained, titillated, and sometimes even moved by the film, and many would fondly remember it even decades later.

Mercury Records released an *Uncle Tom's Cabin* vinyl soundtrack, featuring the bizarre score by German composer/jazz artist Peter Thomas and the spirituals as well as the Eartha Kitt performance not heard in American film prints. (The music had already been successfully released in several European countries on vinyl records that are now highly-sought by collectors.)

Sherman says, "[Babb] went out with salesmen around the country and he pushed this picture. It was a very big success, mainly in the South. He did big, big money. He played less than a third of the country, but they made an enormous sum of money, like $25 million on an investment of maybe a quarter of a million dollars."

In an attempt to get West Coast bookings, Babb set up a disastrous test screening at an urban California theater. "There was a major race riot," Sherman recalls. "And as a result, they wouldn't play it on the West Coast at all. That was the first and last date there. It never played the West Coast, but it continued to play [other areas] for quite some time after that."

In February of 1971 *Uncle Tom's Cabin* played a huge theater in Chicago, with newspaper ads offering half-price tickets "for student and youth groups" through mail order. ("Minimum of 20 for discount to apply.")

Gene Siskel, Chicago *Tribune*: "The G-rated film, with its monotone and out-of-synchronization sound track, is being advertised as if it were a violent skin flick. No such luck. It is a dry and dreary rendering of the archetypal good slave-bad owner theme that manages to keep one's interest by holding out the promise that someone is going to get whupped [sic] by someone else who is going to get his comeuppance. The large audiences prove that black people, like everyone else, enjoy watching stereotypes—even their own."

The same month, the film was at the Fox Theatre in Detroit, where the bottom of the double bill was Babb's release *Walk the Walk* (1971), a low-budget California-shot oddity about a black heroin addict. Over the next year, Babb ended up wasting a good chunk of his hefty profits from *Uncle Tom's Cabin* on his heavy promotion for *Walk the Walk*, which became the showman's last release and one of his few flops.

In November 1975, a promoter named Charles E. Johnson re-released one of Babb's *Uncle Tom's Cabin* prints in a downtown Chicago theater under the new title *Cassy*. For his newspaper ads, Johnson reused Babb's original key art, put his own name over the new title, and added an unofficial PG symbol and the awkward new tag line "Blacks Fought Back With Guns In Mandingo Country," in a feeble attempt to cash in on *Mandingo*, which had enjoyed a long Chicago run several months earlier.

The next year, *Uncle Tom's Cabin* was in the hands of Sam Sherman's Independent-International. "I knew Kroger because I corresponded with him and I was on his subscriber list," Sherman says. "KBA issued a newsletter about exploitation and how to sell films. It was a college course in distribution. It was great. Producer Alex Gordon, a mutual friend, was very close to Kroger and they asked us if we were interested in reissuing *Uncle Tom's Cabin*. Alex pushed this. He said, 'Sam, why don't you take this and put it out and do something.' It didn't strike me as something that I was interested in. I was mainly in other films—horror and exploitation. But my partner, Dan Kennis, felt that this was a very strong picture and he checked with our sub-distributors throughout the South and they said, 'Yeah, the picture was never reissued, it could do big business.' [The film had not played on television.] Based on its big history, Kroger wanted some money up front. I said, 'Kroger, I think [*Uncle Tom's Cabin*] is out-of-date. *Mandingo* and *Drum* were *Uncle Tom's Cabin*-type pictures, but much rougher. You can't come back with something that's G-rated. It's too tame.'"

To make the film more marketable to post-*Mandingo* audiences, *Uncle Tom's Cabin* became one of Independent-International's notorious "patch-jobs," where house director Al Adamson would shoot new footage and add it to an existing movie to create a "new" release. (Sherman and Adamson's "patch-jobs" included *Horror of the Blood Monsters* (1970) and *Dracula vs. Frankenstein*.) Sherman explains, "I talked to our third partner, Al Adamson, who was our head of production. Kroger screened a print for Al, who said he could do something with this. Dan Kennis was anxious to get moving and get the film out into the marketplace. He didn't want us stalling around with a typical Sam Sherman project that took a long time to reach conclusion. Al wrote the script for [the new sequences] handwritten, and said, 'Have one of the secretaries type it.' [Laughs] He picked [the story] up where the slave, Napoleon, jumped off the ship."

In the original version, Napoleon jumped off the riverboat and was munched on by a (laughably-fake) alligator. In Adamson's additions, the slave swims ashore and has consensual softcore sex with a blonde woman (with anachronistic tan lines) before being captured, beaten, anally raped, and covered with boiling tar by three of Legree's drooling, foul-mouthed white henchmen. ("Want us to cut his balls off?" "This mother-fucking cunt-eater's gonna pay!" "I just hope you don't catch nothing from this nigger." "Couldn't be nothing worse than we got from those sheep!" Napoleon retorts with: "Tell Legree to fuck himself!")

Also added was a prologue with the redneck trio raping a slave girl in front of her father and a climax where the henchmen are attacked by three escaped slaves who proceed to castrate one of the white men before hanging all three. ("Now y'all gonna get a taste of black justice!" screams one of the slaves.) The slave girl was played by Marilyn Joi, a gorgeous model and actress (*Hammer*, 1972; *Ilsa, Harem Keeper of the Oil Sheiks*, 1976; *Kentucky Fried Movie*, 1977) who had appeared in several other Independent-International movies as well as in the deleted first act of *Drum*.

Sherman says, "A lot of it was shot in Riverside, California. Al found a place that had trees that looked like the South. Al started shooting and he was shooting some pretty good stuff. I said, 'I'm not ready to finish this yet. I want to add some more.' We played around with this until we had about half the movie in new footage. We shot fifty new minutes and then we took fifty minutes out of the old picture. European pictures, in those years, were always shot without a [sound] track, and then they would dub them for different countries. Who knows who was speaking what before [*Onkel Toms Huette*] got dubbed into English. I told Al that [the new footage] won't match if we shot direct sound. So we dubbed the new footage to match the rest of the picture." Sherman recalls that Adamson shot the new material in "probably three weeks, a week at a time" and that the cost of the alterations was "under $100,000. It wasn't much."

"Well, all of this playing around [took] a considerable length of time," Sherman says. "Dan Kennis was very upset about it as was Harry Clark of Clark Films Releasing in Jacksonville, [Florida,] who was very interested in getting this thing out. Then, around this time, *Roots* came on television and everybody said, 'Well, this is one time you've really fouled up. You've played with this and dragged it out. Now a better thing has been on TV.' Then I began to think, 'Well, we were scooped by *Roots*, let's take advantage of it. So I came up with the campaign: 'Now, all the sensual violence and passions *Roots* couldn't show on TV!' We did a big, fancy campaign with radio and TV spots and trailers and played it up as an all-new version, because we had changed it enough to say that. To save money, we decided that we would print just the new footage and cut it into as many old prints as we could. An old print [from the 1969 release] was matched to the new version and the new footage was printed and cut in."

The shoddy production values, cheap costumes, softcore sex, brutal violence and over-the-top profanity of Adamson's footage clash horribly with the sumptuous images of the original version. Independent-International's ham-fisted removal of scenes from the original prints made mincemeat of the narrative—the essential characters St. Clare and his daughter Little Eva simply disappear from the story after a few vignettes (Adamson cut the little girl's famous death bed scene), and other characters were lost completely.

One-sheet for 1977 release of revised version.

The Independent-International trailer and pressbook, with images from the old and new footage, screamed: "Before *Mandingo* and *Drum* there was *Uncle Tom's Cabin*;" "The REAL Story of how it all happened—The SLAVES, the MASTERS, the LOVERS!;" and "Shocking Savage Version—Never Shown Before!" "Harriet Beecher Stowe's immortal *Uncle Tom's Cabin*" was still promoted as the source, but it's doubtful that any high school English classes took a movie field trip to see this release. The new posters and newspaper ads once again touted "33 International Stars," but except for Herbert Lom,

John Kitzmiller, and Olive Moorefield, the huge original cast was not even listed in the new screen credits. Geza von Radvany wasn't billed as the director this time (nor was Al Adamson), but the movie was still called "A Kroger Babb Presentation."

In March 1977, eight years after Babb had released *Uncle Tom's Cabin*, Independent-International shipped their new R-rated, 108-minute revision. Sherman recalls, "The picture opened and did very good business. It went through the roof. We played it all through the areas that [Babb] had been successful with it. It did well in Memphis territory."

Boxoffice: "Bound to clean up in the wake of *Roots* is a spliced-up version of that old perennial....[Independent-International] added enough nudity, language and violence to earn an R....[The film] has been enlivened by the new footage, directed by Al Adamson, with two good performances from Mary Ann Jensen and Prentiss Moulden, as a lonely white woman and a wounded slave who have a brief affair....One of Independent-International's most exploitable offerings."

Independent-International was also able to play the film beyond Southern territories. On April 27, the film opened at four Washington, DC theaters for a three-week run and grossed $59,263. Sherman says, "We played up in some of those areas. When we went up to Chicago, we opened in one theater—the Oriental—and we did, in one week, a $55,000 gross. The biggest one-week Independent-International gross, ever." (During a June 4, 1978 screening at the Oriental, over two thousand viewers had to miss most of the movie when the building caught fire.)

Sherman says, "It did very well and the question is 'Would it have done just as well if we hadn't re-shot it?' I don't have the answer to that. Our version did play Los Angeles. It didn't mean much out there. But the funny thing was, the L.A. *Times* reviewed it, and the reviewer singled out the love making scene with the white schoolteacher and the black slave as being 'typical European.' [Laughs] He never caught the fact that we re-shot the picture. I don't know if it ever played in New York. There were other areas that never played it. The picture played reasonably well, but it always had a stigma about it. The term 'Uncle Tom' took on a secondary meaning of a subservient black person. [Our version] was pretty rough stuff—those people having sex with the slave [and] tarring him. It was strong in many ways that even *Mandingo* and *Drum* weren't." (Gruesome photos from the tarring sequence were used in the pressbook.)

Since Independent-International did not hold the foreign distribution rights to *Onkel Toms Huette*, their R-rated version was only released to one other country. "We did license our version to Australia," Sherman says. "We had to go back to the German company that represented the film and we had to buy the rights for Australia in order to deliver the film to Australia." Down under, the film was oddly retitled *Cry Sweet Revenge.*

At the end of the 1970s, Independent-International re-released their R-rated *Uncle Tom's Cabin* prints under the title *White Trash Woman* with ads showing a barefoot brunette slipping out of her tattered dress under the tagline: "Her door is open day and night for ANY MAN!" Sherman explains, "I was taking a bunch of films that were inactive and trying to jazz them up with new campaigns. [The *White Trash Woman* campaign had] a sleazy-looking white woman standing outside a cabin. It was awful. That didn't work. It could be classified as 'Going to the well once too often.'"

In 1988 the home video distributor Xenon released Babb's 1969 edit of *Uncle Tom's Cabin* on VHS. Xenon specialized in releasing black-themed films from the 1970s on video, such as *Dolemite* (1974) and other Rudy Ray Moore movies. Sherman recalls, "One day, we found it in a store. I couldn't believe it. A company by the name of Xenon was pirating the picture and making a bloody fortune on this thing. They just found a print and pirated it. I was going to go to court forever against them, but it seemed like not the smart thing to do at the time. So we made a deal with them. They put up money and distributed some of our pictures. They paid us something on *Uncle Tom,* but we never got what we should have gotten. It's just unbelievable what people were doing and are still doing in the video field."

Xenon's video master was a horrendous full-screen presentation (losing over half of the original widescreen image) and originated from a battered, faded-to-pink, heavily-spliced print that looked like it had been abused by a slave driver's whip. The newly-created box art depicted the scarred, naked back and buttocks of a chained male slave. Xenon sold several thousand *Uncle Tom's Cabin* videotapes and since this was the only available dramatization of the classic book, some copies even ended up in school and public library collections (to be shown to unimpressed students during Black History Month).

In August of 2007, an intact (if faded and pinkish) original Superpanorama print of *Onkel Toms Huette* was screened to good response at the Todd-AO 70mm Festival in Karisruhe, Germany. The 141-minute Italian cut was released on DVD in Italy at some point and a Spanish DVD has also been reported.

Independent-International holds film negatives and sound elements for all three versions of *Onkel Toms Huette/Uncle Tom's Cabin.* Sherman says, "All the different versions are copyrighted and owned by us. It's never been on [American] television or cable. It has not been released on DVD. We're still trying to do something with it. The full-length version has never been seen in the United States. It's a good property, a good film."

Slaves (1969)

Slaves is yet another screen version of *Uncle Tom's Cabin* and was created by former Hollywood filmmaker Herbert J. Biberman two decades after he was branded as one of the "Hollywood Ten."

In the 1930s Biberman was with the left-wing dramatic group Theatre Guild in New York before going to California, where he became a successful screenwriter and director (*Meet Nero Wolfe*, 1936; *The Master Race*, 1944) and a founding member of the Screen Directors Guild. In 1947 Biberman (along with nine other film industry veterans) was accused of being a communist and labeled an unfriendly witness by the U.S. House Committee on Un-American Activities. After serving six months in jail for contempt of Congress, he was expelled by the Directors Guild and blacklisted by the film industry. Completely outside of the Hollywood system and with great difficulty, Biberman directed the low-budget feature *Salt of the Earth* (1954), a controversial, pro-union drama about mistreated mine workers in New Mexico. Although *Salt of the Earth* is now considered a classic, it initially failed to find wide distribution and Biberman found a new career as a California land developer.

Since 1952 Biberman had been trying to make films dealing with the history of blacks in America. He briefly worked with two black entrepreneurs to develop a never-made biopic starring Paul Roberson as Frederick Douglass.

In December, 1962—after extensive research which reportedly included the reading of 150 books on American slavery—Biberman completed a screenplay called *Uncle Tom's Cabin*. Using material from the last two-thirds of Harriet Beecher Stowe's book, the script focused on Simon Legree's mistreatment of Tom and the other slaves. John O. Killens, a Pulitzer Prize-nominated black author whose books dealt with racism in America, worked with Biberman on another draft that was finished in September 1963 with the title changed to *The Slave*. Feminist writer Alida Sherman was brought in for later revisions, which continued through 1967.

The final script begins in 1850 when the gentle slave Luke is sold to the cruel cotton lord Nathan MacKay. (Interestingly, although MacKay is vicious towards his slaves, he is fascinated by black history and collects rare African-made sculpture.) On the plantation, Luke befriends other slaves, including Cassy, the master's pampered concubine. (Cassy is the only character name retained from the novel.) After much physical, verbal, and sexual abuse, the slaves revolt and Cassy flees the house. MacKay offers Luke his freedom if he reveals who started the uprising and where Cassy is hiding. (This was Biberman's heavy-handed metaphor for the backstabbing that took place during the Red Scare of the 1950s.) Luke refuses to betray the others and is beaten to death. MacKay's valuable cotton is burned as Cassy and other slaves escape to the North.

Biberman spent years trying to get the film made and was rejected by all of the major studios. He finally raised the $1 million budget through independent sources including Theatre Guild Film Productions and the Walter Reade Organization, which owned a chain of movie theaters.

Under the sixty-eight-year-old Biberman's direction, the film was shot in the summer of 1968 in Shreveport, Louisiana at the Buena Vista, Welcome Hall, and Witherspoon plantations. Producer Philip Langner (*The Pawnbroker*, 1964) told the press, "Under any other circumstances, this wouldn't be such an unusual situation. There are a number of motion pictures that use authentic locales, but in our case, we more or less assumed that we would not be welcomed in the Deep South since our picture would in no way gild the lily in portraying slavery as it really was. Consequently, we had already made arrangements to begin filming in Florida when much to my surprise I was approached by some prominent businessmen in Shreveport to bring the production to Louisiana...I said, 'You don't want this picture. Wait till you read it.' They read it and said, 'This is where you should make it—in the real South.'" (The *Mandingo* and *Drum* movies would also be shot in Louisiana.)

The distinguished cast included Stephen Boyd (*Ben-Hur*, 1959; *Fantastic Voyage*, 1966) as the well-groomed but drunken MacKay, Ossie Davis (*Gone Are the Days*, 1963; *The Scalphunters*, 1968) as the righteous Luke, and Biberman's Oscar-winning wife Gale Sondergaard (*Anthony Adverse*, 1936; *The Spider Woman*, 1944), who was returning to acting after twenty years of being blacklisted like her husband.

Davis' appearance in an *Uncle Tom's Cabin* adaptation was somewhat surprising. In 1967 the actor was one of the many black leaders who was vocally opposed to the announced (but never made) film of *The Confessions of Nat Turner*, based on white novelist William Styron's highly-fictitious account of the infamous slave who led a bloody insurrection. Davis took out space in *Variety* announcing "For a black actor, a black man to lend his craft, his body, and his soul to such a flagrant libel against one of our great heroes, would be to have one of us become an agent for the enemy....It is quite possible I would despise such a man who would do such a thing."

Davis wouldn't agree to play *The Slave* unless his contract gave him final approval over his character's dialogue and actions. "I'm here with a mission," the actor said during production. "One of the great needs today in the black community is a positive male image. Luke is a slave, but more important, he's a positive black male image...Slaves have been shown as buffoons, simpletons, or at best Uncle Toms whose main interest is the welfare of the white masters…Slavery was not moonlight and magnolias. It was the supreme agony…The lesson, as I see it, is that we had better solve racial problems while talk, compromise and mutual adjustments are still possible, rather than wait until extremists on both sides take over."

Boyd said, "Some people have the impression that people are in this picture because they want to say something. I don't have a damn thing to say. [My character] MacKay says it, and what he says, God knows. Show me a business anywhere which is successful, and I will show you a man who could very easily be MacKay. And that, to me, is really the point."

Pop vocalist Dionne Warwick made her movie debut as Cassy. The singer told the press, "I always thought about doing everything in show business, and the two things left for me were movies and a Broadway show. So when *The Slave* came up, I was eager for it. About a year ago, I was playing a concert in upstate New York when the producer and the director came to see me backstage. They told me about the picture and asked if I would like to do it. I said I would love to. Later, they sent me the script, and I thought it was excellent. I asked them if they wanted me to go to dramatic school, since I have never done any real acting. They said not to bother; they wanted the character to become me—they didn't want me to change my personality to fit the role."

Marvin Hodges, a Shreveport businessman and one of the film's bit players, said, "Some people might say this picture is an indictment of the South, but, hell, you can't indict what's already been indicted. It's history which is why we were all for it. I've had 60 letters of appreciation for the picture from local people and only three against it."

Clayton H. Smith, a Shreveport dentist and owner of Witherspoon Plantation, one of the film's locations, said, "I kept telling Mr. Biberman that if the film was derogatory to the South, I did not want him in here. But he assured me it was not, that it's an historical picture of situations in 1850. I sent [the script] to the Chamber of Commerce and a man down there told me he didn't see anything wrong with it."

The filmmakers held a meeting at the battered Morning Baptist Church in the Louisiana backlands to recruit local blacks to be extras during the two weeks of exterior filming. The pressbook noted that "these people were actual descendants of the slaves who lived and worked on the Witherspoon plantation where *Slaves* was filmed." Costar Robert Kya-Hill performed a classic spiritual before Biberman and Davis promised that their important film would explain the origins of racial problems in America.

One crew member recalled, "We were shooting a scene of slaves chained in a wagon and we needed shackles. So we called the sheriff and asked if he knew where we could get 18 pairs of shackles. He said, 'Gee, I don't know. I've got six pairs but I'm using them all now."

One-sheet.

Shortly after production, the title was changed to *Slaves*. Hit songwriter Bobby Scott ("A Taste Of Honey," "He Ain't Heavy He's My Brother") composed the score and songs for the film. The instrumentals and Warwick's three vocal tracks, which included a title single, were released as a soundtrack album.

A lavish world premiere of *Slaves* was held at the Hippodrome Theatre in Baltimore, Maryland on May 6, 1969. Jack Fruchtman, president of the chain that included the Hippodrome, said, "When we first saw *Slaves*, we asked for the world premiere and we think Baltimore is most fortunate to be selected to kick off what will certainly be one of the important pictures of the year."

Richard Lebherz of The Frederick (Maryland) *Post*: "When the film was over, there was a burst of applause mainly for Dionne Warwick (who was present along with Stephen Boyd) but both blacks and white seemed, not stunned exactly, as much as amazed that such an adolescent conception of a touchy area as slavery had been made into film....If *Slaves* had been made in Europe, with English dubbed in, and sent over here to one of our Art Theatres, the film would automatically have been branded as propaganda and judged accordingly as a film that took advantage of our internal social disorders in order to make a point against the white man and the capitalistic system....The producer Philip Langner says of *Slaves* that it is 'the first accurate portrayal of the institution of slavery as it existed in the American South.' If this is true, then the slaves were lucky. Everyone in the film is far too polite. Even on the auction block, the Negroes that are waiting to be sold are treated with such genuine concern (no checking of teeth or for flat feet) that one wonders what it is they were escaping from....If it sounds like I am making fun of *Slaves*, and I am, it is because slavery is not something that can be twisted around for propaganda purposes. The agony of slavery deserves much more than exploitation in a second rate film. The institution was bad enough, but to exploit it in an almost juvenile level is even worse. No wonder the citizens of Shreveport, Louisiana were delighted to have the picture made down there. In many ways, it exonerated them beautifully."

The film attracted crowds during its first and subsequent weeks in Baltimore. Langner reported that many black patrons found *Slaves* to be "cathartic."

Continental Pictures, the distribution offshoot of the Walter Reade Organization, promoted *Slaves* as if it were a Falconhurst paperback. On the one-sheet, the text, "He bought her for $650. But she owned him!" was plastered over a photo of a leering Boyd and a naked Warwick. Other ads screamed: "See! Feel! Taste! The Bloody Whip of Truth!" and "This is the blazing black and white truth! For the slave—courage knew no chains—For the master—desire knew no color in the savage world of the Old South!"

Biberman, John O. Killens, and Alida Sherman were credited with the "Original Screenplay." *Uncle Tom's Cabin* wasn't billed as the source, even though *Slaves* followed the novel as closely as (if not more than) the European movie *Onkel Toms Huette* had.

A paperback novelization by co-screenwriter Killens was released by Pyramid Books. ("Bolder than *Mandingo*! The incendiary novel of a White man who played God—and the Black woman who became his mistress.") *Mandingo* readers were already immune to the depictions of slaves fighting for the amusement of whites, slaves being hung upside down, and slaves getting raped by their masters and birthing the offspring.

Although the MPAA rating system had been established in 1968, most independent distributors still weren't bothering to submit their product, and *Slaves* was released without a rating. (The film did receive an R rating when it was finally submitted in 1979.)

In France—where Biberman's *Salt of the Earth* was considered a masterpiece and had played for ten months during its initial release—*Slaves* was praised and was nominated for the prestigious Golden Palm at the Cannes Film Festival. But the film was poorly-reviewed in America where one critic wrote, "*Slaves* examines a monstrous institution with monstrous incompetence."

Boxoffice: "As an exploitation attraction, *Slaves* certainly has a lot going for it. It's the first film in quite a long time to deal in dramatic terms with the institution of slavery in the Old South, thus providing a unique plot and setting that should get plenty of attention....Saturation bookings and a hard sell will have to put it over, for the film itself is banal, predictable and technically inept....The film is so poorly constructed that, except for a few short moments, the potential historionic [sic] fireworks just sizzle. Miss Warwick looks stunning, but any real judgment concerning her future as an actress will have to await a better showcase."

Variety: "The box office success of *Slaves* will likely depend on the mood and conditions of the black-white situation at the time of the film's general release. It has a good premise and adequate acting, but a rather choppy script and uneven direction....The film's philosophy is a bit heavy handed....The attempts at realistic portrayal of what the situations were like are admirable."

Gary Arnold, *Washington Post*: "*Slaves* is a lousy movie....If you hope to reform an archaic screen tradition, I don't believe you can do it by making a film that's more stilted and confused and archaic than the work you're attacking....*Slaves* bends over backwards to seem 'relevant' and 'true,' but it looks, sounds and moves like the kind of overripe melodrama that went out of style at least 20 years ago....Is it possible to suppress a giggle when Dionne Warwick visits the slave shacks and delivers this tender line to Ossie Davis: 'I brought you some cornbread'? Or the clincher? Boyd's admonition to his henchmen while the cotton barns are on fire: 'Forget the cotton! After the women!'"

Vincent Canby, the *New York Times*: "*Slaves* is a kind of cinematic carpetbagging project in which some contemporary movie-makers have raided the antebellum South and attempted to impose on it their own attitudes that will explain 1969 black militancy. The result...is a pre-fab *Uncle Tom's Cabin*, set in an 1850 Mississippi where everybody—masters and slaves alike—talks as if he had been weaned, at best, on the Group Theater, and, at worst, on silent-movie titles....Mr. Biberman is an intensely earnest propagandist, a man who has committed himself to working for good in his own way, which, unfortunately, does not include the making of good films." (In 1971, two years after completing this last project, Biberman passed away at age seventy-one.)

Slaves had decent grosses in New York and in other northern venues as well as theaters down South. The film got more exposure when it was paired in 1970 with the horror hit *Night of the Living Dead* (1968) for an odd drive-in double bill.

Slaves started appearing on independent TV stations in 1972 in late-night time slots with print ads noting "Mature Audiences." *Leonard Maltin's TV Movies*: "*½....[*Slaves*] might have meant something in the '60s, but now it's just laughable, with Boyd properly embarrassed as Simon Legree-type 'Massa.'" Steven H. Scheuer, *Movies on TV*: "*....[L]ust and villainy on the old plantation....Obviously sincere, but you and me, we sweat and strain while watching it."

Shortly after the Walter Reade Organization filed for bankruptcy in 1977, *Slaves* was obtained by Gaileon International Picture Company. In 1981, 21st Century Distribution, a New York-based exploitation house, used *Slaves* to pad double and triple features at urban grindhouses.

Slaves is now a semi-lost rarity. It has never appeared on home video and has disappeared from TV. Although the trailer has appeared on some compilations, a complete print has not even surfaced on the bootleg/collectors circuit, despite the efforts of diehard film historians and Dionne Warwick completists.

Addio Zio Tom (a.k.a. *Goodbye Uncle Tom* and *Farewell Uncle Tom*, 1971)

When *Mandingo* became a big-selling novel throughout Europe in the 1960s, Dino De Laurentiis wasn't the only Italian who thought that it would make a good film. Gualtiero Jacopetti and Franco Prosperi, creators of the notorious "shockumentary" hit *Mondo Cane* (1962)—an expose of bizarre human behavior filmed throughout the world—were inspired by Kyle Onstott's novel in the late 1960s while preparing their pseudo-documentary on American slavery *Addio Zio Tom*. In the 2003 documentary *The Godfathers of Mondo*, Prosperi explained: "We thought, 'Why don't we do *Mandingo* as a documentary? Like a vintage documentary, in the sense that we imagine being photographers coming to America in the 1800s to observe the situation....I was the one doing the research because of my professorial background. So I read all the documents I could find on the topic of slavery in America."

The worldwide success of Jacopetti and Prosperi's previous "mondo" hits enabled the Italian duo to raise the hefty budget for *Addio Zio Tom* through distribution advances from Japan and other territories. The production was different from their earlier movies, which were made up of real-life footage gathered over several years. Prosperi recalled, "For *Addio Zio Tom*, we planned three months of shooting, like a normal film....It was going to be a fiction for the first time in our lives."

The mostly-Italian crew (and a cast of hundreds) shot in 1968 in Florida, Mississippi, and Louisiana (where De Laurentiis's official *Mandingo* film would later be shot) as well as Haiti (where real-life residents degraded themselves and their screaming infants as completely naked, low-paid extras). Jacopetti said, "It was a new experience: putting on costumes, building sets, and writing dialogue. I had never done that before."

The filmmakers shot a massive amount of footage. Post-production was finally completed in 1971, the same year the film was released in much of Europe.

At times, *Addio Zio Tom* is an unofficial semi-adaptation of *Mandingo*. Jacopetti and Prosperi lifted a number of the book's notorious images including naked slave children roaming a plantation; an elderly slave owner treating his rheumatism by putting his feet on a black boy's stomach; slaves being greased in preparation for auction; female slaves getting checked for odors before being sent to their master's bed; twin slave boys being sold to pedophiles; a virile stud being licensed out to impregnate virgins from other plantations; slaves being given a silver dollar as reward for siring a child; and a slave with three testicles on sale as an oddity.

Also shown are deformed, limbless Haitians crawling across a filthy floor as well as creepy, lingering shots of fully-nude adolescent black girls and boys smiling and gyrating for the camera. (Jacopetti was fond of very young girls. While in his thirties, he married his pregnant thirteen-year-old girlfriend. Later, he spent three months in a Hong Kong jail for a hotel room incident involving two girls under the age of twelve.)

An English-language version (called simply *Uncle Tom*) was prepared by the filmmakers and seen by Dennis Friedland, a twenty-seven-year-old Columbia University law school graduate and chairman of the New York-based distributor the Cannon Group. By 1971, the three-year-old Cannon had co-financed and/or distributed two dozen low-budget features including softcore sex imports (*Inga*, 1967), art-house psychedelica (*Scratch Harry*, 1969), foreign horror movies (*Cauldron of Blood*, *Crucible of Terror*, both 1970); and counterculture comedies (*Guess What We Learned in School Today?*,

1970). The furniture in the company's Manhattan office included a used barber chair and a stack of Colt 45 beer cases.

Cannon's 1970 in-house production *Joe* had become the company's first mainstream critical and financial hit and one of the biggest independent films of the era. The crudely-made dark comedy about a working-class, blue-collar hater of hippies turned Peter Boyle into a star character actor, introduced Susan Sarandon, launched director John G. Avildsen (future Academy Award-winner for 1976's *Rocky*) and got an Oscar nomination for screenwriter Norman Wexler (who went on to write the *Mandingo* and *Drum* scripts). After *Joe* made back its entire $300,000 budget through its initial New York City play dates, Cannon released a mass market paperback of the screenplay, sheet music, and a spoken word LP record with the title character's profane monologues. In a 1970 profile, *Time* magazine said, "Over at Cannon things are in a prosperous uproar….The only way Cannon could lose money on any of its films would be to burn the negative."

Riding high on the success of *Joe* and hoping to cash-in on the blaxploitation genre that had recently been launched with the urban hits *Cotton Comes to Harlem* (1970), *Shaft* (1971) and *Sweet Sweetback's Baadasssss Song* (1971), Friedland formed a limited partnership with nine other New York area entrepreneurs to purchase the American distribution rights to the Jacopetti-Prosperi shocker and release it as *Farewell Uncle Tom*.

Cannon often revised their acquisitions with extensive re-editing and the addition of newly-shot footage. Christopher C. Dewey, Friedland's twenty-six-year-old Cannon partner, said, "I don't know an awful lot about film history, but it seems to me that ten years ago critics got hold of this business of Ingmar Bergman and directors being the creators of films and blew it up out of all proportion. Well, that's all bull. There are a lot of people involved in making a movie, not just the director, and if we see something we don't like, then we're going to change it."

Mindful that bookings for *Farewell Uncle Tom* would be limited due to fears that enraged blacks would riot in the cinemas, Friedland hired New York editors Ken Dewey and Tom Kennedy (assistant editor on *Joe*) to trim some of the more offensive images, notably a modern-day recreation of the Nat Turner massacre where axe- and meat cleaver-wielding blacks with huge afros butcher a white couple and splatter their baby's head against the wall. The young editors also reshuffled most of the sequences, deleted some footage, and inserted about ten minutes of outtakes that had been discarded by the Italians, including reenactments of Harriet Tubman's "underground railroad" and a brutal antebellum slave revolt where whites were slaughtered. This new

Spanish advertisement.

version (featuring the end credit "Prepared for American Release by Ken Dewey and Tom Kennedy") clocked in at 100 minutes. (The original ran 123 minutes.)

Friedland hired the Manhattan firm Solters, Sabinson and Roskin, Inc. to create posters and ads (covered with a self-imposed X rating) and released his new version of *Farewell Uncle Tom* on October 28, 1972 in three New York City theaters, including the huge Cinerama on Broadway. Cannon wasn't listed as the distributor on the prints or any of the lurid ads, which focused on images of caged blacks with the blurb "Beasts of Burden! Tools of Pleasure! Objects of Torture!"

Pauline Kael, *The New Yorker*: "The Italian moviemakers aren't content with simulating the historically recorded horrors of slavery; they invent *outré* ones...so they can mix prurience with their piety about how white Americans are the scum of the universe....No one has ever before attempted a full-scale treatment of slave-ship misery; how degrading to us all that by default it has fallen into the hands of perhaps the most devious and irresponsible filmmakers who have ever lived. They use their porno fantasies as part of the case they make for the slaughter of the whites, who are shown as pasty-face cartoons....Unlike the black hits, the film lacks a central figure for the audience to identify with, but the black audience in the theater was highly responsive to Jacopetti and Prosperi's fraudulent ironies, and in the ads are quotes from black papers saying, 'An all-time great gut-busting flick,' and 'Don't miss *Farewell Uncle Tom*, it is must viewing. Eyeball-to-eyeball confrontation with stark reality and chilling candor.'" (The ads credited that first blurb to *Amsterdam News*.)

In mid-November 1972, the film was booked in Chicago. Roger Ebert, *Chicago Sun-Times*: "The vile little crud-squad of Jacopetti and Prosperi has been getting away with movies like *Farewell Uncle Tom* for so long now that maybe they think audiences will stomach anything. This time they don't even kid us that they're sincere; their vomit-bag of racism and perversion-mongering isn't even covered up with the usual slime of sanctimonious BS. They have finally done it: Made the most disgusting, contemptuous insult to decency ever to masquerade as a documentary....The movie gloats over scenes of human degradation....Unfortunately, Jacopetti and Prosperi have been able to find people willing to undergo the humiliation inflicted on them in *Farewell Uncle Tom*; most of the blacks in the film are apparently Africans [sic] forced by poverty and need to do these things for a few days' pitiful wages. This is cruel exploitation....Make no mistake. This movie itself humiliates its actors in the way the slaves were humiliated 200 years ago.... The fact that this film could find a booking in a legitimate motion-picture theater is depressing."

Farewell Uncle Tom also played at least two weeks in New Orleans, where a newspaper ad depicted a shirtless, meat cleaver-clutching black man under the tagline "300 Years Of Hate Explodes Today!" In a 2003 essay, David Duke, the controversial politician who was once a Louisiana State representative and a Grand Wizard of the Ku Klux Klan, recalled seeing the film at a New Orleans theater as a college student: "Expecting a difficult situation, I drove down from Baton Rouge with two of my bravest and most dedicated LSU [Louisiana State University] friends....[In one scene] a Black revolt occurs, and the screen erupts with revenge-minded Blacks hacking to death White men, women, and children. With each bloody outrage, the audience howled with approval. 'Right on!,' some screamed. 'Rape the bitch! Kill 'em!' The Black crowd laughed and cheered during the goriest scenes of mutilation, rape, and murder....Even after 20 years, I vividly recall the film and the raw hatred it engendered in the Black audience. At the sight of the murders, the audience worked itself into a frenzy. As soon as the credits appeared, my friends and I, sitting in the rear of the theater, grabbed our coats and left quickly."

After less than a month of disappointing business and less-than-expected controversy, Friedland pulled *Farewell Uncle Tom* from distribution to rethink the campaign. In early 1973, a version re-titled as *White Devil, Black Hell* and shorn of even more extreme material was submitted to the MPAA and received an official X rating. But Friedland was able to secure few bookings and *Farewell Uncle Tom* was a huge failure for the distributor. Dewey's plans for Cannon to become "the new United Artist" and "the most important independent in the business" didn't work out. There wasn't a single post-*Joe* hit. The struggling company spent the rest of the decade as a last resort American distributor for imported and domestic sex comedies and subpar Eurocrime and kung fu movies until the early 1980s when Cannon was bought by the Israeli cousins Menahem Golan and Yoram Globus. Friedland and Dewey went on to successful careers on Wall Street. In the early 1990s, Friedland returned to production and distribution as the head of the unsuccessful Arrow Films.

Outside of America, *Addio Zio Tom* was released in most major countries and was heavily promoted. (Soundtrack albums and theme song singles appeared in Japan and Italy while a digest version of "Jacopetti's explosive schocker" was released to the German Super 8mm home movie market). But the film was shunned by the huge international audience that had embraced Jacopetti and Prosperi's earlier movies. Thirty years later, Prosperi reflected, "It is difficult to watch. Understandably so. Maybe we went a little too far and lost sight of the public....It was interpreted as cynicism. It was probably our mistake. We should have stated it clearly: 'Attention: What you are about to see is the viewpoint of men of those times. It is not our viewpoint.'"

Immediately after its release, *Addio Zio Tom* disappeared into obscurity. In the 1980s, the European version was released on VHS in Greece and Australia, while the cut prepared in New York by Cannon turned up in German video stores. Bootleg dubs of these tapes were heavily circulated among American collectors until Blue Underground released the original cut of *Addio Zio Tom* on DVD in 2003. Also discovered and released was an odd, alternate, Italian-language "International Version" which featured footage of Martin Luther King's funeral, the Black Panthers, and a New Orleans funeral procession as well as a creepy (if inaccurate) recreation of the legend of Madame Lalaurie, a sadistic New Orleans slave abuser of the 1800s. Pointless, unrelated footage of naked white hippies with painted bodies and a parade of white drag queens is also in this cut. (Much footage shot by Jacopetti and Prosperi—including more abuse on the slave ship and a scene with a burnt teenage slave getting his hand severed by a machete—has never appeared in any cut.) *Addio Zio Tom* remains one of the most disturbing, shocking, and repulsive cult films ever made.

Quadroon (1971)

The rich history of New Orleans, Louisiana includes tales of the quadroon balls that were held in the French Quarter during the 1830s and 40s, where female quadroons (who were one-quarter black and three-quarters white) were put on display to become the mistresses of wealthy white men. In 1970 R. B. McGowen, Jr., a Texas lawyer and businessman, decided to make a movie about that era called *Quadroon*.

McGowen began dabbling in the movie business by forming Presidio Productions, raising capital and being executive producer on the extremely low-budget horror film *Mark of the Witch*, which was shot in his home state in 1970 and released to Southern drive-ins. Next, McGowen wrote a treatment about a young male teacher from New England who comes to New Orleans in 1835 and falls fatally in love with one of his biracial students. (The film has no relation to Thomas Mayne Reid's 1856 novel *The Quadroon* or the 1970 slaver pulp paperback *Quadroon* by Jonathan Craig.)

McGowen's story was expanded into a screenplay by Sarah Riggs (apparently her only screen credit) with dialogue describing quadroons as "the products of the Creole man and his darker woman…like a sweet drop of cream…schooled in seduction from infancy." Among the Falconhurst-like images in Rigg's script and the finished film were bare-chested slaves being forced to fight for the amusement and financial gain of their masters; lecherous whites fondling young black girls; sadistic whippings and hangings; degrading slave auctions; and an especially-queasy extended scene where a female slave is raped by a slobbering gang of black males.

McGowen wanted to make *Quadroon* "a truly realistic portrait of one of the most fascinating chapters in New Orleans history" by shooting the film in the actual French Quarter. He teamed up with Jack Weis, a New Orleans-based distributor who had secured some play dates for *Mark of the Witch*. *Quadroon* would be the thirty-nine-year-old Weis' first film as producer and director, and he obtained permission from his home city to shoot at several interior and exterior historic sites. McGowen said, "Every effort was made to assure the utmost authenticity for this film. New Orleans is one of the most unique and romantic cities in the world."

Preproduction and casting for *Quadroon* took place in the fall of 1970 for a January 1971 start date. Among those that read for the lead role of Coral was Kathrine McKee, a gorgeous, green-eyed, twenty-year-old actress and dancer. McKee recalls, "It all started in Las Vegas for me. This was, like, 1968. I was having a personal relationship with a guy who had lost all of our money. We didn't have anywhere to stay or any way to get home. I auditioned for a show out of sheer emergency. I was about sixteen years old. I was passing for white and I had a fake ID. I got hired on the spot to work as a dancer at a hotel. That changed my life because I ended up staying in Vegas and one thing lead to another and I auditioned for another show and I got it. That was [the revue] *Viva Les Girls*. I was a lead showgirl. It was a massive show and we played in

Montreal [Canada] for months." She later was a Bunny at the Detroit Playboy club and appeared in Sammy Davis Jr.'s Vegas act.

"Then I ended up coming to L.A.," McKee says. "I was working as an actress then. I had done *The Bill Cosby Show* [1971 season] and a few other things and I got called in for a reading at Crown International Pictures in L.A. When my agent sent me on it, he said, 'They're making this movie called *Quadroon*.' I had never heard of a quadroon. I didn't know what a quadroon was. I investigated and found out. [Quadroons] were in slavery, but they were the girlfriends [of wealthy New Orleans men]. They were held on a higher level than the kitchen slaves or the work slaves because they were light-skinned, they were mixed. Everybody [at the audition] seemed to be very happy to go with me. It didn't seem like I was up against a whole bunch of people for it because I actually was a quadroon. So, they didn't have to put makeup on me, they didn't have to make me be something I'm not. They thought I was perfect for it and they hired me on the spot. The pay wasn't all that great. I remember being paid just the minimum scale wage. But it was my first job, so I took it. I remember thinking that [the script] was very sad. The reality of these women and slave days and what my people had gone through. It was really kind of shocking. Before I knew it, I was on my way to New Orleans to make this incredible movie."

Cast as McKee's love interest, Caleb, was Tim Kincaid. In the 1960s, the young actor had studied in New York with Lee Strasberg before appearing in a tour of *Bye Bye Birdie* with Sheree North, TV commercials, and an episode of *Combat* (season unknown). Kincaid says, "I auditioned the previous year for another movie [*Mark of the Witch*] that the production company was making. It was a standard audition process—reading some scenes with a casting director and some production people (in a mid-town New York office tower, as I remember). Everyone was pleasant and I felt I did well; evidently I came in second. When *Quadroon* came up, the company called the casting director and had her offer me the role of Caleb. [The script] seemed somewhat disjointed, but I assumed they knew what they were doing."

Also hired were Robert Priest as a dashing Creole and George Lupo as the sadistic villain. Priest had bit roles on several TV shows including *Mission Impossible* and *My Three Sons* (seasons unknown). Lupo was a veteran of TV gangster and Western bit roles.

New York actor Madelyn Sanders, who played McKee's mother, said at the time, "At first the producers said I was too young to play the part of the mother in *Quadroon*—until I reminded them that in the early part of the 19th century, young Negro girls were very often mothers when they themselves were little more than children. In fact, *my* mother is only fourteen years older than I am....I really can identify with this role. After all, as you can tell I'm not entirely black....And it's an actual fact that my grandfather bought my grandmother for two dollars and a rifle."

Texas actor Bill McGhee came to New Orleans for a featured role as a bare-chested, bare-fisted slave fighter before returning to his home state to give a memorable performance in the cult classic *Don't Look in the Basement!* (a.k.a. *The Forgotten*, 1973). The smaller *Quadroon* roles were played by local actors.

McKee, who was in New Orleans for the first time, recalls, "We all got down there and for about a week prior to shooting, we had a round table run-through of the script. We'd show up every day in that quadroon ballroom or in another area of the hotel. Everything was done on location. We were there quite a long time. Maybe two months. It was not easy. It was the real world. We had to deal with the heat. We had to deal with mosquitoes. It was a low-budget movie, they didn't have a lot of money. People were wearing a lot of hats making this movie."

The costumes were shipped from California. "I picked out my own wardrobe at Western Costume Company in Hollywood," McKee says. "I was allowed to make the final choices. I went there and I spent two days being fitted and looking. That was fun. Once you put on that wardrobe and you're down there and in these actual places, it's an eerie feeling. It's a lot easier to get into character. There's so much history down there. The character was in the clothes, it would just come out through them like a spirit. Bob Priest used to talk to me about that. He felt the spirit or the soul of the person that he was playing."

In the *Quadroon* pressbook, Priest, a believer in reincarnation said, "The instant I entered the [French] Quarter, a strange feeling came over me. I had a strong sense of having walked these streets before. And when I put on the costume of the period, the feeling became so strong I could no longer ignore it. The clothes felt more comfortable and natural to me than those I wear every day. I even found the house where I believe I lived in the 1800s."

"A lot of crazy stuff happened," McKee recalls. "We were staying in the Bourbon Orleans hotel [in the French Quarter]. It was renowned. A lot of strange things happened in that hotel because that was the real hotel where they had the quadroon ballroom. The hotel was definitely haunted. There's no question about it. They had stories at the front desk about the haunting of this hotel [by] quadroon women who had been murdered or killed or raped. This hotel represented the era of the quadroon ball and the selling of these beautiful women to masters. Many of us had experiences in the rooms where we'd see ghosts out of the corner of our eye at night. [Each of the actors] took one keepsake to take home to cherish. I took a little tiny, two-inch antique photograph of some woman that was a part of the quadroon ball. I think the photograph is haunted because whenever I've [hung] it up, I've experienced strange phenomenon, so I have it wrapped up, put away somewhere."

The Internet Movie Database incorrectly states that Herbert Janneke Jr. co-directed the film with Weis. Janneke was actually the assistant director, but the inexperienced Weis did have help. McKee says, "One of the things that was interesting was that Robert Priest and Tim Kincaid were allowed to direct scenes from time to time. Their goal was to be directors. They did a lot of the directing."

Kincaid says, "I was in the process of raising production funds for my own first movie, which was made the following year. So when I made some (unasked for) suggestions about a scene—only one scene, as I remember—Jack kindly allowed me to block a scene between Kathy and George that involved threats of bodily violence and some bodice-ripping-drama. I believe [Weis] was in a different line of work. This was his first movie. It showed."

McKee says, "Tim was interesting and he was a good actor. Tim was gay and was living in L.A. with a very prominent actor who was in everything—every commercial, every program, had an appearance on *Hollywood Squares* [the TV game show of the 1960s and 70s]. He was a comedic actor. I cannot remember his name."

Kincaid recalls, "[Kathrine and I] struck up a close friendship during the shoot—mostly for the purposes of self-preservation. There was lots of laughing at the absurdity of it all. She was a good egg, and one of the most startlingly beautiful women I had ever laid eyes on. Bob [Priest] also had a great sense of humor about the proceedings. George [Lupo] flat-out couldn't act, but gave it his all. Bill [McGhee] was completely committed to making his role work. As I remember, [screenwriter Sarah Riggs] was a recent college graduate who was glad to be there. New Orleans was a city chockfull of drama and intrigue. So was the *Quadroon* set."

The voluptuous McKee's bare backside and breasts appear onscreen in her nude love scene with Kincaid. "We had a closed set," McKee explains. "We didn't have any clothes on. I just had on some lower underwear. That was one of the harder scene to shoot because we were so close, Tim and I. It was so hard to carry on this romance with him because we were buddies. I knew full well he was gay. I knew his boyfriend. We shot that at the very end of the movie which even made it harder. It would have been easier to have come right in and right on set and do it right away and get it over with. The temperature in that room must have been 116 degrees because we were shooting upstairs over a business in the French Quarter in an apartment with no air conditioning. The [movie] lights were hot. It was miserable."

"[The producers] were looking for somebody to write a haunting theme song for the movie," McKee says. "Right away—because I always was pushing my sister—I said, 'How about my sister? She's a songwriter and she's very talented and she can do this for hardly any money.' So they flew her down. My sister, Lonette, was fifteen. She was still going to school in Detroit, living

Newspaper advertisement. (Collection of Chris Poggiali)

with my parents. She sat for days and days on the piano in the hotel ballroom working on this song. She experienced many ghostly experiences in that ballroom. She saw spirits, she saw ghosts. She saw the ghost of a woman, floating." (Just prior to *Quadroon*, a rhythm and blues songs written and performed by Lonette was a hit on Detroit radio stations.)

McKee recalls, "One night we were all out partying and Lonette was with us. We're all partying with the crew in some club and somebody slipped Lonette a 'Mickey' and tried to get her out of the club to do what they wanted with her, which was, no doubt, some sort of sexual act. She managed to tell us something was wrong, she was dizzy, somebody had drugged her. Then [the male cast and crew] all went on the hunt to find the crew guy that did this to her. They figured out who it was. He's in one of the scenes as an extra where they're beating and raping my [character's] mother. He's a white guy with a beard and long black hair. He never showed up on the set again because not only were they going to beat him to a bloody pulp, they were gonna have him arrested for what he did to Lonette."

Kincaid says, "[*Quadroon*] marked the screen debut of Lonette, who went on to have a fairly big movie career for a while. She came on with one line as a servant, and her long, luxuriant hair completely obscured her face."

"One of my greatest memories is making that movie," McKee says. "I had the most wonderful time. Tom [Smart], the cameraman was giving me the Doris Day treatment. He thought that I was very beautiful and very easy to photograph and he wanted to make certain that everything was perfect when it came to my camera angles. Of course, I loved that. [Laughs] It was mostly us actors that stuck together, which is normal. We all got to know each other very well. There wasn't a night we didn't go out and have a wonderful dinner and several glasses of wine. We were young, we could do it back then. [Laughs] And we all gained weight. [Laughs] Because we were eating that unbelievable, rich, delicious, wonderful French Creole food. They were letting people's costumes out every week and trying to add more pieces."

McKee continues, "I was madly in love with [Robert Priest]. His real name was 'Prete.' 'Priest' was his stage name. We had the most beautiful affair down there—dinner and drinking and holding hands and walking in the moonlight. The last day of shooting, he finally took me aside and decided to tell me the truth. He had a lover in L.A.—a man. I had fallen in love with him and he was gay. He told me and it crushed me. It broke my heart. I couldn't believe that he had kept that from me all these months. I was devastated. Many, many months went by and we didn't speak. Finally I got over it and I contacted him in L.A. and we became friends."

Kincaid says, "The film was made in four weeks, with some nude insert shots of Kathrine made a few months later, in Chicago, to punch up the love scene."

In early February 1971, the Louisiana State Museum Board finally reviewed Weis's five-month-old paperwork requesting permission to film at various French Quarter locations. Due to the script's "objectionable" content the request was denied, but by then the film had already wrapped over a week earlier and the producers had already shot where they wanted. (The Museum was among the organizations thanked in the end credits.) Executive producer

McGowen announced in the press book, "We are grateful to [New Orlean's] citizens for their cooperation."

A few months after filming, a screening of *Quadroon* was held for cast and crew. "They didn't have a big premiere," McKee says. "They had some sort of an event in Los Angeles that I went to. To see yourself on a big screen like that, I was really overwhelmed. I thought I really looked beautiful. Bob Priest went with his friend, but I didn't sit with him and I was trying to just blank that out. I didn't want to know about it."

Kincaid recalls, "I saw the film at a private screening on 42nd Street [in New York] for the top indie/trash distributor on the East Coast. He handled the lowest common denominator material in the business. He passed, citing the unintended racism that informed nearly every scene in the finished product."

The film was given an R rating and opened in its shooting location of New Orleans on June 17, 1971. *Quadroon* played Greenville, Mississippi in July, Atlanta in October, and other Southern venues during the fall (on double bills with Jim Brown movies and sword-and-sandal flicks). It was shown in Baltimore in November, but only after receiving a seal of approval from the Maryland State Board of Motion Picture Censors. (Maryland was the only state that had such a board. It was illegal for theaters to show any film that didn't pass.) In December, the film hit Bridgeport, Connecticut where it was advertised with an X rating and paired with the British sex comedy *Just Like a Woman* (1967).

The poster and the newspaper ads were dominated by a stunning color portrait of McKee with the text: "Now! The shocking truth about the passion slaves of 1835 New Orleans. Rips the veil of secrecy from History's strangest chapter! One Quarter Black, Three Quarters White...All Woman!" Among the publicity stills was one of a shirtless male slave being whipped.

Accompanied by a huge promotional campaign, *Quadroon* played the 2,500-seat McVicker's theatre in Chicago from March to May 1972. Kincaid recalls, "The movie actually broke some records for a week or two in a big theater in the Loop in Chicago."

Variety: "*Quadroon* is a rather flimsy film that appears aimed at both black and white filmgoers, though in terms of its main advertising effort in Chicago, the former seems to get the nod....If there's a surprise in [the] film it's that the three principals, McKee, Kincaid and Priest, occasionally come across in a believable fashion."

Under the headline "*Quadroon* is all garbage" in the popular and influential black newspaper *Chicago Daily Defender*, Sharon Scott wrote: "What is the story? If the filmmakers are trying to show the New Orleans-Creole experience, they have failed. If it is to be a good skin flick which is more or less the image newspaper, billboard, and radio advertisements have projected, it has failed here also."

Defender reader William A. Lewis took it upon himself to submit a *Quadroon* review to the Letters section: "Lured to the McVicker Theatre by the picture of buxom Kathryn [sic] McKee I discovered in a local newspaper, I had great expectations for this film. After all, the ads for it were sensational....All this, plus an 'R' rating, assured me of a little erotic stimulation if nothing else. After the first 35 minutes of phony French accents, incredible bad directing, terrible acting, and an unbelievably rotten script plus a musical score that can be forgotten while it is playing, makes for one big flop all the way. The film shows you what might happen if Hugh Heffner were to finance a high school play. After about 45 minutes of this talent-free production I felt just plain silly sitting there watching it and walked out thereby wasting $2.50 plus CTA fare. The plot...has more inanities than the Pentagon has psychopaths....It's a mess."

McKee wasn't aware that her image was the centerpiece of the promotional campaign. She says, "When that movie came out, I was on the road with Sammy Davis in his nightclub act. We were in limousines, hotels, backstage, and that was it. That went on for a long time. I should have stayed in L.A., pursuing my acting career. I was gone on the road, so that all just blew by me."

With its well-plotted and well-structured screenplay, authentic and photogenic locations, and attractive and appealing lead actors, *Quadroon* could have become an effective low-budget drama instead of just an odd, interesting curio. In Weis's inept hands, the film looks even cheaper than it is. The horrible lighting, static and bland camera angles, poor blocking, and George Lupo's disastrous Creole accent, make *Quadroon* come across like a filmed community theater production. Not good enough to appeal to art house patrons and not trashy enough to become a grindhouse staple, *Quadroon* disappeared into obscurity soon after its regional release across the country and was the second and last film from McGowen's Presidio Productions.

Weis went on to direct three more hopelessly-underfinanced features in New Orleans: *Storyville* (1974)—a drama about jazz musicians in the 1900s—and the dismal horror films *Crypt of Dark Secrets* (1976) and *Mardi Gras Massacre* (1978). (The latter featured Laura Misch from *Mandingo*.) Attempts by several film historians to locate Weis have been unsuccessful. "I heard Jack died several years ago," says Kincaid.

In 1976, Kincaid began directing gay porn features under the name Joe Gage, starting with the acclaimed *Kansas City Trucking Company*. During the direct-to-video boom of the late 1980s, he directed (as Tim Kincaid) several extremely low-budget mainstream movies including *Bad Girls Dormitory* (1986). In 2001 he returned to gay porn, where he continues to direct under the names Joe Gage and Mac Larson.

Priest later appeared in the TV movie *Don't Be Afraid of the Dark* (1973) and an episode of *The Magician* (1973). McKee recalls, "The last time I saw him in L.A., years ago, we had dinner with [comic actress] Rose Marie. He was working with Rose Marie as a manager. He was also involved with [celebrity psychic] Sylvia Browne."

Lonette McKee's long, later career as a singer and actress included the classic movies *Sparkle* (1976), *The Cotton Club* (1984), and *Round Midnight* (1986).

Kathrine McKee made no other features after *Quadroon*, but appeared on TV in episodes of *The Tonight Show Starring Johnny Carson* (with guest host Sammy Davis, Jr., 1973 season), *Sanford and Son* (1972 and 1974 seasons), *Saturday Night Live* (1975, guest-hosted by her then-boyfriend Richard Pryor), and *Police Woman* (1976 season). She explains, "It's a cutthroat business. You really have to be hardnosed and strong and fight your way to make it in that business. I gave up my career in L.A. to raise my son in a healthy environment. I've been back here [in Detroit] doing production work and casting. I've been working for years on a book about the famous men in Hollywood that I was having an affair with or was the girlfriend of." She has a website at kathrinemckee.com.

In September 1982, the decade-old *Quadroon* returned to independent theaters and drive-ins courtesy of the short-lived, Hollywood-based distributor Lone Star Pictures which, like *Quadroon*, was funded by rich Texans.

Quadroon appeared in mom-and-pop video rental shops in 1988 from an obscure fly-by-night video label called Deluxe Movie Ventures that not only retitled the film as *Black Agony: The Color of Truth*, but replaced the main actors' names with fake names. A scratched, faded film print was used for the inept video transfer which was, surprisingly, letterboxed. The box for *Black Agony: The Color of Truth* featured a newly-shot photo of a shirtless black male bound on a leash. Actual copies of this tape are extremely rare but DVD-R dubs are sold on the underground collectors circuit. (*Quadroon* has also appeared online as a torrent file.)

McKee says, "I look at [*Quadroon*] now and I see where I could have done such a better job. But I didn't have an acting coach, I didn't have anyone there helping me. I was on my own. I'm proud of it, still. I've had people call me and say, 'Your movie's on! Your movie's on Channel 22 or whatever.' It's almost got a cult following. It certainly was an interesting, different film."

Mandinga and *Emanuelle bianca e nera* (1976)

Dino De Laurentiis's home country of Italy was one of the many territories where his productions of *Mandingo* and *Drum* were extremely popular. Italy was also where producers cloned many American movies by stripping a hit film's premise to the core, expanding and exaggerating the exploitable elements, and leaving only sex, brutality, and sadism. It was inevitable that there would be "spaghetti *Mandingos*." The Italian movie industry produced entertaining, lower-budgeted rip-offs of American Westerns (*Django*, 1966), demonic possession thrillers (*Chi Sei?*, a.k.a. *Beyond the Door*, 1974), urban crime dramas (*Il Grande racket*, a.k.a. *The Big Racket*, 1976), cannibalistic zombie movies (*Zombi 2*, a.k.a. *Zombie*, 1979), and gory science-fiction films (*Contamination*, 1980), but the country's filmmakers were not successful with the slavesploitation genre.

In 1976 the Rome-based Società Europea Films Internazionali (SEFI), responsible for the banal giallo *Death Carries a Cane* (1972) and the depraved Nazi torture-prison entry *S.S. Experiment Love Camp* (1976), produced a pair of *Mandingo/Drum* copies. *Mandinga* and *Emanuelle bianca e nera* were shot back-to-back, very quickly and extremely cheaply in Spain. (The 1974 French softcore phenomenon *Emmanuelle* inspired numerous unofficial, unrelated European rip-offs. The copycat producers spelled their title heroine's name with only one "m" or one "l.")

Mandinga and *Emanuelle bianca e nera* were each directed by Mario Pinzauti, formerly of subpar Eurocrime and spaghetti Western entries, including *Giunse Ringo e... fu tempo de massacro* (a.k.a. *Ringo, It's Massacre Time*, a.k.a. *Wanted Ringo*, 1970) and *Vamos a matar Sartana* (1971), two of the lesser-known entries with those ubiquitous title characters. (Non-Italian promotional materials for Pinzauti's films sometimes billed him as Peter Launders). Attractive (but uncharismatic) feather-haired model and softcore regular Antonio Gismondo was hired to play the male lead in both films. Model Malisa Longo was the female star of *Emanuelle bianca e nera*. The *Mandinga* leading ladies were Eurosleaze staple Paola D'Egidio (who would re-team with Gismondo for the unrelated rip-off *Emanuelle, Perché violenza alle donne?*, a.k.a. *Emanuelle Around the World*, 1977) and Maria Rosaria Riuzzi (of yet another rip-off: *Emanuelle e Francoise le sorelline*, 1975).

Among the very few cast members who weren't required to provide full-frontal nudity were Serafino Profumo, who played the stereotypical middle-aged plantation lord in both films, and noted character actors Calogero Caruana and Attilio Dottesio (both spaghetti Western veterans) who added some name value for the European market as the respective "guest stars" for *Mandinga* and *Emanuelle bianca e nera*.

There are no writing credits on the English-language prints for either film, but the Internet Movie Database gives sole screenplay credit for *Emanuelle bianca e nera* to Pinzauti and lone writing credit for *Mandinga* to Tecla Romanelli, writer of SEFI's 1977 women-in-Nazi-prison epic *SS Lager 5: L'inferno delle donne* (a.k.a. *SS Camp 5: Women's Hell*). The later American

Mandinga video boxes listed the writers as Pinzauti and Mario Caporali (production manager of both films). But there's not much to give credit for as both movies are virtually plotless.

In *Mandinga*, the treacherous, sexually-insatiable young racist Miss Rhonda (D'Egidio) arrives at the plantation of her cousin, Richard Hunter

Italian poster/locandina.

(Profumo). Hunter rapes Mandingo slave girl Mandy, who dies after secretly giving birth to his child. Twenty years later, Richard's son Clarence (Gismondo) returns from England and marries Mary, the preacher's daughter (Riuzzi). After endless scenes of brutal sex and whippings (at one point, Rhonda and Clarence rape a chained slave couple), there is a sizzling and clever last-minute twist worthy of a Falconhurst novel. Mary gives birth to a black baby and is shot dead by the enraged Clarence. It turns out that Richard's rape of Mandy resulted in Mary, who was raised by the preacher when the baby was left in his church.

("She was all white. No one could'a figured she was a mulatto. It happens sometimes.") Richard strangles the evil Rhonda, holds up his incest-spawned grandson and says: "I shall christen you—Mandingo!"

In *Emanuelle bianca e nera*, Emanuelle Johnson (Longo) is a blonde, vicious, sexually insatiable ruler of a Louisiana cotton plantation (although no cotton is ever seen) whose fiancé (Gismondo) falls in love with the slave girl Judith Emanuelle (played by Rita Manna, a hefty, round-faced Italian wearing an enormous afro wig and one facial expression). The jealous white Emanuelle cries rape after forcing one of her male slaves to bed her, orders her men to kill the slave, and is accidentally shot by the posse. Black Emanuelle holds white Emanuelle's head as the white woman inexplicably expresses redemption before dying.

Like the paperback knock-offs that followed the *Mandingo* novel, the cash-ins of the movie version tried to outdo the original in depravity and shock value with repulsive, prolonged images of salt being poured into whip wounds, master-on-slave rapes with nipple-biting, slaves forced to fight and mate with each other for the amusement of white males, a white woman brutally beating her lover's slave girlfriend, and the sexual violation of chained slaves.

Sexploitation vet Maurizio Centini shot both films and provided plenty of shaky zooms, flat lighting, inept day-for-night shooting, and ugly compositions. (The 2.35:1 ratio was wasted.)

Post-production was done in Italy, where both films were edited by Sergio Leone's tireless former collaborator Eugenio Alabiso, who certainly didn't have much to work with here.

Emanuelle bianca e nera was given a repetitive synthesizer score by exploitation veteran Roberto Pregadio. The equally repetitive *Mandinga* music by the prolific Marcello Giombini was mostly a rip-off of Quincy Jones's hit theme for *Roots*.

Each movie was given a stylized, *Drum*-like credit sequence with abstract red-tinted images. *Mandinga*'s opening had photos of black models who don't appear in the film and the title in the same font that was used for the *Mandingo* credits and ads.

For a final inept touch, the movies received poorly-synced English-language tracks with ridiculous dialogue, often with obviously-white European voice actors trying to sound like blacks from the American South. ("Okay, numbskull, you can bleed all over the cotton;" "We're different colors, but we're all God's children;" "It'll be my pleasure to see you rot in hell, my little nymphomaniac;" "You want I should whip him some?" "I think the times are gonna be changing, Paw;" "You're one of the few beautiful things that this old river has seen while he keeps on rolling and rolling along;" "I don't want to mess you up too much. I sort of go for you;" "You know I want to be your white slave. I'm on fire! Whip me!")

Mandinga and *Emanuelle bianca e nera* are examples of assembly line Eurosleaze at its worse. The tedious, grungy sex scenes with hairy armpits, anachronistic tan lines, and pasty cellulite aren't even up to the standards of typical 1970s European softcore. The crumbling locations in dusty Spain don't pass as luxurious Southern estates, and the tattered antebellum costumes are obviously left over from the cheapest Euro-Westerns. There is almost no action in either film, but the few stunts are awful and the whippings are unconvincing. (*Emanuelle* has talk of a simmering, *Drum*-like slave uprising but it never happens.) Each movie clocks in at less than 90 minutes, but seems endless.

Many of the slaves were played by Spaniards wearing fluffy afro wigs. It's ludicrous to see Paola D'Egidio as a racist white in *Mandinga*, since the actress has darker skin than those playing black slaves. Malisa Longo comes off especially badly as the antebellum belle in the *Emanuelle* movie, with hideous green lace-up boots, ludicrous hair, and heavy blue mascara. The still-active, still-gorgeous model was used to better advantage (with better lighting and makeup) in slicker movies like Terence Young's *The Amazons* (a.k.a. *War Goddess*, 1973).

Hot on the heels of *Mandingo* and *Drum*, the pair of Italian clones were immediately released throughout Europe and other foreign markets, but there was no initial interest from American distributors.

In 1978 *Emanuelle bianca e nera* was sparsely-released to American grindhouses as *Passion Plantation* by the New York-based Howard Mahler Films, a handler of rock-bottom blaxploitation, kung fu, and German sexploitation. The distributor got an official R rating and created a misleading poster with crude artwork (lifted from the 1969 slaver paperback *Muscavado*) of a shirtless male slave lifting a topless blonde woman by her hair under the tagline "Anything can happen on *Passion Plantation* where your real *Roots* were!" (Alternate ads screamed: "ROOTS Were Planted Here!") To hide the film's pedigree, the stars's names were anglicized to "Anthony Gismond" and "Malissa Long." (Some English-language prints billed Longo as "Maria Luisa Longo.")

American trash fans didn't get the chance to see *Mandinga* until 1985, when it was released, along with its sister feature, on VHS and Beta when Wizard Video got hold of a battered print of each movie and cranked out muddy, smeared, cropped video masters. *Emanuelle bianca e nera* became *Emmanuelle Black and White* (two "m"s) with an attractive painting on the oversized box cover that gave no indication that the film was set in the antebellum era and depicted an interracial lesbian coupling (with contemporary underpants) never seen in the movie. The *Mandinga* cover blatantly presented itself as a *Mandingo* knock-off and used artwork lifted from an Italian poster for *Azio Zio Tom. Mandinga* was a far better selling and renting video than

Emmanuelle Black and White, mainly because shop owner and patrons thought they were getting *Mandingo.* Along with numerous other imported softcore epics, *Mandinga* could also be viewed in the late 1980s on the Cinemax pay TV channel.

A decent, letterboxed DVD-R of *Emanuelle bianca e nera* (under the *Passion Plantation* title) is currently available from Something Weird Video. An unwatchable copy of *Mandinga* (apparently originated from an ancient VHS copy) was among the twenty (dreadfully-presented) movies included on a 2007 unauthorized DVD set called *The Grindhouse Experience.*

Roots (TV miniseries, 1977)

In 1974 David L. Wolper—a successful producer of documentaries like *The Rise and Fall of the Third Reich* (TV, 1967–68) and *The Hellstrom Chronicle* (1971) and the feature *Willy Wonka and the Chocolate Factory* (1971)—used his own money to option an unfinished book by African American author Alex Haley. *Roots* told the allegedly-true (but later revealed as mostly-false) story of Haley's ancestors, beginning in the late 1700s when Mandingo teenager Kunte Kinte was captured in Africa by slave traders and transported by ship to Virginia to be auctioned into slavery. "*Roots* was a magnificent story," Wolper recalled in his memoir. "Not a magnificent *black* story, but the kind of universal story that I believed would appeal to people of all races."

Wolper had wanted to make a film on American slavery for some time. In 1967 he bought the film rights to white author William Styron's popular and acclaimed novel *The Confessions of Nat Turner*, based on the famous 1831 slave revolt. After hiring African American Lou Peterson to write the screenplay, Wolper set the project up at 20th Century Fox with James Earl Jones as the star. Directors Norman Jewison and Sidney Lumet were each attached at one point, but the film was aborted due to the studio's financial troubles as well as fears of a boycott by the numerous black activist organizations that hated the book and were vocally opposed to a film version.

Wolper set *Roots* up in development as a potential "Novel For Television" miniseries at the skeptical ABC network. The producer recalled, "There had never been a successful black dramatic series on television, and there was substantial doubt that advertisers would support a miniseries about black history."

Haley—whose only screenwriting credit was on the dreadful *Superfly TNT* (a 1973 sequel that played double features with *Mandingo*)—was still writing the *Roots* book and was not available to write the teleplay for Wolper. He told the producer, "I don't want you hiring writers because of their color, race, or religion. I want you to hire the best writers you can find." William Blinn, creator of the TV-movie classic *Brian's Song* (1971) and the series *Starsky and Hutch* (1975–1979), worked from Haley's early, incomplete *Roots* drafts to adapt the epic story into a workable outline. Ultimately and inevitably, there were substantial story and character differences between the miniseries and the completed book. (The actual teleplay was written by Blinn, James Lee, M. Charles Cohen, and Ernest Kinoy.)

After ABC approved the script and gave *Roots* a $4.5 million budget, executive producer Wolper sent producer Stan Margulies and a largely-black crew to Savannah, Georgia, where the show was shot over several months in the spring and summer of 1976. The directors for the individual episodes were Marvin J. Chomsky, John Erman, David Greene, and Gilbert Moses.

The extraordinary cast included most of the top black actors of the era, many of whom agreed to work for scale: John Amos, Cicely Tyson, Moses Gunn, Louis Gossett, Jr., Leslie Uggams, Richard Roundtree, Ben Vereen, and Georg Stanford Brown. The poet Maya Angelou and football legend/occasional actor O. J. Simpson also turned up briefly. The only black star who declined to appear was Redd Fox, who refused to play a slave. Edward Asner, Chuck Conners, Ralph Waite, Vic Morrow, and Sandy Duncan played reprehensible whites, and each gave one of the best performances of their career.

Ji-Tu Cumbuka, who played the proud, clever, ill-fated slave Cicero in *Mandingo*, appeared in *Roots* as "The Wrestler," the resourceful warrior who is captured with Kunte Kinte and leads an unsuccessful revolt on the slave ship. The actor says, "*Mandingo* [led to] me getting the role of 'The Wrestler.' I told them to watch *Mandingo*, and if they like that, then maybe we can talk. That's what sold me. They told me, 'You look just like the guy that we had pictured.' The Wrestler was 6'5," weighed 220 and had a gap in his teeth. I'm 6'5," I weighed 220, and I had a gap. Alex Haley made the comment, 'If you can act, you got the role because you look the part.'"

Cumbuka recalls competing with some big names for the role: "Jim Brown, Fred Williamson, Bernie Casey, O. J. Simpson. All those football players with the good build. But they were too buff and that's one of the reasons I got the role. I wasn't buff. I was lean and mean, but I didn't get it from playing football or lifting weights. I ran and I hiked and I did my 'daily dozen' like we did in the service. And they needed a really serious actor that could pull it off. I played the role of a guy that lived three hundred years ago and never saw America. O. J. finally took the role of one of the fathers in the film."

Haley wanted the young Kunte Kinte to be played by an extremely dark-skinned actor who would look believable as a pure African. College student

LeVar Burton had never acted on film before, but the nineteen-year-old was chosen out of the hundreds of others who auditioned. Wolper recalled, "A few network executives fought us briefly about him, believing he was too dark-skinned to be acceptable to white audiences—but we refused to back down."

On location, the filming of the early episodes (particularly in the African and slave ship scenes) ate up an unexpected amount of the budget. To insure the overall production values, Wolper decided to put another $1.5 million of his own money into the *Roots* budget, bringing the final cost of the miniseries to $6 million. (Wolper would end up making a fortune from the show.)

Many of the controversial, notorious images in the miniseries were familiar to viewers of the two Falconhurst movies: slave auctions, whippings, brutal uprisings, master-on-slave rape, dismembered limbs, threatened castration, cockfighting (replacing the bloody slave battles of *Mandingo* and *Drum*) and topless black women. "This was the first time that the network permitted any nudity in a dramatic program," Wolper noted. "Unfortunately, we found out, after completing filming, that one of the actresses who had volunteered for a nude role had been underage. We had to identify her on every frame of film and make sure she could not be seen."

ABC decided to run *Roots* as a twelve-hour event (including commercials, recaps of the previous entry, and previews of the next installment) that would run over eight consecutive nights. The anxious network broadcast the first episode on the evening of January 23, 1977, and each entry was watched by an increasing number of viewers. The final episode was the most-watched show in television history (up to that time) and was seen by 100 million American viewers—almost half of the country's population. As Wolper put it, "More people watched *Roots* that week than have seen Shakespeare's plays performed since the day he wrote them."

Variety: "The production and performances are strong....African tribal life is portrayed almost as *Ozzie & Harriet* in blackface and one-dimensional characterization is the rule....But as fresh and innovative television, [*Roots*] stretches the medium, if only a little."

Roots was nominated for thirty-seven Emmys and became an instant television classic, but there were a few negative reviews. *Time*'s Richard Schickel dismissed it as "a middlebrow *Mandingo*;" another critic said it reduced history to "shackles, whips and lust;" and the Ku Klux Klan complained to ABC about how their organization was depicted.

During the *Roots* phenomenon of 1977, numerous African Americans proudly named their children after the characters Kunte and Kizzy and many people of all races were inspired to research their own family tree. The instrumental title theme by Quincy Jones became a radio hit.

The equally-exceptional miniseries *Roots: The Next Generations*, which covered material from the book not seen in the first production, followed in 1979. The 1988 TV movie *Roots: The Gift* was a mediocre, Christmas-themed (and admittedly-fictitious) amendment to the second episode of the original miniseries, with LeVar Burton and Louis Gossett, Jr. recreating their roles. All of the *Roots* entries are readily-available on DVD and can be found in most public libraries.

Ji-Tu Cumbuka, who was featured in *Mandingo* and *Roots*, says, "*Roots* is much better than [*Mandingo*]. And the reason that it's much better is because it is chronological. It started at the beginning and let people know that we weren't always slaves. We were people who had a society, who had a religion, who loved their children. And we were snatched from our environment and our land and put on ships and got off in a strange land where mean, hostile people treated us like animals. We traveled great distances and in my lifetime, I've seen it. We couldn't stop at a hotel, we couldn't eat at a restaurant. It was horrible. Change didn't just come. We had to riot in the streets."

Fuego negro (a.k.a. *Black Fire*, 1978)

Mandingo and *Drum* were blockbusters when released in Mexico, so it's not surprising that a cheap homegrown imitation was produced in that country. *Fuego negro* was made in 1978 by the Mexican company Scope Films and financed through Mexican and Italian sources.

The script (credited in some sources to a Rex Rayter) was about a sugar plantation heir named Gabrielle who sympathizes with her father's overworked slaves and falls in love with the sensitive black Manuel. After a bloody slave revolt, the lovers live together in a hidden cabin. Manuel tries to form an organized, harmonious community of ex-slaves, but his plans are thwarted when the plantation's white former overseer uses violence to force the blacks back into slavery.

Director Raúl Fernández and a skilled local crew shot the film in Oaxaca, a mountainous area in the southern part of Mexico. The stunning Susana Kamini (from the Mexican cult horror films *The Mansion of Madness* a.k.a. *Dr. Tarr's Torture Dungeon*, 1973, and *Alucarda*, 1978) and the trim, handsome Cesar Imbert were cast as the lovers. Busy character actor Rolando Fernandez (often billed as Roland Ferlini in Europe) played the whip-cracking villain.

Director Fernández had previously added dubious marquee value to his 1977 thriller *Ultraje* by adding American ex-teen idol Troy Donahue to the cast. To attract American distribution for *Fuego negro*, the producers hired Yvonne De Carlo to play the plantation matriarch. At this time, the former movie star (*Salome Where She Danced*, 1945; *The Ten Commandments*, 1956) was appearing at dinner theaters and nightclubs while supplementing her income with cameos in things like the unreleased *Arizona Slim* (shot in New York in 1975 by ex-Andy Warhol associate Chuck Wein) and barely-released drive-in fodder like *Satan's Cheerleaders* (1977) and *Nocturna* (1979).

De Carlo explained in her autobiography: "As for my stage and film roles, there was a period of time when I was less selective than I might have been. If a job was offered, and if the price was right, I took it. I needed the money." She is on screen for less than five minutes of *Fuego negro,* in a few scenes clumsily scattered throughout the first half. Her appearance could not have taken more than a day to shoot and it's possible that the she didn't even have to travel South of the Border to shoot the cameo.

Almost all of the black slaves were played by Hispanics wearing heavy blackface makeup and afro wigs, including the prolific actress Aurora Clavel (*Guns for San Sebastian*, 1968; *The Wild Bunch*, 1969) in a hideously-stereotypical performance as a "Mammy."

An opening card states that the film is set in a "remote place in america [sic] where slavery has been abolished," which supposedly means the southern United States shortly after the Civil War. But the heavy dust, the cactus, the dirt mountains, and the dead, bare trees of the shooting location don't create an authentic atmosphere. Nor do the actual straw and clay huts that were used to represent the slave cabins. (Slave quarters on American plantations were made of wood.) The anachronistic costumes (bell-bottomed blue jeans, bright halter tops, floral and polka-dot print skirts) are laughable, although the lead actress does wear a nicely-done copy of Scarlett O'Hara's bonnet and dress from the *Gone with the Wind* barbecue scene.

Included in *Fuego negro* were the expected Falconhurst-inspired images: a helpless slave girl getting raped by a sadistic white; an upside-down male slave getting his (surprisingly non-bare) backside brutally whipped; and an explicit interracial love scene between a white woman and a black man (although in this case the roles were played by a light-skinned Hispanic female and a dark-skinned Hispanic male). There are plenty of deaths, including one by pitchfork, but the gore is mostly restrained, except for one shot where the severed head of a plantation heir is toted on a stick by a rebelling slave.

The soundtrack has minimal sound effects and a library track score that ranges from appropriate (rhythmic drums for a voodoo sequence) to ridiculous (a funky electric guitar and a jazzy piano). All of the actors spoke English during the (silent) filming. An English-language version was recorded with voice actors speaking in Mexican accents. ("You thought you'd get away, you fuckin' nigger. Ha! Ha!;" "Aw, shit!" which comes out as "Aw, sheet!")

Despite its anachronisms, *Fuego negro* is a serviceable, competently-shot, low-budget programmer. It is far superior to the back-to-back Italian *Mandingo* clones. Kamini and Imbert are attractive and appealing as the lovers and Rolando Fernandez is effective as the lecherous, cackling villain. The riot scene is exciting and well-staged, with good stunts. A midnight voodoo chicken sacrifice scene is eerie and moody. Also effective is the odd, downbeat conclusion: Gabrielle is shot dead and the film ends with a sepia-toned freeze-frame of the villain pointing his pistol at Manuel's head.

Fuego negro was released to Mexican theaters in September of 1979. There was no release in America. A poor-quality VHS release of the film (called *Black Fire* on the cover but sans opening and closing credits on the print) came out in Finland in the late 1980s courtesy of a company called Diamond Video. Dupes of this version (which has an English language track and Finnish subtitles) are available from several American underground dealers. Supposedly-authorized VHS copies have also appeared in some Spanish-speaking countries.

Fuego negro is an offbeat curio, but only diehard slavesploitation scholars should bother tracking it down.

Appendix A:
Publication History of the Falconhurst Books (First American and British Editions)

Mandingo by Kyle Onstott (edited by Philip Onstott, uncredited). Richmond, VA: Denlinger, 1957; London: Longman, 1959 (both hardcover)
Drum by Kyle Onstott (with Lance Horner, uncredited). NY: Dial Press, 1962; London: W. H. Allen, 1963 (both hardcover)
Master of Falconhurst by Kyle Onstott (with Lance Horner, uncredited). NY: Dial Press, 1964; London: W. H. Allen, 1965 (both hardcover)
Falconhurst Fancy by Lance Horner and Kyle Onstott. NY: Fawcett, 1966 (paperback); London: W. H. Allen, 1967 (hardcover)
The Mustee by Lance Horner. NY: Fawcett, 1967 (paperback); London: W. H. Allen, 1968 (hardcover)
Heir to Falconhurst by Lance Horner. NY: Fawcett, 1968 (paperback); London: W. H. Allen, 1969 (hardcover)
Flight to Falconhurst by Lance Horner. NY: Fawcett, 1971 (paperback); London: W. H. Allen, 1972 (hardcover)
Mistress of Falconhurst by Lance Horner. NY: Fawcett, 1973 (paperback); London: W. H. Allen, 1973 (hardcover)
Six-Fingered Stud by Lance Horner, (completed by Harry Whittington and Lawrence Blochman, both uncredited). London: W. H. Allen, 1975 (hardcover); Revised for American publication with altered character names to become the non-Falconhurst novel *Golden Stud*, NY: Fawcett, 1975 (paperback)
Taproots of Falconhurst by Ashley Carter (pseudonym for Harry Whittington). NY: Fawcett, 1978 (paperback); London: W. H. Allen,

1978 (hardcover)
Scandal of Falconhurst by Ashley Carter (pseudonym for Harry Whittington). NY: Fawcett, 1980 (paperback); London: W. H. Allen, 1980 (hardcover)
Rogue of Falconhurst by Ashley Carter (pseudonym for Harry Whittington). NY: Fawcett, 1983) (paperback); London: W. H. Allen, 1983 (hardcover)
Miz Lucretia of Falconhurst by Ashley Carter (pseudonym for Harry Whittington). NY; Fawcett, 1985 (paperback); London: W. H. Allen, 1985 (hardcover)
Mandingo Master by Ashley Carter (pseudonym for Harry Whittington). NY: Fawcett, 1986 (paperback); as *Mandingo Mansa,* London: W. H. Allen, 1986 (hardcover)
Falconhurst Fugitive by Ashley Carter (pseudonym for Harry Whittington). NY: Fawcett, 1988 (paperback); London: W. H. Allen, (hardcover)

Notable Additional Editions of *Mandingo*:

Note: This list is not intended to be complete.

Mandingo. NY: Crest, 1958. First American paperback issue.
Mandingo. London: Pan, 1961. First British paperback issue.
Mandingo (*Slaveavl Som Kynisk Forrestning*). Norway: Ponni-bok, no date (probably early 1960s). Paperback with same artwork as original Crest release.
Mandingo. Japan, no date (probably late 1960s/early 1970s). Hardcover.
Mandingo. Greenwich, CT: Fawcett/Crest, 1975. Movie tie-in paperback reissue with movie poster art on cover.
Mandingo. London: Pan, 1975. Movie tie-in paperback reissue with cover photo of Ken Norton and Susan George from the film version.
Mandingo. Milano: Euroclub, 1975 (Italian release) Hardcover with dust jacket photo of Perry King and Brenda Sykes from the film version. Front matter includes a short glossary defining "Masta," "Mista," "Miz," "Pone," "Surrey" and several other slang words found in the novel.
Mandingo (*Sort Sind: Hvid Og Sort Modes I Kaerlighed Og Had*). Denmark: Lademann, no date (obviously 1975 or later). Undersized

hardcover with dust jacket photo of Ken Norton and Susan George from the film version.

Mandingo, Audiotape version (Authorized uncensored abridgment). Publisher: Washington, D.C.: DBPH, 1975; Recording Agency: Dallas Talking Books; Distributor: MTC; Book Number: RC 07845.

Mandingo, Audiotape version. Publisher: Washington, D.C.: National Library Service for the Blind and Physically Handicapped, Library of Congress, 2000. Recording Agency/Distributor: Potomac Talking Book Services; Read by Robert Sams; Book Number: RC 49298; Six cassettes.

Appendix B:
Chronological Story Order of the Falconhurst Books

Note: Some of the novels overlap and/or take place at the same time as others. Any one who plans to read all or several of the novels should still start with Mandingo.

Falconhurst Fancy
Mistress of Falconhurst
Mandingo
Mandingo Master
Flight to Falconhurst
Six-Fingered Stud
Rogue of Falconhurst (Note: This novel negates and replaces *Six-Fingered Stud* as the immediate sequel to *Flight to Falconhurst*)
Falconhurst Fugitive
Miz Lucretia of Falconhurst
The Mustee
Taproots of Falconhurst
Scandal of Falconhurst
Drum
Master of Falconhurst
Heir to Falconhurst

Appendix C:
Additional "Slaver" Paperbacks

Note: This list is not intended to be complete.

Ashanti, Lou Cameron (Lancer, 1969) (sequel to *Mistress of Bayou Labelle*)
Beast, Leslie Gladson (Lancer, 1969)
Beulah Land, Lonnie Coleman (pseudonym for William Laurence) (Hardcover: Doubleday, 1973) (Dell, 1974)
Beauty Beast, MacKinlay Kantor (Hardcover: Putnam, 1968); (Fawcett/Crest, 1968); (Cover blurb: "From the publisher of *Mandingo*")
The Black and the Damned, Harold Calin (Lancer, 1969)
Black Brute, Robert Tralins (Lancer, 1969?)
Black Cargo, Harold Calin (Lancer/Magnum, 1969)
Black Emperor, Stuart Jason (pseudonym for Michael Avallone) (Lancer, 1971)
Black Gold , William H. A. Carr (Lancer, 1969)
Black Hell, Harold Calin (Lancer, 1969?)
Black Ivory, S. J. Treibich (Lancer, 1969)
Black Lord, Stuart Jason (Lancer, 1970); Reissue: *Royal Stud* (Manor Books, 1976)
Black Love, Stuart Jason (pseudonym for Michael Avallone) (Lancer, 1969)
Black Master, Stuart Jason (pseudonym for Michael Avallone) (Lancer, 1970)
Black Hercules, Stuart Jason (pseudonym for Michael Avallone) (Lancer, 1969)
Black Vengeance, Norman Gant (pseudonym for George Wolk)(Lancer, 1968) (Sequel to *Chane*) Reissued in England as *Vengeance of Chane* (New English Library, 1969)
The Bond-Master, Richard Tresillian (Warner Books, 1977) (Cover

blurb: "Harder than *Mandingo*")
Brood of Fury, Jess Shelton (Crest Giant, 1961)
Brute Force, Robert Tralins (Lancer, 1969?)
Chains, Justin Adams (Dell, 1977)
Chane, Norman Gant (pseudonym for George Wolk) (Lancer, 1968) British reissue: (New English Library, 1969)
Dark Master, Raymond Giles (Fawcett/Crest, 1970) (Cover blurb: "From the publisher of *Mandingo*")
Delta Stud, Stuart Jason (pseudonym for Michael Avallone) (Manor, 1976)
Dragonard, Rupert Gilchrist (Bantam Books, 1976)
Dragonard Rising, Rupert Gilchrist (Golden Apple, 1984)
Flamingo, Mark Oliver (Dell, 1970)
Generation of Blood, I.A. Grenville (Manor, 1961)
Kingblood, Stuart Jason (pseudonym for Michael Avallone) (Paperback Library, 1969)
King's Blacks, Leslie Gladson (Lancer, 1969)
Legacy of Beulah Land, Lonnie Coleman (pseudonym for William Laurence) (Hardcover: Doubleday, 1980) (Dell, 1981)
Look Away, Beulah Land, Lonnie Coleman (pseudonym for William Laurence) (Hardcover: Doubleday, 1977) (Dell, 1979)
Machismo, Gramm Hill (Lancer, 1971)
Mistress of Bayou Labelle, Lou Cameron (Lancer, 1968) (Cover blurb: "In the Brutally Honest Tradition of *Chane* and *Mandingo*")
Muscavado, Eleanor Heckert (Hardcover: Doubleday, 1969), (Dell, 1969) (Cover blurb: "As Scorching as *Mandingo*")
The Plantation, George McNeill (Bantam, 1975)
Plantation Breed, Hugo Paul (Prestige Books, 1969)
Quadroon, Jonathan Craig (Lancer, 1970) (no relation to the film of the same title)
Rafe, Peter Gentry (NY: Fawcett Gold Medal, 1976)
Ratoon, Christopher Nicole (Hardcover: St. Martin, 1962) (Bantam Books, 1963) (Cover blurb: "Even More Explosive than *Mandingo*"); Reissue: (Bantam, 1968) (Cover blurb: "As Savage and Lusty as *Mandingo*")
Rebels of Sabrehill, Raymond Giles (Fawcett/Gold Medal, 1976)
Rogue Black, Raymond Giles (Fawcett/Crest, 1973) (Cover blurb:

"From the publisher of *Mandingo*")
Royal Master, Stuart Jason (pseudonym for Michael Avallone) (Manor Books, 1976)
Sabrina, Joseph Chadwick (Paperback Library, 1970)
Sabrehill, Raymond Giles (Fawcett, 1974)
Slave, Eric Corder (Pocket, 1968)
Slave Empire, Norman Gant (pseudonym for George Wolk) (Lancer, 1969) (Sequel to *Black Vengeance*)
Slave Queen, Norman Gant (pseudonym for George Wolk) (Dell, 1970) (Cover blurb: "Not Since *Mandingo*!")
Slaver, Leslie Gladson (Lancer, 1968) (Cover blurb: "In the Blazing Tradition of *Mandingo* and *Chane*")
Slave Ship, Eric Corder (Hardcover: McKay, 1969); (Pocket Books, 1970)
Slave Ship, Harold Calin (Leisure Books, 1977)
Slaves, John O. Killens (Pyramid Books, 1969) Novelization for the film of the same title; (Cover blurb: "Bolder Than *Mandingo!*")
Slaves of Sabrehill, Raymond Giles (Fawcett, 1975)
The Slave Stealer, Boyd Upchurch (Hardcover: Weybright & Talley, 1968); (Signet, 1969) (Cover blurb: "In the pulsating tradition of *Mandingo*")
Sparhawk Lionel Webb (Lancer, 1968) (Cover blurb: "In the Brilliant, Brutal tradition of *Mandingo*"), Reissue: (Award Books, 1976) (Cover blurb: "In the daring, explosive tradition of *Mandingo*")
Voodoo Slave, Norman Daniels (Paperback Library, 1970); Reissue: (Warner Books, 1974)
The Wrath of Chane, Norman Gant (pseudonym for George Wolk) (Lancer, 1970?); (Thick compilation of the previously-released *Chane*, *Black Vengeance*, and *Slave Empire*)

Appendix D:
Credits for Broadway Production of *Mandingo*

Cast: Franchot Tone (Warren Maxwell), Dennis Hopper (Hammond Maxwell), Brooke Hayward (Blanche Maxwell), Duke Farley (Calvin Brownlee), Georgia Burke (Lucretia Borgia), Clark Morgan (Memnon), Philip Huston (Doc Redfield), Vinie Burrows (Tense), Rockne Tarkington (Mede), Maurishka Ferro (Ellen), Fran Bennett (Lucy), Verta Smart (Big Pearl), Arnold Soboloff (Neri), John A. Topa (Remick), Coley Wallace (Topaz), Arnold Moore (Meg), Ronald Moore (Alpha). Also: A number of unbilled actors played non-speaking Townsmen and Slaves. Understudies: Philip Huston (Warren Maxwell), Lane Bradbury (Blanche Maxwell, Ellen), Ken Menard (Memnon, Mede, Topaz), Miriam Burton (Lucretia Borgia, Tense, Lucy, Big Pearl), John A. Topa (Calvin Brownlee), C. C. Boyd (Hammond Maxwell), Pierre Epstein (Remick, Neri, Doc Renfield). (None of the understudies were needed during the run.)

Production Credits: Play by Jack Kirkland. Based on the novel by Kyle Onstott. Directed by Louis Macmillan. Presented by Billy Baxter and Edward Friedman. Production Designed and Lighted by Frederick Fox. General Manager: Irving Cooper. General Press Representative: Bill Doll. Production Stage Manager: James Gelb. Stage Manager: Pierre Epstein. Casting Director: George Repp. Master Carpenter: Richard Nolan. Master Electrician: Sam Knapp. Assistant Electricians: Al Manganaro, Milton Saltstein. Master of Properties: Mike Bobrick. Wardrobe Mistress: Muriel King. Assistant to the Producers: Hilda Simms. Scenery: Nolan Scenic Studios. Lighting Equipment: Century

Lighting Company. Costumes: Eaves Costuming Company. Sound Equipment: Masque Sound, Inc. Lighting Fixtures: Knickerbocker Lighting Company. Carpenting: Hotel and Theatrical Carpet Company. House Physician: Dr. Benjamin A. Gilbert.

Location: Lyceum Theatre, 149 West 45th St., New York City
Preview: Wednesday, May 17, 1961. Total previews: Five (?)
Opening Night: Monday, May 22, 1961. Closing Night: Saturday, May 27, 1961. Total performances: Eight.

Settings:
Act I: Falconhurst - The Maxwell Plantation near Benson, Alabama. The year 1832.
Act II: The Maxwell Plantation - Six months later.
Act III: A tavern yard in the town of Benson.

Appendix E: *Mandingo and Drum* Filmographies

***Mandingo** (1975)*

Cast: James Mason (Warren Maxwell), Susan George (Blanche), Perry King (Hammond Maxwell), Ken Norton (Mede), Brenda Sykes, (Ellen), Richard Ward (Agamemnon), Lillian Hayman (Lucrezia Borgia), Roy Poole (Doc Redfield), Ji-Tu Cumbuka (Cicero), Paul Benedict (Brownlee), Beatrice Winde (Lucy), Ben Masters (Charles), Debbi Morgan (Dite), Irene Tedrow (Mrs. Redfield), Ray Spruell (Wallace), Louis Turenne (De Veve), Duane Allen (Topaz), Earl Maynard (Babouin), Reda Wyatt (Big Pearl), Simon [a.k.a. Simone] McQueen (Madame Caroline), Evelyn Hendrickson (Beatrix), Stanley J. Reyes (Major Woodford), John Barber (Le Toscan), Durwyn Robinson (Meg), Kerwin Robinson (Alph), Deborah Ann Young (Tense), Debra Blackwell (Blonde Prostitute), Kuumba (Black Mother), Stocker Fontelieu (Wilson), Rosemary Tichenor (German Widow at Auction) (uncredited), Laura Misch (Prostitute) (uncredited), Warren Kenner (Slave) (uncredited), Deleted Scenes: Sylvester Stallone (Young Man in Crowd), Edwin Edwards (Gambler)

Production Credits: Directed by Richard Fleischer. Produced by Dino De Laurentiis. Screenplay: Norman Wexler. Based on the Novel by Kyle Onstott and on the Play Based Thereon by Jack Kirkland [Note: Kirkland's credit was due to a dispute between De Laurentiis and one of the play's producers. In fact, the screenplay contained nothing that had been created by Kirkland for his stage adaptation.] Executive

Producer: Ralph Serpe. Director of Photography: Richard H. Kline, A.S.C. Production Design: Boris Leven. Casting: Lynn Stalmaster. Music Composed and Conducted by Maurice Jarre. Song "Born in This Time" Music by Maurice Jarre, Lyrics by Hi Tide Harris [also producer, uncredited], Sung by Muddy Waters. Production Manager: Peter V. Herald. First Assistant Director: Fred Brost. Costume Design: Ann Roth. Editor: Frank Bracht, A.C.E. Assistant Editor: Chris Kaeselau. Sound Effects Editor: James Nelson. Music Editor: Milton Lustig. Post Production Supervisor: Stanley Neufield. Assistant to Producer: Frederico De Laurentiis. Script Supervisor: Alvin Greenman. Second Assistant Directors: Gary D. Daigler, Albert Shepard. Location Contact: Albert J. Saizer. Set Decorator: John Austin. Property Master: William Wainess. Stunt Coordinators: Joe Canutt, Alan Oliney. Production Sound: William Randall. Boom Operator: Raul A. Bruce (uncredited). Technical Director of Sound: Donald C. Rogers (uncredited). Makeup: George "Hank" Edds. Special Effects: Ira Anderson, Jr. Wardrobe: Jack Martell. Hair Stylist: Maryce Blymer. Gaffer: Ross Maehi. Head Grip: Gene Kearney. Location Auditor: Robert Koucerek. Titles and Optical Effects: Pacific Title. Color by Technicolor. Filmed on Location in Baton Rouge and New Orleans, Louisiana and at Paramount Studios, Hollywood, California. Aspect Ratio: 1.85:1.

A Dino De Laurentiis Presentation. American Distributor: Paramount Pictures.
American Version Running Time: 127 minutes. MPAA Rating: R.

Drum (1976)

Cast: Warren Oates (Hammond Maxwell), Isela Vega (Marianna), Ken Norton (Drum), Pamela Grier [a.k.a Pam Grier] (Regine), Yaphet Kotto (Blaise), John Colicos (Bernard DeMarigny), Fiona Lewis (Augusta Chauvet), Paula Kelly (Rachel), Brenda Sykes (Calinda), Lillian Hayman (Lucretia Borgia), Royal Dano (Zeke Montgomery), Rainbeaux Smith [a.k.a. Cheryl Smith] (Sophie Maxwell), Alain Patrick (Lazare Le Toscan), Clay Tanner (Mr. Holcomb), Lila Finn (Mrs. Holcomb), Henry Wills (Mr. Gassaway), Donna Garrett (Mrs. Gassaway), Harvey Parry (Doc Redfield), May R. Boss (Mrs. Redfield),

Ilona Wilson (Elly Bee Rowe), Monique Madnes (Mary Ruth Rowe, Eddie Smith (Bruno), S.A. Lewis (Babouin), Harold Jones (Slave #1), Maurice Emanuel (Slave #2), Larry Williams (Slave #3), Julie Ann Johnston (Woman Guest #1), Jean Epper (Woman Guest #2), Bob Minor (Minor's performance as Omo was completely deleted from the film; he plays Tamboura in one shot in the completed film and is credited as playing Cuban Slave), Roger E. Moseley (Tamboura) (uncredited) (most of Moseley's performance was deleted from the completed film and his face is not seen. He is only seen from the back.), Cynthia James (Julita) (uncredited) (her role was deleted completely, except for one glimpse of her figure in bed with Tamboura.)
Cast Deleted from Completed Film: John Vernon (Don Cesar), Gene Evans (Lazare Le Toscan) [replaced by Alain Patrick], Robert Alda (Don Gregorio), Majel Barrett (Eva), Don "Red" Barry (Auctioneer), Peter Savage (Don Raimundo), Esther Sutherland (Mama Baba), Ann McRae (Anita), Ned Wertimer (Cuban Aristocrat), Harry Caesar (Clemente), Harold Jones (M'Dong), Ann Summerfield (Pia), Marilyn Joi (Maria Luz), Genji James (Edna), Norma Smith (Elvira), Alberto Morin (Cuban Artist), Jane Actman (Sophie Maxwell) [replaced by Rainbeaux Smith], Amedee Frederick (Jacque)

Production Credits: Directed by Steve Carver [and Burt Kennedy (uncredited)]. Producer: Ralph B. Serpe. Screenplay: Norman Wexler [and Richard Sale (uncredited)]. Based on the Novel by Kyle Onstott [and Lance Horner (uncredited)]. Director of Photography: Lucien Ballard, A.S.C. [and Robert Hauser (uncredited)]. Production Design: Stan Jolley. Film Editor: Carl Kress [and Harold F. Kress (uncredited), Thomas Stanford (uncredited), Stuart H. Pappe (uncredited)]. Music by Charlie Smalls. Casting: Jack Baur. Costume Design: Ann Roth. Art Director. Bill Kenney. Set Decorator: John McCarthy. Unit Production Manager: Darrell Hallenback. Assistant to Producer: Jann Carver. Assistant Director: Peter Bogart. Second Assistant Director: Al Shepard [also Assistant Production Manager (uncredited)]. Men's Costumer: Tony Scarano. Women's Costumer: Jennifer Parson. Makeup: Bill Turner [and Don Cash (uncredited)]. Hair Stylist: Kathy Blondell [and Gladys Witten (uncredited)]. Assistant Film Editor: David Ramirez. Apprentice Film Editor: Lorraine Catalano. Script Supervisor: Terry

Terrill. Special Effects: Roger George [and Jack DeBron (uncredited)]. Prop Master: Sam Moore, Bud Shelton. Stunt Coordinator: Eddie Smith. Gaffer: Ted Holt. Key Grip: Clyde Hart. Camera Operator: Roger Shearman, Jr. Camera Assistant: Harry Young. Production Secretary: Anna Zappia. Sound Mixer: Robert Gravenor. Re-Recording Mixer: Bill Varney. Music Conductor and Arranger: Charles H. Coleman. Music Editor: Ken Wannberg. Additional Music: Richard P. Hazard. Sound Effects Editors: Gil Marchant, Gordon Daniels, Neiman-Tillar Associates. Title Design: Don Record. Titles: Pacific Title Company. Lenses and Cameras by Panavision. The following were all uncredited: Stunts: Jophery C. Brown, Tony Brubaker, Jim Burk, Gary Combs, Jadie David, J.D. Davis, James M. Halty, Bill Hart, Chuck Hayward, Henry Kingi, William T. Lane, Julius LeFlore, S.J. McGee, Bob Minor, Alan Oliney, Russell Saunders, Richard Washington, George P. Wilbur, Henry Wills, Eddie Smith, Bob Yerkes. Production Accountant: Steve Fisher. Assistant Auditor: Debbie Kocourer. Secretary to Producer: Kathy Boone. Extras Casting: Sally Perle. Additional Casting: Bill Kindelon, Carl Joy. Set Designers: Sig Tinglof, William Lindstrom. First Assistant Director: David Hamburger. Second Assistant Directors: Arne Schmidt, Al Murphy, Stephen J. Lim, Miles Tilton. Assistant Cameraman: Jose Hernandez. Assistant to Ms. Roth: Mary Malin. Costumers (Men): Silvio Scarano, Jack Spangler, Wayne Reed. Costumer (Women): Francine Jamison. Costume Assistant: Edgar Soberón Torchia. Assistant Makeup: Mike Bacaarella, Dee Manges. Body Makeup: Dorothy Parkison. Supervisory Sound Mixer: James H. Pilcher. Sound: Willie Burton. Boom: Cal Marks, Joseph Kite. Production Stills: Bruce McBroom, Elliott Marks. Publicist: Louis Dyer. Lead Men: Jimmie Heron, Jim Duffy. Second Grip: LeRoy Lydia, Jr.. Best Boys: Roger E. Redel. Elisha Harris. Electricians: Dean Harris, Joseph Cardoza, Jr.. Lamp Operators: Mickey A. Welsh, Jon Antunovich, Harry Dial, Jr. Dolly Grips: Pat Campea, Charles "Tex" Williams. Assistant Special Effects: Art Eishtadt. Construction Coordinator: Wally Graham. Construction Foreman: Silvio Fama. Painter: Harry Welton. Standby Painter: Glen W. Cooper. Drapery: Ragnar Antonsen. Transportation Coordinators: Dale Henry, Alan Henry. Assistant Transportation: Joseph Benet. Drivers: Cary Kelley, Dave Shafer, Gaylene Sagonna, Alan Henry. Cinemobile Driver:

Bill Van Hoek. Honeywagon Driver: Dick Schultz. Crane Operator: Pat Walke. Livestock Supervisors: Kenneth Lee, Lou Schumacher. Wrangler: David Richardson. Craft Service: Doug Vaughn. Production Assistants: Jane Burkett, Ellen Gordon, Diego de la Texera. First Aid: Rick Canelli. Filmed on Location in San Juan, Puerto Rico and New Orleans, Louisiana and at Paramount Studios, Hollywood, California. Aspect Ratio: 1.85:1.

A Dino De Laurentiis Presentation (uncredited in English-speaking territories). American Distributor: United Artists
American Version Running Time: 102 minutes. MPAA Rating: R.

Appendix F:
Mandingo Radio Spot Transcript

(60 seconds)

Announcer (White, male): Expect the savage.
White male: Violent.
Older white male: Very violent.
Older white male: Bloody.
White female: Gory, but good.
Announcer: Expect the sensual.
Young black female: That's the way they really treated women in the South.
Young black male: It was alright for a white man to get a black woman, but it was wrong for a black man to touch a white woman.
Black male: They're using each other.
Older white female: I can't get over it.
Announcer: Expect the shocking.
Black female: It was horrible.
Black female: Very revealing.
Black male: It was terrifying.
White male: Very surprising.
Older white female: It's what happened.
Announcer: Expect all that a motion picture screen has never dared to show before.
Older White Female: I don't think that, five years ago, they could have presented this without having a riot.
Announcer: Expect the truth.
Young black female: Very accurate.
Older white female: True.

Black male: It turned me around.
Young black female: It was true to life.
Announcer: Now you are ready for *Mandingo.*
Black male: Terrific.
White female: Sensational.
White female: Beautiful.
Black female: Depressing.
White male: Exciting.
White female: Great.
White male: Realistic.
White male: Excellent.
Older white male: Terrific.
Young black female: That's the way it really is.
Announcer: *Mandingo* starring James Mason, Susan George, Perry King, Brenda Sykes, and introducing Ken Norton as Mede.
Black male: Ken Norton was beautiful. Beautiful.
Announcer: *Mandingo.* From Paramount Pictures. Rated R, under 17 not admitted
without parent.
Black male: It's an education to the young and a reminder to the old.

Bibliography

Interviews: (Conducted by Paul Talbot)

Steve Carver (September 3, 2003, September 4, 2003 and September 14, 2003)

Ji-Tu Cumbuka (December 14, 2008)

Richard Fleischer (August 28, 2003)

Tim Kincaid (a.k.a. Joe Gage) (March 9, 2008)

Kathrine McKee (February 10, 2008)

Laura Misch (November 18, 2007)

Ken Norton (August 13, 2003)

G. Franklin Rothwell (November 15, 2007)

Sam Sherman (October 4, 2006)

Books:

Irving C. Ackerman and Kyle Onstott, *Your Dog as a Hobby* (NY and London: Harper & Brothers Publishers, 1940)

Frederick Bancroft, *Slave-Trading in the Old South* (Baltimore: J. H. Furst Company, 1931)

Harry Birdoff, *The World's Greatest Hit: Uncle Tom's Cabin* (NY: S. F. Vanni, 1947)

Thomas L. Bonn, *Undercover: An Illustrated History of American Mass Market Paperbacks* (NY: Penguin Books, 1982)

Tim Brooks and Earle Marsh, *The Complete Directory to Prime Time Network TV Shows: 1976–Present* (NY: Ballantine Books, 1979)

Jim Brown with Steve Delsohn, *Out of Bounds* (NY: Zebra Books, 1989)

Jeff Canja, *Collectable Paperback Books: A New Vintage Paperback Price Reference*, Second Edition (East Lansing, MI: Glenmoor Publishing, 2002)

Susan A. Compo, *Warren Oates: A Wild Life* (Lexington, KY: University

of Kentucky Press, 2009)
Jean-Pierre Coursodon with Pierre Sauvage, *American Directors Volume II* (NY: McGraw-Hill Book Co., 1983)
Alexander Davidson and Bernard Stuve, *Complete History of Illinois from 1673-1873* (Springfield, IL: D. L. Phillips, 1877)
Kenneth C. Davis, *Two Bit Culture: The Paperbacking of America* (Boston: Houghton Mifflin, 1984)
Yvonne De Carlo with Doug Warren, *Yvonne: An Autobiography* (NY: St. Martin's Press, 1987)
David Duke, *Jewish Supremacism: My Awakenings to the Jewish Question* (Mandeville, LA: Free Speech Press, 2003)
John Gregory Dunne, *The Studio* (NY: Farrar, Straus & Giroux, 1969)
Richard Fleischer, *Just Tell Me When to Cry* (NY: Carroll & Graf, 1993)
David F. Friedman with Don De Nevi, *A Youth in Babylon* (Buffalo, NY: Prometheus Books, 1990)
Ellis Ford Hartford and James Fuqua Hartford, *Green River Gravel: A Heterogeneous Collection of Historical and Humorous Bits Concerning Life and Times in the Counties South of Green River* (Utica, KY: McDowell Publications, 1983)
Lesley Henderson, editor, *Twentieth-Century Romance and Historical Writers* Second Edition (Chicago and London: St. James Press, 1990)
Larry Holmes with Phil Berger, *Larry Holmes: Against the Ropes* (NY: St. Martin's Press, 1998)
Lance Horner, *Rogue Roman* (NY: Pyramid Books, 1965)
P. B. Hurst, *The Most Savage Film: 'Soldier Blue,' Cinematic Violence, and the Horrors of War* (Jefferson, NC: McFarland and Company, Inc., 2008)
Pauline Kael, *When the Lights Go Down* (NY: Holt, Rinehart, Winston, 1980)
Jurate Kazickas, "The New, Young Capitalists: Getting Rich on Their Own Terms," *The New York Times* (April 18, 1971)
Burt Kennedy, *Hollywood Trail Boss: Behind the Scenes of the Wild, Wild Western* (NY: Boulevard Books, 1997)
Tullio Kezich and Alessandra Levantesi, *Dino: The Life and Films of Dino De Laurentiis* (NY: Hyperion, 2004).

Bill Landis and Michelle Clifford, *Sleazoid Express* (NY: Fireside, 2002)

Mark Thomas McGee, *Fast and Furious: The Story of American International Pictures* (Jefferson, NC: McFarland and Company, Inc., 1984)

Harry and Michael Medved, *The Golden Turkey Awards* (NY: Perigee Books, 1980)

Harry Medved with Randy Dreyfuss, *The Fifty Worst Films Of All Time* (NY: Popular Library, 1978)

Christina and Richard Milner, *Black Players: The Secret World of Black Pimps* (Boston: Little, Brown and Company, 1973)

Sheridan Morley, *James Mason: Odd Man Out* (London: Weidenfeld & Nicolson, 1989)

Jon Musgrave, *Slaves, Salt, Sex & Mr. Crenshaw: The Real Story of the Old Slave House and America's Reverse Underground R.R.* (Expanded Edition) (Marion, Illinois: IllinoisHistory.com, 2005)

Peter Noble, *The Negro in Films* (Port Washington, NY: Kennikat Press, 1969)

Ken Norton with Marshall Terrill and Mike Fitzgerald, *Going the Distance* (Champaign, IL: Sports Publishing, Inc., 2000)

Russel B. Nye, *The Unembarrassed Muse: The Popular Arts in America* (NY: Dial Press, 1970)

Kyle Onstott, *The Art of Breeding Better Dogs* (Washington, DC: Denlinger's, 1946)

Kyle Onstott, *Beekeeping as a Hobby* (NY and London: Harper & Brothers Publishers, 1941)

Original Paperback Cover Artwork from the Pan Archive (Auction Catalog) (London: W. & F. C. Bonham & Sons, Ltd., 1991)

Danny Peary, *Cult Movie Stars* (NY: Simon & Schuster/Fireside, 1991)

Ulrich B. Phillips, *A Documentary History of American Industrial Society Vol. 1–2: Plantation and Frontier, 1649–1863* (Cleveland: The Arthur H. Clark Co., 1910)

Fred Peterson Ragsdale, *The Contract Tree* (Chicago: Adams Press, 1993)

Elena Rodriguez, *Dennis Hopper: A Method to His Madness* (NY: St. Martin's Press, 1988)

Steven H. Scheuer, editor, *Movies on TV: 1978–1979 Edition* (NY:

Bantam Books, 1977)

Kenneth M. Stamp, *The Peculiar Institution: Slavery in the Ante-Bellum South* (NY: Random House, 1956)

Cobbett Steinberg, *Reel Facts: The Movie Book of Records* (NY: Vintage, 1982)

Kevin Sweeney, *James Mason: A Bio-Bibliography* (Westport, CT: Greenwood Press, 1999)

Troy Taylor, *Haunted Illinois* (Alton, IL: Whitechapel Productions, 1999)

James Vinson, editor, *Twentieth-Century Romance and Gothic Writers* (Detroit: Gale Research Co., 1982)

David L. Wolper with David Fisher, *Producer* (NY: Scribner, 2003)

Robin Wood, *Sexual Politics and Narrative Film: Hollywood and Beyond* (NY: Columbia University Press, 1998)

Articles:

Don Alpert, "Bad Guy Never Had It So Good," *Los Angeles Times* (August 6, 1967)

Dave Anderson, "Is Norton worrying about film career?" *The New York Times* (September 26, 1976)

Jeremy Arnold, "How I Got to Call the Shots," *Movie Maker* (Issue 38) (Spring 2000)

James Bacon, "Louis Picks Norton to Whip Ali," *Los Angeles Herald-Examiner* (Monday, March 15, 1976)

Earl F. Bargainnier, "The Falconhurst Series: A New Popular Image of the Old South," *The Journal of Popular Culture*, (Vol. 10, No. 2) (Fall 1976)

Barbour, Chris, "Cheryl 'Rainbeaux' Smith: The Life, Times, Death and Letters of a Drive-In Diva," *Bill George's Red Hot Planet.net* (May 2005)

http://www.redhotplanet.net/hof_rainbeaux_cheryl.htm.

Brian Baxter, "Obituary: Richard Fleischer, Reliable Hollywood director with a penchant for crime thrillers" *Guardian* (March 28, 2006)

"Best-Seller Breed, The" *Newsweek* (May 13, 1957)

Boxoffice (announcements and advertisements in various issues, circa 1970s and 1980s)

Jack Bradshaw, Jr., "Best in Movieland Show is Saint Bernard," *American Kennel Gazette* (July 1927)

Ian Cameron, Douglas Pye, "Richard Fleischer on *Mandingo*," *Movie* (Spring 1976) (No. 22)

Vincent Canby, "Sequels Are a Sign of Fear," *The New York Times* (May 25, 1975)

Vincent Canby, "Some Big Moneymakers With Little Redeeming Value," *The New York Times* (January 2, 1977)

Vincent Canby, "What Makes a Movie Immoral?," *The New York Times* (May 18, 1975)

"Carver Named *Drum* Director," *Variety* (February 19, 1976)

Othon Castillo, "Candilejas: Isela Vega Conquista Hollywood," *Los Angeles Opinion* (March 18, 1976)

"Catholic Conference 'Condemns' *Drum*," *Variety* (August 31, 1976)

"A Conversation With Richard H. Kline, ASC," American Society of Cinematographers website (theasc.com) (September 20, 2005)

Diane Dalbey, "Perry King: How his 'perseverance' paid off!" *Nighttime TV Stars* (December 1984)

"De Laurentiis Dismisses Altman From *Ragtime*," *Variety* (June 22, 1976)

"De Laurentiis Next Three Start Jan. 12; 'One To San Juan,'" *Variety* (December 24, 1975) (281:19)

"Delta Lady," *Playboy* (February 1975) (Vol. 22, No. 2)

"Dog Days Nip Chi 1st-Runs; *Drum* And *Horse* Out Front," *Variety* (August 25, 1976)

"*Drum* Opens With Big 21G In Frisco, *Clockmaker* Nice 7G," *Variety* (August 26, 1976)

Drum review, *Coast Week* (July, 1983) (newspaper of Mombasa, a city in the Republic of Kenya, Eastern Africa)

"*Drum*, With Sizzling 212G In Four Sites, The Big News At Windy City Box-Office," *Variety* (August 18, 1976)

"18 Key Situations Produce $1,187,138 for UA's *Drum*," *Box Office* (August 30, 1976)

"EMI To Distribute De Laurentiis Pix In British Market," *The Independent Film Journal* (October 15, 1975) Vol. 76, No. 10)

Stephen Farber, "The Campaign to Suppress *Coonskin*," *The New York Times* (July 20, 1975)

Neil Feineman, "*Blueboy* Interview: Perry King," *Blueboy* (October 1978)
Guy Flatley, "The Girl Who Made *Straw Dogs* Bark," *The New York Times* (March 5, 1972)
"For Ken Norton: Boxing, Now Nude Scene" *High Point* [N.C.] *Enterprise* (Associated Press) (July 25, 1976)
Ed Franklin, "Perry King," *In Touch* (1978)
"Frankovich, Self Set Two Features For De Laurentiis," *Variety* (August 27, 1975)
"French Quarter Use Disallowed," *High Point* [N.C.] *Enterprise* (Associated Press) (February 13, 1971)
Gerhard Fromm, "The Work of Jan Jacobsen," *In 70mm: The 70mm Newsletter* (June 1999) (Issue 57)
Alan L. Gansberg, "Susan George: 20 Years A Film Star," *The Hollywood Reporter* (October 8, 1985)
Jay A. Gertzman, "Softcore Publishing: The East Coast Scene," in *Sin-A-Rama: Sleaze Sex Paperbacks of the Sixties*, edited by Brittany A. Daley, et al. (Los Angeles: Feral House, 2004)
Kris Gilpin, "The Return of Rainbeaux," in *Invasion of the Scream Queens* edited by Bill George and Donald Farmer (Cookeville, TN: Mondo Press, 1989)
Larry Greenberg, Ted Bolman, Gwynne Kelly, and James Cohen, "More Rainbeaux," in *Invasion of the Scream Queens* edited by Bill George and Donald Farmer (Cookeville, TN: Mondo Press, 1989)
Ki Hackney, "Eye View," *Women's Wear Daily* (February 4, 1972)
Sheryl Hayward, "Perry King: Nice Guy or Bad Boy?" Alan Mercer.com (2003)
(www.alanmercer.com/perrykingprofile.htm)
Ed Hirshberg, "Meet Ashley Carter, Clay Stuart, Harry White, Hondo Wells and Harriet Kathryn Myers," *Florida Accent* (March 12, 1978)
"Hollywood Report: Jack Haley and Julia Phillips Featured in UA's *NY, NY* [sic]," *Box Office* (August 30, 1976)
Harlan Jacobson, "De Laurentiis 100% Yank; To Roll 14, 2 with Bergman," *Variety* (April 30, 1975)
Pauline Kael, "Notes On Black Movies," *The New Yorker* (December 2, 1972)
"Ken Norton prefers ring to film fame," *Greeley* (CO) *Tribune* (UPI)

(April 2, 1976)
"The Kids at Cannon," *Time* (August 31, 1970)
Peter Kihss, "More Film Makers Tied to Publishing," *The New York Times* (October 20, 1975)
Ronald E. Kisner, "Seldom Seen Side of Yaphet Kotto—Filmland's Tough Dude," *Jet* (September 16, 1976)
David Konow, "#1 Bad Ass: An Interview with Stuntman-Actor Bob Minor," *Shock Cinema* (Spring-Summer 2005) (No. 28)
John S. Lang, "Slavery Epic Is Filmed in South," Associated Press (1968)
Robert Lindsey, "All Hollywood Loves a Blockbuster—and Chips Off the Old
Blockbuster," *The New York Times* (May 30, 1976)
Richard R. Lingeman, "Paperbacks: Middletown Now," *The New York Times* (February 26, 1967)
"*Lipstick* Enters Production," *The Independent Film Journal* (November 12, 1975) (Volume 76, No. 12)
Nicanor Loreti, "The Rules of the Game: An Interview with Isela Vega," *Shock Cinema* (Number 34) (Winter 2008)
Bob Lucas, "Pam Grier Is Big In Talent, Too," *Jet* (December 16, 1976)
Dorothy Manners, "Film Violence Reflects the Streets," *Los Angeles Herald-Examiner* (May 23, 1976)
Andy Marx, "Lost and Found: Exit Stage Left," *Variety* (April 11-17, 1994)
Rudy Maxa, "The Master of Mandingo," *Potomac* (The Sunday Magazine of the *Washington Post*) (July 13, 1975)
James Meade, "The Lively Arts," *The San Diego Union* (March 1976)
Thomas Meehan, "He Makes Movies That Make Money," *The New York Times* (July 27, 1975)
Jeff Millar, "A Silk Purse Out of a Sow's Ear?" *Los Angeles Times* (April 6, 1975)
Julian Mitchell, "A Last Look at the Season," *Theatre Arts* (July 1961)
Paul I. Montgomery, "Pulp Sex Novels Thrive as Trade Comes Out into the Open," *The New York Times* (September 5, 1965)
Jon Musgrave, "History comes out of hiding atop Hickory Hill," *Springhouse* (December 1996)

"Negro Beefs Loom Vs. 'Mandingo,' Malenotti-Lattuada's Upcoming Pic," *Variety* (January 22, 1969)

Phillip Nobile, "Alex Haley's Hoax," *The Village Voice* (February 23, 1993)

Leo Noonan, "Where Do You Go After *Mandingo*?" *Fighting Stars* (April 1976)

Kevin Nudd, "Collecting Pan Books," *Book and Magazine Collector* (October 1990) (No. 79)

Kyle Onstott, "Cruel Masters," *True: The Man's Magazine* (October 1959) (Vol. 40, No. 269)

George Panton, "How shall we tell the story [?]," *The Sunday Gleaner* (Kingston, Jamaica, W.I.) (May 31, 1970)

"Paper Back Talk," *The New York Times* (January 11, 1976)

"Paper Back Talk," *The New York Times* (February 22, 1976)

"Paper Back Talk," *The New York Times* (March 7, 1976)

Louella O. Parsons, "Revised 'Uncle Tom's Cabin' Is Being Prepared For Movie," *Anderson* (IN) *Daily Bulletin* (March 31, 1960)

"People," *Time* (March 24, 1975)

Mary Ellen Perry, "'Slave gothics' put publishers in tall cotton," *Chicago Tribune* (May 24, 1977)

"Personalities: A Star Unborn, A Role Deleted," *Washington Post* (January 28, 1975)

Clarence Petersen, "Paperbacks: Status situation," *Washington Post* (February 9, 1969)

Chris Poggiali, "*Shock Cinema* Talk with '70s B-Movie Starlet Marilyn Joi," *Shock Cinema* (Spring–Summer 2000) (Number 16)

Pat Putnam, "The Bugle Call Champion," *Sports Illustrated* (June 12, 1978)

"Rap with Ken Norton, Movie Star," *Black Sports* (February 1975) (Vol. 4, No. 8)

Louie Robinson, "Pam Grier: More than just a sex symbol," *Ebony* (June 1976)

John Sandilands, "Warren Oates Collects," *Honey* (February 1972)

Andrew Sarris, "*Othello* It Ain't," *Village Voice* (May 26, 1975)

Andy Sawyer, "Magnolia Blossom and Whiplash," *Million* (March–April, 1992).

"Star Gossip," *The Star* (July 6, 1976)

Louis M. Starr, "Uncle Bob, Almost 110, Still Manages a Song for

Visitors" *Chicago Tribune* (September 24, 1945)
Ted Stewart, "Hollywood's prettiest black star," *Sepia* (January 1975) (Vol. 24, No. 1)
Norma McLain Stoop, "Perry King: Boundaries Bore Him," *After Dark* (January 1977)
"'Street-Bright' Actress Favors Instinct," *The New York Times* (August 31, 1984)
Bob Thomas, "Dionne Warwick Turns to Acting," Associated Press (July 6, 1968)
Richard Trubo, "The black star who won't act in black movies," *Sepia* (September 1975) (Vol. 24, No. 9)
Neil Tweedie, "Susan George: By George, I think she's still got it," *Telegraph* (September 27, 2007)
"UA Takes *Drums* [sic]; Par [sic] Passed On It in Anticipation Of X," *Variety* (June 30, 1976)
"UA's *Drum* Pulls In $1.2-Mil In 18 Theatres," *Variety* (August 25, 1976)
"'Uncle Bob,' 112, was Illinois' oldest vet," *Elgin* (IL) *Daily Courier-News* (April 12, 1948)
James Verniere, "An Interview With Susan George: The Work, The Work: Good, Bad Or Indifferent," *The Anquarian* (September 5, 1984)
Mel Watkins, "In The Ghettos," *The New York Times* (February 25, 1968)
"West End Returns Dip, But *Drum* Is Lively Entry," *Variety* (September 24, 1976)
Harry Whittington, "I Remember It Well," introduction to *The Dimes of Harry Whittington* (Disc-Us Books, Inc., 2000)
Earl Wilson, "It Happened Last Night," column, *New York Post* (August 10, 1974)
"Wm. Baxter Sues De Laurentiis On Now-Completed 'Mandingo'," *Variety* (March 12, 1975)
Kathryn Wright, "'Mandingo's' author had his dog days," *Billings* (MT) *Gazette* (May, 30, 1975)
"X (As In Nix) Sends *Drum* Searching A Paramount Sub," *Variety* (June 2, 1976)
Dick Young, "Norton: Young's right counter quick" *The New Mexican* (Santa Fe, N.M.) (April 30, 1976)

Pressbooks/Press Kits:

Drum, Bound Promotional Press Booklet with Stills, United Artists, 1976

Drum Pressbook, United Artists, 1976

Mandingo Pressbook and Merchandising Manual, Paramount Pictures, 1975

Mandingo Press Kit, Paramount Pictures, 1975

Quadroon Pressbook, Presidio Productions, 1971

Slaves Pressbook, Continental, 1969

Uncle Tom's Cabin Pressbook, Independent-International, 1976

Screenplays:

Drum, "Revised Final Script," A Screenplay by Norman Wexler, Based on the novel by Kyle Onstott, Draft dated November 17, 1975, with additional revised pages dated November 26, 1975; December 1, 1975; December 4, 1975; December 8, 1975; December 15, 1975; December 17, 1975; and December 18, 1975.

Drum, Production Revisions by Richard Sale, pages dated February 16, 1976; February 17, 1976; February 24, 1976; February 25, 1976; March 1, 1976; March 9, 1976; March 15, 1976; March 16, 1976; and March 18, 1976.

Mandingo, "Second Revised Screenplay" by Norman Wexler, from the novel by Kyle Onstott and a script by Roberto Malenotti, Damiano Damiani, Beverly Bennet, Draft dated August 3, 1974, with additional revised pages dated June 3, 1974; June 5, 1974; June 26, 1974; July 15, 1974; and July 23, 1974.

Play Scripts:

Mandingo by Jack Kirkland, based on the novel by Kyle Onstott

Handwritten first draft play script, not dated (circa 1960-1961).

Mandingo by Jack Kirkland, based on the novel by Kyle Onstott

Clean carbon typescript of handwritten first draft play script, not dated (circa 1960-1961).

Mandingo by Jack Kirkland, based on the novel by Kyle Onstott

"Master Script B, Final revision before rehearsal," 1961 (Typescript with handwritten revisions and additions taped or stapled in).

Location: Jack Kirkland Papers (1928-1969), Billy Rose Theatre

Collection, The New York Public Library for the Performing Arts

Theatre Programs:
Playbill: Mandingo (May 22, 1961) (Vol. 5, No. 21)

Brochures:
Bonnie Sisk, *The Old Slave House*. Tourist Brochure (Junction, Ill: privately printed by owners of the house, not dated [1940s?])

Documents:
Certificate of Death: Kenric Lance Horner; Department of Health and Rehabilitative Services, Division of Health, Office of Vital Statistics, State of Florida; State File No. 73-051739 (Certified Copy)

Websites:
Advanced Book Exchange (abenooks.com)
absolutelyperryking.com
Amazon.com
British Film Institute (www.bfi.org.uk)
eBay (ebay.com)
Gale Literary Databases: Contemporary Authors (www.galegroup.com)
Genealogy.com
Internet Broadway Database (ibdb.com)
Internet Movie Database (imdb.com)
Wikipedia (wikipedia.org)

Documentary:
The Godfathers of Mondo (2003). A Blue Underground Presentation. Director: David Gregory. Producers: Joyce Shen, Michele De Angelis.

Index

N

O

P

T

U